Exploring the Qur'an

Context and Impact

Muhammad Abdel Haleem

I.B. TAURIS
LONDON · NEW YORK

MIX
Paper from
responsible sources
FSC
www.fsc.org
FSC® C007584

Published in 2017 by
I.B.Tauris & Co. Ltd
London • New York
www.ibtauris.com

ISBN: 978 1 78076 365 1
eISBN: 978 1 78672 165 5
ePDF: 978 1 78673 165 4

A full CIP record for this book is available from the British Library
A full CIP record is available from the Library of Congress

Library of Congress Catalog Card Number: available

Typeset by Riverside Publishing Solutions, Salisbury, SP4 6NQ
Printed and bound in Sweden by ScandBook AB

Muhammad Abdel Haleem, OBE, is King Fahd Professor of Islamic Studies at the School of Oriental and African Studies, University of London, and one of the world's leading authorities in Qur'anic studies. He is the author of *Understanding the Qur'an: Themes and Style,* also published by I.B.Tauris, and his major new translation of the Qur'an, with parallel Arabic text, was published by Oxford University Press in 2010.

'This is a learned yet accessible work born of deep erudition and familiarity not only with the complexities of the Arabic language but also with the underlying spirit of Islamic thought and tradition. At a time when Muslims are assailed from within and without by zealots intent on denigrating their faith, Professor Haleem's book provides thoughtful and incisive counter-arguments to their heated rhetoric. The reader cannot help but be impressed by the author's careful and insightful engagement with some of the most important Qur'anic verses that are being deliberately misconstrued today, by extremists from both Muslim and non-Muslim backgrounds. *Exploring the Qur'an* is a compelling study that will be of great interest to specialists and non-specialists alike.'

Asma Afsaruddin,
Professor of Islamic Studies,
Indiana University, Bloomington

'*Exploring the Qur'an: Context and Impact* combines a judicious critique of aspects of Western Qur'an studies – and aspects too of the Qur'anic exegetical tradition – with an acutely perceptive and detailed analysis of the language and thought of the Qur'an. It conclusively establishes that all attempts to interpret the Qur'an without a thorough familiarity with its nuanced *Arabic* text will remain inadequate. Muhammad Abdel Haleem's important and groundbreaking book makes a singular contribution to Qur'anic studies.'

Mustansir Mir,
University Professor of Islamic Studies,
Youngstown State University

'Muhammad Abdel Haleem is one of the foremost Arabists and scholars of the Qur'an today. His translation of the Islamic sacred scripture is widely known and appreciated, as are his other scholarly works. The present volume, again dealing with the Qur'an, is a major addition to his corpus and to literature in the field in general. This new book reflects mastery of the material as well as deep faith in the sacred nature of the Qur'an itself. *Exploring the Qur'an* makes a very substantial and a very important contribution to Qur'anic studies in the English language.'

Seyyed Hossein Nasr,
University Professor of Islamic Studies,
The George Washington University

Contents

Acknowledgements vii

Introduction 1

Part I: Teachings

1 The 'Sword Verse' Myth 7

2 Qur'anic *Jizya*: Tax Defaulters 29

3 Qur'anic *Jihād* 49

4 Qur'anic Paradise 69

Part II: Style

5 Legal Style: Qur'anic *Sharī'a* – Avoiding the Application of the Ultimate Penalties 89

6 Euphemistic Style: Sexual Etiquette 111

7 Narrative Style: Repeating Stories – Noah 119

8 Coherent Style: How to Read the Sura 141

9 Evidential Style: Divine Oaths in the Qur'an 177

10 Rhetorical Style: Arabic of the Qur'an 213

Part III: Impact

11 The Arabic Qur'an in the Muslim World 237

12 English Translations of the Qur'an: The Making of an Image 249

Acknowledgements

Some of the chapters in this book are elaborations on my previously published material. I would like to acknowledge the kind permission of:

Edinburgh University Press (Chapters 2, 3, 6, 7 and 8). Published in various issues of the *Journal of Qur'anic Studies.*

E. J. Brill (Chapter 4). In their forthcoming book, Sebastian Günther and Todd Lawson (eds), *Roads to Paradise.*

(Chapter 10). Published as 'Arabic of the Qur'an: grammar and style', in C. Versteegh (general ed.), *Encyclopedia of Arabic Language and Linguistics* (Brill 2009), Vol. IV (Q–Z), Qur'an, pp. 21–32.

Harper Collins (Chapter 11). Published as 'Qur'anic Arabic: its characteristics and impact on Arabic language and literature and the languages and literatures of other Islamic peoples', in Seyyed Hossein Nasr (ed.), *The Study Qur'an* (New York, 2015), pp. 1626–43.

I would also like to thank Hannah Erlwein, who formatted the whole final text and made very good suggestions. My most sincere thanks go to my wife, Harfiyah, who has typed every part of the material throughout and has also made many useful suggestions. Many thanks for her patience and encouragement.

Acknowledgements

Introduction

This book challenges the image of the Qur'an put forward by many Western and Muslim authors, both classical and modern, and particularly by modern extremists from all sides. It argues that the image they produce is highly selective, hastily produced and actually ignores important parts of the Arabic text of the Qur'an, sometimes even from within the same verse from which they are quoting. At times they ignore the context, style and rhetorical aspects of the Qur'an that are essential for determining the correct meaning. They often force norms of Arabic grammar and rhetoric on to the English, producing an Arabised, rather than an eloquent English translation, while also disregarding the power of the original Arabic. Sometimes they overlook the Qur'anic text and base their views on the tradition of exegesis (*tafsīr*) or images and ideas that have accumulated in the West over centuries. Those who do this unwittingly emulate the pagan Arabs, described by the Qur'an as follows:

When it is said to them, 'Follow the message that God has sent down,' they answer, 'We follow the ways of our forefathers.' What! Even though their forefathers understood nothing and were not guided?

Q. 2:170

They say, 'We saw our fathers following a tradition; we are guided by their footsteps.'

Q. 43:22

The present book explores what such writers have neglected, that is, the Arabic text of the Qur'an itself, rather than views expressed in imperfect *tafsīrs* or translations, or polemical readings of the text which subvert its original meaning. Linguistic analysis is then used, paying due regard to the Qur'anic context, style and habits of expressing its message. The objective is to challenge tradition or convention where it stands in contradiction to the Qur'an; however, just as my intention is not to criticise all Muslim writers, it is certainly not my aim to criticise all Western writers on the Qur'an either, many of whom, based on the rich cultural heritage existing in various Western countries, have made significant contributions to Qur'anic studies. They have complemented the scholarship of Muslim authors and have expended huge efforts enriching our understanding of the text, especially when such scholarship has been marked by true academic objectivity.

The material in this book is presented in three categories: teachings, style and impact. The first part (Chapters 1–4) covers certain illustrative controversial issues. The second (Chapters 5–10) covers questions where the Qur'anic style gives rise to a number of common misunderstandings. The final part (Chapters 11–13) deals with some issues relating to the impact of the Qur'an within and outside the Muslim world. These issues, apart from Chapter 11, have been selected because Western authors themselves have highlighted them in their discussions on the Qur'an.

Chapter 1 discusses the so-called 'Sword Verse' to show that a web of myth has been created around it, based on the selection of one single verse, cutting it off from its textual context before and after, and also its historical context. This has led to a misunderstanding of the purpose of the words within that verse. In fact, not one single person was killed as a result of this verse at the time it was revealed. For polemical reasons, what the Qur'an actually says on the subject has been ignored.

Chapter 2 on the *jizya* verse exposes scholars' disregard of what the Qur'an says on this issue and their misunderstanding of why it speaks in the way it does, as well as of basic terms such as *dīn*. The image has instead been taken from later *tafsīr* and *fiqh* works, the history of hostile rivalry between faiths and the views of modern extremists.

Chapter 3 shows how the general impressions regarding *jihād* in certain circles, both Eastern and Western, ignore what the Qur'an actually says, namely that it is only for defence and is limited by the best humanitarian restrictions. This is directly contrary to what many have said outside the Muslim world as well as many extremists within the Muslim world, classical and modern.

Chapter 4 discusses the Qur'anic view of Paradise. It argues that the general picture given by many Western writers and the media, and indeed by many Muslim extremists now, who argue that *jihād* is their surest way of achieving Paradise, is far from that actually given in the Qur'an. In particular, it shows that sensual pleasure in Paradise has been highly exaggerated and is certainly not its most important feature.

Chapter 5, the first on style (legal style), shows that the general picture of the *sharīʻa* in the West and indeed as given by many Muslim authors past and present, is not a true one. The ultimate penalties, which are very limited in number (four), are given in the Qur'an to deter and they carry with them many ways of avoiding their application. The question of 'beating' wives is also discussed here.

Chapter 6, on euphemistic style, discusses the sensitive issue of sexual etiquette. It demonstrates that the general view actually overlooks the wording of the Qur'an. Far from using coarse language, it deals with the subject using figurative speech that shows dignity, respect and obedience to God, while allowing the enjoyment of what God has ordained for humans.

Chapter 7, on narrative style, shows that the impression of the Qur'an as being repetitive in telling stories does not reflect the reality. The story of Noah is given in various places in the Qur'an as illustrative material to convey differing messages. It serves the Qur'anic purpose of instilling the basic elements of faith and teachings in the minds of Muslims at different points, so that they are aware at all times.

Chapter 8, on coherent style, shows that the picture given of the suras of the Qur'an as being chaotic, disordered and switching from one theme to another is contrary to what actually appears in the suras. This becomes evident when Qur'anic habits and stylistic features are understood. Three suras are analysed as examples.

Chapter 9, on evidential style, shows a feature of the Qur'an used to provide arguments and evidence for its statements. The theme of divine oaths is selected here due to its being seriously misconstrued and its objectives disregarded. This is again true both in some classical *tafsīrs* and in Western writings, with these misunderstandings being handed down from generation to generation.

Chapter 10, on rhetorical style, demonstrates how the priority of creating effect through rhetorical style sometimes overrides formal grammatical considerations. This is in keeping with the way Arabs already used their language at the time of the revelation and beyond. Many Western scholars seem unaware of this aspect of the Qur'anic language and imagine grammatical errors where they do not exist.

Chapter 11 gives a picture of the wide impact of the Qur'an on the languages, literature and cultures of the Muslim world. This has been little appreciated in the non-Muslim world, as is subsequently demonstrated in Chapters 12 and 13.

Chapter 12 shows that translations of the Qur'an into English started over a thousand years after the Arabic original was revealed. History shows that translations on the whole have missed very important considerations of the style and effect of the Arabic Qur'an. They therefore contained serious flaws, which were copied by others (as shown in Part I of this book), and so gave a detrimental image of the Qur'an and Islam. Seven translations have been selected as examples.

Finally, Chapter 13 reveals the negative effect of inadequate translation on interfaith relations, particularly between Muslims, Jews and Christians.

Overall this book demonstrates that, due to various factors, the true nature of the Qur'an has repeatedly been neglected in one way or another and an inadequate picture given. This flawed portrayal has been handed down from one generation to another, hindering a genuine understanding of the Qur'an. At times, I have quoted extensively from the Qur'an to help show the full picture and allow the Qur'an to speak for itself.

Unless otherwise indicated, the translation quoted is that of M. Abdel Haleem (Oxford University Press, 2010).

PART I
Teachings

1

The 'Sword Verse' Myth

The 'Sword Verse' is perhaps one of the most famous Qur'anic verses and one of the most often quoted by propagandists, extremists and by some modern academics. For example, Michael Cook gives the following translation of Q. 9:5:

> *Then, when the sacred months are drawn away, slay the polytheists wherever you find them, and take them, and confine them, and lie in wait for them at every place of ambush. But if they repent, and perform the prayer, and pay the alms, then let them go their way: God is All-forgiving, All-compassionate.*

He then interprets the verse as follows:

> In other words, you should kill the polytheists unless they convert. A polytheist (*mushrik*) is anyone who makes anyone or anything a 'partner' (*sharik*) with God; the term extends to Jews and Christians, indeed to unbelievers.[1]

This is an extraordinary assertion when applied to the Qur'an, which has very definite separate terms for Jews, Christians and unbelievers. Moreover, as will be shown conclusively in the discussion below, the verse is talking about just one group of polytheists, not all of them, and the instruction absolutely does not 'extend to Jews and Christians, indeed to unbelievers'.

Cook uses Q. 9:5 in his discussion to contrast this interpretation of the Qur'anic verse with 'a modern Western society, where it is more or less axiomatic that other people's religious beliefs [...] are to be tolerated and perhaps even respected'.[2]

This particular criticism of Islam has become widespread. Even Pope Benedict XVI in his Regensburg lecture said:

> ... surah 2,256 reads: 'There is no compulsion in religion'. According to the experts, this is one of the suras of the early period, when Mohammed was still powerless and under threat. But naturally the emperor also knew the instructions, developed later and recorded in the Qur'an, concerning holy war.[3]

Indeed this verse has been similarly interpreted by many Muslims in the past and in modern times, including extremists and terrorist groups who wish to justify their views and actions. This chapter undertakes a close analysis of the text alongside an examination of the opinions expressed by such authors as the modern academic Michael Cook and the fifth/eleventh-century writer Ibn Salāma. I thereby aim to show that a mythology has been created and maintained about this verse and anti-Islamic polemicists and propagandists actually stand on the same ground as Islamic extremists and terrorists in this regard.

The Historical Background

In order to embark on a proper reading of the 'Sword Verse', it is necessary to look at the historical background against which it was revealed. We must therefore go back in time to the Treaty of Hudaybiyya between the Prophet Muhammad and the Meccans in the sixth year of the *hijra* (Islamic Era). Those who doubt the accuracy of the Muslim historical sources referred to below, however, will find that the text of the Qur'an itself gives a sufficiently clear explanation of the events and the justification for them.

When the Muslims went peacefully from Medina towards Mecca to perform the *'umra* (minor pilgrimage), in fulfilment of a vision of the Prophet, the Meccans refused to allow them to come near the city. After lengthy negotiations it was agreed the Muslims would go back without performing the *'umra* in that year and return the following year to do so. The Meccans did not want it to be seen in Arabia that they were coerced into allowing the Muslims to enter Mecca to perform pilgrimage.[4] A ten-year truce was agreed, even though the terms were disadvantageous to the Prophet and the Muslims, but peace was a goal which the Prophet eagerly sought.[5] One of the terms was that whoever wanted to ally themselves with Muhammad and his camp was allowed to do so and whoever wanted to ally themselves with the Meccans should be allowed to do so.[6] Within two years, however, the Meccans broke the treaty by helping the Banū Bakr with men and arms to attack and kill a number of the Banū Khuzā'a (allies of the Muslims) even though the Banū Khuzā'a sought refuge at the Ka'ba. The Banū Khuzā'a sent a delegation to the Prophet informing him that the Meccans had broken the treaty and killed some of them in the Sanctuary while they were kneeling and prostrating in prayer. As a result, the Muslims marched on Mecca, and took possession of the Ka'ba and the Sacred Precincts. It is worth noting that, in approaching Mecca on this occasion, the Prophet sent emissaries to call out to the Meccans, 'Whoever stays in his house is safe, whoever enters Abū Sufyān's house is safe, whoever enters the Sanctuary is safe.'[7] He did not say, however, 'Whoever becomes Muslim is safe or renounces polytheism is safe.' Many Meccans entered Islam following the surrender of the city, but many living inside and outside the boundaries of Mecca remained polytheists.

In 9 AH, the Prophet led a Muslim expedition to Tabūk to meet the Byzantine army who were thought to be marching to attack the Muslims. Some of the polytheists who had entered into treaties with the Prophet, whether at Hudaybiyya or subsequently, believed this was going to be the final and complete end of the Muslims, who could not possibly stand up to the mighty Byzantine army, and so openly reneged on their treaty.[8] The Prophet and the Muslim army returned from Tabūk without engaging the enemy in combat, having found that the Byzantines were not coming after all. Later that same year, in the month of Dhu'l-Qa'da, the Prophet appointed Abū Bakr to lead the Muslims to Mecca on pilgrimage. Soon afterwards, the beginning of Sura 9 was revealed:

A release by God and His Messenger from the treaty you [believers] made with the polytheists [is announced] – you [polytheists] may move freely about the land for four months, but you should bear in mind both that you will not escape God, and that God will disgrace those who ignore [Him]. On the Day of the Great Pilgrimage [there will be] a proclamation from God and His Messenger to all people: 'God and His Messenger are released from [treaty] obligations to the polytheists. It will be better for you [polytheists] if you repent; know that you cannot escape God if you turn away.' [Prophet], warn those who ignore [God] that they will have a painful punishment. As for those who have honoured the treaty you made with them and who have not supported anyone against you: fulfil your agreement with them to the end of their term. God loves those who are mindful of Him. When the [four] forbidden months are over, wherever you find the polytheists, kill them, seize them, restrict them, sit watching out for them at every look-out post – but if they turn [to God], maintain the prayer, and pay the prescribed alms, let them go on their way, for God is most forgiving and merciful.

The Prophet then sent his cousin 'Alī to join the pilgrimage and to make the proclamation referred to in verse 3. On the appointed day, he announced to the assembly of pilgrims, Muslims and polytheists alike, that the Prophet had sent him to proclaim four messages: first, that after that year, no idolater would be allowed to perform the hajj;[9] second, that no one would be allowed to perform the circumambulation of the Ka'ba naked (this was the practice of some idolaters);[10] third, that 'only believers will enter Paradise';[11] and fourth, that the terms of any treaty should be observed.[12] It is reported that a leader of the polytheists, on hearing this, responded to 'Alī by saying, 'Tell your cousin that we have broken the treaty and there is nothing between him and us other than stabbing with spears and striking with swords.'[13]

Analysis of the Qur'anic Text

As should become clear in the following discussion, verse 5 of Sura 9 cannot be correctly understood when isolated and ripped out of its context. Such a strategy, which is the basis for interpretations often adopted by Islamic extremists and terrorists as well as anti-Islamic propagandists, is misleading and contrary to sound linguistic norms and proper academic practices. In fact, the verse should be read together with the whole of the first section of the sura (verses 1–28), which are all interconnected and deal with one and the same theme. This section will thus provide a contextualised analysis of Q. 9:5 in the light of these verses, as they are presented in the Qur'anic text. Arberry's translation of verse 5, used by Cook, will be used for this purpose.

1. '*Then, when the sacred months are drawn away, slay the polytheists*'

In their announcement of the impending termination of '*the treaty you [believers] made with the polytheists*', verses 1 and 2 of Sura 9 define the target audience 'polytheists' referred to in Q. 9:5 as 'the polytheists with whom you [the Muslims] made a treaty'. It further announces that '*you [polytheists] may move freely about the land for four months*', meaning that, even after the polytheists had broken the treaty, the Muslims were not permitted to enter into a state of war with them at once. Four months' grace was declared, during which the polytheists could go about their ways as before, without any interference, although they were reminded that God has the power to disgrace them. It is truly remarkable that, so early in history, an enemy was given so much notice. The announcement was made in a way that ensured it reached all parts of Arabia, at the peak of the pilgrimage: '*On the Day of the Great Pilgrimage [there will be] a proclamation from God and His Messenger to all people*' (Q. 9:3). As always with the Qur'an, it leaves an opening and gives advice, '*It will be better for you if you repent.*' Even before coming to the crucial verse 5, it makes an exception, stating: '*those polytheists who honoured the treaty you made with them, and who have not supported others against you: fulfil your agreement with them to the end of the term. God loves those who are mindful of Him*' (Q. 9:4).

As a result, verse 5 clearly and very explicitly deals only with those polytheists who did not honour their treaty and who 'supported others against the Muslims'. In other words, those who, by breaking the peace treaty and supporting others against the Muslims, had themselves entered into a state of war. The definite article '*al-*' in 'kill *al-mushrikīn*' is not a generic '*al-*' (*al-jinsiyya*), but a specific '*al-*' (*al-'ahdiyya*), referring only to those *mushrikūn* mentioned in verses 1–4. '*Al-*' *al-'ahdiyya* is a basic rule of Arabic grammar. Cook misinterpreted this '*al-*' because he relied on English translations, not on the Arabic text. Moreover he isolated verse 5 from everything around it. If read in the original Arabic, or even in translation, with its surrounding verses (verses 4, 5 and 6 onwards) the correct interpretation becomes clear. In Cook's discussion the Arabic text and context are both neglected.

Another point of note is that the four months' notice, during which Muslims were not permitted to fight these polytheists, started on the ninth day of the Arab month of Dhū'l-Ḥijja, '*the day of the Great Pilgrimage*'. It so happens that the rest of Dhū'l-Ḥijja and the following month of Muḥarram are part of the normal Sacred Months during which, by Arab tradition and by Islamic law, no fighting should take place. However, the four months given in verse 5 would continue after that until 9 Rabī' al-Thānī. It is therefore misleading to call them the 'sacred months' as in the translation quoted by Cook; the normal Sacred Months would have come to an end at a maximum of 50 days after the declaration was made. Verse 5 therefore gives a special period of grace to these people over and above the Sacred Months.[14] Correct translation of the Arabic text of the Qur'an is crucial here.

Similarly, Cook's interpretation of the imperative 'kill the polytheists' is also misleading and should actually mean 'you *may* kill the polytheists'. In Arabic linguistics and in Islamic jurisprudence, the imperative form covers a vast range of meaning (Ṣāliḥ surveyed 15 different meanings, including orders, permissibility, advice and encouragement).[15] The usage of the imperative in this instance conforms to the juristic rule (deduced from analysis of the text of the Qur'an and agreed by the majority of jurists) *al-amr ba'd al-ḥaẓr li'l-ibāḥa*, 'an imperative form that comes after prohibition means permissibility'.[16] To give one example of the 'imperative of permissibility': in Ramadan Muslims refrain from eating and drinking during the daytime. When the Qur'an tells them, 'When night time falls, eat and drink', it is not *ordering* them to eat and drink, it merely brings them back to the original state of permissibility.[17] In accordance with this, the end of the four months' notice, during which Muslims were not permitted to fight the polytheists who broke the treaty, did not actually *order* them to fight, but rather put the Muslims back into the original state of permissibility. It simply meant that there was no further obligation to refrain from fighting the polytheists. Thus, al-Rāzī categorically states: 'When the four months are ended, God Almighty permitted (*adhina fī*) four things.'[18]

It is interesting that Cook's interpretation is apparently in accord with that of the modern Islamic scholar Sayyid Quṭb, regarded by many as holding a number of extremist views and executed in Egypt in 1965. In his famous work *Fī ẓilāl al-qur'ān,* he states: 'God has ordered (*amara*) the Muslims, when the forbidden months are over, to kill every polytheist wherever they find him, or arrest him, or …'[19]

2. '*wherever you find them, and take them, and confine them, and lie in wait for them at every place of ambush*'

There are several further problems with Cook's translation of the initial part of Q. 9:5, which seriously hinder an accurate understanding of the verse's intent. The phrase Arberry translates as 'wherever you find them' in reality means 'inside or outside the Sanctuary'[20] and what he gives as 'confine them' actually means 'restrict their movement', that is, do not allow them to come to the Sanctuary, or to the Muslim area.[21] This understanding is supported by the use of the very same word, *uḥṣirtum* ('you are prevented') in Q. 2:196, which instructs the Muslims to '*complete the pilgrimages, major and minor, for the sake of God. If you are prevented* (*uḥṣirtum*) *from doing so, then send whatever offering for sacrifice you can afford.*' Thus, the root *ḥ-ṣ-r* is used in Q. 2:196 in the context of the Muslims on their way to Mecca being prevented from reaching the sanctuary and in Q. 9:5 for preventing the polytheists from doing so.

Furthermore, Arberry's translation 'lie in wait for them at every place of ambush' is also incorrect. The Qur'an says no more than 'sit watching out for them at every look-out post' (*wa-q'udū lahum kulla marṣad*). In times of war, all countries watch out for enemies entering their territory.

Last but not least, Arberry seems to misunderstand the use of the particle '*wa*', which he translates as 'and'. It is not conceivable that the Qur'an would order the believers to kill *and* arrest the polytheists *and* confine them: logic alone dictates that if someone is killed they cannot after that be arrested, confined and watched out for at every look-out post. Arabic grammar recognises the usage of '*wa*' in such sentences as 'or', rather than simply 'and'.[22] In contrast to Cook's reading, which serves to exacerbate the sense of directed persecution, the fact that the Qur'an resorted to such a series of options only serves to direct the Muslims' attention away from killing.

3. '*But if they repent, and perform the prayer, and pay the alms, then let them go their way: God is All-forgiving, All-compassionate.*'

As mentioned in the introduction to this chapter, Cook makes the exegetical statement 'in other words "kill them unless they convert"' in his discussion of the second half of Q. 9:5. However, when the verse is examined in context, it becomes clear that this reading cannot be correct, since killing is only one of four permitted alternatives mentioned, the others being, as mentioned above, 'arrest them', 'restrict their movement' and 'watch their movements'. The rest of Q. 9:5 reads, '*if they repent, maintain the prayer, and pay the prescribed alms, let them go on their way, for God is most forgiving and merciful.*' This should not be read as a condition for not killing: it does not mean that Muslims should go on killing polytheists until they repent. When one looks at the Qur'anic text carefully, one notices the use here of the particle '*in*', meaning 'if'. This is in contrast to the alternative particle '*hattā*' which has two meanings: *ta'līl*, indicative of purpose ('so that') and *ghāya*, indicating a limit ('to the point of', 'until'), used, for example, in Q. 2:193, '*Fight them until there is no more persecution*'. Hence, Q. 9:5 does not say, 'kill them, arrest them [...] until (or: so that) they repent and perform the prayer'. Likewise, the verse does not use *illā* ('unless', 'except'): it does not say, 'unless (*illā*) they repent'.[23] In Qur'anic usage it is clear that '*in*' refers to possibilities and options. Hence in Q. 9:11–12, '*if* they repent ...' and '*if* they break their oath, after having made an agreement with you, and revile your religion, then fight them' and Q. 9:74, '*if* they repent, it will be better for them, and *if* they turn away, God will punish them in this world and the hereafter'.

Thus, a more accurate reading of the intention behind Q. 9:5 '*if they repent, perform the prayer ...*' would be that it aims to restrain Muslims from pursuing those who have been fighting them even if they say they have repented and will perform the prayer and so on. There are similar examples of restraining Muslims elsewhere in the Qur'an. In Q. 4:94 Muslims are warned:

... be careful when you go to fight in God's way, and do not say to someone who offers you a greeting of peace, 'You are not a believer,' out of desire for the chance gains of this life – God has plenty of gains for you. You yourself were in the same position [once], but God was gracious to you, so be careful: God is fully aware of what you do.

The Prophet is also reported to have condemned a Muslim who killed an enemy in battle even after the latter gave him the Islamic greeting, thinking that the man was merely trying to save himself.[24]

The instruction in Q. 9:5, '*If they repent [...] let them go on their way, for God is most forgiving and merciful*', means that 'you too should forgive them and not continue to pursue them'. This interpretation is confirmed by Q. 9:11, that says: '*If they repent, keep up the prayer and pay the prescribed alms, then they are your brothers in faith.*' This statement also opened the door for any polytheist who wished to take this option. It is worth noting that the verse does not say, 'if they repent [...] don't kill them, restrict their movement ...'. It merely says, 'let them go on their way' (that is, to the Ka'ba), which suggests that the focus in this verse is on watching them and keeping them away from the Sanctuary and from coming into the Muslim area.

Cook's interpretation 'kill them unless they convert' is further refuted by verse 6: '*If any of the idolaters should seek your protection, Prophet, grant it to him so that he may hear the word of God, then take him to a place safe for him, for they are people who do not know.*' It is significant that, immediately following the 'Sword Verse' the Qur'an advocates giving protection to non-believers and conducting them to a place of safety, while not stating that it is incumbent on them to become Muslims to receive this treatment.

Verses 7–13 go on to explain the various ways the polytheists have dishonoured their treaty and why Muslims should not continue honouring such a treaty. Verse 7 reads: '*How could there be a treaty with God and His Messenger for the idolaters ... ?*' And before this question is completed, there is a repetition of the exception: '*Except for those with whom you made a treaty at the Sacred Mosque,*[25] *so long as they remain true to you, be true to them. God loves those who are mindful of Him.*' Then the original sentence is resumed: '*How, when, if they were to get the upper hand over you, they would not respect any tie with you of kinship or of treaty?*'

The interruption of the sentence in the way observed here is noteworthy. It has been seen that in verse 4 the exception is placed even before verse 5 and not inside it. This is an example of the way the Qur'an is so restrictive and careful whenever it deals with the theme of fighting.[26] This level of caution is observed in the passage under discussion in the repetition of the conditional 'if' (verses 3, 5, 6, 11 and 15). There is also repetition of '*illā*', 'except for' (verses 4 and 7). Restriction can also be seen at the ends of the verses, where Muslims are urged: '*God loves those who are mindful of Him*' (verse 4); '*let them go their way, God is most forgiving and merciful*' (verse 5); '*remain true to them, God loves those who are mindful of Him*' (verse 7); '*God will accept the repentance of whomever He wishes, God is all knowing and wise*' (verse 15); and '*God knows well all that you do*' (verse 16).

Verse 10 provides further justification: '*Where believers are concerned, they [the polytheists] respect no tie of kinship or treaty. They are the ones who are committing aggression.*' Even after this, verse 11 comes to repeat, '*If they repent, keep up the prayer, and pay the prescribed alms, then they are your brothers in faith.*' This reminder that polytheists could become their brothers in faith further restrains the Muslims from pursuing them with hostility, just as they were told in Q. 4:94 quoted above: '*You yourself were in the same position [once], but God was gracious to you, so be careful: God is fully aware of what you do.*'

'God is fully aware of what you do', both in Q. 4:94 and 9:16 is a warning to the Muslims to follow His instructions and not to exceed the limits set for them. The Qur'an is consistent in its teachings, its phraseology and its habit of restriction when dealing with the issue of fighting.

In verse 12 permission to fight is again given, not because the enemy have not repented, kept up the prayer or paid the prescribed alms, but because of their breaking their oath and reviling the religion of the Muslims. Fighting is clearly directed at the 'leaders of disbelief', who (after pretending to repent)[27] instigate such hostility towards the Muslims, rather than 'all polytheists': '*But if they break their oath after having made an agreement with you, if they revile your religion, then fight the leaders of disbelief – oaths mean nothing to them – so that they may stop*' (Q. 9:12).

This confirms that the instruction in verse 5 is merely permissive, and is in harmony with verse 28, '*Believers, those who ascribe partners to God are truly unclean: do not let them come near the Sacred Mosque after this year.*' This verse indicates fairly conclusively that polytheists are still expected to be a living presence, and that rather than being annihilated or imprisoned, they are simply to be prevented from entering the Sacred Mosque. Just as those who come to the Prophet asking for safe conduct are exempt, so also are those who do not come near the mosque the following year.

This series of exceptions shows that the original permission to kill was not an imperative of obligation.

Q. 9:5 gives permission, not an order, but in case it became necessary to defend the Muslims it was important that people should not be afraid to fight to defend themselves and others. The Muslim community included new converts, less firm in faith, less committed people and hypocrites who pretended to be Muslims. It is clear from verse 13 and following that at least some of these Muslims were hesitant about obeying the instructions given in verse 5, and needed to be urged:

How could you not fight a people who have broken their oaths, who tried to drive the Messenger out, who attacked you first? Do you fear them? It is God you should fear if you are true believers. Fight them: God will punish them at your hands, He will disgrace them, He will help you to conquer them, He will heal the believers' feelings and remove the rage from their hearts. God turns to whoever He will in His mercy; God is all-knowing and wise.

These verses give reasons and encourage such Muslims, if they are afraid, to engage the polytheists, saying that claiming to be believers without being ready to sacrifice '*and seek help only from God, His Messenger and the Believers*' will not be allowed to go untested (verse 16).

Verses 17–22 try to remove from the minds of hesitant Muslims any hesitation on the grounds that the polytheists were maintaining the mosque and giving drinks to the pilgrims. It also informs the polytheists that such acts will not make them equal to those who believe and are ready to struggle, with themselves and their possessions, in the way of God.

Verses 23–4 are directed at those Muslims who may refrain from following the instructions in verse 5 on the grounds of having some relatives among the polytheists, or that their trade or property might suffer or because of fear.

Verse 27, as always in the Qur'an, again opens the way for the disbelievers to return to God and urges the Muslims to forgive them as God is forgiving and merciful.

Verse 28, as already stated, only restricts polytheists from entering the Sacred Mosque '*after this year*', for they are unclean. (It is noteworthy that even Muslims themselves are not allowed to enter the mosque if they are in a state of ritual pollution (*janaba*)[28] until they have had a full wash.) The verse ends with, '*If you are afraid you may become poor,*[29] *[bear in mind that] God will enrich you out of His bounty if He pleases: God is all knowing and wise.*'

Here ends the entire passage, which deals with one and the same issue: permission, after the lapse of the four months' notice, to fight those polytheists who had broken their treaty.

Is There Anything New in the 'Sword Verse'?

Sura 9 is, chronologically speaking, the last sura to mention fighting. The permission it gives to fight and arrest those polytheists who had broken their treaty and were thus in a state of war with the Muslims did not bring anything new. The verse revealed first permitting fighting states: '*Permission is given to those who have been attacked, because they have been wronged and God is able to support them*' (Q. 22:39). From year 2 of the *hijra*, after the Battle of Badr and seven years earlier than the 'Sword Verse', comes the following revelation:

> *[Those] who, whenever you [Prophet] make a treaty with them, break it, for they have no fear of God. If you meet them in battle, make an example of them to those who come after them, so that they may take heed, and if you learn of treachery on the part of any people, throw their treaty back to them, for God does not love the treacherous.*
>
> Q. 8:56–8

'*Throw their treaty back to them*' is mirrored in Q. 9:7–8, '*How could there be a treaty between such polytheists and God and His Messenger?*' Following this, Sura 2 was revealed, including the verses: '*Fight, in God's cause, against those who fight you, but do not overstep the limits. God does not love those who overstep the limits*' (Q. 2:190–4). Here, the Muslims are forbidden to overstep the limits; Q. 9:10 describes the polytheists as the ones who overstep the limits. Again, in Sura 2 we read: '*Kill them [those who fight you] wherever you encounter them,*[30] *and drive them out from where they drove you out*' (Q. 2:191). This is no different from Q. 9:5, saying: '*Kill them [the polytheists who have broken the treaty] wherever you encounter them.*' Similarly, Sura 4, another Medinan sura, earlier than Sura 9, referring to the hypocrites and warning the Muslims against allying themselves with them, states: '*If they turn on you, seize them and kill them wherever you encounter them*' (Q. 4:89). The same sura states:

> *You will find others who wish to be safe from you and from their own people, but whenever they are back in a situation when they are tempted to fight you, they succumb to it. So, if they neither withdraw nor offer you peace, nor restrain themselves from fighting you, seize and kill them wherever you encounter them. We give you clear authority against such people.*
>
> Q. 4:91

All of these verses, which echo the same instructions and the same crucial words and phrases, date from the Medinan period, and can be seen to correspond with those found in the 'Sword Verse'. In fact, the only new things in the 'Sword Verse' are:

1. The phrase '*restrict [the polytheists'] movement*' – although even that is heralded earlier in '*expel them from where they expelled you*' (Q. 2:191);
2. The injunction to '*sit watching for [the polytheists] at every look-out post*';
3. The announcement that the polytheists were to be given four months' notice before any of this came into effect;
4. The description of the polytheists as being unclean and therefore not to be allowed into the mosque.[31]

On this basis, Q. 9:5 cannot mean, as Cook emphatically says, 'kill them unless they convert'. Nor, by any stretch of the imagination, does the 'they' it describes include – as asserted by Cook – Christians, Jews and unbelievers. When he says, 'a polytheist is a *mushrik* [...] and the term extends to Jews and Christians and indeed to unbelievers', his statement causes confusion where there is none in the Qur'an. The terms *mushrikūn* (polytheists), *kuffār* (unbelievers) and *ahl al-kitāb* (People of the Book, that is, Christians and Jews), are recognised as referring to quite distinct groups of people. If Cook's claim were true, how does he account for the largely peaceful co-existence of Christians, Jews and other non-Muslims in Muslim lands over the last 14 centuries? Many of these have made brilliant contributions to Islamic civilisation and culture, for example, the Christian translations of Greek works into Arabic which were readily adopted by Muslim scholars and resulted in a tremendous flourishing of Islamic philosophy and sciences. It is quite obvious from the beginning of Sura 9 that it is dealing only with '*the polytheists with whom you have a treaty*'.

Abrogation

We have seen that the 'Sword Verse' was dealing with a state of war brought about by some polytheists breaking their treaty with the Muslims. The only new additions this verse brought to the Qur'anic teachings about fighting the polytheists were that it gave them four months' notice and stopped access of polytheists to the mosque. None of these could conceivably abrogate '*there is no compulsion in religion*' at the beginning of Q. 2:256. Yet this claim has been made and persistently reported by Muslim extremists of various shades, as well as by anti-Islamic propagandists and some non-Muslim academics, past and present. Rather than isolate a few words, four in Arabic in this case, and base claims upon them, as such people have done, it is essential here to quote the whole verse of Q. 2:256:

There is no compulsion in religion: true guidance has become distinct from error, so whoever rejects false gods and believes in God has grasped the firmest hand-hold, one that will never break, and God is all-hearing and all-knowing.

This verse begins with the phrase *lā ikrāha fī'l-dīn* (there is no compulsion in religion). It is introduced by '*lā*', the particle of absolute negation in Arabic, which negates absolutely the notion of compulsion in religion. Religion in the Qur'an is based on choice, and true choice is based on knowledge and making matters clear for people to choose. The rest of the '*there is no compulsion in religion*' verse gives reasons justifying and explaining this statement. The structure of the sentence includes *faṣl* (removing the conjunction: in this case 'because'). This is a well-known convention in the Arabic language used to show concisely that what follows the *faṣl* is the reason for what comes before it; the structure is also quite obvious in the English rendition above. It is inconceivable that the Qur'an would abrogate any of this, including, '*true guidance has become distinct from error. God is all-hearing and all-knowing*'. Neither does it make sense linguistically to abrogate something and leave its reasons operative.

The preceding verse, the so-called 'Throne Verse' (Q. 2:255), which shows the glory of God, making Him clearly distinct from the false gods the polytheists worship, should also be borne in mind when reading the 'no compulsion' verse. It is because this True God is clearly distinguished from false gods that there is no need for compulsion in religion. As Abū Muslim and al-Qaffāl, two eminent exegetes, state: 'The verse means that God did not base the matter of faith on compulsion or coercion; rather on choice.'[32] To argue this case, al-Qaffāl states:

Having explained [in the 'Throne Verse'] the evidence of *tawḥīd* (oneness of God), in a thorough manner which leaves no excuse, God said the disbeliever no longer has any excuse for upholding his disbelief unless he is forced and coerced to embrace the faith, and this is not allowed or permissible in this world, which is meant to test people to see how they behave, and compulsion and coercion nullify the notion of testing, on which the Final Judgement is based. This is parallel to God saying, '*Let whoever wishes to believe do so, and let whoever wishes to disbelieve do so*' (Q. 18:29); '*If your Lord had wished so, all those on earth would have believed. Can you [Prophet] compel people to believe?*' (Q. 10:99); '*Are you, [Prophet] going to worry yourself to death because they will not believe? If We had wished, We could have sent them down a sign from heaven at which their necks would stay bowed in utter humility*' (Q. 28:3–4). What confirms this view is that God Almighty said, after 'no compulsion in religion', 'true guidance has become clear from error' [...] Coercion negates *taklīf* (individual responsibility which will be the basis for the Final Judgement).[33]

It is difficult to see how any of this can be abrogated by Q. 9:5, the 'Sword Verse', which gives the Muslims permission to fight some Arab polytheists who had broken their peace treaty. It is also important to note the following statement in Q. 2:256: '*Whoever rejects false gods and believes in God has grasped the firmest handhold, one that will never break.*' It does not say, 'whoever rejects false gods [...] will save himself from being killed', nor does it say, 'whoever embraces false gods will be killed or taken captive'.

Ibn Kathīr records a narration from a man named Asbaq, who stated:

I was a Christian slave owned by 'Umar Ibn al-Khaṭṭāb. He used to suggest to me that I become a Muslim but I would refuse, upon which he would say, 'There is no compulsion in religion' and would add, 'Asbaq, if you become a Muslim, we could use your services on matters concerning the Muslims.'[34]

Here is 'Umar, the head of the Muslim state, some years after the revelation of the 'Sword Verse' and the death of the Prophet, not thinking of coercing his own slave to become a Muslim. His stated motivation is obedience to the 'no compulsion' verse, which certain people claim to have been abrogated.

Thus, the claim by propagandists that Q. 2:256 is a Meccan verse, where Muhammad was at a disadvantage, having to deal with the strong pagans in Mecca, and that the 'Sword Verse' and others like it are Medinan verses, allowing the Muslims to compel non-Muslims to accept Islam, is baseless. Q. 2:256 comes towards the end of Sura 2 of the Qur'an, which is entirely Medinan, and not one single verse of it is reported by Qur'anic scholars, Muslim or non-Muslim, to be Meccan. Yet propagandists have used such incorrect dating and fallacious claims to advance their argument. For example, we see once again the author of the website islamreview.com, Abdullah Al-Araby, writing:

In Mecca Mohammed was weak, struggling to be accepted, often mocked at and ridiculed. He tried to appeal to the people of Mecca by being compassionate and loving. His teachings condemned violence, injustice, neglect of the poor. However, after he moved to Medina and his followers grew in strength and number, he became a relentless warrior, intent on spreading his religion by the sword. This change in Mohammed's personality becomes apparent by comparing the Meccan and the Medinan suras. The following are some examples: [...] In Sura 2:256 God tells Mohammed not to impose Islam by force 'There is no compulsion in religion.' While in verse 193 God tells him to kill whoever rejects Islam, 'Fight (kill) them until there is no persecution and the religion is God's.' [...] To justify this sudden change in the Qur'an's mood from peaceful to militant, conciliatory to confrontational, Mohammed claimed that it was God who told him so. It was God who abrogated the peaceful verses and replaced them by harsh ones.[35]

There are at least five fallacies in this piece of propaganda:

1. The implication that verse 256 of Sura 2 is Meccan and verse 193 is Medinan; verse 193 and verse 256 of Sura 2 are both Medinan;
2. The equation of 'fighting' with 'killing' in Al-Araby's statement, 'God tells him to kill whoever rejects Islam "Fight (kill) them until there is no persecution"'; 'fight' is different from 'kill';
3. The attribution of 'them' in Q. 2:293 to 'whoever rejects Islam', rather than to the actual subject, 'those who fight you' (mentioned in Q. 2:190);
4. The unsupported assertion that 'Muhammad claimed that it was God who told him so'; without giving any reference from the Qur'an or Hadith;
5. The representation of the statement that Muhammad himself said that 'it was God who abrogated the peaceful verses and replaced them with harsh ones' as established fact; in actuality, only extremists have alleged this.

Another recent instance of this perennially repeated incorrect assertion about the abrogation of Q. 2:256 came from quite another quarter. In connection with a reference to the Byzantine emperor Manuel II Paleologus (d. 1425), Pope Benedict XVI stated in his Regensburg lecture:

In the seventh conversation edited by Professor Khoury, the emperor touches on the theme of the jihad (holy war). The emperor must have known that sura 2:256 reads: *There is no compulsion in religion.* It is one of the suras of the early period, when Mohammed was still powerless and under threat. But naturally the emperor also knew the instructions, developed later and recorded in the Qur'an, concerning holy war.[36]

Whatever the emperor may have thought about this, his views on Islam would naturally have been coloured by the threat of Constantinople's imminent demise. Furthermore, the term 'holy war', used here, is certainly not an Islamic one.

There are also those within the Islamic tradition itself who have adopted the view that the 'Sword Verse' abrogated the 'no compulsion in religion' statement, especially those writing on the phenomenon of *naskh* (abrogation) in the Qur'an. This *naskh* phenomenon shows itself in two ways:

1. It is used by jurists, who confine it to replacing one legal ruling with another, due to the termination of the effective period of the earlier ruling. Examples frequently cited are the gradual increase in restriction on intoxicating substances, ending in a total ban as well as the gradual introduction of ritual prayers up to the final obligatory five daily prayers, and the verse dealing with the change of the prayer direction from Jerusalem to Mecca (Q. 2:144). In the first two examples, the 'abrogated' verses remain effective, but are superseded by a verse revealed later. Thus, '*do not come to prayer intoxicated*' (Q. 4:43) remains effective after the introduction of a total ban on intoxicants (Q. 5:90). However, abrogation in English means 'repeal, cancellation, annulment', and what we have here is extension rather than annulment. Scholarship in Qur'anic/Islamic studies should actually re-examine the universally accepted translation of *naskh* as 'abrogation'. In the third example, there is no abrogated verse in the Qur'an about praying towards Jerusalem, only the previous practice of the Prophet.

   Muslim jurists are more restrictive over the issue of *naskh* than exegetes and preachers. One jurist, for example, argues as follows:

   > It is not permissible for a Muslim to say something is abrogated without basing this on certainty, since it affects the *sharīʿa*, and you cannot rely for that on statements made by the common exegetes, or the *ijtihād* (independent reasoning) of any scholar without a true, transmitted, textual basis. Thus it is not admissible to rely on *ijtihād* without evidence, on statements of exegetes without evidence, nor on seeming contradictions between texts, nor on the fact that a text comes in the Qur'an after another, because the Qur'an is not arranged chronologically.[37]

2. The proponents of *naskh*, in a much wider sense, are neither jurists nor are they exegetes of recognised importance. Because common exegetes and preachers joined in claims about *naskh*, the number of verses that are taken to have been affected by *naskh* have increased over the centuries, with people widening the meaning of *naskh* to include any specification or exception in a given verse. Thus al-Zuhrī (d. 124/742)

> mentions 48 abrogated verses, al-Naḥḥās (d. 338/950) 138, Ibn Salāma (d. 410/1020) 238, Ibn al-'Atā'iqī (d. 790/1300) 231 and al-Fārisī (d. 461/1069) mentions 248.[38] Those who reacted against this trend include al-Suyūṭī (d. 911/1505), who confined the number to 20 verses in the whole Qur'an, some of which he considered disputable.[39] Shah Waliullah al-Dehlawi (d. 1762) reduced the number to just five.[40]

Hibat Allāh Ibn Salāma (d. 410/1020), in his book *Al-nāsikh wa-l-mansūkh* (*The Abrogating and the Abrogated*) – in the introduction he is described as an exegete, a grammarian and a teacher of recitation of the Qur'an[41] – is an extreme example of someone who adheres to the second, more general, concept of *naskh*. According to him, the 'Sword Verse' abrogated 124 verses in the Qur'an.[42] Amazingly, he considers the first main clause of the verse, '... *kill the polytheists wherever you find them*', as abrogated by its end '*but if they repent and perform the prayer, and pay the prescribed alms, let them go their way*'.[43] Not only that, but he then goes on to state that God made a further abrogation of the repentance verse by saying in verse 6, '*and if any of the polytheists should seek your protection [Prophet], grant it to him so that he may hear the word of God*'.

Ibn Salāma also considers that verse 7, '*except for those with whom you made a treaty at the Sacred Mosque: as long as they remain true to you, be true to them ...*', has been abrogated by '*kill the polytheists wherever you find them*' in the 'Sword Verse' before it.[44] According to this logic, if you say in English 'the class came, except for John', 'the class came' abrogates and annuls 'except for John', so we are left with no indication that John did not come. To call this exception *naskh* is a misconception of the meaning of *naskh*. Furthermore, how can a verse that has been abrogated by its own end and the following verse, still survive to abrogate another later verse and indeed a total of 124 verses of the Qur'an?

With such logic, no wonder Ibn Salāma considers this verse to be one of the amazing verses of the Qur'an! It shows something of how he understands the word 'abrogation', and how this understanding leads him to make such sweeping claims about abrogation in the Qur'an. Unfortunately, what he said is still being repeated. This gives us an example of how, in the Islamic tradition, authors often accumulate and include any claims or statements made by their predecessors. Although this practice may be considered to illustrate academic integrity in that it actively works against the suppression of information, on close examination much of what Ibn Salāma said will not stand up to proper linguistic or textual analysis. In fact, Ibn Salāma shows total disregard for context and wrenches short statements out of place. A few examples of what he thinks the 'Sword Verse' abrogated will suffice us here:

1. Q. 2:83. '*We took a pledge from the Children of Israel: Worship none but God, be good to your parents and kinsfolk, to orphans and the poor; speak nicely to people*'.[45] Ibn Salāma considers the order *'speak nicely to people'* to be abrogated by the 'Sword Verse'.[46] Yet how can a description of an instruction given at the time of Moses to the Children of Israel be abrogated by a permission given to the Muslims at the time of Muhammad to fight the polytheists who had broken the treaty with them? This clearly shows Ibn Salāma's total disregard for context just as he totally disregarded the context in reading Q. 9:5, the 'Sword Verse'.
2. Q. 40:11–12. Verse 11 talks about the polytheists in Hell, admitting '*Lord [...] now we recognise our sins. Is there any way out?*' in response to which, in verse 12, they are told by the angels, '*This is all because, when God alone was invoked, you rejected this, yet when others were associated with Him you believed. Judgement belongs to God, the Most High, the Most Great.*' Ibn Salāma blatantly and mysteriously asserts, against the context: 'The meaning of the ruling on this verse in this world is abrogated by the Sword Verse.'[47] What he considers abrogated in Q. 40:12 are the words '*Judgement belongs to God, the most great*'. It is amazing that this reported statement, made by the angels to those in Hell in the Hereafter, could be abrogated by a verse giving permission to fight the polytheists who broke the Hudaybiyya treaty.
3. Q. 76:5–6. God speaks of the *righteous* on the Day of Judgement '*drinking from a spring for God's servants, which flows abundantly at their wish.*' In verse 7 it gives, as a reason for this grace, the fact that '*they fulfilled their vows, they fear a day of widespread woes; they give food to the poor, the orphan and the captive, though they love it themselves, saying, "We feed you for the sake of God alone*"'. Yet Ibn Salāma tells us that giving food to the captive was abrogated by the 'Sword Verse'.[48]
4. Q. 15:88. '*[Prophet] do not look longingly at the good things we have given some to enjoy. Do not grieve over the disbelievers, but lower your wings over the believers*' is also abrogated, he thinks,[49] by the 'Sword Verse'.[50]

At the end of his book, Ibn Salāma asserts:

> Everything in the Qur'an of the type 'turn away from them', 'bear patiently with what they say', 'ignore them', 'be patient as befits you', 'bear with them graciously' and all similar verses are abrogated by the Sword Verse.[51]

Ibn Salāma and others like him thus scan the entire Qur'an for anything which goes against killing the disbelievers – he does not even say the polytheists – and claim that it has been abrogated, giving no other authority. If this principle were applied now, in the way Ibn Salāma and others have understood it, for instance to English law, it would create havoc. In fact, none of the present-day extremists and terrorists who cite the 'Sword Verse' in their arguments have gone as far as Ibn Salāma.

Conclusion

This chapter has partly been devoted to exploring the theological and ideological edifices constructed around the 'Sword Verse' by two specific figures, Michael Cook and Ibn Salāma, and illustrating that these are no more than myth. On the one hand, Michael Cook makes this verse the basis for an injunction to 'kill' all polytheists, including Christians, Jews and disbelievers. He then goes on from this baseless claim to describe this alleged aggression against other religions as being a mark of Islam that distinguishes it from the modern Western, 'tolerant' civilisation, in a clear example of anti-Islamic polemic. On the other hand, Ibn Salāma has been seen to be extreme and inconsistent, sometimes incoherent, in his view of the 'Sword Verse' and what it abrogated.

Other anti-Islamic propagandists not only repeat such extremist views but, as we have seen, go even further to claim, against all historical fact, that the 'no compulsion in religion' verse was revealed in Mecca and therefore was abrogated by the 'Sword Verse', revealed at a later stage. Present-day Muslim extremist preachers and terrorists hold a very similar, if not the same, view and use the same methodology on the 'Sword Verse'. Thus Sheikh Abdullah al-Faisal (original name Trevor William Forrest), a fiery Jamaican preacher formerly living in South London, repeatedly quoted the 'Sword Verse' in his taped sermons, which were on sale in London and elsewhere until he was arrested, prosecuted and convicted in 2003, and sentenced to seven years imprisonment.[52] In this particular case, Sheikh Faisal even went so far as to cut off the beginning of the verse, '*when the four months are over*', and simply quoted, '*kill the polytheists wherever you find them*'.

Putting these individuals aside, the main aim of this chapter has been to employ a close contextual, linguistic analysis of the actual verses of the Qur'an (rather than claims made about them on the basis of wrenching a few words out of their original context). This has been done in an attempt to place Q. 9:5 in its proper context and define exactly the area of its application: the permissibility of fighting and restricting the movement of the enemy in times of war, and preventing them from entering the Muslim Sanctuary. This approach has demonstrated that, in the final analysis, Q. 9:5 does not differ in any significant way from other Qur'anic instructions, some of them having been revealed before the 'Sword Verse', permitting the Muslims to defend themselves. It deals with the situation of war in which an enemy had declared that they had broken their treaty and would resort to spears and swords. The verse simply makes the declaration that God and His Messenger are no longer bound by the treaty the enemy has broken, and gives this enemy a whole four months' notice before hostilities may begin. It is also notable that the verse merely gives permission for the Muslims to fight or restrict their enemies' movements, and then only those polytheists who have broken the treaty, not any other polytheists. Even within the boundaries of its permissive scope, it puts restrictions on the Muslims, as the Qur'an always does when mentioning the theme of fighting, allowing the Muslims no more than self-defence and what is now permitted in international law, that is, the right not to allow the enemy to enter one's territory. It opens the way for the enemy to cease fighting, mend their ways, to request and receive safe conduct, to hear the word of God if so wished and urges the Muslims to forgive people who do this.

It is not surprising, then, that not a single person is reported to have been killed or arrested as a result of this verse. The 'Sword Verse' was revealed in 9 AH, only a year before the Prophet went on his final pilgrimage, three months after which he died. Authors on *sīra* (the biography of the Prophet), the most famous being Ibn Isḥāq, and on *maghāzī* (military campaigns), of whom the best known is al-Wāqidī, meticulously recorded the number and names of individuals, Muslim and non-Muslim, who fought and died in those campaigns, but did not record the name of one person killed on the basis of the 'Sword Verse'.

Perhaps the most surprising thing about this verse is that some people insist on calling it the 'Sword Verse', in spite of the fact that the word 'sword' (*sayf*) does not occur anywhere in the Qur'an.[53] It is also incredible that it has become so often quoted by both Muslim extremists and Western propagandists as an example of Islamic aggression against other religions.

The above discussion and analysis of the actual Qur'anic text have shown that selective quotation, total disregard for context and historical background, misinterpretation of the concept of *naskh* (abrogation), incorrect dating of verses, confusion of terms, fallacies, unfounded claims and propagandist zeal have all contributed to the construction of a whole web of myth around the 'Sword Verse'. Some, unfortunately, insist on clinging to myths.

Closely related to fighting in relation to the so-called 'Sword Verse' is fighting tax defaulters in the *jizya* verse, and this is the subject of Chapter 2.

2

Qur'anic *Jizya*: Tax Defaulters

I swear by God that if they refuse to pay me even a camel-halter which they used to pay to the Prophet, I will fight them for it.[1]

This oath by the first Caliph Abū Bakr (r. 632–4 CE), swearing to fight those Muslims who refused to pay *zakāh* (the obligatory tax on Muslims and one of the pillars of Islam) after the Prophet died, should be compared with Q. 9:29, which deals with fighting People of the Book (those who received divine scriptures, meaning particularly Jews and Christians) who refused to pay the *jizya* tax. The so-called *jizya* verse has been translated by Arberry as follows:

Fight those who believe not in God and the Last Day and do not forbid what God and His Messenger have forbidden – such men as practise not the religion of truth, being of those who have been given the Book – until they pay the tribute out of hand and have been humbled.[2]

The *jizya* verse has been the basis of a huge amount of writing by Muslims in Islamic law and Qur'anic exegesis, as well as by non-Muslim scholars writing about Islam. It continues to be used by some academics, media and anti-Islamic propagandists to denigrate Islam and its treatment of non-Muslims, especially the aforementioned People of the Book.[3]

This chapter aims to examine the verse afresh, using close linguistic analysis and paying due regard to the linguistic and historical contexts of the verse with all their elements, as well as the general style of the Qur'an and what it says outside the confines of this verse. Such analysis will prove the picture that has been drawn from this verse, based on various historical contingencies, both by Muslim exegetes and jurists and non-Muslim writers, is post-Qur'anic, inaccurate and far removed from the actual picture as given in the Qur'an itself.

Cook, talking about tolerating the beliefs of others, states, 'The Qur'an has much to say about the treatment of false belief, but the traditional Muslim scholars saw the core of it in two verses.'[4] Cook here refers to Q. 9:5, known as the 'Sword Verse', which was discussed in the previous chapter, and Q. 9:29, the *jizya* verse. Again, it is clear that he neglected the Arabic text of the Qur'an and was relying on what he calls 'the traditional Muslim scholars'.[5]

Literal translations of the *jizya* verse, such as Arberry's quoted above, make it more difficult for a reader[6] to recover the real meaning of the Arabic text. Beyond this initial hurdle, there is the interpretation of crucial elements of this verse. Seven points are counted in this one verse which have given rise to misunderstandings and each will be discussed phrase by phrase as follows:

1. '*Fight those who believe not in God and the Last Day* (*qātalū'lladhīna lā yu'minūna bi'llāhi wa-lā bi'l-yawmi'l-ākhir*)'

For reasons we explain later, even some Muslim exegetes have taken this phrase literally and set out to explain how the People of the Book, to whom this verse refers, do not believe in God and the Last Day; that the Jews and Christians associate others with God, for example, by seeing Ezra and Jesus as 'sons of God'.[7] These exegetes also explain that Jews and Christians do not really believe in the physical resurrection[8] and therefore cannot be said to believe in the Last Day.[9] Such explanations run counter to what we know of Qur'anic style. The Qur'an often speaks of belief in God and the Last Day to emphasise a point; if you believe in God and the Last Day, you should refrain from such and such, or do such and such. This rhetorical expression is found, for example, in instructions advocating good treatment of women in divorce situations (see Q. 2:232, Q. 8:41 and Q. 65:2). It is also very common in the Hadith, for instance, 'Let him who believes in God and the Last Day not harm his neighbour' and 'Let him who believes in God and the Last Day say what is good or keep silent'.[10] In Q. 5:81, in connection with the People of the Book, the Qur'an says, '*If they had believed in God, the Prophet and in what was sent down to him they would never have allied themselves with the disbelievers, but most of them are rebels.*' This does not negate the belief of the People of the Book in God, the Prophet[11] and Scripture; but rather simply states that they do not act on such belief because they are rebellious. Commenting on the *jizya* verse, Abū Ḥayyān (d. 745/1344) states, 'they are so described because their way [of acting] is the way of those who do not believe in God'.[12] According to him, the meaning in Q. 9.29 then is 'who do not truly believe'. In any case, there is nothing in the Qur'an to say that not believing in God and the Last Day is in itself grounds for fighting anyone.

2. '*And do not forbid what God and His Messenger have forbidden* (*wa-lā yuḥarrimūna mā ḥarrama'llāhu wa-rasūluhu*)'

Many exegetes have interpreted this phrase as asserting that '*what God and His Messenger have forbidden*' includes such things as eating pork and drinking wine. However, this cannot be correct since Islamic law does not require the People of the Book to refrain from these and indeed Muslims should not interfere with them in these matters; any Muslim who pours away their wine or forcibly appropriates it is liable to pay compensation.[13] Other explanations given by Abū Ḥayyān are that the People of the Book do not forbid lying about God. For instance, they say, '*We are God's sons and beloved*' (Q. 5:18) or '*Nobody will enter the Gardens unless they are Jews or Christians*' (Q. 2:111). '*What God has forbidden them*' also means usury and unlawful consumption of the property of gentiles (Q. 3:75), according to Abū Ḥayyān;[14] however, these actions do not constitute grounds for fighting the People of the Book.

The context of this phrase in the *jizya* verse requires that the thing being forbidden is something that the People of the Book ought not to be doing according to their belief in God and their own prophets, but must also connect to non-payment of *jizya*, which is the cause for fighting them. It cannot relate to their food and drink or what they say about God, because these are not given as causes for fighting them, and after paying the *jizya* they will still be consuming these things and saying these things without being fought. The closest and most viable cause must relate to their obligation to pay *jizya*, that is, unlawfully consuming what belongs to the Muslim state, which, al-Bayḍāwī (d. *c*.685/1286) explains, 'has been decided that they should give',[15] since their own scriptures and prophets forbid breaking agreements and not paying what is due to others.[16]

'*His Messenger*' in this verse has been interpreted by exegetes as referring to the Prophet Muhammad or the People of the Book's own earlier messengers, Moses or Jesus, but the latter must be the correct interpretation as it is already assumed that the People of the Book did not believe in Muhammad or forbid what he forbade. They are condemned for not obeying their own prophet who told them to honour their agreements. To make sense in the context of the *jizya* verse, this must mean 'they do not forbid breaking an agreement – something that God and His Messenger forbid'. The agreement here was to pay *jizya*. It is not likely to mean that they should pay *jizya* when initially asked to do so. God and their prophets did not forbid refusing to pay what one is simply being asked to pay, but they did forbid going back on an agreement which has been entered into. They forbid refusing to pay what is due to others (Q. 3:75–8).

3. '*Such men as practise not the religion of truth* (*wa-lā yadīnūna dīna'l-ḥaqq*)'

Dawood translates this phrase as referring to those 'who do not embrace the true faith'[17] and Alan Jones gives 'who do not follow the religion of truth'.[18] These interpretations, and indeed the interpretations of many Muslim exegetes, are based on a hasty reading of the Arabic text. The main meaning of the Arabic *dāna* is 'he obeyed', and of the many meanings of *dīn* is 'behaviour' (*al-sīra wa'l-'āda*). Al-Fayrūzabādī (d. 817/1415) gives more than 12 meanings for the word *dīn*, placing the meaning 'worship of God, religion' lower in the list.[19] *Al-Mu'jam al-wasīṭ* gives the following definition: '*dāna* is to be in the habit of doing something good or bad; "*dāna bi-* something" is to take it as a religion and worship God through it'. Thus, when the verb *dāna* is used in the sense of 'to believe' or 'to practise a religion', it takes the preposition '*bi-*' after it (e.g. *dāna bi'l-islām*) and this is the only usage in which the word means religion.[20] In the *jizya* verse, it does not say *lā yadīnūna bi-dīni'l-ḥaqq*; rather *lā yadīnūna dīna'l-ḥaqq*.[21] The meaning that fits into the *jizya* verse is thus 'those who do not follow the way of justice (*al-ḥaqq*)', that is, by breaking their agreement and refusing to pay what is due.

4. '*Being of those who have been given the Book* (*mina'lladhīna ūtū'l-kitāb*)'

'*Min*' here has normally been explained by exegetes as *bayāniyya* ('explanatory'), that is, it explains who is meant by 'those who do not believe in God' and so on, which gives the impression that all the People of the Book are to be fought. The first meaning of '*min*' in Arabic is *tab'īḍiyya* ('partitive'), meaning 'of' or 'from among': hence 'those *of* the People of the Book'. In fact, in Qur'anic usage, whenever '*min*' occurs with the People of the Book it is partitive (compare Q. 2:109, Q. 3:69, 75 and 113, Q. 5:80 and Q. 9:34). The distinction is crucial because, according to the partitive sense, only those of the People of the Book should be fought who did not truly believe and followed neither what their God or their prophets said, nor the way of justice. The Qur'an does not say, 'Fight the People of the Book until they give *jizya*', but 'Fight *those of them* who do not truly believe, do not forbid [...] until they give the *jizya*'.

Significantly, in the *jizya* verse, the Qur'an introduces the causes of the offence of those to be fought before identifying the guilty ones as being from among the People of the Book. The offence is failing to pay what is due to the Muslim state in which they live. The earlier part of the verse condemns their behaviour, which leads them to the real offence for which they are to be fought. The whole text is addressed to the Prophet as the head of the Muslim state and the Muslims as citizens of that state.

5. '*Until they pay the tribute* (*ḥattā yuʿṭūʾl-jizya*)'

It is significant that the verse does not say, 'fight them until they agree to pay the *jizya*', but that this phrase, when seen in the context of the verse as a whole, implies that the People of the Book had already agreed to pay *jizya*: if they did not pay, they would be fought until they paid.

Jizya is discussed in the *Encyclopaedia of the Qur'ān* under the title 'Poll Tax',[22] which immediately brings in connotations and associations of a much-resented and failed foreign system. In fact, 'poll tax' does not translate the Arabic word *jizya*. It is also inaccurate because women and old men, clerics and children normally did not have to pay the *jizya*, nor did anyone who could not afford to pay, unlike a poll tax, which by definition is levied on every individual (poll meaning head) regardless of gender, age or ability to pay. Such inaccurate translations ignore the Qur'an and can contribute to a negative image of Islam. The root verb of *jizya* is *j-z-y*, 'to reward somebody for something', 'to pay what is due in return for something' and, as will be explained later, it has a positive connotation. The important question now is, what was the *jizya* paid in return for? Many exegetes and Western scholars take this to mean that it was in return for allowing Christians and Jews to live in the Muslim state, practising their religion and being protected. From the practice of the early Muslim community it is known that Christians and Jews were not obliged to join the Muslims in fighting to defend the state. For example, the Prophet's treaty with the Christians of Najrān stipulated that they should not be obliged to join the Muslim army (*lā yuḥsharūn*).[23] This was so because military *jihād* has an Islamic religious connotation and was therefore not imposed on them. As Muḥammad 'Imāra puts it, 'those who did volunteer to fight with the Muslims against the Persians and Byzantines were exempted from the *jizya* and shared the battle gains with the Muslims'.[24] *Jizya* in this sense can be considered, as 'Imāra states, '*badal jundiyya*' ('in exchange for military service'), not in exchange for the People of the Book being allowed to keep their own faith.[25]

Moreover, Abū 'Ubayda, one of the Prophet's companions and commander of the Muslim army, during his campaign in Syria in 15/635, when it became clear to him that he could not defend a community that paid *jizya*, returned the *jizya* to them saying, 'As we cannot defend you, we have no right to charge you the *jizya*'.[26] Beyond the sphere of protecting them, paying *jizya* is clearly meant to be a contribution to the state. In the Muslim state, Muslims have to pay *zakāh*. People of the Book, who enjoy the benefits of living in the Muslim state, are exempted from *zakāh* because there is a religious, Islamic side to it, since it is a pillar of Islam.

6. '*Out of hand* (*'an yadin*)'

The expression *'an yadin* is most controversial and has given rise to numerous interpretations. Abū Ḥayyān[27] presented a long list of interpretations including: that they should give the *jizya* 'by their own hand'; 'prompt and not delayed payment'; 'with the hand of the giver being under the hand of the receiver'; 'admitting [that they should be paying]'; 'as a result of power and coercion and humiliation by the Muslims and the fact that their order is carried out'; 'as a sign of favour to the payers' or 'out of their wealth and ability, so that it is not taken from the poor'. Al-Zamakhsharī (d. 538/1143) explains that 'hand' could be interpreted either as the hand of the giver, in which case it means 'willingly, without resisting', 'in currency, not postponed, and not sent by an intermediary', or it is the hand of the receiver, in which case it means the powerful hand of the Muslim over the givers or 'the generous hand' because it is accepting the *jizya* and refraining from killing them, 'which is a great favour'.[28]

Interpreting this phrase as referring to the hand of the receiver seems to be far-fetched because the subject of the verb *yu'ṭū* ('they give') is definitely the givers, with no mention of a receiving hand. Abū Ḥayyān, writing in the eighth/fourteenth century, in the footsteps of numerous other exegetes, had accumulated all their views (an example of a practice well known in classical Muslim scholarship, where authors felt it was a matter of integrity to acknowledge and include the views of other scholars), and cites more than 30 opinions. He admitted that the Qur'an said nothing about any of these.[29]

However, al-Ṭabarī, who died in 310/922, about four centuries before Abū Ḥayyān, gives only one explanation: 'it means "from their hands to the hands of the receiver"; just as we say "I spoke to him mouth to mouth" we also say "I gave it to him hand to hand".'[30] Al-Ṭabarī's explanation is the most obvious and natural on the basis of the Arabic expression as attested by Arabic lexicographers. All the other explanations seem to have been introduced later, contaminated by historical factors and by the particular interpretation of the following phrase in the text referring to their having been humbled (discussed in point (7) below). Those who follow such explanations have neglected the Qur'an and relied instead on the practice of Muslim communities in later centuries.

We know that the Qur'an comments on existing, actual situations at that time. It would not have said *'an yadin* unless it was talking about some people who were delaying payments or trying to get out of paying.

7. '*And have been humbled* (*wa-hum ṣāghirūn*)'

This is a circumstantial (*ḥāl*) clause. Again, Abū Ḥayyān gives a list of five ways in which the People of the Book can show their humbleness, including that they should stand and the recipient be sitting; that they should not be thanked for giving *jizya*; that the receiver should say to the giver, 'Pay the *jizya*', and smack him on the back of his neck; or that someone should take hold of his beard and hit him under the jaw. Other ways mentioned by al-Rāzī are that the payer should come by himself, walking, not riding. Abū Ḥayyān comments that the verse does not mention any of this (*lam tata'arraḍ li-ta'yīn shay' minhā al-āya*), thus rejecting these interpretations.[31]

In contrast to all this, there is a straightforward explanation, more in keeping with Islamic teaching, which is mentioned by al-Rāzī and Abū Ḥayyān. According to this, the meaning of *ṣāghirūn* is merely that instead of considering themselves above payment, the very act of paying the *jizya* in itself constitutes their submission. Any suggestion or notion of humiliation, not simply submission, associated with this word must have come after the time of the Prophet. It is attributed to Ibn 'Abbās, a companion of the Prophet, that the payer should be made to pay and his back pushed even if he is already paying.[32] This notion of humiliation also runs contrary to the Qur'an itself, for example Q. 29:46, '*Do not dispute with the People of the Book except in the best manner*', as well as a Prophetic Hadith, stating: 'May God have mercy on the man who is liberal and easy-going (*samḥ*) when he buys, when he sells and when he demands what is due to him.'[33] The reports of the actual practice of the early caliphs and Muslim rulers show quite the opposite to the views of the *mufassirūn* (exegetes). They would not permit any humiliation or ill-treatment of anyone required to pay the *jizya.* On the contrary, they were magnanimous in instructing that non-Muslims be treated with respect, that payment be deferred if they were in difficulty and waived if they were unable to pay.[34]

In view of the ethics of the Qur'an and Hadith, it is unthinkable such practices as mentioned above could be based on the Qur'an. In this context, *wa-hum ṣāghirūn* simply means 'submitting to the tax'. In modern Arabic taxation, governments have departments of *al-khuḍū' al-ḍarībī,* which lists everyone who is subject to taxation. Lane's entry for the word *khuḍū'* in his *Lexicon* lists it as meaning 'being lowly, humble or submissive', while Hans Wehr[35] gives 'submission, obedience, humility, subjection'. The fact is that everybody, Muslim or otherwise, is subject to taxation and there is no humility or shame in this.

In the application of the *jizya* verse, Muslim jurists have been shown to be influenced by the earlier taxation systems of the Persian Sassanids and the Byzantine Romans.[36] The views of the exegetes on *'an yadin wa-hum ṣāghirūn* must have been coloured by the actual situations in their times when the enmity between Muslims and Christians in Muslim lands, such as Iraq, Syria, Egypt and beyond, had accelerated during the Crusades and, in modern times, with colonial occupation. Such situations were different from those in the Prophet's lifetime. Abū Hayyān's statement that 'the Qur'anic verse mentions nothing of this' is very telling here. Many exegetes were distorting what the Qur'an said.

In view of the many interpretations exegetes gave for different elements of this verse, it may be assumed that the verse appears to foster a host of opinions and is somewhat open to the vagaries of interpreters. However, such vagaries were actually the result of the traditionally atomistic approach of exegetes who dealt with a word or phrase in isolation. Al-Zamakhsharī, for instance, in his *tafsīr,* deals only with certain words or phrases, a practice likely to isolate them from the context of the whole verse. He suggests a possible meaning and sets out to support it by saying 'a poet said' or 'the Arabs said', then goes on to suggest another meaning and says, 'a poet says' or 'Arabs said'. They may have said this, but in what context? Does such a meaning fit in the context we have in hand or does the meaning of a word change in a different context? Less able exegetes came up with interpretations that were far removed from the context and from what we know of the Qur'an as a whole. The practice of including everything anybody ever mentioned often did not help clarifying the intent of a verse. Al-Rāzī starts his discussion of *'an yadin* by saying '*wa-ikhtalafū fī-qawlihi*' ('they differed over God's saying'), then lists all the information that was available at his time.[37] Al-Bayḍawī gives it in the form of '... or ... or ...'. By the time of Abū Ḥayyān, the list had grown further, however, he dealt a blow to this multiplicity of interpretations by stating categorically that the verse gave no concrete grounds for many of the opinions proffered. Had many exegetes paid regard to context and dealt with the verse as a unified, coherent unit, we would not have witnessed such variations.

Just as we explained under *'an yadin,* here again the Qur'an would not have said *wa-hum sāghirūn* if it were not talking about people who arrogantly refused to submit to the *jizya* system.

The Occasion of Revelation (*sabab al-nuzūl*)

The *sabab al-nuzūl* of the *jizya* verse is reported by al-Ṭabarī as follows: 'It was said that this verse was revealed to the Prophet when he was ordered to fight the Byzantines, so he embarked, after its revelation, on the Tabūk expedition.'[38] Al-Ṭabarī does not give any basis for this assumption. The clause 'it was said' would, in Hadith scholarship, be called a form of *taḍ'īf* ('weakness in the trustworthiness of the Hadith') since the source is left unclear. It is significant that al-Rāzī, who normally records *asbāb al-nuzūl,* does not mention any such story.[39] More importantly, nor does al-Wāḥidī (d. 468/1075), who wrote an entire book on *asbāb al-nuzūl,* though he gives the *sabab* for the previous verse.[40] When we come to al-Suyūṭī (d. 911/1505), in his book on the occasions of revelation, again he does not give any *sabab* for verse 29, though he gives one for verse 28 and then moves on to verse 30.[41] However, al-Ṭabarī's statement was taken verbatim by Abū Ḥayyān who gives the claim as an established fact.[42] It is possible to accept al-Ṭabarī's statement about the time of revelation, but it does not say the order to fight was in connection with Tabūk itself or that those who refused to pay *jizya* were from Tabūk. In Tabūk there were Byzantines, not Jews, but Jews were definitely included in the *jizya* verse, as they are referred to specifically before the Christians in verses 30, 31 and 34.

Abū Hayyān states,[43] immediately following the claim that it was to do with Tabūk: 'It was said that the verse was revealed with regard to Banū Qurayẓa and Naḍīr', two Jewish clans in Medina. This could well be the correct reason and time for the revelation; if the verse does have anything to do with Tabūk, we would have to assume that their refusal to pay *jizya* occurred just before Muslims were going to Tabūk.

Regrettably, therefore, we do not have in the literature any decisive *sabab al-nuzūl* for the *jizya* verse, and so have to rely on linguistic analysis, the context of the verse and what the Qur'an says in other places.

As previously pointed out, we know that the Qur'an is a reactive text. It responds to situations that occurred while it was being revealed: '*Fight those who fight you*' (Q. 2:190); '*Permission is given to those who are being fought*' (Q. 22:40); and in situations other than fighting, '*Believers, do not approach the prayer when intoxicated*' (Q. 4:43); '*Perish the hand of Abū Lahab*' (Q. 111:1). This habit of the Qur'an is an important factor that should be borne in mind in the present situation. It would not have used the word *ṣāghirūn* unless those liable were refusing to pay; if the *jizya* had been introduced in this verse for the very first time, rather than being enforced, we could expect the Qur'an to say, 'take from them the *jizya*', in analogy to Q. 9:103 which introduces the giving of alms with the words, '*[Prophet], take alms out of their property (khudh min amwālihim ṣadaqatan)*'. This would be consistent with the Prophet's practice as recorded in the Hadith, whether referring to the polytheists or the People of the Book:[44]

> Give them three alternatives, whichever of them they accept (*fa-in hum ajābūka*), take it from them and leave them alone (*fa'qbal minhum wa-kuff 'anhum*). Ask them first to become Muslims. If they accept, you should accept this from them and leave them alone; if not, ask them to pay *jizya*. If they accept, take it from them and leave them alone, and if not, fight them.

Nor would the Qur'an have said earlier in the *jizya* verse, '*who do not forbid what God and His Messenger forbids and who do not behave according to the rules of justice*', unless they were breaking an earlier agreement to pay. Breaking an agreement is forbidden by their own prophets and by the rules of justice and fair play, which also demand keeping one's agreement and paying taxes in a state in which one lives, benefiting from its protection and welfare provisions.

It is reported that the second Caliph 'Umar b. al-Khaṭṭāb (r. 634–644 CE) passed by the door of people at which there was a beggar who was an old blind man. 'Umar struck his arm from behind and asked, 'To which People of the Book do you belong?' He said, 'I am a Jew.' 'Umar said, 'What has compelled you to beg?' The man replied, 'I am begging in order to get money to pay for *jizya* and my need, as I am old.' Then 'Umar held his hand and took him to his house and gave him gifts and money. He then sent him to the Treasurer (the keeper of the *bayt al-māl*) who had been instructed to take care of the man and whomsoever was like him. 'Umar added, 'We have not done justice to this man as we took *jizya* from him when he was young, but we forsook him when he was old. Verily, the *ṣadaqa* is for the poor and destitute. And this man is a destitute from the People of the Book.' Thus 'Umar exempted taking the *jizya* from him.[45]

It is important to note that the disagreeable behaviour of the People of the Book is expressed in Q. 9:29 in three negative clauses, stating what they fail to do: '*who do not believe in God*'; '*who do not forbid what God and the Messenger forbid*'; and '*who do not behave according to the rule of justice*'. This intimates another negative 'who have not paid'. The three negative clauses are shown as failure on the part of the People of the Book to do what they should do, made more serious by stating after it that they have been given the Book (*ūtū 'l-kitāb*) in accordance with which they should conduct themselves. In contrast, the reasons given in the Qur'an for fighting the polytheists are put in positive sentences, basing it on certain actions ascribed to them: they fight the Muslims (Q. 2:190); they break their treaties with them and revile their religion (Q. 8:56–7, Q. 9:5 and 12). Q. 9:5, which is about fighting those who broke their agreement, gives us an indication of how Q. 9:29, the *jizya* verse, has to be read. So the sense would be: 'Fight them until they accept to pay the *jizya* that has been agreed upon before.'[46] Based on the above analysis, this emerges to be the original meaning of Q. 9:29, but apparently because it is the only verse in the Qur'an that deals with *jizya*, jurists and exegetes take it to apply to all situations, whether the People of the Book have agreed to pay beforehand or when payment is initially demanded from them.

Q. 9:28, the immediately preceding verse, says:

Believers, the [polytheists] are truly unclean. Do not let them come near the Sacred Mosque after this year. If you are afraid you may become poor, God will enrich you out of His bounty if He pleases: God is all knowing and wise.

The fact that this verse is adjacent to the *jizya* verse has led some to conclude that the *jizya* was introduced to compensate the believers for the loss of trade with the polytheists. Indeed, al-Qurṭubī (d. 671/1272) states the Muslims felt concerned about the cessation of trade that the polytheists brought to Mecca, 'so God Almighty said, "If you are afraid you may become poor" in this verse, then made taking the *jizya* lawful in verse 29'. He goes on to say it had not been taken before, thus making it a compensation for trade that would be lost.[47] Al-Qurṭubī does not give a reference for this assertion about compensation, but even if it were to be well founded, what verse 29 introduces is *enforcing* payment and the wording of the verse makes it unlikely that it was *introducing jizya* for the first time, as explained above.

The *jizya* verse states that it only applies to *some* of these People of the Book, that is, the ones who are misbehaving, as mentioned above. Thus, for example, there is no order recorded that the Christians of Najrān, who honoured their treaty with the Prophet and paid their *jizya*, should be fought. Discussion on the *jizya* verse, as we said, comes after discussion of fighting the polytheists. Polytheists are described earlier in the same sura: '*Where believers are concerned, they [the polytheists] respect no tie of kinship or treaty. They are the ones who are committing aggression [against the Muslims]*' (Q. 9:10). The Qur'an urges the Muslims strongly in various ways to fight such people (Q. 9:1–15) and again, in the *jizya* verse, which, as is suggested, deals with people who have broken an agreement, we find the same exhortation to fight them. This starts immediately by showing their misbehaviour: they do not truly believe in God and the Last Day and do not obey the teachings of their own prophets, but they should be true to their word. Nor indeed do they adhere to the normal requirements of justice. Q. 9:30–5 are no more than further urging of the believers; if these People of the Book attribute children to God, in a way similar to earlier pagans,[48] taking '*their rabbis and monks as well as Christ as their lords*' and trying '*to extinguish God's light with their mouths*', and if many of their rabbis and monks '*wrongfully consume people's possessions and turn people away from God's path*', it is not surprising that they should refuse to pay the *jizya* that was due to the state. The behaviour of these rabbis and monks, in consuming people's possessions wrongfully, and the statement that they were taken as lords to be obeyed, suggest, in the author's view, that these religious leaders incited their followers not to pay *jizya* or at least did not command them to honour their commitment to pay as members of the state they lived in. This is the wider context of the *jizya* verse in the Qur'an: Q. 9:30–5 is not given as reasons to fight the People of the Book or as descriptions of them in general. These verses first and foremost pertain to certain Jewish and Christian leading figures and portray them in a light that highlights their lack of responsibility. The Qur'an sets out its general assessment of the People of the Book elsewhere, saying:

> *They are not all alike: there are some among the People of the Book who are upright, who recite God's revelation during the night, who bow down in worship, who believe in God and the*

Last Day, who order what is right and forbid what is wrong, who are quick to do good deeds. These people are among the righteous and they will not be denied [the rewards] for whatever good deeds they do: God knows exactly who is conscious of Him.

Q. 3:114–15

Similarly:

There are People of the Book who, if you [Prophet] entrust them with a heap of gold, will return it to you intact, but there are others of them who, if you entrust them with a single dinar, will not return it to you unless you keep standing over them, because they say, 'We are under no obligation towards the Gentiles.' They tell a lie against God and they know it. No indeed, God loves those who keep their agreements and are mindful of Him.

Q. 3:75–6

It would not be surprising if those who would not hand over one dinar that was in their custody 'unless you keep standing over them' would refuse the one dinar of *jizya*. Those Jews who would return a whole ton of gold intact would not need to be fought for one dinar of *jizya*. This supports our interpretation of '*min*' in the *jizya* verse as being 'of' or 'from among' and referring to certain people, not the People of the Book in general.

In Q. 9:34 too, the Qur'an discriminates clearly and does not say that *all* rabbis and monks, at different times and places, consume people's wealth wrongfully, but *many* of those the Qur'an addresses do. It shows that it is only those who refuse to pay the agreed *jizya* who should be fought, as they do not keep to their agreements, thus demonstrating that they do not truly believe in God and the Last Day (i.e. the day they will be judged for their behaviour in this life) and do not forbid what God and His Prophet forbid or act according to the rule of justice. Breaking agreements is very strongly condemned in the Qur'an, whether this is done by the People of the Book (Q. 5:13), Muslims (Q. 13:25 and Q. 16:91–2) or idolaters (Q. 8:55–6, Q. 9:5 and 10); the latter verses come only a page before the *jizya* verse.

Most Muslim exegetes, unfortunately, take Q. 9:30–5 as an elaboration or explanation of how People of the Book generally do not believe in God and the Last Day. Al-Rāzī says, 'Know that God Almighty, having ruled in the previous verse [Q. 9:29] that the Jews and Christians do not believe in God, explains this in this verse [Q. 9:30].'[49] Likewise, Sayyid Quṭb states, 'then God explains in the following verses [Q. 9:30 ff.] how they [the People of the Book generally] do not believe in God and the Last Day, do not forbid what God and His Prophet have forbidden and do not follow the true religion.'[50]

We have shown earlier that Q. 9:29 certainly does not claim that all People of the Book do not believe in God and the Last Day, just that the behaviour of some of them shows they do not. These individuals do not really and truly believe in God and the Last Day, just as the Prophet said that a Muslim while committing adultery or stealing is not a believer.[51] This shows that reference to their lack of true belief is rather a turn of phrase or a mode of expression; however, the question arises as to why the Qur'an urges the Muslims so strongly to fight to enforce payment of the *jizya*. Urging is a general feature of the Qur'an.[52] Fighting was, naturally, not an easy matter ('*wa-huwa kurhun lakum*', Q. 2:216) and the Muslim community included people who were faint-hearted, new to Islam and still not strongly committed to the cause, let alone the hypocrites. Fighting also involved asking people to break commercial, tribal and even close family ties. Thus in Q. 9:24, the Prophet is told to say:

If your fathers, sons, brothers, wives, tribes, the wealth you have acquired, the trade which you fear will decline and the dwellings you love are dearer to you than God and His Messenger and the struggle for His cause, then wait until God brings about His command. God does not guide those who break away [from His orders].

Urging people to follow the order to fight was to be expected, since there was no question of *forcing* people to join the Muslim army. The Prophet did not have a conscripted army, and going to battle could mean losing one's life and leaving families without support. Strong urging was similarly needed when asking people to pay in charity (compare Q. 2:261–81). Refusal by any section of society to pay tax is not something to be lightly tolerated. The first Caliph Abū Bakr enforced payment of tax on the Muslim groups who refused to pay, as mentioned above.

Perhaps it is appropriate now to give a different, clearer translation of the *jizya* verse as an alternative to the one given at the beginning of this chapter:

Fight those of the People of the Book who do not [truly] believe in God and the Last Day, who do not forbid what God and His Messenger have forbidden, who do not behave according to the rule of justice, until they pay the tax and submit to it.

In my translation, instead of using a noun (*al-mumtaniʿīn*), a relative clause, 'those who do not believe', has been substituted (*al-taʿrīf bi'l-mawṣūl*) for rhetorical purposes as scholars of *balāgha* (rhetoric) put it. According to *ʿilm al maʿānī* in *balāgha*, substituting 'those who do not believe in God [...]

according to justice' serves two purposes: first, it exposes the reasons that lead them to refuse to pay what they should pay; they do not truly believe, nor forbid what God and His Messenger forbid, nor behave according to the rule of justice. Second, it exposes their shortcomings in this respect.[53]

Linguistic Analysis

Having explained why many Muslim exegetes were so extreme in their interpretations of elements of the *jizya* verse, and having also explained why the Qur'an urges the believers in the way it does concerning enforcement of *jizya*, we should perhaps now summarise the causes of difficulty when interpreting this particular verse. Again, taking Arberry's translation used by Cook, it will be discussed phrase by phrase from the beginning to the end of the verse.

1. '*Fight those who believe not in God and the Last Day* (*qātilū'lladhīna lā yu'minūna bi'llāhi wa-lā bi'l-yawmi'l-ākhir*)'

The interpretation of the phrase '*those who believe not*' depends on whether one takes this as a factual statement or a figure of speech. As a figure of speech, it questions the sincerity of people's belief on the grounds that it has not produced the expected fruit of good behaviour, as if their faith did not exist. The Qur'anic usage of similar references to unbelief in other places supports the figurative interpretation, thus there is no assertion that these people are real *kuffār* ('disbelievers').

2. '*Do not forbid what God and His Messenger have forbidden* (*wa-lā yuḥarrimūna mā ḥarrama'llāhu wa-rasūluhu*)'

The reason for the ambiguity in interpretation here is the omission (*ḥadhf*) of what exactly it is they do not forbid and substitution of a noun clause beginning with '*mā*', a relative particle of generalisation (*ta'mīm*). So instead of saying, 'they do not forbid breaking their agreements', it puts instead a description which, general as it is, shows strong condemnation of their action by stressing the aspect that God and His Messenger (whether Muhammad, Moses or any other messenger sent by God) have forbidden such an action.

3. '*Such men as practise not the religion of truth* (*wa-lā yadīnūna dīna'l-ḥaqq*)'

The difficulty here is that the words *yadīnūna* and *dīn* have a multiplicity of meanings, as explained earlier, and some interpret them as pertaining to 'religion', not being alert to the fact that they are not accompanied by the preposition *'bi-'*, which is the only situation in which the meaning of the word *dīn* is associated with religion. The contextual interpretation is '*behave* according to the *rule* of justice'.

4. '*[Being of] those who were given the Book* (*mina'lladhīna ūtū'l-kitāb*)'

'*Min*' has multiple meanings, a phenomenon referred to as *ishtirāk* or *ta'addud al-ma'nā* in Arabic. It can be seen as explanatory or partitive. In the second case, it means 'from among' or 'of', so the condemnation is directed only at those individuals or tribes from among the People of the Book who broke their agreement, not the People of the Book in general.

5. '*Until they pay the tribute* (*ḥattā yu'ṭū'l-jizya*)'

It is important to be alert to the fact that the Qur'an does not say, 'until they agree to pay', but 'until they pay'. This indicates that the agreement had been reached previously.

6. '*Out of hand* (*'an yadin*)'

Again this is open to different interpretations. The deciding factor in selecting any specific meaning will be the context, which requires paying promptly, hand to hand.

7. '*And have been humbled* (*wa-hum ṣāghirūn*)'

This, too, is open to different interpretations, which has led some exegetes to give extraordinary and incredible views. The multiplicity of interpretations proffered can be in the degree of *ṣaghār* or the meaning or method of the presumed humiliation. We have seen that the context, the Qur'anic attitude in general and usage require that the phrase simply means, 'those who do not pay because they think of themselves as too proud or too big (*kabīr*) to pay, and by paying they come down from being *kabīr* to being *ṣaghīr*.'

This is a summary of the linguistic difficulties. Again in summary, the solutions for these were found in the following aspects: first, the style of the Qur'an (*'ādāt al-kitāb*) and how it negates a belief because it does not result in good behaviour; second, the crucial role of the context; third, avoiding atomistic analysis, instead of treating all the elements together with due regard to the others (for example, the phrase '*who do not forbid*' was taken by many in isolation, which produced inappropriate meanings with no relation to the immediate context of the rest of the verse); and finally, paying regard to the teachings of Islam in general while trying to interpret any specific phrase, sentence or verse (some explanations of *ṣāghirūn* are so bizarre, as has been seen, that they not only ignore but starkly contradict the teachings of the Qur'an and the practice of the Prophet).

The Meanings and Significance of Crucial Terms

In this study we have concentrated on the Qur'anic text itself. Abū Ḥayyān's statement with regard to humiliation that 'the verse did not mention any of this' should always be borne in mind. It is the Qur'anic text which is the authority and not the views of jurists or exegetes who were influenced by historical contingencies such as were described earlier. Our analysis of the Qur'anic text is above all linguistic. We will now apply this in considering the main terms of this whole question of *jizya.* The term *jizya,* especially in the writings of non-Muslims, has acquired strongly negative connotations, but in the Qur'an the word is quite different. In fact it is a positive expression and can be said to show generous cooperation between the payer and the recipient. We have noted that the root means 'to reward' and that people only give rewards for services rendered. In paying the *jizya,* the People of the Book are giving a reward to the Muslim state in return for not obliging them to engage in *jihād* for the Muslim state, which might be against their faith, or obliging them to pay *zakāh,* which is a pillar of Islam, supporting the Islamic edifice, and allowing them to live completely according to their own faith, even in matters which Islam does not accept, such as questions of food and drink. In Muslim societies, non-Muslims were allowed to trade in such products between themselves and they and all their property were protected from any attackers from within or outside the Muslim state.[54] The only thing the Islamic state demanded in return was that those men who could fight and afford to pay should pay a small tax, estimated normally as one dinar a year.[55] It is relevant here to recall the statement by the Christians in Syria, to whom Abū 'Ubayda returned their *jizya* because he was not able to defend them. They replied, 'We would prefer paying *jizya* to you to the treatment we would receive from the others [the Byzantine Christians].'[56] Part of the *jizya* pact was protection, and the Prophet was very clear about this; he declared that those who paid the *jizya* were under the protection (*dhimma*) of God and His Prophet, saying:[57]

> If anyone wrongs someone who is protected by a treaty or disparages him or charges him with more than he can bear or takes anything from him without him willingly giving it, I personally will be his adversary on the Day of Resurrection.

The word *dhimmī* ('protected') again has acquired very negative connotations in Western writing about Islam, when in fact it is a very powerful and positive word in Arabic.[58] Clearly the Prophet felt that, with the wide sweep of Islam and a few non-Muslims being allowed to live in the Muslim state while adhering to their own religion rather than accepting Islam, some Muslims might, out of their zeal, harass or mistreat them. This explains the need he evidently felt to make a strong stand on this and assert that these minorities were under the protection of God and His Prophet. As God and His Messenger are the highest authorities in Islam, this means that they are to be protected by the whole Muslim community, just as people's religious freedom in society now is protected by law.

The *jizya* verse talks about Christians and Jews as '*those who were given the Book* (*alladhīna ūtū 'l-kitāb*)', which again confers great honour; they are people who had been recipients of divinely inspired Scripture, confirmed by the Qur'an. So *jizya, dhimmī* and *ahl al-kitāb* ('People of the Book') are Qur'anic terms and should be understood on the basis used in the Qur'an and not corrupted in the way they so often have been.

The *jizya* is a very clear example of the acceptance of a multiplicity of cultures within the Islamic system, which allowed people of different faiths to live according to their own faiths, all contributing to the well-being of the state; Muslims through *zakāh* and the *ahl al-dhimma* through *jizya*. In the Qur'an we find an excellent example of interfaith relationships, pluralism and multiculturalism, concepts that have come to be regarded as important values of Western liberal democracies as well, the exact meaning of which still remains a matter of controversy.

It is clear that the treatment of the Christians and Jews in the early years of Islam, before the compilation of *fiqh* (Islamic law) and *tafsīr* (Qur'anic exegesis) works, was based on the Qur'anic principle of *birr* ('kindness', mentioned in Q. 60:8), keeping one's agreements (as in the case of Abū 'Ubayda mentioned above) and on the proper understanding of the *jizya* verse to mean that it was only those refusing to pay who could be fought to enforce payment.

It was the concept of *ahl al-kitāb, dhimma* and *jizya*, in spite of all the misinterpretation and misapplication in some Muslim lands in later years, which ensured the continued existence of Christians and Jews there up to the present time;[59] this was not the fate of Muslims in Christian countries like Spain. When the Jews were expelled from Spain, along with the Muslims, they found refuge in many Muslim countries.

The *jizya* institution is now relegated to history, having been replaced by modern taxation in Muslim countries, which applies to everyone regardless of faith, but the Qur'anic teachings about *jizya* still stand as an example of how people in one society should cooperate to the good of all and no one should be allowed to avoid taxation. In the same way as Abū Bakr, then the head of the Muslim state, fought those Muslims who refused to pay *zakāh* to enforce payment of what was due to the state, Q. 9:29 allows the Muslim state to fight those who refuse to pay *jizya* to enforce payment of what was due to the state in which they lived.

Having talked about the 'Sword Verse' myth and about the *jizya* verse, it is suitable to move on and to explain the meaning of *jihād* in the Qur'an.

3

Qur'anic *Jihād*

The word *jihād* is one that has been much discussed and which is often interpreted with some degree of sensationalised polemic. It has become, to some extent, divorced from its significance as a Qur'anic term. Our approach in this study is therefore to deal with the subject on the basis of the Qur'an alone, on the basis of linguistic analysis of the text of the Qur'an itself, as a term which forms an important theme in the Qur'an. In particular, our analysis will not ignore the linguistic context that is crucial in understanding any text. The picture that emerges from this study and approach will differ from that held by many, both Muslims and non-Muslims, who have arrived at a perception of the meaning of *jihād* on a basis other than what is found in the Qur'anic text. Indeed, it is clear that there are those in both East and West (not only extremists, but also journalists and academics) who hold the same views on this emotive subject, views which run counter to what is found in the Qur'an.

Words based on the root *j-h-d*, from which *jihād* is derived, occur in the Qur'an a total of 35 times, in 15 suras, four Meccan and 11 Medinan.[1] The verb root means 'to exert effort', and the form *fi'āl*, as in *jihād*, is reciprocal, 'exerting effort in the face of an exertion by something or someone else'. Such effort includes *jihād* by the tongue and even by the heart.[2] In this sense it occurs in Q. 25:52, instructing the Prophet, '*so do not give in to the disbelievers: strive hard against them with this [Qur'an]* (*jāhidhum bihi jihādan kabīran*)'.[3] In addition to this verbal *jihād*, there is also *jihād bi-amwālihim* ('using one's wealth to support a cause') as found in Q. 8:72 as well as Q. 9:20, 41 and 86, which is normally used in a wider context than to simply denote military *jihād*, even in a sura which is alluding to a situation where actual fighting is taking place. *Jihād* is also used twice in the Qur'an (Q. 29:8 and Q. 31:15) to indicate the efforts exercised by pagan parents to convert their children from Islam back to paganism. There is also another *jihād* that has nothing to do with fighting (Q. 9:73, Q. 22:78, Q. 25:52, Q. 29:69, Q. 66:9). In Q. 66:9, '*Prophet, strive hard against the disbelievers and the hypocrites* (*jāhidi'l-kuffāra wa'l-munāfiqīn*). *Deal with them sternly. Hell will be their home, an evil destination!*', the word *jihād* occurs in the context of a warning to the Prophet's own wives, whose divulgence of a private conversation was disapproved of, that they should not be like the unbelievers or hypocrites against whom he must strive. This particular verse, however, has, on occasion, been grossly misunderstood and mistranslated on occasion. For example, in his translation of the Qur'an, Dawood translates the phrase *jāhidi'l-kuffār wa'l-munāfiqīn* in both Q. 66:9 and Q. 9:73 as '*Prophet, make war on the unbelievers and the hypocrites*',[4] ignoring the historical context and the Qur'anic teachings as a whole; the Prophet had no authority from the Qur'anic revelation to make actual militant war on the hypocrites.

Often, however, when the Qur'an combines allusions to striving with one's wealth and one's person, this does indicate the *jihād* of fighting; for example, Q. 9:20, '*those who believe, who migrated and strove hard in God's way with their possessions and their persons* (*hājarū wa-jāhadū fī sabīli'llāhi bi-amwālihim wa-anfusihim*), *are in God's eyes much higher in rank; it is they who will triumph*'; Q. 9:41, '*so go out, no matter whether you are lightly or heavily armed, and struggle in God's way with your possessions and your persons* (*jāhidū bi-amwālikum wa-anfusikum*): *this is better for you, if you only knew*'; Q. 9:44 and 81 as well as Q. 61:11, '*have faith in God and His Messenger and struggle for His cause with your possessions and your persons* (*tujāhidūna fī sabīli'llāhi bi-amwālikum wa-anfusikum*) – *that is better for you, if only you knew*'. It is *jihād* in person (*jihād bi-anfusihim*) that normally refers to participation in warfare and can involve actual fighting (*qitāl*).[5]

This *jihād* is more inclusive than *qitāl*, which is specific to actual fighting. *Qitāl* is a reciprocal form, the root of which (*q-t-l*, 'to kill') occurs in the Qur'an more frequently than the root for *jihād*, and is used with a wide historical and geographical range, including, for instance, Cain's killing of Abel (Q. 5:30) and David's killing of Goliath (Q. 2:251). It occurs in the Qur'an, in various derivations, less than 60 times in the semantic sense of combative *jihād* (e.g. see Q. 2:190, Q. 4:76, Q. 8:79, Q. 22:39 and Q. 47:20).

One further point that must be made before moving on to discuss the connotative range of the Qur'anic usage of *jihād* is that there is a specific historical background to which the Qur'anic verses are responding, and which serve to contextualise the verses on *jihād*; permission to fight was given in the second year following the *hijra*, when the Muslims left Mecca and founded a new community in Medina.

According to the traditional historical accounts, while in Mecca, the Muslim community was small, oppressed and on two occasions groups of them were forced to emigrate to Abyssinia for protection.[6] Faced with escalating persecution, Muslims began to flee to Yathrib (the former name of Medina), leaving homes and possessions behind. Sensing that the situation would get out of their control, the Meccans plotted to kill the Prophet (Q. 8:30). He then also fled to Yathrib under cover of darkness. Having settled there in the thirteenth year of the Islamic mission, the situation changed and the Muslim community began to feel safe. Early in the Medinan period, verses ordered the believers to show restraint and, as in Mecca, stick to their prayers and almsgiving (Q. 4:77, Q. 2:109). But, as became apparent from developments that followed within five years, their Meccan adversaries were not going to leave the Muslims in peace in their new home, and it is against this background, in the second year of the *hijra*, that permission was given for Muslims to defend themselves.

It has been argued that once Muhammad felt strong in Medina, he decided to fight, which he did not when he was weak in Mecca.[7] This assumes that he changed religious teachings according to whim or political expedience. It also assumes that Islam was meant to consist only of the few teachings that were revealed in the Qur'an in Mecca, that the Muslims should always accept oppression and be forced to flee in the face of aggression and that the Prophet should lay himself open to being killed, a paradigm that clearly was not meant for Muhammad, his mission and followers. Islam was obviously meant to grow into a much greater entity than it was in Mecca. In fact, only two of the Five Pillars of Islam were introduced in Mecca, the creed and the five daily prayers. Fasting in the month of Ramadan, which one would assume was suitable for Mecca, was introduced only in the second year in Medina, shortly before permission for military defence. *Zakāh* (obligatory tax on Muslims) and hajj were introduced later, so were the laws of marriage, divorce and trading, for example.

Permission for Muslims to defend themselves and retaliate could not have been introduced in Mecca for two reasons: first, they would have laid themselves open to being wiped out, a fate that Islam would not impose on its followers; the Qur'an forbids Muslims to cast themselves into destruction with their own hands (Q. 2:195). When the Prophet saw that his enemies surrounded his house, planning to kill him, he did not await his fate passively, but instead slipped out and away to Medina. Second, in Mecca, Muslims and their opponents were living among each other rather than being two separate communities. Persecution was thus normally carried out by individuals against individuals. Emigration to Medina changed the situation drastically. For the first time the Meccans and their allies were a separate camp and could march on the new community in Medina.

Justifications for Fighting in the Qur'an

The Qur'anic texts on *jihād* and *qitāl* will now be analysed but, in keeping with the approach taken in this study, which is the approach of the Qur'an itself, cohesive passages will be introduced. These will be analysed as entire passages, meant to impact as such on the listener/reader, and not as extracts wrenched out of context. It will be seen that this is the surest way of discovering a true picture of Qur'anic teaching.

> *Those who are attacked are permitted to take up arms because they have been wronged – God has the power to help them – those who have been driven unjustly from their homes only for saying, 'Our Lord is God.' If God did not repel some people by means of others, many monasteries, churches, synagogues, and mosques, where God's name is much invoked, would have been destroyed. God is sure to help those who help His cause – God is strong and mighty – those who, when We establish them in the land, keep up the prayer, pay the prescribed alms, command what is right, and forbid what is wrong: God controls the outcome of all events.*
>
> Q. 22:39–41

This first passage justifies armed resistance by '*those who have been wronged* (*ẓulimū*)', in the passive form, a word that will recur in other passages justifying war; here '*those who [...] are permitted to take up arms*' have been driven out of their homes and properties specifically for worshipping God. Such justification of giving permission to the believers to take up arms is a crucial feature of all verses on *jihād* and fighting, as it is with all teachings in the Qur'an that demand doing or abstaining from something.[8] Even such fundamental aspects as the Qur'an's exhortations for belief in the oneness of God, Muhammad's prophethood and the Resurrection, as well as advocating the protection of children and of women, are always supported by rational justifications. In the passage under discussion here, thus, the

Qur'an first gives a moral argument in favour of defending oneself against injustice. Then it gives another argument, based on the nature of how things work in the world and what has happened in history, and on the necessity of *daf'* ('driving back evil forces'), as stated in Q. 2:251, '*David killed Goliath and God gave him sovereignty [...] If God did not drive some back by means of others, the earth would be completely corrupted, but God is bountiful to all*'.

Armed resistance here is described as necessary for the protection of all houses of worship, not just mosques, in fact mosques come last on the list. The passage ends by reminding those who have been given permission to defend themselves that God will help only those who, when established in the land, will behave righteously and '*keep up the prayer, pay the prescribed alms, command what is right, and forbid what is wrong*' and that '*God controls the outcome of all events*', including battles, and so they should take heed of His teachings. Permission to fight, then, is not given in the form of a simple instruction to 'go forth and fight', but is couched in justifications, restrictions and reminders of God's power and the believers' duty to Him. This nuanced approach to the issue of 'taking up arms' is one that is too often unacknowledged in discussions on *jihād* by academics, let alone by the media and propagandists, which only leads to consolidating the popular image of *jihād*.

After permission was given to the Muslims to defend themselves, teaching was given on how to act on this permission:

> *Fight in God's way against those who fight you, but do not overstep the limits: God does not love those who overstep the limits. Kill them wherever you find them, and drive them out from where they drove you out, for [their] persecution is more serious than [your] killing. Do not fight them at the Sacred Mosque unless they fight you there. If they do fight you, kill them – this is what such disbelievers deserve – but if they stop, then God is most forgiving and merciful. Fight them in order to put an end to persecution, and so that [your] worship is devoted to God [without fear]. If they cease hostilities, there can be no [further] hostility, except towards aggressors. A sacred month for a sacred month: violation of sanctity [calls for] fair retribution. So if anyone attacks you [in a sacred month], attack him as he attacked you, but be mindful of God, and know that He is with those who are mindful of Him. Spend in God's cause: do not contribute to your destruction with your own hands, but do good, for God loves those who do good.*
>
> Q. 2:190–5

This passage requires detailed discussion, as it has given rise to numerous misinterpretations which have contributed to the popular image of *jihād* in the Qur'an. The phrase '*kill them wherever you come up against them*'

(Q. 2:191) has been repeatedly misrepresented. James Busuttil, for example, has made it the title of an article, '"Slay them wherever you find them": Humanitarian Law in Islam'.[9] As in the case of the so-called 'Sword Verse' discussed in Chapter 1, the phrase has been wrenched from its context, cutting the pronoun 'them' off from what it refers to in the previous verse (this being '*those who fight you*'), making it a general rule for how Muslims should treat non-Muslims. Similarly, Ella Landau-Tasseron, in the *Encyclopaedia of the Qur'ān*, describes the understanding of this as 'warfare against infidels'.[10] This understanding is incorrect: the object of fighting is '*those who fight you*', also described as those who '*drove you out [of your homes in Mecca]*'. Similarly, '*kill them wherever you find them*' has frequently been misinterpreted. In their discussions of this verse, *mufassirūn* (Qur'anic exegetes) such as al-Rāzī (d. 606/1209) contextualise this verse with the information that it was revealed in response to the Muslims' concern that, if their enemies attacked them within the Meccan sanctuary while they were performing hajj and they replied in kind, they would be violating the sanctity of the sacred site by killing them, and so they were instructed to kill their attackers wherever they came up against them, inside or outside the sacred area.[11] In the same way, Q. 2:194 gives permission to fight back if attacked during a sacred month. This is confirmed in Q. 2:217:

They ask you [Prophet] about fighting in the sacred month. Say, 'Fighting in that month is a great offence, but to bar others from God's path, to disbelieve in Him, prevent access to the Sacred Mosque, and expel its people, are still greater offences in God's eyes: persecution is worse than killing.'

It is also confirmed in Q. 9:36:

God decrees that there are twelve months – ordained in God's Book on the Day when He created the heavens and the earth – four months of which are sacred: this is the correct calculation. Do not wrong yourselves in these months – though you may fight the idolaters at any time, if they first fight you – remember that God is with those who are mindful of Him.

These passages confirm the sanctity of the Sacred Months, but still give Muslims permission to fight back if they are the victims of aggression.

To return to the six verses that comprise the passage under discussion, Q. 2:190–5, they contain many restrictions and are couched in restraining language that appeals strongly to the conscience; in them we find four prohibitions, seven restrictions (one 'until', 'if' four times, 'those who fight you' twice) as well as such cautions as '*in God's way*', '*be mindful of God*',

'*God does not love those who overstep the limits*', '*He is with those who are mindful of Him*', loves '*those who do good*' and '*is most forgiving and merciful*'. Restrictions abound from beginning to end.[12] At a grammatical level, it is a rule in Arabic that omission of the object of the verb, as we have here, makes it open to the widest possible application. Thus al-Bayḍawī (d. 791/1388) explained this verse indicates that the Muslims should not initiate fighting or fight non-combatants, be disproportionate in their response or continue to fight when the enemy have stopped.

Some classical exegetes, however, maintained that these core restrictions on initiating combat were rescinded in later revelations, specifically Q. 9:1–14:

> A broad consensus amongst medieval exegetes and jurists exists on the issue of waging war. The simplest and earliest solution of the problem of contradictions in the Qur'ān was to consider Q. 9:5 and Q. 9:29 as abrogating all the other statements [...] all restrictions were removed and all treaties with infidels were repudiated by Q. 9:1–14 and the ultimate divine orders were expressed in Q. 9:5 and Q. 9:29.[13]

This statement ignores what the Qur'an actually says and instead is based on *tafsīr* works (Qur'anic exegesis). I would argue that this interpretation of Q. 9:1–14 only seems valid if one consciously disregards the connection of Q. 9:5 (the 'Sword Verse') with its surrounding verses, and that, in fact, these core restrictions remained unchanged in the Qur'an in the light of later revelations. In the 'Sword Verse' Muslims were ordered to fight only those polytheists who had repeatedly broken all treaties with the Muslims and had continued their hostilities, as shown in Q. 9:1–14, and thus it is a generalisation to apply what in the Qur'an is particular to one group of polytheists to all 'treaties with infidels'. The text itself shows that other treaties with 'infidels' remained intact.[14]

A second source of much misinterpretation can be found in translations of the phrase *wa'l-fitnatu ashaddu mina'l-qatl* in Q. 2:191, which should read '[their] persecution *(al-fitna)* is more serious than *(ashaddu min)* [your] killing *(al-qatl)*' The specific term that has been subject to misinterpretation in this case is *fitna*. Dawood, for example, has translated this phrase as '*idolatry is worse than carnage*'. Al-Rāzī gives a report explaining what has made people think that *fitna* means *kufr* (unbelief) in his commentary on the phrase '*if they stop, then God is forgiving and merciful*' in Q. 2:192.[15] According to this report, some argue that 'stop' must here mean 'stop their *kufr*', because otherwise God would not be forgiving and merciful to people who disbelieve. This can only be so if one assumes that the phrase '*God is most forgiving and merciful*' is addressed to the disbelievers, whereas in my opinion it is addressed to the Muslims, telling them to overlook and forgive what their enemies have done, rather than taking up arms, remembering that God is forgiving and merciful. There are parallels to this in other parts of the Qur'an (Q. 4:149 and Q. 24:22). My interpretation here can be seen to be confirmed in the following verse, Q. 2:193, which ends, '*if they stop, there can be no [further] hostility, except towards aggressors*'.

An alternative interpretation of *fitna*, one that is adopted by Arberry[16] and most recent translators of the Qur'an into English, is 'persecution', which better fits the context and agrees with numerous other citations in the Qur'an.[17] For example, see Q. 2:217, '*they will not stop fighting you [believers] until they make you revoke your faith*', a verse which refers to the polytheists' persecution of the Muslims in an attempt to force them to give up their religion.

What, then, is the context of the statement, *wa'l-fitnatu ashaddu mina'l-qatl*, coming after the order to '*fight those who fight you*'? The Muslims were hesitant about fighting in the Sanctuary, considering it a serious offence.[18] So the Qur'an sought to remove this sense of guilt by stating that the persecution these individuals inflict on the Muslims for believing is more serious than the latter's killing them in the Sanctuary in self-defence,[19] just the same as it said about fighting back against aggressors during a sacred month (Q. 2:217). No other explanation makes sense in the context. In grammatical terms, an important point to note here is the significance of the function of the definite article '*al-*' in *al-fitna* and *al-qatl*. This is not functioning as a generic (*jinsiyya*) definite article signifying persecution in general, but is specific (*'ahdiyya*), referring to something already known: the persecution they inflict on you is more serious than the killing you subject them to. This grammatical structure is well known in both Arabic grammar in general and in Qur'anic usage specifically. So, the function of this statement in context and the correct grammatical interpretation are essential for interpreting the statement.

Moving on to the following verse, Q. 2:193, we again find another phrase that has given rise to serious misinterpretation, *wa-qātilūhum ḥattā lā takūna fitnatun wa-yakūna'l-dīnu li'llāh* ('*Fight them in order to put an end to persecution, and so that [your] worship is devoted to God [without fear]*'). Dawood translates this as '*fight them until there is no more idolatry and God's religion reigns supreme*'. We have already dealt with his translation of *fitna* as 'idolatry', but we have here another issue; how to read the word *dīn*. *Dīn* is often (as here) translated as 'religion' but the word has many meanings in Arabic (al-Fayrūzabādī gives more than 15, and 'religion' comes near the end of the list).[20] The meanings that fit here are 'worship' or 'obedience'; thus, it expresses the idea that 'if persecution stops, you will be able to worship God without oppression or concealment'. It has nothing to do with fighting until God's religion (i.e. Islam) becomes supreme as this has no relation to the beginning or end of the passage, '*fight those who attack you [...] whoever attacks you, attack him*', and it goes against such Qur'anic statements as '*most people will not believe*' (Q. 12:103) and '*they will always be different*' (Q. 11:118).

Akin to this type of permission for Muslims to fight on the basis of self-defence are verses giving permission to fight '*those [...] who, whenever you [Prophet] make a treaty with them, break it*' (Q. 8:56) and who '*if they get the upper hand over you would not respect any tie of kinship or treaty*' (Q. 9:8).

In addition to self-defence, in Q. 4:75 the Qur'an specifically permits fighting in defence of '*helpless men, women, children and old people who are oppressed and cry out, "Lord, rescue us from this town whose people are oppressors! By Your grace give us a protector and a helper"*'. In this passage, we find again the use of the passive form, those '*who are oppressed*' in a town '*whose people are oppressors* (*al-ẓālimi ahluhā*)'. Even when coming to the aid of the oppressed, however, the cause of permitting Muslims to fight is, as usual, restricted, as can be seen from Q. 8:72, '*if they seek help from you against persecution it is your duty to assist them, except against people with whom you have a treaty: God sees all that you do.*' Self-defence and defending such oppressed, helpless people are, in fact, the only justifications found in the Qur'an for Muslims to fight non-Muslims. Thus, statements such as '[o]n the basis of the sword verse (Q. 9:5) and the *jizya* verse (Q. 9:29) it is clear that the purpose of fighting the idolaters is to convert them to Islam, whereas the purpose of fighting the People of the Book is to dominate them'[21] are inaccurate and misleading if one examines the actual text of the Qur'an.

Both the 'Sword Verse' and the *jizya* verse discussed in previous chapters have been addressed in separate studies.[22] However, it is worth mentioning here that the purpose of fighting those given the Book (an honorific title applied by the Qur'an to Jews and Christians) in the *jizya* verse was to compel those who refused to pay their taxes to the state in which they lived to conform to the law, just like Muslim citizens of the state who paid their taxes. If there is any domination advised in this verse, it is only that of the state over its citizens to enforce tax regulations. Thus, for example, when some Muslim tribes, following the death of the Prophet, refused to pay *zakāh,* Abū Bakr sent Muslim armies to fight them and enforce payment.

Who is to be Fought?

The object of the verb 'fight' (*q-t-l*) is, in fact, often crucial in clarifying the causes of combat in a Qur'anic context. Sometimes the object of the verb indicates the cause for fighting, as in '*fight, in the cause of God, those who fight you*' (Q. 2:190) and in '*if anyone attacks you, attack him as he attacked you*' (Q. 2:194). Sometimes the object does not give the cause for conflict itself, but merely describes the enemy, as in Q. 8:15, '*believers, when you meet the disbelievers* (*alladhīna kafarū*) *in battle* (*zaḥfan*), *never turn your backs on them*'. Here, it is implicit that 'meeting the disbelievers in battle' is the cause for the order, and not the fact that those being met in battle are disbelievers. The verse gives regulations and tactics for a battle already in progress. In cases where the object is *al-mushrikīn* (idolaters), as in Q. 9:36, '*fight the idolaters at any time as they fight you*', the underlying point is, again, when this phrase is examined in context, not an issue of whether the enemy are idolaters, but of whether the Muslims can fight back when attacked during the Sacred Months, which the idolaters, in accordance with their belief system, are able to postpone as a device to permit fighting. Sometimes, the cause of conflict is not given in the same verse but in an earlier or following verse. This is the case in Q. 8:55–7, for example: '*the worst of creatures in the sight of God are the disbelievers, those with whom you made treaties but they broke them every time, so if you meet them in battle, make a fearsome example of them to those who come after them, so that they may take heed.*'

Likewise, on some occasions in which the Qur'an refers to 'idolaters' as the enemy, the definite article '*al-*' in *al-mushrikīn* is *'ahdiyya* (specific) and thus refers to an earlier citation in which the cause for fighting them in this particular instance is given. Taking the 'Sword Verse' (Q. 9:5) as an example, which starts '*when the forbidden months are over, wherever you encounter the idolaters, kill them*', the earlier verses, Q. 9:1–5, and indeed the following verses up to Q. 9:15, give justifications for the conflict. The underlying reason for identifying the adversary as 'disbelievers' or 'idolaters', apart from stigmatising them, is that the only parties involved in warfare in Qur'anic terms were the Muslims, the disbelievers and the idolaters. As is discussed in Chapter 2, references to fighting the People of the Book, as they are referred to in the so-called 'Tribute Verse' (Q. 9:29), was to enforce payment of due taxes. In Q. 9:123, '*believers, fight the disbelievers near you and let them find you standing firm*', the description of the disbelievers as being 'near you' refers to a matter of tactics, as will be discussed later. In short, the relationship between those who are to be fought and the causes of the conflict with them is crucial to a correct understanding when discussing military *jihād* and war in the Qur'an.

In addition to the two types of situation discussed above (self-defence and the aid of the oppressed), the Qur'an contains plenty of material on the theme of fighting, but this is to do with tactics or urging and persuading the Muslims to do their duty and fight as permitted. There are also some regulations on captives, safe passage, distribution of war gains, truces and peace treaties in general.

Qur'anic Exhortation: Persuasion and Dissuasion

The Qur'an's discussion of the themes of military *jihād* and fighting does not include detailed descriptions of the battlefield or how the battle was managed. This clearly is not the intention; rather, the Qur'an seeks to draw lessons from reference to past events.[23] Orders to carry out military *jihād* and fight are also relatively few. There are some references to war tactics, as we will see later, but, in contrast, there is plenty of material on justification, urging the Muslims to fight and providing persuasion and dissuasion. Again, it is important to distinguish verses relating to tactics and persuasion from those relating to the causes of war. Such a lack of distinction leads to misunderstanding and confusion.

In terms of the Qur'anic use of persuasion and dissuasion, it should be remembered that, when looked at in a historical context, unlike modern states which can force their citizens to join the army and pay them salaries, and give social security to their families if they die, the newly emerging Muslim community in Medina to which the Qur'an addresses itself had no conscripted army. Going to battle, which took male breadwinners from their families, to put their lives at risk in defence of the community, was a lot to ask. Consequently, the Qur'an uses various techniques of persuasion and dissuasion. For instance, taking persuasive verses first, we have:

> *Those believers who stay at home, apart from those with an incapacity, are not equal to those who commit themselves and their possessions to striving in God's way. God has raised such people to a rank above those who stay at home – although He has promised all believers a good reward, those who strive are favoured with a tremendous reward above those who stay at home.*
>
> Q. 4:95

And:

God has purchased the persons and possessions of the believers in return for the Garden – they fight in God's way: they kill and are killed – this is a true promise given by Him in the Torah, the Gospel and the Qur'an. Who could be more faithful in his promise than God? So be happy with the bargain you have made. That is the supreme triumph.

Q. 9:111

References to the Torah and the Gospel here reinforce the appeal to take on this difficult task, in similar vein to the introduction of the obligatory fast '*as it was prescribed for those before you*' in Q. 2:183:

[Prophet,] do not think of those who have been killed in God's way as dead. They are alive with their Lord, well provided for, happy with what God has given them of His favour; rejoicing that for those they have left behind, who have yet to join them, there is no fear, nor will they grieve; rejoicing in God's blessing and favour and that God will not let the reward of the believers be lost.

Q. 3:169–71

These verses do indeed describe great rewards, but, in fact, we find in the Qur'an that God has promised all believers, both men and women, '*gardens graced with flowing streams where they will remain; good, peaceful homes in gardens of lasting bliss; and – greatest of all – God's good pleasure: that is the supreme triumph*' (Q. 9:72). The picture painted in this verse describes rewards that are in fact greater than the one given to those who fought alongside the Prophet with their possessions and persons, a few lines later in Q. 9:89. (It should also be pointed out here that the rewards in Paradise for those who carry out *jihād* and *qitāl* and die as martyrs do not, as popularly held, include houris. In fact, the descriptions of Paradise which include houris come in the Meccan suras, such as Q. 52, Q. 56 and Q. 78, and do not occur in the passages that mention *jihād* and *qitāl*.)

As regards dissuasion, in Q. 61:2–4 there is castigation of those who break their promise to fight:

You who believe, why do you say things and not do them? It is most hateful to God that you say things and do not do them; God truly loves those who fight in solid lines for His cause, like a well-compacted wall.

This is built on in the following verses:

[Prophet], do you not see those who were told, 'Restrain yourselves from fighting, perform the prayer, and pay the prescribed alms'? When fighting was ordained for them, some of

them feared men as much, or even more than, they feared God, saying, 'Lord, why have You ordained fighting for us? If only you would give us just a little more time!' Say to them, 'Little is the enjoyment of this world. The hereafter is better for those who are mindful of God: you will not be wronged by as much as the fibre of a date stone. Death will overtake you no matter where you may be, even inside high towers.

Q. 4:77–8

Believers, why, when it is said to you, 'Go and fight in God's way,' do you feel weighed down to the ground? Do you prefer this world to the life to come? How small the enjoyment of this world is compared with the life to come! If you do not go out and fight, God will punish you severely and put others in your place, but you cannot harm Him in any way: God has power over all things. Even if you do not help the Prophet, God has helped him.

Q. 9:38–9

According to the *asbāb al-nuzūl* (the occasions or causes of revelation), this last passage refers to a request that people go to battle in Tabūk, far away in the north of Arabia, in the heat of the summer. Anyone who did not go was in effect forsaking the Prophet at the *sā'at al-'usrā*, the hour of adversity, mentioned in Q. 9:117. Such blame for laggards is paralleled in the Qur'an with those who failed to respond readily to Saul's (Q. 2:246) and Moses' calls to battle (Q. 5:21–4).

It should be remembered that the Muslim community in Medina being addressed here by the Qur'an consisted of those who were truly committed to the faith for the long haul as well as newcomers, some of whom were even branded as hypocrites,[24] and it is they who were the main objects of castigation. Castigating the laggards, however, is not confined in the Qur'an to the area of military *jihād* and fighting. The same technique of castigation is applied to those who were tardy in giving charity and those who tried to acquire property unlawfully as, for example, in Q. 4:9–10 and Q. 20:21.

Battle Tactics

As mentioned above, some verses, such as Q. 9:36, deal with issues relating to such aspects of warfare as the months in which fighting is prohibited. In addition, a few verses deal with battle tactics; for example, Q. 8:15–16, '*believers, when you meet the disbelievers in battle, never turn your backs on them: if anyone does so on such a day – unless manoeuvring to fight or join a fighting group – he incurs the wrath of God and Hell will be his home, a wretched destination.*' In modern armies, deserters are liable to a severe penalty. Similarly, in Q. 9:36 we are told, '*fight the idolaters at any time if they first fight you*'. This verse addresses the issue of the permissibility of going to battle during the months in which fighting is prohibited. Another, tactical, interpretation of this verse is '*fight them all together as they fight you all together*'.

In Q. 9:123, '*believers, fight the disbelievers near you and let them find you standing firm. Know that God is with those who are mindful of Him*', practical advice on how to comport oneself on the battlefield is given, but the permission to fight itself comes earlier, at the beginning of the sura. Likewise, the preceding verse, Q. 9:122, gives another piece of tactical advice that the believers should not all go out to battle together, but some should go to study. Q. 4:71, is also tactical, '*believers, be on your guard. March to battle in small groups or as one body*' as well as Q. 8:12 and Q. 47:4, '*when you meet the disbelievers in battle, strike them in the neck and once they are defeated, bind any captives firmly – later you can release them by grace or ransom – until the toils of war have ended*'. 'Striking the neck' has often been quoted as showing abhorrent violence in the Qur'an, but the underlying reason for this verse can be seen as persuasive, urging on a Muslim community which was afraid to meet its enemies on the field. Since the beginning of Islam, they had been oppressed by them, with the enemies always in far greater numbers, so here they are being urged to be bold and strike effectively. War involves killing and it could be argued that killing by cutting the neck is more humane and fast than many other ways. The fear of the Muslim community in the face of their considerably more numerous opponents is well attested in the Qur'an: Q. 9:13 asks, '*are you afraid of them?*' and Q. 33:10–11 states, '*your eyes rolled with fear, your hearts rose into your throats [...] there the believers were sorely tested and deeply shaken*'.[25]

Another often misquoted verse, Q. 8:60, which relates to preparing forces to deter the enemy, occurs in the middle of the following passage, which is quoted in full here:[26]

The worst creatures in the sight of God are those who reject faith and will not believe; who, whenever you [Prophet] make a treaty with them, break it – for they have no fear of God. If you meet them in battle, make a fearsome example of them to those who come after them, so that they may take heed. And if you learn of treachery on the part of any people, throw their treaty back at them, for God does not love the treacherous. The disbelievers should not think they have won – they cannot escape. Prepare against them whatever forces you [believers] can muster, including warhorses, to frighten off [with this preparation] God's enemies and yours, and warn others unknown to you but known to God. Whatever you give in God's cause will be repaid to you in full, and you will not be wronged. But if they incline towards peace, you [Prophet] must also incline towards it, and put your trust in God: He is the All Hearing, the All Knowing. If they intend to deceive you, God is enough for you.

Q. 8:55–63

Upon grammatical analysis, it is clear that this verse should be read contextually, in connection with people who were always breaking their treaties; fighting them was to be undertaken to make an example of them for others who behave in the same way. Q. 8:60, '*prepare against them [...] forces*', also refers to such people, but has been misrepresented as referring to all non-Muslims, using the well-tried practice of isolating the pronoun (here 'them') from the noun it refers back to. Furthermore, the forces Muslims should prepare are, as clearly stated, a deterrent to '*frighten off*' the enemy, not an aggressive military force. Deterrence is one of the main reasons that all countries, past and present, have prepared armies, to frighten off others from attacking them. Yet, this phrase has been used, isolated from its context and from its reference 'those who break treaties', to connect Islam to terrorism. In Q. 8:61 we are told that, even with regard to those who regularly break their treaties, if they ask for peace, the Prophet must accede, despite any danger of further treachery.

As can be seen from this discussion, it is essential in dealing with verses that urge fighting and verses that talk about tactics that they should be seen as techniques for winning a war rather than as advocating engaging in aggressive military action. Confusion over this gives rise to serious misunderstandings.

Military *Jihād* as the Business of the State

When the Muslims moved from Mecca to Medina, the community effectively became a state responsible for its own protection. The Prophet became the head of state. It is made clear in the Qur'an that it is the head of state who initiates *jihād*. The Prophet is asked to urge the believers to fight (Q. 8:65). It is he who gives permission for some not to fight (Q. 9:54–5) and he who excludes some people from going (Q. 9:83). It is he who orders preparations to be made (Q. 9:92–3). He goes out leading the army (Q. 3:121 and Q. 8:5). It is he who decides on peace and the end of hostilities (Q. 8:61). It is he who decides on the distribution of battle gains (Q. 8:1). Believers who are able-bodied (Q. 4:95, Q. 9:91–2 and Q. 48:17) are expected to hear and obey the head of state (Q. 24:51) and to go out to battle with him, unless given permission not to do so (Q. 9:44). It is the head of state (or his appointee) who assigns them where to stand in the battlefield (Q. 3:121). It was the Prophet who decided and declared war and it was he who decided on cessation of hostilities. He is addressed in Q. 8:61–2, '*if they [the enemy] incline to peace, you [Prophet] must also incline towards it and put your trust in God. He is the All-Hearing, the All-Knowing, and if they intend to deceive you, God is enough for you.*' It is the head of state who decides on taking captives: '*later you can release them by grace or ransom*' (Q. 47:4). It is not up to any individual Muslim to take up the tasks assigned to the head of state. Nowhere in the Qur'an do we find permission to do so.[27]

Conclusion: The Consistency of Qur'anic Teachings on *Jihād* and *Qitāl*

As has hopefully become clear from the previous discussion of the relevant passages and verses of the Qur'an, if one bases a reading of the Qur'an's teachings on *jihād* and *qitāl* on the text itself, from the time permission was given to Muslims who were attacked to fight back (Q. 22:39) in the second year of the *hijra* to the last teachings in Sura 9, shortly before the Prophet's death and the end of Qur'anic revelations, Qur'anic teachings on *jihād* and *qitāl* remained the same both in terms of the objectives of war and the style the Qur'an employs. We have seen that in the oft-misquoted passage Q. 2:190–5, the object of the verb '*fight them*' is '*those who fight you*', and that snatching snippets out of context and ignoring what the pronoun 'them' refers to has led to misinterpretation, mistranslation and misrepresentation of the true Qur'anic teachings in this passage, leading to it being attributed with a universal nature. In fact, what this passage does is rather to introduce restrictions on the original permission to fight in self-defence granted in the text. In similar vein, Q. 4:90–1 stipulates:

> *if they withdraw and do not fight you, and offer you peace, then God gives you no way against them [...] if they neither withdraw, nor offer you peace, nor restrain themselves from fighting; you, seize and kill them wherever you encounter them.*[28]

Likewise, in Q. 8:57, which deals with the first battle fought by the Muslim community, we find mentioned '*those who, whenever you [Prophet] make a treaty with them, break it. If you meet them in battle, make a fearsome example of them*' and in Sura 9, which provides, according to traditional chronology, the last Qur'anic teaching on fighting, we read in connection with the 'Sword Verse' (Q. 9:10–12), '*they do not respect any tie with you of kinship or treaty [...] they have broken their oaths*'.

Nevertheless, the reading of a 'universal' aspect to *jihād* persists in the minds of many. To return to just one example from recent academic writing in English we have already mentioned, the chapter on 'Jihād' in the *Encyclopaedia of the Qur'ān*, Q. 9:5 and Q. 9:29 are described as being viewed by many as containing an order to fight unconditionally. A similar claim is made about Q. 2:216, Q. 8:39 and Q. 47:4. Given that Q. 2:216 states '*fighting is prescribed for you though you dislike it. You may dislike something though it is good for you, or like something though it is bad for you: God knows and you do not*', it is difficult to see how this can be read as meaning 'fighting unconditionally without restraint'. The clear meaning here is that fighting is an unwelcome necessity that has been prescribed; it is the means for *daf'* ('pushing back'), without which corruption would prevail and houses of worship would be destroyed (Q. 2:251 and Q. 22:40). Likewise, Q. 8:39, which states '*[believers,] fight them until there is no more persecution, and all worship is devoted to God alone: if they desist, then God sees all that they do*', only by wrenching out of context and misinterpreting it, can it be made to mean 'unconditional fighting'.[30] Q. 47:4 is actually addressing actions in battle, not advocating battle per se, as is, again, clear from reading the sura.

Just as it is argued that the Qur'anic teachings on *jihād* remain constant, so too does the style of presenting the Qur'anic teachings on *jihād*. In the very first teaching that permits taking up arms, God reminds the believers that He will only help those who, '*when We establish them in the land, keep up prayer, pay the prescribed alms, command what is right and forbid what is wrong*' and that '*God controls the outcome of all events*' (Q. 22:41). In the last instruction to take up arms, where the Qur'an states that '*God has purchased the persons and possessions of the believers in return for the Garden – they fight in God's way: they kill and are killed*' (Q. 9:111–12), immediately after this it describes them as '*those who turn to God in repentance; who worship and praise Him; who bow down and prostrate themselves; who order what is good and forbid what is wrong and who observe God's limits*'. It then adds: '*Give glad news to such believers.*' So here we have the first and last instructions describing those who are permitted to fight.

Again (and broadly speaking), the tendency in discussions of *jihād* in the West appears to be not to take account of this, but to zoom in on '*they kill and are killed*' and '*God has purchased their persons and possessions*'. No attention is given to the fact that the famous passage of Q. 2:190–5, which has given rise to exaggerated assertions about fighting in Islam, was revealed to allay the fears of Muslims who thought that the Meccans might fight them in the Sanctuary when they went to perform *'umra* (pilgrimage) in the seventh year of the *hijra* according to the provisions of the Treaty of Ḥudaybiyya. It is remarkable that no fighting took place on that occasion. Likewise, little reference is made to the historical accounts reporting that when the Muslims marched on Mecca in 8 AH, reportedly with 10,000 men, practically no fighting took place; only three Muslims were killed and 17 Meccans. Finally, not one single polytheist is reported to have been killed as a result of the so-called 'Sword Verse' in the traditional accounts.[31]

The fact is that the Muslims who were addressed in the first place by the Qur'anic teachings on *jihād* and *qitāl* did not take verses out of context. They were affected by the Qur'anic teaching as a whole, and that is why, for all the wars they fought in the nine years during the Prophet's lifetime, very few people were actually killed. Muḥammad 'Imāra gives a full list of all the battles, with dates as well as the numbers of Muslims and non-Muslims killed.[32] On the same page he comments:

> The 600 people who were killed from Banū Qurayza in 5 AH were not killed in the wars. Rather they were killed as a sentence after arbitration which they themselves chose, as a result of their high treason against the Muslims. So, they cannot be counted as having been killed in battle.

Even if we do include these additional numbers, the figure would still be less than a thousand.[33] What is significant about this is that Muslim scholars in the Arab world have now turned to criticising the Orientalist and Western image of Islam, including *jihād*, and making comparisons to show that the West, which concentrates on denigrating the Muslim tradition, keeps silent about its own. They see the speck in other people's eyes and ignore the plank in their own. This exercise of refuting Western accusations was first strongly and repeatedly expressed by the Egyptian writer 'Abbās Maḥmūd al-'Aqqād (d. 1964). In his book, *Ḥaqā'iq al-Islām wa-abāṭīl ḥusūmihi*, he refutes Orientalist and missionary claims about war in the Qur'an and quotes the Old Testament for comparison, citing Deuteronomy 20:10–18:[34]

> When you march up to attack a city, make its people an offer of peace. If they accept and open their gates, all the people in it shall be subject to forced labour and shall work for you. If they refuse to make peace with you in battle, lay siege to that city. When the Lord your God delivers it into your hand, put to the sword all the men in it. As for the women, the children, the livestock and everything else in the city, you may take these as plunder for yourselves.

And you may use the plunder the Lord your God gives you from your enemies. This is how you are to treat all the cities that are at a distance from you and do not belong to the nations nearby.
However, in the cities of the nations the Lord your God is giving you as an inheritance, do not leave alive anything that breathes. Completely destroy them – the Hittites, Amorites, Canaanites, Perizzites, Hivites and Jebusites – as the Lord your God has commanded you. Otherwise they will teach you to follow all the detestable things they do in worshipping their gods, and you will sin against the Lord your God.

He also quoted, in connection with the treatment of cities where people worship a god other than the God of Israel, Deuteronomy 13:15–16:

Thou shalt surely smite the inhabitants of that city with the edge of the sword, destroying it utterly, and all that is therein, and the cattle thereof, with the edge of the sword.
And thou shalt gather all the spoil of it into the midst of the street thereof, and shalt burn with fire the city, and all the spoil thereof every whit, for the LORD thy God: and it shall be a heap for ever; it shall not be built again.

Regrettably, such accusations and counter-accusations only serve to polemicise the discussion of such potentially sensitive subjects as *jihād*.

In conclusion, *jihād* is undoubtedly an important subject in the Qur'an, whether it is non-military or military. Military *jihād* is prescribed only for self-defence and defence of the oppressed. It serves the function of *daf'*, without which, as the Qur'an says, '*the earth would be corrupted and houses of worship wherein God's name is mentioned would be destroyed*'. The Qur'an sets very stringent conditions and limitations for fighting, which is to be carried out by the Islamic state. It is indeed fortunate that the Qur'an, which deals with all aspects of life, dealt also with this subject; one could speculate that if the rules of engagement had been left unregulated, they would have been open to the whims of any ruthless state or commander. However, even then, in order to understand the proper picture of Qur'anic *jihād*, close linguistic analysis of the Qur'anic text is essential and context is crucial. Without taking context into account, as we have seen, gross and wild misunderstandings of the subject have arisen. The Qur'an itself recognised the dangers of such practices and, in Q. 5:13 and 41, condemns those who *yuḥarrifūna'l-kalima 'an mawāḍi'ihi* ('*distort the meaning of [revealed] words*' or '*take words out of their contexts/places*'). This, unfortunately, is something that has been done both by Muslims and non-Muslims.

Muslim extremists and anti-Muslim propagandists hold the same views on *jihād* and stand on the same ground. Both deviate flagrantly from the teachings of the Qur'an. From the first to the last sura to give instructions on fighting, the aims and restrictions outlined remain the same:

God helps those who, when established in the land, establish prayer, pay the poor due, command what is right and forbid what is wrong: God controls the outcome of all events.

Q. 22:41

those who turn to God in repentance; who worship and praise Him; who bow down and prostrate themselves; who order what is good and forbid what is wrong and who observe God's limits. Give glad news to such believers.

Q. 9:111–12

In the following chapter we will deal with Qur'anic descriptions of Paradise to see whether *jihād* is the surest way of going to Paradise, as claimed by extremists and propagandists.

4

Qur'anic Paradise

The afterlife is an inevitable reality in Islam, the crucial point of which is judgement followed by requital, whether bliss in Paradise or torment in Hell. Since the Qur'an is the supreme authority in Islam and the starting point of everything Islamic, and since it is considered by Muslims to be categorically and thoroughly authentic, this chapter on Paradise will examine the subject only in relation to the Qur'an. The subject occupies a very important position in the text and naturally much has been written about it by Muslims and non-Muslims. This chapter examines three questions: (1) who will get to Paradise? (2) what qualifies them to do so? and (3) what can they expect when they get there? The examination will be based on close linguistic analysis of the text of the Qur'an. This will require extensive quotation from the text to let the Qur'an itself speak about the subject. The material will be examined critically, paying regard to the context, the questions of quantity and quality, the relative values the Qur'an assigns to any given rewards, and the way Paradise is presented in the Qur'an in general. This examination will show that much of what has been written on the three questions above, by Muslims and non-Muslims alike, involves misinterpretation of some aspects of the Qur'anic picture of Paradise and mistranslation into English of some crucial terms.

The Inevitability of Judgement

The Resurrection and Judgement are fundamental in Islamic theology. Without them, creating humans would be in vain: '*Did you think We had created you in vain, and that you would not be brought back to Us? Exalted be God!'* (Q. 23:115–16). Without them, divine justice would be compromised: '*Would We treat those who believe and do good deeds and those who spread corruption on earth as equal?*' (Q. 38:28). Likewise: '*What makes you, then, deny the judgement? Is God not the most just of all judges?*' (Q. 95:7–8). Justice entails final recompense: whatever recompense people may have in their life on earth is not comprehensive, or lasting; it is also mixed with the imperfections of this world (Q. 2:155, Q. 42:30, Q. 87:17). Thus the divine scheme from the beginning was to have two worlds, *al-ūlā* ('*the first*') and *al-ākhira* ('*the last*'), both occur in the Qur'an 115 times. Linguistically, it is impossible to use one of these two terms without it recalling the existence of the other. A good prayer for Muslims is to ask God to grant them happiness in both homes (*al-dārayn: al-ūlā wa'l-ākhira*).

This scheme is unalterable. There is no escape from the Day of Resurrection: '*Say [Prophet], "God gives you life, then He causes you to die, and then He gathers you all to the day of resurrection about which there is no doubt*"' (Q. 45:26). It is described as '*a day that cannot be averted*' (Q. 42:47).

There is no escape from judgement either: '*People will come forward after resurrection in separate groups to be shown their deeds*' (Q. 99:6) and '*every soul will be repaid in full for what it has done. God knows best what they do*' (Q. 39:70).

Who Will Get to Paradise?

Anyone, male or female, found at the judgement to have the required qualifications will get to Paradise: '*Anyone,*[1] *male or female, who does good deeds and is a believer will enter Paradise and will not be wronged by as much as the dip in a date stone*' (Q. 4:124) and '*Those who believe and do good deeds will have gardens of bliss*' (Q. 31:8, see also Q. 4:57 and 122).

Q. 4:122 states that their entry into Paradise '*is a true promise from God*' and asks, '*Who speaks more truly than God?*' (see also Q. 46:16, Q. 3:194, Q. 28:61 and Q. 40:8).

The inhabitants of Paradise will not be alone, but will have the company of all the good members of their families: '*They will enter the perpetual gardens along with their righteous ancestors, spouses and descendants*' (Q. 13:23). They will be '*among those God has blessed: the messengers, the truthful, those who bore witness to the truth and the righteous – what excellent companions these are!*' (Q. 4:69). All these are the people of Paradise.

What are the Qualifications for Entry into Paradise?

It is clear throughout the Qur'an that there are two essential qualifications for entry into Paradise: *īmān* (belief) and *'amal ṣāliḥ* (good deeds), which frequently collocate in the Qur'an,[2] making it clear that one is not enough without the other. Paradise is a reward for '*what [the blessed believers] have done*' (Q. 56:24). So fundamental is *'amal* that '*God has created death and life to test you and reveal which of you is better in actions*' (Q. 67:2).

If belief is a condition for being admitted into Paradise, then an important question is, belief in what? Qur'anic exegetes normally seem to take this as known and do not comment on it. The answer can be sought in the Qur'an itself.

The Messenger believes in what has been sent down to him from his Lord and so do the believers. They all believe in God, His angels, His scriptures and His Messengers – we make no distinction between any of His Messengers. They say, 'We hear and obey. Grant us Your forgiveness, our Lord. To You we all return!'

Q. 2:285

This is not just for the believers in the message of Muhammad, but it applies to belief in all other messengers sent by God throughout human history (Q. 2:285), right from the beginning. When Adam and his wife were sent out of the garden, God spoke: '*Get out, all of you, but when guidance comes from Me, as it certainly will, there will be no fear for those who follow My guidance nor will they grieve*' (Q. 2:38).

Later on, the Qur'an states:

God took a pledge from the Children of Israel. We made twelve leaders arise among them and God said, 'I am with you: if you keep up the prayers, pay the prescribed alms, believe in My messengers and support them, and lend God a good loan, I will wipe out your sins and admit you into gardens graced with flowing streams.'

Q. 5:12

Here the belief and required actions are the same as those required of Muhammad's followers and the result is the same, that is, wiping out their sins and admitting them to gardens.

After listing Zechariah, John, Mary and Jesus, Abraham, Moses and Aaron, Ishmael and Idrīs, the Qur'an continues:

These were the prophets God blessed, from the seed of Adam, of those We carried in the Ark with Noah, from the seed of Abraham and Israel – and those We guided and chose. When the revelations of the Lord of Mercy were recited to them, they fell to their knees and wept [...] those who repent, who believe, who do righteous deeds will enter the garden. They will not be wronged in the least: they will enter the garden of lasting bliss promised by the Lord of Mercy to His servants.

Q. 19:58–61

There are in addition sundry references with regard to Moses in Q. 7:156 and Q. 7:169–70; to Abraham in Q. 28:82–5; and to Joseph in Q. 12:101, asking to be joined with the righteous in Paradise. The Qur'an tells us that the scriptures of Abraham and Moses (Q. 87:17–19) testify that the hereafter is better and more lasting. More generally:

The [Muslim] believers, the Jews, the Christians and the Sabians – all those who believe in God and the last day and do good deeds will have their rewards with their Lord. No fear for them, nor will they grieve.

Q. 2:62 (see also Q. 4:163 and Q. 5:69)

In respect of the People of the Book (Jews and Christians), the Qur'an emphasises:

They are not all alike. There are some among the People of the Book who are upright, who recite God's revelations during the night, who bow down in worship, who believe in God and the last day, who order what is right and forbid what is wrong, who are quick to do good deeds. These people are among the righteous and they will not be denied the reward for whatever good deeds they do.

Q. 3:113–5

With regard to belief in God as an entry requirement to Paradise, it should be noted that the Messiah (in the Qur'an usually referred to as Jesus son of Mary) is quoted as saying: '*Children of Israel, worship God, my Lord and your Lord. If anyone associates others with God, God will forbid him the garden, and Hell will be his home*' (Q. 5:72).

Significant also is the fact that belief in God's messengers should be without distinction between them, that is, believing in some and not in others: '*God will give due rewards to those who believe in Him and His Messengers and make no distinction between any of them*' (Q. 4:150–1). In the Qur'an, all these messengers are represented as preaching the same fundamental message, the later ones confirming the earlier (Q. 3:3 and 82).

The entry requirement being the same for all, the Qur'an stresses that, with regard to the requirements of belief and good deeds, Muslims have no right to expect any different treatment from that given to the People of the Book, or vice versa:

It will not be according to your hopes, or those of the People of the Book: anyone who does wrong will be requited for it and will find no one to protect or help him against God; anyone, male or female, who does good deeds and is a believer will enter Paradise and will not be wronged by as much as the dip in a date stone.

Q. 4:123–4

Good deeds (*'amal ṣāliḥ*) are the second requirement for entry into Paradise. In its various forms, this phase occurs over 380 times in the Qur'an, strongly connected with entry into Paradise: '*This is the garden you have been given as your own because of what you used to do*' (Q. 43:72). Here, the emphasis is on good deeds, and the Qur'an frequently repeats the collocation of good deeds and belief when it speaks of '*those who believe and do good deeds*' (*alladhīna āmanū wa-'amilū 'l-ṣāliḥāt*). A sure way of identifying good deeds is to trace the ones the Qur'an itself lists as good deeds that lead to the garden. For example:

Hurry towards your Lord's forgiveness and a garden as wide as the heavens and earth prepared for the righteous, who give both in prosperity and adversity, who restrain their anger and pardon people – God loves those who do good – those who remember God and implore forgiveness for their sins if they do something shameful or wrong themselves – who forgives things but God? – and who never knowingly persist in doing wrong. The reward of such people is forgiveness from their Lord and gardens graced with flowing streams, where they will remain. How excellent is the reward of those who labour!

Q. 3:133–6

There is a similar long list in Q. 25:64–76, ending with:

Those who pray, 'Our Lord, give us joy in our spouses and offspring. Make us good examples to those who are aware of You.' These servants will be awarded the highest place in Paradise for their steadfastness. They will be met with greetings and peace. There they will stay – a happy home and resting place.

Likewise:

We have commanded man to be good to his parents: his mother struggled to carry him and struggled to give birth to him [...] when he has grown to manhood and reached the age of forty, he [may] say, 'Lord, help me to be grateful for Your favours to me and to my parents; help me to do good work that pleases you; make my offspring good.' We accept from such people the best of what they do and overlook their bad deeds. They will be among the people of Paradise, the true promise that has been given to them.

Q. 46:15–16

And:

The righteous fulfill their vows [...] for the love of Him, they give food to the poor, the orphan and the captive [...] 'We feed you for the sake of God alone. We seek neither recompense nor thanks from you.'

Q. 76:7–9

It is important to note that, in these lists, the Qur'an does not speak of any single deed that will lead to *janna* (Paradise), but gives a whole list. That is why each passage should be read as a whole, as shown above. In this way it becomes clear how the Qur'an itself speaks about these deeds and we understand more perfectly the comments it makes on them, which give them their respective values and show the Qur'an's persuasive rhetoric (*targhīb*). When Muslims read these passages, especially in Arabic, they experience the contents in a way that cannot be obtained by extracting and analysing them. Q. 46:15–16, for example, can be reduced to the instruction to be good to ones parents, thus losing all its persuasive force.

Sometimes the Qur'an does not list deeds as entry requirements, but just gives the general expression '*those who believe and do good deeds*', or simply talks about *al-muttaqīn* ('*those who are mindful [of their Lord]*', Q. 44:51, Q. 52:17, Q. 54:54 and Q. 77:41), or *man khāfa maqāma rabbihi* ('*those who fear [the time when they will] stand before their Lord*', Q. 55:46 and Q. 79:40). These two descriptions cover every good deed because such people will stay away from whatever is bad and do whatever is good.

Is *Jihād* the Best Way to Get to Paradise?

From the above discussion it becomes clear that those jihadists or extremists who are reported by the media to think that *jihād* alone will get them to Paradise are evidently mistaken. In fact, faith and good deeds, any good deeds, are said in the Qur'an to be the way to Paradise. *Janna* and *jannāt*, referring to Paradise, occur in the Qur'an over 130 times and in no more than about half a dozen of these is *jihād* said to be a way to it (Q. 2:218, Q. 3:169, Q. 9:111 and Q. 61:11). Indeed, sometimes, in the same sura, there is entry to Paradise by deeds that include *jihād* and deeds which do not. The rewards are more elaborate and better for those that do not. For example, in Sura 9, it is good deeds in general that are first mentioned to lead to Paradise (Q. 9:71–2), and only a few verses after this (Q. 9:88–9), admission into Paradise is linked with *jihād*:

The believers, both men and women, support each other; they order what is right and forbid what is wrong; they keep up the prayer and pray the prescribed alms; they obey God and His Messenger. God will give His mercy to such people: God has the power to decide. God has promised these believers, both men and women, Gardens graced with flowing streams, where they will remain; good, peaceful homes in Gardens of lasting bliss; and – greatest of all – God's good pleasure. That is the supreme triumph.

Q. 9:71–2

The Messenger and those who believed with him, strove hard with their possessions and their persons. The good things belong to them. It is they who will prosper. God has prepared Gardens graced with flowing streams for them and there they will stay. That is the supreme triumph.

Q. 9:88–9

Even those who went to defensive *jihād* with the Prophet himself are not shown to get better treatment than ordinary believers.

Where is the *Janna*?

The Qur'an does not specify where exactly the *janna* will be. This is perhaps part of the mystery of Paradise which makes it part of *al-ghayb* (what has been kept hidden) for the pious. Related to this is that what is given in the Qur'an is only a *mathal* (a likeness) of something indescribable. Accordingly, the exact structure of Paradise is not specified. However, the Qur'an tells us that '*its breadth is like the breadth of the heaven and earth*' (Q. 3:133 and Q. 57:21), so it cannot be anywhere just on earth as we know it. It is also described as being *'āliya* ('*high*' or '*lofty*', Q. 69:22 and Q. 88:10). It has *abwāb* ('*gates*', Q. 13:23, Q. 30:13 and Q. 39:73), which are opened to welcome the blessed, with angels to greet them, whereas the gates of Hell are closed and are opened when a consignment of the damned arrives (Q. 39:71).

Names of Paradise

Janna is the generic name, occurring more than 66 times in the Qur'an, with the dual *jannatān* twice in the next world and twice in this world, and the plural *jannāt* 69 times. The root of the verb *j-n-n* indicates being covered and protected, apparently in this world it indicates being concealed and protected from the sun by the branches of the trees. Some suggest that *janna* is taken from the Hebrew word *gan* in Genesis 2:8.[3] However, the root is well known in Arabic: *junna* is a shield, *jinn* are unseen. Speculation about non-Arab origins[4] remains speculation. Whatever may be said in that respect, the fact is, when the Prophet was reciting the Qur'an to the Arabs, he was naturally using words they would understand, simply because they were part of the language they knew and used. Whatever foreign origin there may have been does not in any case affect the whole picture of Paradise in the Qur'an. Christians and Jews see Paradise in the Qur'an as different from the one in their texts, otherwise they would not have criticised the Islamic version. The Qur'an is an Arabic text. The Muslims who received it were native speakers of Arabic. They knew what words meant for them. They also believed that all that was said about Paradise was there to be seen as a reward for good deeds.

The words *janna* and *jannāt* often come in possessive constructions (*iḍāfa*), being joined with another term, such as *jannāt al-ma'wā* ('*garden of abode*', Q. 32:19 and Q. 79:39), *jannāt al-na'īm* ('*gardens of bliss*', for example Q. 22:56 and Q. 31:8). Paradise is also described in a number of other ways, among them *dār al-salām* ('*home of peace*' or '*home of wholeness*', Q. 6:127 and Q. 10:20) and *dār al-khuld* ('*the eternal home*', Q. 41:28). People in Paradise are said to be in *maqām amīn* ('*a secure dwelling*', Q. 44:51). Paradise is also described as *al-dār al-ākhira* ('*the last home*', Q. 40:39) and *al-ḥusnā* ('*the best*', Q. 10:26 and Q. 13:18). The Qur'an also speaks of *jannāt al-firdaws* (Q. 18:107). Whatever was the origin of the word *firdaws* when it came into Arabic in pre-Islamic times,[5] the general meaning for Muslims is that it is a high, selected place in Paradise, hence the common phrase *al-firdaws al-a'lā* ('*the lofty Paradise*'). All the names and adjectives of Paradise give a picture of a good and highly desirable place.

Janna, jannāt, jannatān

Al-janna as a singular refers to the garden, the abode of the good, in contrast to *al-nār*, the fire, the abode of the bad. As such, *al-janna* collocates with the word *aṣḥāb* ('*the companions*', Q. 36:55), *udkhulū* ('*enter*', an imperative form, Q. 43:70), *abshirū* ('*rejoice in the good news*', Q. 41:30), *ūrithtumūhā* ('*have been given as an inheritance*', Q. 43:72), *mathal* ('*the likeness of*', Q. 13:35 and Q. 47:15), *uzlifat* ('*brought near*', Q. 50:31 and Q. 81:13), *farīq fī'l-janna* ('*a group in the garden*', Q. 42:7) and *baytan fi'l-janna* ('*a house in the garden*', Q. 66:11). When it is indefinite, it is a garden inside the main garden, as also when it is in the plural and the dual.

Jannāt in the plural indicates greater privilege from God and collocates with *lahum* ('*for them*', Q. 85:11), *jazā'uhum* ('*their reward*', Q. 98:8), *athābahum* ('*He rewarded them*', Q. 5:85), *la-udkhilannahum* ('*I will certainly admit them*', Q. 3:195), *yubashshiruhum bi-* ('*He gives them the good news of* ...', Q. 9:21), *wa'ada* ('*He promised*', Q. 9:72), *a'adda lahum* ('*He prepares for them*', Q. 9:89) and *fī jannāt* ('*in gardens*', Q. 22:56). In very few places does it take the definite article '*al-*'. Out of the 69 occurrences, 40 come with *anhār* ('*streams*') and 29 without.

Jannatān ('*two gardens*') occurs only twice, in Sura 55, verses 46 and 63; two gardens for the better class of believers and two others for the less deserving (see Q. 56: 10–40). Annemarie Schimmel observes[6] that 'the Qur'anic description of Paradise is rather consistent [...] but our imaginative faculty becomes slightly confused when, in Surat al-Rahman (Sura 55/36–73), two gardens are mentioned, with two fountains of running water and two kinds of every fruit.' John Wansbrough discussed the two versions occurring at the end of Sura 55 and argued that 'version A [55:46–61] represents an elaboration of version B [55:62–77] both by rhetorical device and exegetical gloss.'[7] He goes on to reduce the whole figure to one garden; however, this ignores the context of the sura itself, which is built on duality from beginning to end, and the principle that different parts of the Qur'an explain each other. Indeed, two and a half lines after the end of Sura 55, in Sura 56 we have an explicitly expressed tripartite division similar to the one in Sura 55, one for those brought near, another for those on the right hand and the third of the trio refers to the fire. The two gardens in Sura 56 are different in quality like those in Sura 55 which conclusively proves that the numbers are as stated in Sura 56 and cannot be reduced in the way Wansbrough argued.[8]

Nor is there any need for our imaginative faculty to be confused: *Sūrat al-Raḥmān* (Q. 55) mentions two pairs of gardens as understood by Annemarie Schimmel. The question arises, why two gardens for those brought near and two for the less deserving? The answer to this can be found in the Qur'an when it refers to the people of Sheba:

> *There was a sign for the people of Sheba. In their dwelling places: two gardens, one on the right and one on the left: 'Eat from what your Lord has provided for you and give Him thanks, for your land is good and your Lord most forgiving'.*
>
> Q. 34:15

To have two gardens, one on the right and one on the left, represent the ultimate luxury.[9]

This is further confirmed in the parable of the two gardens in *Sūrat al-Kahf* (Q. 18:32 ff.), where the use of two gardens shows more privilege given by God. So *jannatān* in Sura 55 cannot merely, as suggested by Schimmel, be explained away as caused by the necessity of the rhyme in the dual, provoked by the initial word *al-Raḥmān.*[10]

What Awaits Those Qualified to Enter?

Although the Qur'an tells us in Q. 32:17 that '*no soul knows what joy is kept hidden in store for them as a reward for what they have done*', let us attempt to explore what is not hidden but given as hints and images (*mathal*) of this joy. We will begin from the beginning.

> *On the day when you see the believers, both men and women, with their light streaming ahead of them and to their right, 'The good news for you today is that there are gardens, graced with flowing streams, where you will stay. That is the supreme triumph.'*
>
> Q. 57:12

After being given such excellent news,

> *Those who were mindful of God will be led in throngs to the garden. When they arrive, they will find its gates wide open and the keepers will say to them 'Peace be upon you, you have been good. Come in, you are here to stay,' and they themselves will say, 'Praise be to God, who has kept His promise to us and given us this land as our own. Now we may live wherever we please in the garden. How excellent is the reward of those who labour!' You will see the angels surrounding the Throne, glorifying their Lord with praise.*
>
> Q. 39:73–5

Essential Components of Paradise

The essential component of Paradise is flowing water. This is logical since God says, '*We made every living thing from water*' (Q. 21:30). No garden can exist without water, whether the damp equatorial heat, the dry heat of Arabia,[11] or the well-watered lands of the temperate zones.[12] Springs and fountains are '*flowing*' (*tajriyān*, Q. 55:50) and '*gushing*' (*naḍḍākhatān*, Q. 55:66); the righteous cause the spring to gush (Q. 76:6). Such verbs indicate life, energy and plenty,[13] and carry a healing connotation:

We shall have removed all ill-feeling from their hearts: streams will flow at their feet. They will say, 'Praise be to God who guided us to this: had God not guided us we would never have found the way'.

Q. 7:43

Water comes mainly in the form *tajrī min taḥtihā'l-anhār*, literally '*running from beneath it*' or '*beneath the trees*'. The term *anhār*, referring to these waters, always appears in the plural and is always connected with the idea of running. The question now is what these *anhār* (sing. *nahr*) are? The normal translation is rivers; however, this does not seem to fit the image. To have rivers everywhere under Paradise or under the trees would be too wet. Nor does the translation as 'rivers' agree with the original root verb *n-h-r*, 'to flow'. *Nahr* is *al-mā' al-'adhb al-jārī* (fresh running water).[14] *Anhāra al-'irq* means 'the vein kept flowing'.[15] What seems to be important in Paradise is fresh, running water, so the most suitable translation in the context of *jannāt tajrī min taḥtihā'l-anhār* seems to be 'gardens graced with running streams'. In Q. 47:15 there is a description of '*rivers of water, forever pure, rivers of milk, forever fresh, rivers of wine, a delight for those who drink, and rivers of honey clarified and pure*', all running, they seem to suggest fresh, plentiful and continuous supply, rather than major, or any other kind of, rivers.[16]

Annemarie Schimmel writes that 'the most famous detailed description of these rivers can be gathered from Sura 47:16ff. [...] The idea of the four rivers [...] Thus agreeing with the concept of four rivers, which many Western writers seem to repeat and some relate it to the four rivers in Genesis.'[17] Bell, for example, says the details have their parallels in Christian and Jewish literature and he quotes Horovitz and Grimme.[18] The fact is that the quote above mentions there are more than four rivers, but they are not necessarily taken from any biblical source. What is described is in fact four types of drink, each type in plentiful supply, described as rivers (*anhār*).[19] Nor is there any need to go to the Bible for a source or parallel.[20] In fact, the source is in the Qur'an itself in Q. 16:65–9 where the four types of drink are mentioned in exactly the same order as they are in Q. 47:15 ff., that is, water, milk, wine and honey. All are given to show the power and grace of God to all people, not just the believers. In fact, this passage and this part of the sura is addressed to the polytheists of Mecca who consumed all these four drinks in a Meccan sura (Q. 16) which predates Sura 47, a Medinan sura.

Other components of Paradise include tall, shady trees,[21] laden with an unceasing supply of fruit that hangs within reach and is not forbidden. The blessed, with their spouses (Q. 36:56), will be seated comfortably (*muttaki'īn*, often mistranslated as 'reclining'),[22] on upholstered seats, *surur* (Q. 56:15) and *arā'ik* (Q. 83:23), which are things to sit on, not beds but chairs. Seated on them, the people of Paradise look around (*yanẓurūna*, Q. 83:23 and 35), clearly enjoying the scene around them. There will be what delights the eyes (Q. 43:71) and nothing to jar the ears: '*There you will hear no idle talk*' (Q. 88:11), '*no vain or lying talk*' (Q. 78:35). They wear green silk garments and gold and silver bracelets (Q. 18:31 and Q. 76:21).

The Qur'an describes food and drink in Paradise, mainly fruit such as they choose; meat of any bird they like (Q. 56:21), wine that never intoxicates or loosens their tongues in idle talk (Q. 52:23); and their Lord gives them a pure drink (Q. 76:21), flavoured with ginger (Q. 76:17), a very healthy diet, one may say. The Arabs who first received the Qur'an were people who celebrated with meals of camel, goat and sheep meat, but none of this is mentioned in Paradise. What is described in Paradise is more in the nature of light snacks and, together with everything else given in Paradise, it will be offered by God who will tell the blessed: '*This is a reward for you: your striving has been thanked*' (Q. 76:22).

Women in Paradise

God will not allow the deeds of believing women to be wasted but will reward them, like men, in Paradise:

> *I will not allow the deeds of any one of you to be lost, whether you are male orfemale, each is like the other [in rewards]. I will certainly wipe out the bad deeds of those who emigrated and were driven out of their homes, who suffered harm for My cause, who fought and were killed. I will certainly admit them to Gardens graced with flowing streams, as a reward from God: the best reward is with God.*
>
> (Q. 3:195)

Thoroughly studied, but also criticised in non-Islamic circles is the topic of the women granted to the faithful as a celestial reward in the Qur'anic Paradise.[23] To describe the women as being granted to the faithful as a celestial reward actually is a misrepresentation of the Qur'anic picture, since a reward is mentioned in the Qur'an not just referring to women, but to the whole picture of what has been promised in long passages, for example, Q. 52:17–28; 55:46–60; 56:11–26; 76:7–22. To think that the reward given to men is women shows very odd selectivity and reductionism, and neglects or ignores what the Qur'an actually says. The Qur'an tells us that '*God has promised the faithful, men and women, gardens graced with flowing streams, there to stay, and goodly dwellings in eternal gardens and – greatest of all – God's good pleasure*' (Q. 9:72).

In Q. 33:35, '*God has prepared forgiveness and a rich reward [...] for Muslim men and women, believing men and women, obedient men and women, truthful men and women, patient men and women*' and in Q. 36:56, '*the people of Paradise [...] and their spouses are seated on chairs in the shade*'. So the believing women of this world will be resurrected, judged and rewarded in Paradise. Just as men, they will be '*created anew in a form they do not know*' (Q. 56:61), God will create women anew (*ansha'nahunna*), '*virginal, loving, of matching age* (*atrāb*)' (Q. 56:35); everyone in Paradise will be young again, male and female and they will not suffer from old age. They will praise God, who settled them in the everlasting home, where no toil or fatigue will touch them (Q. 35:35). The women seen in Paradise are described as *kawā'ib* (Q. 78:33). Much has been made of the word *kawā'ib*, which occurs only once in the Qur'an. As the author of *al-Ṣiḥāḥ*[24] explains, *al-kā'ib wa-hiya al-jāriya ḥīn yabdū thadyuhā li-nuhūd* – a *kā'ib* is a young girl when her breast shows as it develops, so what is intended here is clearly their youthfulness rather than the swelling breasts that regularly recur in Western writing.[25] According to Lane, *jāriyatun kā'ib* is a girl whose breasts are beginning to swell, or become prominent or protuberant,[26] so the first meaning here is that the breasts are beginning to swell. It should be remembered that the dictionaries mention a *jāriya*, a young girl. Those who exaggerate the physical aspects of the Qur'anic Paradise choose a further stage in her development. In colloquial Arabic people express the same concept by saying *al-bint bazzazat* ('the girl has developed breasts'), even when they are just beginning to appear. The boys will be *wildān mukhalladūn* (Q. 76:19), of an age matching the girls. In fact, physical description of the people of Paradise is very sparse: *Ḥūr 'ayn*, '*with beautiful large eyes*', is mentioned only twice (Q. 52:20 and Q. 56:22); and Q. 55:56 mentions, '*they are like rubies and brilliant pearls*'. The physical description for both men and women is: '*You will recognise in their faces the radiance of bliss*' (*naḍrat al-na'īm*, Q. 83:24). Nowhere are they seen in any sexual situations or even sleeping. In fact, what is clear in the descriptions is that they are sitting in groups all the time,[27] facing each other as seen in Q. 15:47 that states: '*We shall remove any bitterness from their hearts. [They shall] be seated, facing each other, as brothers*'; and Q. 37:42–4 adds, '*They will be honoured in gardens of bliss, seated facing each other.*' They will be '*on seats lined up in rows*' (Q. 52:20) and '*pass around a cup which does not lead to any idle talk or sin*' (Q. 52:23).

With such sparing descriptions, Muslims usually express great surprise that many Westerners seem to criticise the physical pleasures in the Qur'anic Paradise. Some have expressed their disapproval of such Western thinking in strong language.[28]

Physical and Non-Physical Rewards in Paradise

As Ibn Rushd explains, the representation of existence in the afterlife as being bodily and not merely spiritual is more suitable for the majority of people, as it is easier to understand and more moving.[29] Figurative representation of spiritual realities may be appropriate only for speculative thinkers, whereas the simpler religious explanations are aimed primarily at the great majority. Scriptures address human beings of all varieties of mental, psychological and cultural backgrounds, at all times and in all parts of the world: '*We sent you [Prophet] only to bring good news and warning to all human beings (kāffatan li'l-nās)*' (Q. 34:28).

Such minimal physical descriptions as are present in the Qur'an would thus be fitting for some of the people the Qur'an addresses. Similarly, the philosopher Abū Manṣūr al-ʿĀmirī (d. 381/992) said, 'It is inevitable that the rewards [in Paradise] should be made in a way that is pleasing (and torment be made in a way that is painful) and that its nature cannot be apprehended except by giving a standard or a gauge for it of what human senses have experienced.'[30] The fact is that humans are not angels or any other different beings and should be addressed only as humans (Q. 17:95).

According to the picture given in the Qur'an, when humans go to Paradise they will not be turned into angels; they will still be a class of creatures different from the angels. The angels will be carrying the throne of God (Q. 69:17), or '*surrounding the throne, glorifying their Lord with praise*' (Q. 39:75). Angels also come and greet the new arrivals in Paradise and welcome them (Q. 13:23–4 and Q. 39:73).

Even the physical comforts of Paradise are shown in the Qur'an as a mark of honour and appreciation from God (Q. 70:35 and Q. 76:22), a grace from Him (Q. 44:57).

In Q. 47:14, in addition to the plentiful supplies of four different drinks (*anhār*) and '*fruit of every kind*', the blessed will have '*the forgiveness and pleasure of their Lord*'.

God's providing for the people of Paradise in the plural of majesty ensures a very special privilege: '*We have made them enter*' (*adkhalnāhum*), '*We have provided them*' (*amdadnāhum*) and '*We have joined/paired them*' (*zawwajnāhum*). When provision is attributed to Him in the singular it is expressed through God's role as Sustainer (*rabbuhum*) (e.g. Q. 2:63, Q. 3:169, Q. 42:22, Q. 45:30, Q. 68:34 and Q. 76:21) or in the form of '*My servants*' (Q. 21:105 and Q. 89:29).

Being seated comfortably with their spouses, surrounded by beautiful scenery, wearing green silken robes, does not in any case detract from feeling spiritual. One does not have to be naked or shabbily clothed, sitting in a rough place, segregated by gender, in order to feel spiritual.

Say, 'Who has forbidden the adornment and the nourishment God has provided for His servants?' Say, 'They are [allowed] for those who believe during the life of this world: they will be theirs alone on the day of resurrection.'

Q. 7:32

Should the reward of good be anything but good?

Q. 55:60

The people of Paradise feel that they have been given such good things as a grace from God, which enhances their spirituality and makes them more thankful. Even before they reach Paradise, they receive the blessing of being protected from the fire of Hell and they themselves are aware of this and thankful for it (Q. 35:35 and Q. 52:27). When they are inside Paradise, they have a chance to see the sufferings of those in Hell and recognise the blessing of God in not being there (Q. 37:57). The Qur'an always brings out the contrast between hellfire and the garden of Paradise. The believers have all along recognised that whoever God sends to Hell is put to shame (Q. 3:192).

On the Day of Judgement, after being spared the suffering and shame of being taken to Hell,

the believers, both men and women, will be seen with their light streaming out ahead of them and to their right and they will be told, 'The good news for you today is that there are gardens graced with flowing streams where you will stay. This is truly the supreme triumph.'

Q. 57:12

The believers will be addressed: '*You, soul at peace, return to your Lord, well pleased and well pleasing; go in among My servants; and enter My garden*' (Q. 89: 27–30). A great number of verses express the greater honour of being among God's servants:

He will admit them by the gate of honour, by a gate that is well pleasing to them.

Q. 4:31 and Q. 22:59

For them there will be no fear, no grief, no shame.

Q. 10:62 and Q. 66:8

Their efforts will be appreciated.

Q. 76:22

Whoever does good, God is thankful and all-knowing.

Q. 2:158

The blessed will have a sure footing with their Lord.

Q. 10:2

They will live securely in gardens and rivers, secure in the presence of an all-powerful sovereign.

Q. 54:54–5

There will be radiant faces, looking towards their Lord.

Q. 75:22–3

God is well pleased with them and they are well pleased with Him.

Q. 98:8

God has promised the believers, both men and women, gardens graced with flowing streams, where they will remain; good peaceful homes in gardens of lasting bliss; and – greatest of all – God's good pleasure: that is the supreme triumph.

Q. 9:72

They will have the good company of their good spouses, parents and children.

Q. 13:23 and Q. 52:22

[they] will be among those He has blessed: the messengers, the truthful, those who bear witness to the truth, and the righteous. What excellent companions these are!

Q. 4:69

They will be in dār al-salām ('the home of peace').

Q. 6:127

They rejoice that they will not die.

Q. 37:59

They are there forever and will not be expelled.

Q. 15:48

In fact, the examination of Qur'anic material reveals that the number of references to spiritual and moral rewards in Paradise exceeds those to material rewards.[31]

Figurative Language

With all the descriptions and details given in the Qur'an, it still tells us that what has been given is only *mathal al-janna* (*'a picture of the garden'*, Q. 13:35 and Q. 47:15). Describing the purity of boys in Paradise, it uses similes: they are *'like hidden pearls'* (*ka-annahum lu'lu' maknūn*, Q. 52:24). The same simile is used for the women in Q. 56:23. In Q. 37:49 another simile is used: *'as if they were hidden eggs'* (*ka-anna bayḍun maknūn*).[32] In Q. 76:19, the *wildān mukhalladūn* (*'people forever young'*) in Paradise are also described metaphorically as *'you would think them scattered pearls'* (*ḥasibtahum lu'lu'an manthūra*). The fruit the people of Paradise are given will resemble what they were given before (Q. 2:25).

What God has for the righteous is *'better'* (*khayr*, Q. 3:198) and *'more lasting'* (*abqā*, Q. 87:17) than the life and rewards of this world. The Qur'an does not say how much or in what way it is better. According to Arabic rhetoric, leaving it unspecified indicates that what is talked about is indescribable. It must be remembered on that day *'the earth is turned into another earth, the heavens into another heaven'* (Q. 14:48). Ibn 'Abbās aptly observed, 'there is nothing this world shares with *al-janna* except the names of things.'[33] What is described is only what the good receive on arrival (*nuzūlan*, Q. 18:107 and Q. 41:32). *Nuzūl* is what has been prepared for a guest.[34] The command *udkhulū* (*'enter!'*) is used in many places (Q. 7:49, Q. 15:46, Q. 16:32, Q. 39:73, Q. 43:70 and Q. 50:34). In many situations, the Qur'an says no more than *'they will have whatever they wish for'* (Q. 25:16, Q. 39:34, Q. 42:22) and *'they will have all that they wish for there, and We have more for them'* (Q. 50:35).

With all the details the Qur'an gives of Paradise, it remains in reality part of *al-ghayb* (the unseen/unknown) and one of the first characteristics of the believer is that they believe in *al-ghayb* (Q. 2:3). Q. 32:17 clarifies: *'No soul knows what joy (qurrat a'yun) is kept hidden in store for them [the believers] as a reward for what they have done.'*

The expression *qurrat a'yun* has been variously translated as 'comfort to the eye', 'joy', and 'bliss'. When Moses' mother had her baby restored to her after she put him in the river, when he was picked up by Pharaoh's household, this was so that *taqarra 'aynuha* (*'her eye might be comforted'*, and not grieve, Q. 28:13). What is kept hidden now will become clear and real when the good arrive in Paradise, and no wonder that even after being there for a long time, they will not wish to leave (Q. 15:41 and Q. 18:108). Why should they desire to leave when they have already achieved *al-fawz al-'aẓīm* ('*the supreme achievement*', for example in Q. 57:12)?

In the *Encyclopaedia of the Qur'ān,* after describing the women granted to men as a celestial reward and the delicacies of eating, drinking and palaces, the author of the chapter on Paradise[35] goes on to say: 'Such pleasures and those like them are often defined as "[the great] triumph" (fawz).' This seriously misrepresents what *al-fawz al-'aẓīm* stands for in the Qur'an. The author gives a list starting with Q. 4:13, which mentions nothing of the physical details being discussed. It merely says: '*God will admit whoever obeys God and His Messenger to gardens graced with flowing streams, and there they will stay: that is the supreme triumph.*' Q. 5:119 is also cited, but again does not mention the details:

> *God will say, 'This is a day when the truthful will benefit from their truthfulness. They will have gardens graced with flowing streams, there to remain forever. God is pleased with them and they with Him: this is the supreme triumph.'*

Cited also in the list is Q. 9:72, but all we have in the verse is:

> *God has promised the believers, both men and women, gardens graced with flowing streams where they will remain. Good, peaceful homes in gardens of lasting bliss and, greatest of all, God's good pleasure: that is the supreme triumph.*

Q. 9:89 and 100, also included in the author's list, are even briefer. Added to this list of verses mentioning *al-fawz al-'aẓīm* could be Q. 45:30, '*Those who believed and did good deeds will be admitted by their Lord into His Mercy: that is the clearest triumph*' (similarly Q. 48:5, Q. 57:12, Q. 61:12 and Q. 64:9), as well as Q. 85:11, '*Those who believe and do good deeds will have gardens, graced with flowing streams: that is the great triumph.*'

None of these mention the delights claimed in the *Encyclopaedia of the Qur'ān* to be *al-fawz al-'aẓīm.* The true blessing of Paradise for the believers, then, is to be admitted by their Lord to the joy kept hidden in store for them (Q. 9:72 and others, see above) 'and, greatest of all, God's good pleasure'.

In the next chapter we shall go on to deal with a subject much talked about, but showing surprising neglect of the Qur'anic teachings, *sharī'a.*

PART II
Style

5

Legal Style: Qur'anic *Sharīʿa* – Avoiding the Application of the Ultimate Penalties

The Meaning of *Sharīʿa*

The basic lexical meaning of *sharīʿa* in Arabic is 'way to water', 'watering place' or simply 'path'; however, in the religious context it has the following three meanings:

1. In the Qur'an it is used in the sense of 'religion' (Q. 45:17–18). After stating that He has given the Children of Israel the scripture, wisdom and prophethood, God says: '*Now we have set you, Muhammad, on a clear religious path, so follow it.*' This path includes both beliefs and practices. This is the broadest meaning of *sharīʿa*.
2. There is another technical meaning that sets the *sharīʿa* as the laws (*aḥkām*) of Islam in contrast to the beliefs (*ʿaqīda*). For example, the famous jurist and rector of Al-Azhar, Mahmūd Shaltūt (d. 1963), employed it in this meaning in his celebrated book entitled, *Al-Islām: ʿāqīda wa-sharīʿa*.[1] Similarly, Al-Azhar University has a faculty of *uṣūl al-dīn* (basic principles of the faith) and a faculty of *sharīʿa* (law), covering specifically religious laws for prayer, fasting, giving charity, pilgrimage and all other aspects of law in its widest, general sense. Throughout the Muslim world this usage is the one generally associated with *sharīʿa*.
3. There is also the concept of *sharīʿa* as commonly understood by many people in the West, including the media, in which it is confined to the

> penal code, covering matters such as adultery, theft, highway robbery and apostasy, to which some may add the treatment of women and non-Muslims. For many of those who campaign for the application of the *sharī'a*, whether Muslim extremists or moderates, it is this particular area that they mean, and it is not enough in their opinion that other aspects of Islamic law may already be applied in Muslim countries. The reality is, however, that these penalties occupy only a very small percentage of the whole panoply of Islamic law. In the Qur'an, verses relating to the penal code are 30 out of a total of 6,236,[2] and even in this small area it will be seen that the tendency in the Qur'an is to avoid the application of the ultimate penalties stipulated.

It is this limited area of *sharī'a* that we will examine in this chapter, looking directly at the Qur'anic texts to see how the Qur'an deals with the application of the specified penalties. We will, moreover, examine where the Qur'an actually means the penalties to be applied and who has the authority to apply them.

Types of Penalties

In Islamic Law, penalties are divided into three types, outlined below.

The first type is the *ḥudūd* (plural of *ḥadd*). The basic lexical meaning of *ḥudūd* is 'the limits set by God that should not be exceeded'. Technically, it means a penalty specified in the Qur'an or the Hadith (traditions of the Prophet), set to guard God's limits. These are limited in number. According to some jurists the maximum is seven, but the Qur'an mentions only four: *ḥirāba* (traditionally translated as 'highway robbery'), *sariqa* (theft), *zinā* (fornication/adultery) and *qadhf* (slander). *Ḥudūd* thus deal with what are considered major crimes affecting society.

Murder, homicide and physical injury make up the second type of penalty, referred to as *qiṣāṣ* (retribution). In Islamic law, murder, homicide and physical injury are considered to be a separate category, for which the injured party or (in the case of murder and homicide), their family have the right to *qiṣāṣ*. This allows them to exact a penalty equal to what has been committed, to waive the penalty and accept compensation (*diya*), or indeed pardon the culprit as an act of charity. This does not apply in any of the *ḥudūd*, which must be applied once legally established.

The third type of penalty, *ta'zīr*, is technically defined as discipline for an offence which is neither *ḥadd* nor *qiṣāṣ*. Lexically, it is derived from a verb meaning, in this field, to 'restrain' or 'deter'. The *ta'zīr* penalty is left to the discretion of legislators and judges. The vast majority of laws in a modern Muslim country like Egypt fall under this heading and are regulated by legislative bodies; hence they vary and change from time to time.

Qiṣāṣ: Fair Retribution

Let us first deal with *qiṣāṣ* and how the Qur'an treats it. The Qur'an was primarily concerned with equality, since powerful tribes used to be excessive when seeking retribution; however, it also encourages waiving penalties:

> *You who believe, fair retribution is prescribed for you in cases of killing: the free man for the free man, the slave for the slave, the female for the female, but if the culprit is pardoned by his aggrieved brother, this shall be adhered to fairly and the culprit shall pay what is due in a good way. This is an alleviation from your Lord and an act of mercy. If anyone then exceeds these limits, grievous suffering awaits him. Fair retribution saves life for you, people of understanding.*
> Q. 2:178

This prescribes a penalty equal to, but not exceeding the crime committed, but then suggests an alternative, even encouraging and reminding both culprit and the family of the victim that they are still brothers in faith and that this is an act of mercy from God. In murder and homicide, the intended effect is that giving compensation is more useful for the family.[3] The family of the victim has been reminded that God has given them the right to retaliation, but they should not be excessive in exacting that right (Q. 17:33). The Qur'an here is dealing with a situation in which, if a woman was killed, a more powerful tribe would insist on killing a man from the other tribe in return, or a free man for a slave or more than one person in return for one person.[4] From these two examples it becomes clear that the language of the Qur'an is not that of a legal text in the modern sense of law, rather it is couched in rhetorical and emotional expressions to persuade and dissuade. The Qur'an is a book of guidance (*hudā*).

Ḥudūd

We shall now deal with the *ḥudūd* one by one. We have seen that there are only 30 verses in the Qur'an dealing with penalties. It should be noted that the Qur'an legislates in response to actual situations that arose at different times and mostly in answer to a question. It did not set out from the beginning to write a chapter on penalties as is done now in modern law.

The *ḥudūd* penalties are derived from various parts of the Qur'an revealed in Medina at different times, when the Prophet Muhammad was in effect the head of the Muslim state.

Ḥirāba

Ḥirāba is the verbal noun of *ḥāraba,* 'to wage war', and is mentioned only once in the Qur'an, in Q. 5:33:

> *The penalty of those who wage war on God and His Messenger (alladhīna yuḥāribūna'llāha wa-rasūlahu) and strive to spread corruption in the land is death or crucifixion or amputation of an alternate hand and foot or banishment from the land: a disgrace for them in this world and then a terrible punishment in the Hereafter, unless they repent before you overpower them – in that case, bear in mind that God is most forgiving, most merciful.*

This refers to bands of armed criminals who attack people, committing such crimes as murder, rape and robbery. As usual, the language of this passage is highly emotive. Instead of using a noun as a technical term, for example 'the assailant', it uses a relative clause to rhetorically scandalise what they do, describing it as waging war against God and His Messenger and seeking to spread corruption in the land.[5]

It is significant that a series of alternative penalties are given. As a result, the passage does not insist on applying the ultimate penalty, death, but leaves it to the law enforcement authorities to select the appropriate punishment from the alternatives given, according to the seriousness of the crime committed, whether murder, robbery, rape or general violence and corruption.[6] Stating that the punishment will be a disgrace for them in this world and that they will have a terrible punishment in the hereafter is intended to deter. *Ḥirāba* involves committing multiple heinous crimes, yet the Qur'an still opens the door further to avoiding the application of the ultimate and even lesser penalties. It states, '*if they repent before you overpower them, then bear in mind [or: know] that God is most forgiving, most merciful*', using the intensive adjectival forms, *ghafūr* and *raḥīm,* to refer to God. The implication is that God Himself shows mercy to them, so the society and the law enforcement authority should not apply the penalty in such cases, but should likewise show mercy. '*If they repent before you overpower them*' encourages the criminals to desist and spare society from further attacks by them.

It is clear from this verse that the Qur'an, in setting out these aspects of the *sharīʿa,* tempers the severe, punitive language of the law with more emotive appeals for ceasing hostility and for mercy.

Sariqa: *theft*

Soon after the passage on *ḥirāba* the Qur'an introduces the penalty for theft, in Q. 5:38–40, the only place where it is mentioned:

As for the thieves, male or female, cut off their hands as payment for what they have done – a deterrent from God: God has the power to decide. But if anyone repents after his wrongdoing and makes amends, God will accept his repentance: God is most forgiving, most merciful. Do you [Prophet] not know that control of the heavens and earth belongs solely to God? He punishes whoever He will and forgives whoever He will: God has power over everything.

The passage starts very sternly: '*cut off their hands as payment for what they have done*'. Again, after the stern, punitive language, the Qur'an states that this is meant to deter, telling the thieves that God has the power to decide on their penalty. It then goes on to emphatically state that if the thief repents and makes amends, God will certainly accept his repentance (*fa-inna'llāha yatūbu 'alayhi*). In anticipation of some being surprised at such magnanimity from God, the Qur'an flatly asks in the subsequent verse (Q. 5.40), '*Do you [Prophet] not know that control of the heavens and earth belongs solely to God? He punishes whoever He will and forgives whoever He will: God has power over everything.*'

All this clearly indicates that the intention is to keep people away from theft and its penalty. In fact, in the case of theft it can be seen that the Qur'an tries more to coax people to reform their ways. In cases of *ḥirāba* they have to repent before they are overpowered, but not in the case of theft; the door appears to remain open after they have been caught. This analysis is based on what the Qur'an actually says and on how it is stated in the two different verses.

Despite this, according to al-Rāzī, the majority of jurists insist that the penalty still has to apply even after the thief has repented. Apparently this opinion was influenced by the fact that in Q. 5:33 on *ḥirāba,* the guilty person has to repent *before* being caught. He notes, however, that some early successors of the *Ṣaḥāba* (the Prophet's companions) held that the penalty would not apply if the thief repents.[7]

If after taking the thief to court and before amputation is applied the owner of the property declares that he gives it to the thief as a gift, Mālik and Shāfi'ī said the penalty still applied, but Abū Hanīfa and some others said it did not.[8]

The view that the penalty still has to apply even after the thief has repented can be challenged by comparing the Qur'anic statement on theft with that on *ḥirāba*. In the case of *ḥirāba* the Qur'an specifies two penalties (Q. 5:33): one characterised as '*a disgrace in this world*' and another one described as a '*severe punishment in the life to come*'. When God accepts the repentance of a culprit it means waiving both stated penalties. In the case of theft, there is only one penalty mentioned: '*cut off their hands*'. No penalty is mentioned for the life to come, so when God accepts the repentance of a thief the effect must be referring to the only penalty mentioned in the verse, the cutting off of the hand. A few scholars are of the opinion that repentance and putting things right (i.e. returning goods or paying compensation), can avoid the penalty and that the door is open for people to repent and escape the penalty.[9] Actually, there are other penalty cases in the Qur'an where repenting and putting things right stops the application of a worldly penalty, such as in the case of *zinā* in Q. 4:16 and in the case of disqualifying the testimony of a slanderer in Q. 24:4, both discussed below.

Even those jurists who insist on applying the penalty of amputation[10] allow some concessions where the penalty is not applied: in times of famine, in cases of doubt or when stealing what may partly belong to the thief, such as public funds.[11] Given that such important jurists as Abū Hanīfa, Ibn Ḥazm and others argued that the penalty should not be applied in certain cases, some modern jurists have, and continue to adopt such views. These opinions of jurists left aside, in this book we are dealing with what the Qur'an itself states about theft and the style and context it uses on the subject. We cannot ignore the way the Qur'an presents its message for the sake of any jurist.

Zinā: *extramarital sexual intercourse*

This is forbidden in the Qur'an. During the Meccan period of revelation (lasting 13 years), in describing the true believers it states that '*they guard their private parts*' (Q. 23:5–6, Q. 25:67 and Q. 70:29) and says, '*do not come near zinā because it is an abomination and bad way to go*' (Q. 17:32). No punishment was mentioned during the Meccan period except in the world to come (Q. 25:68–71). In Medina, in addition to the normal prohibition, the Qur'an gradually introduced penalties in this world. In Q. 4:15–16 it states:

For those of your women who commit fāḥisha, call four witnesses from among you. Then if they testify to their guilt, keep the women at home until death comes to them or until God shows them another way. As for any two of you who commit fāḥisha, hurt them both; if they repent and mend their ways, leave them alone – God is always ready to accept repentance: God is full of mercy.

Verse 15 is clearly about women who are said to '*commit lewdness*' or *fāḥisha. Fāḥisha* means something abominable, going far beyond what is acceptable. The word applies to *zinā* and lexically it can apply to any other serious infringement which breaks the bounds. Exegetes understand it to mean sexual infringement and because the verse here talks only about women, some assume this must be about lesbianism. According to al-Rāzī, Abū Muslim thinks that both verses 15 and 16 are to do with homosexuality;[12] however, the majority of exegetes take it to refer to *zinā. Fāḥisha*, in these verses, like *zinā* has to be established by four trustworthy male witnesses who have seen the full sexual act itself. The verse goes on to say, '*if these witnesses testify to their guilt, keep the women at home*'. This makes it strange to think that the verse refers to lesbianism: keeping a woman at home does not preclude other women being in or coming into her house and behaving in this way. The more likely explanation is that punishing them by keeping them at home indicates that these were women who would deliberately go out seeking illicit relationships, as al-Bayḍāwī puts it, *al-ta'arruḍ li-rijāl* ('showing their availability to men'),[13] and that this is what keeping them at home was seeking to avoid. They were to be kept at home until death came to them or God made a way out for them. Exegetes agree that the way out could include getting married and so having a man of their own.[14] This in itself tends to disprove the lesbian theory.

Another indication that verse 15 cannot be referring to lesbianism is that, if it were, it would have said, 'if two women' in the Arabic dual rather than in the plural. This is what we find in the subsequent verse (v. 16): it deals with two individuals and the pronoun is masculine dual (*alladhāni*). This led many exegetes to think this must refer to male homosexuality; however, in Arabic grammar, when talking about a male and female together, either one can use a conjunction like 'and' or 'he and she' or the masculine dual pronoun. In Arabic, the male form is used when referring to males and females together according to the rule of preponderance (*taghlīb*). Another possibility is that this verse is talking about a man and a woman involved in illicit sexual relations (*fāḥisha*).

The stated penalty in verse 16 is to hurt them, which exegetes say is confined to verbal hurt. Al-Rāzī states: 'There is agreement that there must be verbal hurt. As to hurting by beating, some argued that it might include beating although the first opinion was preferable.'[15] Verse 15, however, does not include even verbal hurt; it refers merely to a mechanism to stop such women going out to seek illicit relations. The penalty for actual illicit sexual relations is stated in verse 16.

One further argument against the homosexuality theory relates to the surrounding context of the verses. These two verses come immediately after a passage on inheritance, and following on from verses 15–18 the discussion is mainly on marriage and which women are lawful for marriage. To establish inheritance it is necessary to establish legitimacy of children and marriage. Neither of these in the Qur'an result from homosexual relations. It is far-fetched to think that within Sura 4, which is about rights, inheritance and marriage, after inheritance the subject of homosexuality should intrude. The natural assumption is rather that the two verses in question are about *zinā* (adultery or fornication).

Before verses 15 and 16 were revealed, there was no penalty mentioned in the Qur'an for illicit sexual intercourse and, one may say, the penalty revealed in these verses is a very light one. Even so, the Qur'an still opens the way to repentance: '*if they repent and mend their ways, leave them alone – God is always ready to accept repentance: God is full of mercy.*' Yet, there are also limitations:

> *But God only undertakes to accept repentance from those who do evil out of ignorance and soon afterwards repent: these are the ones God will forgive: He has the knowledge to decide. It is not true repentance when people continue to do evil until death confronts them and then say, 'Now I repent,' nor when they die defiant.*
>
> Q. 4:17–18

During the Medinan period, the only other reference in the Qur'an to a penalty for adultery[16] seems to refer to the law of the Torah, which was clearly still available to the Jews at that time. A Jewish couple of high standing were accused of adultery, so some rabbis suggested they go to the Prophet Muhammad and ask him for a ruling. '*If he gives you a lenient option,' they said, 'take it, if not, be careful*' (Q. 5:41). When they came to the Prophet, he said, 'But you have it in the Torah'. They denied it was there, so the Prophet asked a young Jewish scholar, whom the Jews accepted as an arbiter, to confirm whether or not it was in the Torah. He replied, 'Now that you ask me by God in this way, I confirm that the penalty is there.' At this, some Jews leapt out to attack him, so he responded, saying, 'I was afraid that if I lied, God would bring down punishment upon us.' At this,

Al-Rāzī quotes a report that the Prophet ordered the stoning penalty to be administered.'[17]

As regards the penalty for *zinā* for Muslims, an important event took place in the fifth or some say sixth year of the *hijra*. On the way back to Medina after a campaign, as the camp was about to depart, the Prophet's wife 'Ā'isha discovered that she had lost her necklace while away from the people to answer a call of nature. She went back to search for it and was unknowingly left behind by the caravan. A tardy Muslim saw her and escorted her back to Medina. A few individual Muslims then began to spread rumours about this. For a month the Prophet waited for a revelation until eventually he received the early part of Sura 24, entitled *al-Nūr* (Light). Unlike other suras this one starts in a very decisive, direct manner:

This is a sura we have sent down and made obligatory: We have sent down clear revelations in it so that you may take heed. Strike [ijlidū] the adulteress and the adulterer one hundred times. Do not let compassion for them keep you from carrying out God's law – if you believe in God and the Last Day – and ensure that a group of believers witnesses the punishment. The adulterer is only fit to marry an adulteress or an idolatress, and the adulteress is only [fit] to marry an adulterer or an idolater: such behaviour is forbidden to believers.

Q. 24:1–3

This ruling for the adulterer and the adulteress gives the ultimate (*ḥadd*) penalty in the Qur'an and has remained permanently without any abrogation, alteration or addition. Clearly any penalty mentioned in Q. 4:16 was a preliminary measure later superseded by Q. 24:1–3 which give the final, ultimate penalty; however, it is reported that 'Umar, the second caliph, said:

There was a verse in the Qur'an which was removed (during the time of the Prophet) and if I had not been afraid that people would say that 'Umar had added to the Qur'an, I would put it back. 'If an old man and an old woman (*shaykh* and *shaykha*) commit adultery, stone them definitely (*al-battata*), a deterrent from God: God has the power to decide.'

Hadith according to Mālik[18]

Those who uphold the stoning penalty argue that this verse was removed verbally but the ruling was retained; however, the concept of abrogating words and retaining the ruling is extraordinarily strange. In any case, even if it is true that this was part of the Qur'an and was removed, the removal confirms that stoning is not part of the Qur'an in its final, revealed form.

There is a further issue involved. The above report gives the stoning penalty only for the 'old', leaving the youth and the middle-aged, who are far more likely to fall into adultery, without any penalty. We can therefore confirm that stoning was never mentioned in the Qur'an except, as reported by one single narrator, for those who are old and even this, according to the report itself, was permanently removed.

Those who uphold the stoning penalty, in the face of Q. 24:2 above, argue, without any basis from the Qur'an, that the adulterer and adulteress in the verse mean only virgins who have never been married before. They are driven to this restriction because they say that, although stoning is not in the Qur'an, it was part of the Sunna (custom) of the Prophet. Therefore, they argue, the verse must be construed to apply only to virgins. The strongest argument against this, which jurists and exegetes do not seem to have considered, is the context in which Q. 24:2 was sent down. The whole passage was revealed as a result of an accusation made against a married woman, the Prophet's wife. The context of the text before and after the verse is very decisive and categorical about the rulings. Verses 5 and 6 talk about accusing chaste women, married or unmarried, giving the same penalty of 80 lashes for accusing a chaste woman, married or unmarried. It appears strange to argue that only verse 2 should apply to virgins and not married people.

On the other hand, it is reported that the Prophet did order the stoning of at least three individuals, a man called Māʿiz, a woman called al-Ghāmidiyya and a wife who committed adultery with her husband's employee (*ʿasīf*). The Prophet ruled that the employee, being unmarried, would have 100 lashes and the wife, if she admitted to adultery, would be stoned.[19] These are the three cases regularly quoted by those who uphold stoning for married people. In all these cases the Prophet did not summon the offender, rather they came of their own accord. The Prophet also tried repeatedly to put them off their confessions and sent them away without pursuing them. They insisted on coming back and requesting the application of penalties in order to purify themselves.

Then there is another crucial issue: when did these three events of stoning take place? Was it before the revelation on adultery quoted above (Q. 24:1–2) or after? If they happened before, there is no problem because the verse could be argued to have ended the rule of stoning. One of the Companions of the Prophet was actually asked whether the stoning took place before or after the verse and he said he did not know.[20] So the doubt as regards timing clearly was there from the beginning and no one seems to have categorically established the dates of these events.

M. S. El-Awa[21] argues it can be deduced that the stonings happened after the revelation of Q. 24:2, commanding lashing, because among the narrators there is Abū Hurayra who came to Medina no earlier than the seventh year of the *hijra* and Ibn 'Abbās who was brought when young to Medina with his mother in the ninth year. The reference to Ibn 'Abbās is not a strong argument. Having been brought to Medina with his mother only one year before the death of the Prophet, according to this report, he is more likely to have heard it from others. Likewise, Abū Hurayra could also have heard it from others, and a decisive, crucial issue like death by stoning needs to be established by stronger, more decisive evidence. El-Awa is perhaps the strongest exponent among modern scholars of the continuation of the stoning penalty, but he does not specify whether Abū Hurayra or Ibn 'Abbās had actually witnessed a stoning event themselves or simply heard about it from others.

Even in the cases of Māʿiz and al-Ghāmidiyya, the Prophet tried hard to dissuade them from confession and sent them away two or three times. Māʿiz insisted on confessing and indeed requested the Prophet to apply the penalty, despite the Prophet's suggestions that perhaps he committed lesser acts (he is reported to have said: 'Perhaps you just kissed her, or put your thighs on hers?'). Māʿiz insisted and wanted to be purified, so the Prophet ordered him to be stoned. While being stoned he cried, 'Take me back to the Prophet', but those in charge of the stoning refused and carried on until he died. When the Prophet heard that he had asked to be brought back to him, he reprimanded them, 'You should have brought him back to me'.[22]

In another example, a pregnant woman is reported to have confessed to adultery and the Prophet told her to go away until she gave birth. When she came back he said, 'Go away until you have suckled him.' So she came back after weaning him and said, 'Here, I have weaned him and he now eats food.'[23]

The tendency of the Prophet to avoid the application of penalties can also be seen from other similar examples. In one report, a man came to the Prophet after praying behind him in the mosque and said, 'I have committed a deed and you should apply the *ḥadd* on me.' The Prophet said to him, 'Have you not just prayed with us?' He said, 'Yes', and the Prophet sent him away saying, 'God has forgiven you your sin.'[24]

We also find Huzzal went to the Prophet and gave testimony that Māʿiz had committed adultery. The Prophet said to him, 'You should have covered him, even with your own garment.'[25]

The Prophet is also reported to have said:

> If any of you commits any dirty actions (*qādhūrāt*) he should cover himself with the covering God has given him, because if anyone comes to us we would have no choice but to apply the law to him.[26]

It is clear that the Prophet's practice was to avoid applying the *ḥadd* penalty. He tried to put off confessions and if the guilt was to be established by testimony he insisted on having four trustworthy Muslim men to testify that they had seen the actual act, 'like the stick in a kohl pot' (*al-mirwad fī'l-mukḥula*), something most unlikely to happen. If less than four come and accuse a person, they themselves become liable to the penalty of 80 lashes for slander, as will be seen below. Both the Qur'an and the Prophet's practice show that the penalty is clearly intended to deter, rather than to be put eagerly into action.

To go back to Q. 24:2, commanding 'strike (*ijlidū*) each of them 100 times', it is not meant as full lashing of the offender's skin as is commonly understood. From the time of the Prophet there are reports of striking with the hand or with a garment. There is also one case when a leper was reported to the Prophet for having committed adultery with a slave girl. The Prophet instructed, 'Take one bunch of a hundred stripped date stalks [that is, sometimes used as a broom] and strike him once with it.'[27] Even after the time of the Prophet, when the *sharī'a* became legalised by later jurists, they agreed that the one administering the strokes should not raise his arm so his armpit becomes seen, in an endeavour to make it less painful, and the offender's clothes must not be stripped from him before the beating.[28]

To return to Q. 4:15, speaking about confining women who committed an act of lewdness to their homes, some assume there is a connection between this verse and Q. 24:2, commanding lashing. There is a Hadith narrated by 'Ubāda b. al-Ṣāmit that the Prophet said in connection with Q. 4:15:

> Take it from me, take it from me, God has made a way out for them: virgins fornicating with virgins should have 100 lashes and banishment for a year, and non-virgins 100 lashes and stoning.[29]

Jurists and exegetes keep quoting this Hadith when in fact there is a serious problem with it. To say 'God has made a way out for them' is the expression used in the Qur'an for making something easier. In Q. 65:2–4, '*God will find a way out [of difficulty] for those who are mindful of Him and will provide for them from an unexpected source'*. This is a well-established meaning for the expression, but 100 lashes on their own or combined with stoning and banishment cannot possibly be said to be an easier way out. Besides, 'Ubāda's Hadith does not provide any penalty for a virgin and non-virgin fornicating together, nor does it apply to verse Q. 4:16 where the penalty is merely '*hurt them*', 'by words only'. The better understanding is, as some exegetes[30] suggested, that the 'way out' could be getting married. 'Ubāda's Hadith, narrated only by him, is thus used to increase the penalty hugely even though it contradicts the meaning of the Qur'anic words as established by usage in the Arabic language. It is strange that while Q. 4:14 directs keeping women at home to protect them within the family, this Hadith gives the punishment of banishing them to a far off land *taghrīb*. Al-Rāzī states that this Hadith was abrogated by the second verse of *Sūrat al-Nūr*, adding weakness to its application.[31]

It is interesting to note here that stoning for adultery was strongly denied by the Khawārij, a splinter group that emerged in the early days of Islam, on the following grounds:

1. It cannot be halved to cater for slave women whose penalty is always half that of free women.
2. The Qur'an gives less detail about the rulings for disbelief, murder and theft than it does about *zinā*: God forbade *zinā* and threatened people with Hell for it, then stated lashing, done in the presence of other Muslims, and said that compassion should not restrain anyone from applying the punishment. In addition, the Qur'an made the penalty of slander 80 lashes, which it did not do for slandering someone in respect of murder or disbelief, acts more heinous than *zinā*, and stated that one should never accept the slanderer's testimony, ever afterwards. It also introduced the penalty for slandering between husband and wife, and stated that an adulteress is only fit for marriage to an adulterer or an idolater.[32] Moreover, the Qur'an demanded that guilt be established by four witnesses. With all this detail regarding *zinā*, it would not be at all fitting for the Qur'an to neglect the most important rule, which has the most profound consequences: stoning to death.[33]
3. Q. 24:2 demands that all adulterers should be lashed. To restrict the verse and impose stoning on some on the basis of a Hadith of one man alone means specifying and restricting what is general in the Qur'an on the basis of a report by one individual. Such a report cannot be decisive as a text against the established text of the Qur'an.

Whatever reply others may have produced, these arguments by the Khawārij still have undeniable force, particularly the second and third, and no strong rebuttal seems to have been offered.

Arguments such as those by the Khawārij listed above and the fact that the timing of the stoning events, whether before or after the lashing penalty, has not been convincingly established, have led some modern scholars to re-open this subject and conclude that stoning, though it may have been part of the Islamic penal system early in Medina, was not in fact a permanent part of the penal code. El-Awa mentions a number of such modern scholars, including Muhammad Azza Darwaza, 'Ali al-Khafīf, Muhammad Abū Zahra, according to some reports, and finally Councillor 'Ali Mansur, a high court judge who participated in laying down Libyan law on the penalty for adultery (1973), which resulted in a single unified penalty of 100 lashes for virgin and non-virgin offenders alike.[34]

Zinā can be established by the four stated witnesses, by admission on the part of the culprit or by pregnancy if the woman is unmarried; however, if she claims that she has been coerced or that she was fast asleep, or that she is married to the man, the *ḥadd* penalty should not be applied.[35] It should be pointed out here that Islamic marriage (*nikāḥ*), which makes the relationship between the couple permissible, does not have to be registered with any authority. It is sufficient that the two persons agree to get married in front of two witnesses, and a bride gift is agreed between them. In the past, as girls were often married below the age of consent, the guardian (*walī*) was considered essential to the validity of the marriage. A woman who has been married before does not need a *walī*.

Since this book is about the Qur'an, it must be concluded that the only ultimate penalty for unlawful sexual intercourse, if well-established according to the stringent rules stated in the Qur'an, is 100 lashes, with lashes being interpreted as defined above. Yet, as we have seen, Islamic *sharī'a*, as found in the text of the Qur'an, tries by various strategies to avoid implementation of the ultimate penalties.

Qadhf: *slander*

As for those who accuse chaste women of adultery, and then fail to provide four witnesses, strike them eighty times, and reject their testimony ever afterwards: they are the lawbreakers, except for those who repent later and make amends – God is most forgiving and merciful.

Q. 24:4–5

The Qur'an strongly warns, in Q. 24:19, '*Those who love indecent slander to spread among the believers will have painful punishment in this world and the next. God knows and you do not.*'

We have seen that the Prophet said to someone who came to inform on a man committing adultery, 'Could you not have covered him, even with your own garment?' Slandering someone, in addition to defaming their name in society, could contribute to them receiving the strict penalty for adultery. In light of this, the Qur'an specifies for slanderers the penalty of 80 lashes, in addition to which they are to be disqualified from giving any testimony ever afterwards unless they repent and make amends. As always, the Qur'an opens the way for people to be corrected. If they repent and mend their ways, then God is most forgiving and merciful, and the penalty of disqualifying their testimony comes to an end. The fact that repentance does not stop the application of 80 lashes shows the seriousness of the offence. The culprit cannot avoid the consequences of inflicting harm on a victim by merely resorting to repentance. It is clear that the Qur'an restrains individuals from slandering others by requiring them to produce four reliable witnesses who have seen the act of sexual intercourse taking place, something not possible to achieve under normal circumstances. If they cannot, they themselves will be penalised.

The only *ḥudūd,* then, mentioned in the Qur'an are four: *ḥirāba,* (highway robbery), *sariqa* (theft), *zinā* (fornication or adultery) and *qadhf* (slander). Based on the discussion above, the Qur'an appears to mention the *ḥudūd* penalties in very limited circumstances and mainly as a deterrent. Indeed, it actually tends to avoid the application of these ultimate penalties by such means as setting strict conditions for the establishment of guilt, providing alternatives, opening the way to repentance, using terms that are open to various interpretations, gradual introduction of legal directives and not stating the stoning penalty in the Qur'an.

We have also seen that the Prophet himself tried to avoid application of these penalties. In addition to this, there is a rule for judges: 'avert application of the *ḥudūd* from Muslims as much as you can. If there is any way out for the culprit, let him off, because it is better that the leader errs in pardoning than in applying the penalty.'[36] All crimes other than the *ḥudūd* come under the category of *taʿzīr,* where a suitable punishment, other than *ḥadd,* can be applied. This is left to the legislators and the judges to decide on as they see fit. As already mentioned, this means that a huge area of the penal system is actually left open to be decided according to circumstances, times, places and so on. If the *ḥudūd* penalties are not deemed applicable, the authority can still use *ta'zīr* penalties if found suitable,[37] so that criminals are still deterred.

It is clear from the Qur'an that the *ḥudūd* verses were revealed only in Medina and were addressed to the Prophet as head of the Muslim state and the Muslim community of believers. Most commentators and jurists agree that the application of the penalties should be carried out only by the authorities and only in a Muslim state, and that no individual has the right to take the *ḥudūd* punishment into their own hands at their discretion.

Ḥudūd Penalties not Established by the Qur'an

I will deal here with two controversial issues, apostasy and consumption of intoxicants, both mentioned in the Qur'an, which have been much highlighted as part of the 'barbaric' *sharī'a* system, in particular in the case of apostasy.

Ridda: *apostasy*

The Qur'an does not specify any penalty in this world for apostasy from Islam; however, it states:

They will not stop fighting you [believers] until they make you revoke your faith, if they can. If any of you revoke your faith and die as disbelievers, your deeds will come to nothing in this world and the Hereafter, and you will be inhabitants of the Fire, there to remain.

Q. 2:217

You who believe, if any of you go back on your faith, God will soon replace you with people He loves and who love Him.

Q. 5:54

Those who return to unbelief after God's guidance has been revealed to them, are seduced by Satan and inspired by him.

Q. 47:25

Some of the People of the Book said [to each other], 'At the beginning of the day, believe in what has been revealed to these believers [the Muslims], then at the end of the day, reject it so that they too may turn back'

Q. 3:72

In the Hadith, however, there are certain statements on which jurists have based the penalty of death for apostasy from Islam. Among them we find: 'The Prophet said, addressing his companions, "Whoever exchanges his religion [for another] (*man baddala dīnahu*), kill him".'[38]

This Hadith and other similar ones should be seen in the context of Q. 3:72 above. In the context of the time, such a person would clearly be joining an enemy camp; another Hadith talks about the apostate as 'leaving his religion (*al-tāriku li-dīnihi*) and breaking away from the community (*al-mufāriqu li'l-jamā'a*)'. This indicates that the issue is not just leaving the religion in the sense of losing faith, but also breaking away from the community.[39] In the context of the Muslim community in Medina at the time, breaking away meant siding with the enemy camp. In modern times, breaking away from one's camp and joining the enemy camp is likewise treated as high treason and punished by death in many laws, even if nowadays the two camps are often no longer divided on religious, but rather on national or other grounds. This then explains why the Hadith mentions 'religion' alongside 'community'; what defined the two camps struggling with each other was primarily their religious identity. One problem is that many jurists do not seem to pay sufficient regard to the contexts of such Hadiths. Some statements have been taken in isolation from their contexts and this has at times caused serious misunderstandings of many Hadiths. Neither do jurists seem to have discussed how the penalty they insist on for apostasy fits with the Qur'an's categorical statement that '*There is no compulsion in religion*' (Q. 2:256). This comes towards the end of a Medinan sura revealed late in the life of the Prophet and seems therefore unlikely to have been abrogated.

What supports my explanation about the Hadiths quoted above is stated decisively in the following passage in Q. 4:88–91, especially verses 90 and 91, about a group of hypocrites who declared themselves to be Muslims[40] and then reverted and joined the polytheists. This action made some think they were Muslims and others that they were non-Muslims. The verses show that they did in fact become non-Muslims. Yet, even so, and more importantly, the Muslims are instructed *not* to fight them if they do not attack Muslims and instead show them peace. The Muslims have no way against them, except when they attack Muslims. There is no question of any penalty for apostasy alone being applied to them, and the only instance where fighting them is permitted for Muslims is when these people fight them. Sura 4 is late Medinan and it cannot be claimed that this was only in the early times of Islam. The whole passage is quoted to let the Qur'an itself show the rules:

[Believers], why are you divided in two about the hypocrites, when God Himself has rejected them because of what they have done? Do you want to guide those God has left to stray? If God leaves anyone to stray, you [Prophet] will never find the way for him. They would dearly like you to reject faith, as they themselves have done, to be like them. So do not take them as allies until they migrate [to Medina] for God's cause. If they turn [on you], then seize and kill them wherever you encounter them. Take none of them as an ally or supporter. But as for those who seek refuge with people with whom you have a treaty, or who come over to you because their hearts forbid them to fight against you or against their own people, God could have given them power over you, and they would have fought you. So if they withdraw and do not fight you, and offer you peace, then God gives you no way against them. You will find others who wish to be safe from you, and from their own people, but whenever they are back in a situation where they are tempted [to fight you], they succumb to it. So if they neither withdraw, nor offer you peace, nor restrain themselves from fighting you, seize and kill them wherever you encounter them: We give you clear authority against such people.

Sukr: *consumption of alcohol and intoxicants*

The Qur'an does not mention any worldly penalty for this. It introduces prohibition of intoxicating substances (*khamr*) gradually, through the following four stages:

We give you a drink [...] From the fruits of date palms and grapes you take sweet juice [intoxicants (sakaran)] as well as wholesome provisions.

Q. 16:66–7

The mere contrast here with 'wholesome provisions' hints at disapproval. Then we find:

You who believe, do not come anywhere near the prayer if you are intoxicated.

Q. 4:43

Since the prayers are performed five times a day this had the effect of curbing drinking. Then:

They ask you [Prophet] about intoxicants and gambling: say, 'There is great sin in both, and some benefit for people: the sin is greater than the benefit.'

Q. 2:219

Finally:

Intoxicants (khamr) and gambling, idolatrous practices, and [divining with] arrows are repugnant acts – Satan's doing: shun them so that you may prosper. With intoxicants and gambling, Satan seeks only to incite enmity and hatred among you, and to stop you remembering God and prayer. Will you not give them up?

Q. 5:90–1

Only the first of these passages comes from the Meccan Qur'an; the other three come from the Medinan Qur'an and none of the four mentions any penalty. Ranking intoxication along with the other stated acts and their consequences shows very strong disapproval.

In the Hadith, however, penalties of 40 or later 80 lashes are reported when people reverted to drinking heavily. The caliph 'Umar varied the penalty according to circumstances. Sometimes he banished the offender or shaved his head.[41] This suggests it can be left to the legal authorities to decide. In any case, the present book is about the Qur'an and although the Qur'an expresses disapproval of consuming intoxicants many times, as seen above, it does not mention any penalty for it in this world.

The present chapter has investigated some of the legal verses in the Qur'an. It has been seen that the Qur'an exhibits a clear intention of avoiding the application of the ultimate penalties. Penalties are definitely mentioned, but so are ways of avoiding them, as has been explained.

It is clear in the Qur'an that all the *ḥudūd* verses were addressed to the Muslims with the Prophet as the head of the Muslim state, not to anyone outside it; for example, jurists themselves put as a condition for applying the penalty of *zinā* that it should have taken place in a Muslim land (*Dār al-Islām*).[42] The application of the *ḥudūd* punishments is the prerogative of Muslim state machinery, not of any individual. In this respect, any recent talk of applying the *sharī'a* in Britain, meaning these *ḥudūd*, as hyped by some parts of the media or imagined by some Muslim extremists, has no basis whatsoever in the Qur'an.

Having emphasised that the Qur'an clearly tends to avoid application of the ultimate penalties (*ḥudūd*), it may be suitable, at the end of this chapter, to deal briefly with a similar situation from beyond the penal code. The Qur'an's declaration in Q. 4:34, addressing husbands with regard to their wives from whom they fear *nushūz*, '*and hit them*' is much talked about as one harsh teaching of the *sharī'a*. In reality, however, the same tendency to avoid, by various means, the application of a strict rule can also be seen in this case.

In Sura 4 (entitled *Women*), verses 34, 35 and 148 refer to *nushūz*. It is Q. 4:34–5 that is much talked about. From the beginning, Sura 4 concerns the financial rights of women, children, orphans and then heirs (verses 1–13 and 20–1). It talks again about financial rights in verses 29–34, establishing the rights of wives to be supported by their husbands in verse 34: '*Husbands should take good care of their wives with [the bounties] that God has given some more than others and out of what they spend of their own money.*'[43] Verse 34 goes on to state that good wives, first of all, guard their chastity in the absence of their husbands, because God Himself commands it to be guarded. Husbands are not given any authoritative role over good wives. In contrast to these women, there are the wives in *nushūz*. What exactly constitutes *nushūz* should be understood first in the light of this obvious contrast with the behaviour of good wives and, second, in the light of what the Prophet said in his final address to believers before he died.[44] It is on these two grounds that I am defining what *nushūz* means in Q. 4:34. Both relate to chastity. When an offence takes place, we see again how the Qur'an tries to avoid punishment.

There are three stages of dealing with the situation. Even though the Qur'an presents these in the imperative form, the majority of commentators have rightly noted that, in accordance with the rules of the Arabic language, they should be understood as permissions.[45] The first stage is to 'remind' the wife, that is, of God and His teachings. The second is to ignore her in bed. Then, if this does not work, 'hitting' is allowed as a last resort, but the Qur'an then seeks to avoid it again by immediately placing the condition, '*if they obey you then you have no right to act against them*' with the reminder for the husband, '*God is high and great*', that is, above them and the intentions they might have. Obedience here must be understood to mean ceasing the offensive behaviour. Then there is further avoidance of trouble by addressing the couple's relatives and society around them, '*If you fear that the couple may break up, appoint two arbiters, one from his family and one from hers, to try to put things right between them*' (Q. 4:35). This can happen before or after the three stages mentioned. Following all this, in verse 36 comes the order to all believers to worship God, be good to parents and a long list of other relatives, orphans, poor people and near and distant neighbours. It is just inconceivable to think that it is intended that husbands should be good to all these people, but are at the same time encouraged to beat their wives.

Worship God; join nothing with Him. Be good to your parents, to relatives, to orphans, to the needy, to neighbours near and far, to travellers in need, and to your slaves.

Q. 4:36

The Prophet Muhammad was the most obedient Muslim to God and the Qur'anic teachings. The Qur'an shows that at times he experienced difficulties with his wives, mentioning at least three occasions (Q. 33:28–35, Q. 66:2–5 and Q. 24:11–23). In none of these cases or at any other time in his life did he hit any of his wives. Muslims read these verses and learn from the Prophet whom the Qur'an describes as a '*good example*' (Q. 33:21) for the believers. He strongly condemned those who beat their wives: 'How does anyone of you beat his wife as he beats the stallion camel and then he embraces [that is, sleeps with] her?'[46] In all these cases, all he did was talk to the wives in question.

In Q. 4:128 when the *nushūz* is on the part of the husband rather than the wife, it is combined with *i'rādan* (rejection):

If a wife fears nushūz or i'rādan from her husband, neither of them will be blamed if they come to a peaceful settlement, for peace is best.

This again is dealt with by the couple making a peaceful settlement between them, this being recommended as the best way. They are reminded that if they do good, they will be rewarded by God. If it is not possible to bring reconciliation between them, it is advised that they leave each other amicably, with the promise that God will give each of them something better (verses 129–30). Again, this avoids difficulties and turning the marriage into the opposite of what God intended it to be: '*repose, affection and mercy between the two*' (Q. 30:21). It is obvious that in the case of *nushūz* either by the wife or the husband, the Qur'an recommends amicable settlement between the couple.[47]

As we have seen throughout this chapter, any penalties or punishments stated are actually meant to deter, rather than to be applied.

6

Euphemistic Style: Sexual Etiquette

Your women are a tilth for you[1]

This statement in the Qur'an is sometimes thought to show disrespect for women. I have heard this from my own BA students who thought that it meant that women were just there for the husband to have pleasure with, on demand. A contrasting view was that medieval Christian polemicists said the Qur'an was obscene on the grounds that it even mentioned coitus in this verse[2]; no mention of degrading women there.

This study will illustrate some of the mechanisms by which the Qur'an has been misinterpreted and misrepresented with regard to women's status, and more generally. In the above verse, as elsewhere, such mechanisms include:

1. Wrenching a short statement out of its textual context.
2. Cutting a statement off from its social and cultural context.
3. Lack of regard for the style of the Qur'an in treating various subjects.

Discussing this issue will also be useful in explaining how Qur'anic discourse deals with intimate physical matters.

The starting point in our discussion will be to state the textual context of this verse where wives are compared to a 'tilth' (Q. 2:222–3):

They ask you, Prophet, about menstruation. Say, 'Menstruation is a painful condition, so keep away from women during it. Do not approach them until they are cleansed and when they are cleansed, you may approach them as God has directed you. God loves those who turn to Him and He loves those who keep themselves clean. Your wives are [like] your fields, so go into your fields whichever way you like and send forward [good deeds] for yourselves. Be mindful of God: remember that you will meet Him.' [Prophet,] give good news to the believers.

It may well be asked, 'Why should the Qur'an speak about menstruation?' The obvious answer here is that some men around the Prophet asked the question, as part of a series of six questions, starting from Q. 2:215, about spending money, about wine and gambling and so on, and then about the issue of menstruation. However, it was not about menstruation in itself, but whether they were permitted to have intercourse with their wives at such times. This is clear from the reply the Qur'an gives to the question and also from the way it posed the previous questions.[3] The Qur'an has to answer them especially in a basic area that has such effects on people's lives. Women menstruate for a large part of their lives, and men's desire for intercourse[4] is an important issue in their lives that needs to be addressed. Before instructing them, the Qur'an gives justification for the instructions; it gently directs men that menstruation is a painful condition (*adhā*), which has also been interpreted as 'a messy condition' or 'a pollution'.[5] Then comes the instruction for husbands therefore to keep away (*iʿtazilū*), a euphemism for avoiding intercourse at that time. 'Do not approach them (*lā taqrabūhunna*)' is lexically listed[6] as a euphemism in Arabic for 'having sexual intercourse with women'.[7] '*When they are cleansed you may approach them as God has directed you*' (Q. 2:222): this is another gentle hint to announce the following instruction that intercourse should be done in the way God has allowed. God has ordained for them to fulfil their sexual urge, but in a lawful way. Before it specifies this, it reminds the husband[8] that '*God loves those who come back to Him [after erring, that is] and who keep themselves clean*' (Q. 2:222). All this is introduced in the wake of the instruction that they should abstain from intercourse during menstruation.

Then we come to the crucial statement, '*Your women are [like] fields to you*' (Q. 2.223). The use of the image of fields in fact further reinforces the instruction to abstain during menstruation since it is not a time for sowing or casting seeds to grow. It also directs them away from practising anal intercourse on the same grounds. By its imagery the verse suggests that sodomy was practised by some, and certain Hadiths contained in al-Bukhārī's *Ṣaḥīḥ* make it clear that it was prohibited.[9] The single image of *ḥarth* ('field') has the double effect of forbidding two practices and, as we will see later, it is an example of the style of the Qur'an in gently touching on such intimate matters.

'*Come to your fields whichever way you like*' is an interesting instruction that alludes to cultural and social issues in the society in Medina. When the Meccan Muslims immigrated to Medina and intermarried there, they discovered the difference of cultural habits. The Meccans were used to being more open in their habits of sexual intercourse, coming from behind, opening them wide from the front.[10] The Medinan women were more shy and modest and raised objections. Discussion ensued as to what was appropriate in such matters. The Meccan men also learned that the Jewish community in Medina held that a child born from a woman approached from behind would have a squint, and that this was in the Torah.[11] The Prophet was asked about this and he said 'they lied'.[12] This is the context in which the Qur'an tells husbands that approaching one's wife is like going to one's field to sow it, from whichever direction or way they may desire (*annā shi'tum*), provided that the seed is sown where it can grow and provided nowhere else.

'*Send forward [good deeds] for yourselves*' in the Qur'an means that by obeying God's commands so far mentioned they would be storing up good rewards for their next life. It can also be interpreted as 'make preparation for yourselves beforehand', suggesting that husbands should be gentle with their wives and prepare them psychologically and physically.[13] This is in keeping with the Prophet's instructions in such matters. He said: 'Let a man not fall on his wife like a donkey. Let him send a messenger beforehand.' When he [the Prophet] was asked what sort of messenger, he said, 'A kiss, for instance.'[14] The Prophet reportedly forbade men to have intercourse with their wives without foreplay: 'When one of you has intercourse with his wife, he should truly love her, and if he finishes before her, he should not hurry her until she has gained her satisfaction.'[15]

Verse 223 continues, '*Be mindful of God. Know that you are going to meet Him. [Prophet] give good news to those who believe.*' This reinforces abstinence from disobedience as well as obedience to the teaching, including proper conduct towards one's wife in such an intimate situation. All this is part of the passage that begins with, '*Your wives are [like] a field for you*' (Q. 2:222). Those who wrench the statement from its context are not aware of how the Qur'an develops a whole web of instructions on cleanliness, proper conduct and treating one's wife decently, making all this part of being aware of God and respecting His teachings. It reminds Muslim husbands, even in this situation, that they will meet God and will have to account for their treatment of their wives, so they should place themselves in a position to receive good news in this life and the next. Sensationalists and

Islamophobes who object to the statement '*your wives are a tilth for you*' (Q. 2:222) show no awareness of this.

In plain terms, these two interconnected verses do no more than answer two questions raised by some Muslim men in Medina over 14 centuries ago:

1. whether they were permitted to have intercourse with their wives during menstruation, to which the answer is: they must not; and
2. whether they were permitted to practice sodomy with their wives, the answer being: they must not.

Contrary to claims that in Q. 2:222 the Qur'an speaks in a demeaning way about women, the answers the Qur'an gives in fact show respect to women, their female workings, their reproductive needs and functions. It shows that men should be considerate and not be governed merely by indiscriminate sexual urges.

The status of women in these verses should be derived from the entire answers the Qur'an gives to these two questions and not from wrenching a short statement out of its context and cut off from the extended teachings given in the two verses.

In contrast to the early allegations by detractors of Islam in medieval Europe who said that the Qur'an was obscene since it speaks of coitus,[16] the style of the Qur'an in dealing with such sensitive matters is euphemistic and relies mainly on imagery. The image presented here is that of a field where seeds are sown, of fertility and productivity. It touches a deep chord in the minds of men and women, whether they are aware of it or not. The rich image reminds men that their children are their own seeds, grown into a new life. Such linguistic devices are seen in other parts of the Qur'an as well. For instance, in relaxing the regulations to allow intercourse between spouses on the nights of the fast, the Qur'an intimates the need they have for each other using, in Q. 2:187, the image of garments (*libās*) to express the need for protection, covering and comfort which each spouse derives from the other: '*Your wives are a garment to you and you are a garment to them.*' Some exegetes[17] take the word *libās* to mean not 'garment' but to stand for an active participle, *mulābisāt,* meaning 'in close contact'. This fits the context, showing that husband and wife are close to each other and not 'out of sight, out of mind', so they are likely to wish to have relations during the night of the fast. Therefore God, in His grace, relented and allowed them to do this. It is significant that the Qur'an here reminds men that they need the comfort and protection of women before saying that women are in need of them, too.

The Qur'anic vocabulary is expressive: *i'tū* ('come' to them) and *taqrabū* (lit. 'come near' to them) in Q. 2:222 are both euphemisms for sexual intercourse. When it is preventing men from intercourse during menstruation the Qur'an uses *i'tazilū* (lit. 'keep away'); but the Hadith, as well as all exegetical works and Islamic legal texts, make clear that this does not mean that men have to isolate themselves from women, as was the habit in some cultures and as some Arab men understood until the Prophet corrected their misunderstanding.[18] The Qur'anic text only means 'refrain from full sexual intercourse'. Similarly, the Qur'an elsewhere employs a short, comprehensive and euphemistic expression for abstaining from illicit intercourse: *al-ḥāfiẓūna furūjahum* which means those who 'guard, protect, preserve or control their private parts'. This phrase is used frequently to describe how believers behave.[19] No one should come near them, that is, the private parts, illicitly, and both men and women should prevent illicit contact.[20] Individuals should be possessive and protective of such important parts; this is all implied in *ḥāfiẓūna*. The Qur'an also describes these parts as *'awra*,[21] denoting something that is vulnerable to being exposed and invaded and needs protection, again an expressive image to reinforce all the other images and terms used in this whole, delicate side of human life.

Another expressive term the Qur'an uses is *zīna*, the first meaning of which is 'ornaments' such as jewellery. After telling believing men to restrain their glances, the Qur'an uses *zīna* also to express the attractions of women's bodies that should not be flaunted. It also tells the believing women in Q. 24:31:

> *They should restrain their glances, guard their private parts and not display their attractions (zīna) beyond what is acceptable to reveal. They should let their scarves fall to cover their necklines and not reveal (yubdīna) their attractions except to their husbands, their fathers …*

The Qur'an recognises that these parts of women's bodies are attractive and make women desirable. Such attractive and beautiful parts are special. They should not be exposed, except for '*what is acceptable*'.[22] The word *zīna*, being only one short word, provides an expressive metaphor for these parts.[23] The term *yubdīna* here refers to 'flaunting' and 'exposing', implying the deliberate intention of uncovering and showing. For covering the breast area, it uses the euphemism of making women's scarves cover their necklines (*juyūb*) or the neck-openings of their shirts. It is clear that the Qur'an uses imagery and not exact expressions of measurements. It makes a main point but does not go into details, which explains how some interpret these instructions with what can be seen as excessive restriction, while others are more liberal. In Muslim countries there are women who opt for total covering, including the *burqa*, whereas others do not consider leaving their heads uncovered to be in contradiction to being obedient to God. There are all shades of opinion.

This passage on covering (Q. 24:31) should be read in parallel with Q. 33:59: '*[Prophet] tell your wives, your daughters and women believers to make their outer garments hang low over them (yudnīna 'alayhinna), so they can be recognised and not molested.*' The Arabic words *yudnīna 'alayhinna* are an expression for lengthening the garments so that the legs are not exposed.[24] This is a recognised idiom although most English translators[25] take it to mean 'draw their garments close around them'. This latter interpretation would seem to involve making the garments tighter, which might expose the shape beneath. Jurists, however, say that women's garments should not be transparent or chosen deliberately to reveal the shape.[26] The interpretation of the meaning of Q. 33.59 suggested here is supported by the Qur'an at the end of Q. 24:31, which says that women should '*not swing their legs (lā yaḍribna bi-arjulihinna) when walking so that the attractions (zīnatihinna) they conceal become known*'. *Zīna* here is not just ornaments and *yadribna* does not just mean 'stamp their feet',[27] as some translators have offered. *Arjulihinna* in Arabic can mean 'their feet', but also 'their legs' (lexically, *rijl* can mean foot or leg, from the hip to the foot).[28]

In keeping with its euphemistic style, the Qur'an also uses the verbs *lāmasa* ('reciprocal touching') (Q. 5:6) and *bāshara* ('reciprocal skin-to-skin touching') (Q. 2:187) for sexual intercourse. The disapproving word *rafath* is used for sexual intercourse when it is forbidden, for instance during the hajj pilgrimage (Q. 2:197). *Fawāḥish* (sing. *fāḥisha,* lit. 'breaking the bounds', that is, gross indecency, foul deed or abomination), is used for an illicit sexual act in Q. 6.151: '*Do not kill your children, fearing poverty – we will provide for you and for them – stay well away from committing fawāḥish, whether openly or in secret, do not take life*'.[29]

So far it has been seen that, when it is lawful and desirable, sex is described in appealing terms, but when it is forbidden the words used imply strong disapproval. The Qur'an never uses basic, crude or even straightforward Arabic terms either for licit or illicit sex. It clearly avoids such language.

One important feature of the Qur'an in dealing with this subject is the use of persuasion and dissuasion. In trying to divert men from having intercourse during menstruation in Q. 2:222–3, it starts by saying that it is a painful or messy condition, but when women have been cleansed, husbands can come to them. The Qur'an stresses God loves those who come back to Him (having stopped doing something blameworthy) and those who seek cleanliness. In directing men to have intercourse in the appropriate place, women are compared to a field to evoke the image of sowing, plantation, harvest and plenty. The Qur'an reminds those who disobey, in a warning tone, in Q. 2:223: '*Be mindful of God, know that you are going to meet Him.*' It then says: '*Give good news to those who do good.*'

In relaxing the regulation for sexual conduct during the night of the fast, the Qur'an reminds men in Q. 2:187:

God was aware that you were betraying yourselves [by infringing the regulations], so He turned to you in mercy and pardoned you: so now you can lie with them – seek what God has ordained for you – eat and drink until the white thread of dawn becomes distinct from the black, then fast until nightfall.

In asking women to cover their legs, it gives them a reason for this, which is that they can be recognised[30] and not molested, and then it goes on to say that '*God is most forgiving, most merciful*' (Q. 33:59), forgiving any previous misbehaviour.

Contrary to the impression created by the distorting, sensationalist mechanism of wrenching a short statement from its context, as well as by misunderstanding its real intent resulting from the failure to grasp the Qur'anic style, enjoying intimate relations between husbands and wives is made appealing in the Qur'an and expressed in rich euphemisms. It is all presented as part of God's grace:

Seek what God has ordained for you.

Q. 2:187

One of His signs is that He created spouses from among yourselves, for you to live with them in tranquillity. He ordained love and kindness between you. There truly are signs in this for those who reflect.

Q. 30:21

7

Narrative Style: Repeating Stories – Noah

The Qur'an justifies its teachings using logical arguments, often based on God's creation and grace in nature and reference to past history, the future and what will happen on the Day of Judgement. The employment of the histories of prophets previous to Muhammad is a salient feature of the Qur'anic discourse. As al-Shāṭibī (d. 790/1388) rightly observed, in strengthening Muhammad in the face of various forms of denial and obstinacy from his opponents at different times, earlier prophets were cited and 'the particular form of the narrative varies according to the situation, while all of it is true, factual, with no doubt about its being correct.'[1] On this basis, this chapter surveys the various Qur'anic Noah accounts, which vary in length, form, content and tone, according to their contexts.

The view of Noah as being 'the first prophet of punishment' is stated categorically in the first and second editions of the *Encyclopaedia of Islam*,[2] and Richard Bell includes the Noah story under the heading 'Stories of Punishment' in his *Introduction to the Qur'an*, in which he says: 'In the Qur'an the people of Noah are frequently referred to as having been destroyed for unbelief.'[3] David Marshall, in describing the punishment story in his chapter on the subject in the recently published *Encyclopaedia of the Qur'ān*, remarks, 'It is to be noted that these stories depict a punishment inflicted by God in this world rather than in the afterlife', and states that 'their primary purpose was to warn of a punishment from God that would fall upon the Meccan unbelievers if they did not repent and accept Muhammad's message.'[4] He goes on to claim that such accounts are 'linked to form a chain of punishment stories suggesting that human history has been a sequence of such encounters between God, messengers and unbelievers'.[5] However, although the theme of divine punishment is, undeniably, an element that occurs in nearly all the Noah accounts in the Qur'an – almost all of which explicitly mention the flood – such a reductionist reading of Noah's Qur'anic persona misrepresents his presence in the text. A close reading of the Qur'anic accounts of the Noah story shows that the view put forward by Bell and Marshall on the Qur'anic approach to prophetic history is, in reality, divergent from that found in the actual text of the Qur'an.

Noah in the Qur'an

Noah is normally mentioned at the head of chronological lists of the prophets in the Qur'an,[6] and his story is related in ten accounts: Q. 7:59–64; Q. 10:71–3; Q. 11:25–49; Q. 21:76–7; Q. 23:23–30; Q. 26:105–21; Q. 29:14–15; Q. 37:75–82; Q. 54:9–16; and Q. 71:1–28, in addition to which there are also other brief references to the story. According to Theodor Nöldeke's chronology, Suras 54, 37, 71, 26, 23 and 21 (revealed in this order) are all from what he terms the first Meccan period, and Suras 11, 29, 10 and 7 (again in this order) date from the second Meccan period.[7] Quantitatively, these occurrences of the Noah accounts can be put in the order as shown in Table 1.

Table 1. Occurrences of the Noah story in the Qur'an

Sura Number	*Lines in Arabic*
21	2
29	2.5
37	3.5
54	4.5
10	6
7	7
26	9.5
23	11
71	22
11	38

The Noah accounts are described by the Qur'an itself (in Q. 11:47) as being *min anbā' al-ghayb* (*'some of the stories of the unseen'*).[8] As we will see, in the Qur'an the material presented in each account is selected solely to illustrate specific points, hence none of the passages offer a full version of Noah's life, nor even of his prophethood. Although the accounts vary in length (from 2 to 38 lines), tone and content, every single account begins with 'We sent Noah' and ends with God delivering him and his people and drowning others – stressing 'there is a sign in this' – but goes no further. We are not even told of Noah's death. This basic message is repeated throughout the long period of his prophetic mission to reiterate the most fundamental elements of the faith; that is, the unity of God, Judgement Day and prophethood.[9] This reflects the fact that the Qur'an does not present itself as a history book, but a book of guidance. If this is the objective of the Qur'an in telling stories of previous prophets, then it would miss the point to expect that any of the accounts should be a complete story. The suggestion that other versions should be seen in relation to that notional complete story and are in abridged forms, as well as the attempt to find and extract a 'complete story' on the part of scholars such as Wansbrough embodies an approach that is fundamentally unsound.[10]

Main Themes of the Qur'anic Noah Accounts

We will now address these Qur'anic passages according to Nöldeke's scheme, so as to examine the main themes of each in chronological context.

Q. 54:9–16

The part of Noah's story told in this first account begins right at the end of his mission. The initial verse, '*Before them, the people of Noah rejected the truth: they rejected Our servant, saying, "He is mad!" Noah was rebuked*' (Q. 54:9), reflects the context of the narrative given in verses 2 to 5 that the people of Mecca had rejected Muhammad, turned away from every sign and mocked his claim to prophecy. Verse 9 sums up in three phrases the similar way Noah was received by his people; they rejected him, called him mad and rebuked him. This rebuke is expanded in later accounts. Noah calls upon his Lord, saying, '*I am defeated: help me!*' (Q. 54:10), and there follows a powerful description of how the sky and earth produced great torrents of water. (This description is found only here and fitting to the tone of this sura, which recounts various stories in brief, admonitory style and finally addresses the Meccan disbelievers, challenging them that they are no better themselves than the disbelievers of the stories and warning them that they have no guarantee of immunity from punishment.) The punishment of drowning is not mentioned on this occasion, merely alluded to in verse 12: '*the waters met for a preordained purpose*'. The use of this wording, as well as the absence of the element of the water subsiding, which is already implicit in the very fact of its being preordained, points to the purpose of this account. What is highlighted is God's grace shown to Noah, carried on a mere vessel of planks and nails (there is no description of how it was built, this being irrelevant to the purpose of the story), floating '*under Our watchful eye, a reward for the one who had been rejected*' (Q. 54:14). The tool of God's grace, the Ark, is left '*as a sign*' (Q. 54:15). Only at the very end of this passage is the torment mentioned: '*How [painful] was My torment and [the fulfilment of] My warnings!*' (Q. 54:16).

Q. 37:75–82

The early parts of this sura describe how the Meccans rejected and ridiculed Muhammad (Q. 37:12–15) and, in the verses immediately prior to the Noah account, God reminds His Prophet that most people before the disbelievers of his time also went astray (Q. 37:71), then says, '*See how those before them met their end, not so the true servants of God*' (Q. 37:73–4). Here again the account begins at the end of Noah's mission, with him calling to his Lord for help, as in Q. 54.10 (above) and Q. 21:76 (below), and depicts the nature of God's response: '*Noah cried to Us, and how excellent was Our response! We saved him and his people from great distress, We let his offspring remain on the earth, We let him be praised by later generations: "Peace be upon Noah among all the nations!"*' (Q. 37:75–9). '*This,*' we are then told in verse 80, '*is how We reward those who do good*', not just Noah, who was '*truly one of Our faithful servants*' (Q. 37:81).[11] In the previous account, as we have seen, the nature of the punishment is not even explicitly mentioned. Here, the punishment which awaits those who do not do good gets only four words: '*We drowned the rest*' (Q. 37:82). We shall see that, as here, in the other Noah accounts the description of the punishment is mentioned only briefly, by use of this same phrase, 'they drowned', in comparison with long descriptions of how God was gracious to Noah. Noah and all the other prophets mentioned later in the sura are said to be the true servants of God, who are assured of help (Q. 37:171–3). The sura ends with '*Peace be upon the messengers*', a phrase which gives a touch of graciousness to the messengers and which is used as a refrain after each story, and finally with '*Praise be to the Lord of all the Worlds*' (Q. 37:181–2).

Q. 71:1–28

This account of Noah is unique in that it occupies the entire sura (thus its name *Sūrat Nūḥ*, Nūḥ being the Arabic version of Noah) and mentions no other prophet. Much of it consists of material that is not mentioned in the other Qur'anic accounts of Noah (e.g. verses 4–28), with the exception of one element, *ughriqū* ('*they were drowned*', Q. 71:25). As with the accounts in suras 7, 11, 23 and 29 it begins with God commissioning Noah as His Messenger: '*We sent* (*arsalnā*) *Noah to his people: "Warn your people, before a painful punishment comes to them."*' (Q. 71:1). The Qur'an gives no information on Noah before this point in his life, but it refers to the early stages of Noah's mission and the way he calls upon his people, day and night, openly and in private, but they maintain their rejection of him:

He said, 'My Lord, I have called my people night and day, but the more I call them, the further they run away: every time I call them, so that You may forgive them, they thrust their fingers into their ears, wrap themselves in their garments, persist in their rejection and grow more insolent and arrogant. I have tried calling them openly. I have tried preaching to them in public and speaking to them in private.'

Q. 71:5–9

Noah tries various means of persuasion, by promising that God will give them, in addition to forgiveness, other rewards, chiding them for having no fear of the majesty of God even though He created them, and pointing out to them signs in nature proving God's providence and lordship:

Ask forgiveness of your Lord: He is ever forgiving. He will send down abundant rain from the sky for you; He will give you wealth and sons; He will provide you with gardens and rivers. What is the matter with you? Why will you not fear God's majesty, when He has created you stage by stage? Have you ever wondered how God created seven heavens, one above the other, placed the moon as a light in them and the sun as a lamp, how God made you spring forth from the earth like a plant, how He will return you into it and then bring you out again, and how He has spread the Earth out for you to walk along its spacious paths?

Q. 71:10–20

But they put their fingers in their ears and persist in their arrogance. Eventually he calls upon God in frustration, saying:

My Lord, they have disobeyed me and followed those whose riches and children only increase their losses; they have hatched a mighty plot, saying to each other, 'Do not renounce your gods! Do not renounce Wadd, Suwāʿ, Yaghūth, Yaʿūq or Nasr!' They have led many astray. Lord, bring nothing but destruction down on the evildoers.

Q. 71:21–4

So, for these sins the disbelievers are drowned and will face the final punishment in Hell (Q. 71:25). Noah is harsher at the end of this sura than anywhere else, first asking God, '*Lord, do not leave any of the disbelievers on the earth*' (Q. 71:26) because they will only beget disbelievers and lead others astray, then '*Forgive believing men and women but bring nothing but ruin down on the evildoers!*' (Q. 71:28).

What is interesting, in the light of Marshall's assertion that the punishment in the Noah story is one of this life only, on this occasion, at the beginning of the sura, Noah is asked to warn his people before '*a painful punishment* (*ʿadhāb alīm*)' comes to them.[12] Likewise, in the accounts in Suras 7, 11 and 23, he also warns of '*an awesome day* (*yawm alīm*)'. That this refers to the punishment of the Day of Judgement, not one of this world, is attested by other similar references throughout the Qur'an to *ʿadhāb alīm* or *ʿadhāb yawm al-ʿaẓīm*, which usually occur in the Qur'an in the context of the commissioning of prophets to warn of the Day of Judgement.[13] This reading of the '*painful punishment*' as referring to the Day of Judgement is also supported in Q. 11:36–7:

It was revealed to Noah, 'None of your people will believe, other than those who have already done so, so do not be distressed by what they do. Build the Ark under Our [watchful] eyes and with Our inspiration. Do not plead with Me for those who have done evil – they will be drowned.'

Here it is made clear that Noah only learns of a punishment in this world at the end of his long mission of effort, when he is told to build the Ark. At this point, Noah is shown as being unaware of what specific punishment his people would receive; he declares, '*I do not know the unseen*' (Q. 11:31) and in Q. 11:34 he says, '*My advice will be of no use to you if God wishes to leave you to your delusions: He is your Lord and to Him you will be returned.*' Thus, when Noah tells his people, '*Serve God, be mindful of Him and obey me. He will forgive you your sins and spare you until your appointed time – when God's appointed time arrives it cannot be postponed. If only you understood!*'

(Q. 71:3–4), he is referring to their being spared from eschatological punishment, rather than punishment in this world. This is confirmed by Q. 71:25, '*[The evildoers] were drowned and sent to Hell for their evildoings*', in which the Qur'an clearly announces that the punishment imposed on the disbelievers was both worldly (for their evildoings the disbelievers '*were drowned*') and eschatological ('*and sent to Hell*') as Noah warned them at the beginning of the sura.

Q. 26:105–22

This relatively short Noah account occurs in the context of a series of linked prophetic stories within the sura addressed to Muhammad in response to his distress at his lack of success in persuading people to believe. In verse 3, Muhammad is asked, '*Are you going to worry yourself to death because they will not believe?*' Then he is shown how the disbelievers before his time reacted to their prophets in a series of accounts which put forward the stories of the rejection of Moses (Q. 26:10–68), Abraham (Q. 26:69–104) and Noah (Q. 26:105–22), followed by the people of 'Ād's rejection of the messengers (Q. 26:123–40), that of the people of Thamūd (Q. 26:141–59), of Lot (Q. 26:160–75) and finally of the Companions of the Wood (Q. 26:176–91), following which are a number of verses of reassurance to Muhammad. This Noah account begins with the words '*The people of Noah, too, called the messengers liars*' (*kadhdhabat qawmu Nūḥin al-mursalīn*) (Q. 26:105).[14] Noah, here uniquely described as 'their brother', responds in a gentle and persuasive tone: '*Will you not be mindful of God? I am a faithful messenger sent to you: be mindful of God and obey me. I ask no reward of you, for my only reward is with the Lord of the worlds: be mindful of God and obey me*' (Q. 26:106–10). His opponents object, '*Why should we believe you when the worst sort of people follow you?*' (Q. 26:111)[15] and threaten him, '*Noah, if you do not stop this, you will be stoned*' (Q. 26:116), at which Noah immediately asks God to judge between them. God responds, using the plural of majesty, '*We saved him and the believers in the fully laden ship, and drowned the rest*' (Q. 26:119–20). The account ends by saying, '*There truly is a sign in this, though most of them do not believe: your Lord alone is the Almighty, the Merciful*' (Q. 26:121–2). Thus, although the judgement of the disbelievers and their punishment with the flood is mentioned, it is, again, mentioned only briefly and backgrounded; the main focus of the account reflects that of the Qur'an's message to Muhammad that he should not grieve, but remember that, with all his persuasive teachings, Noah was rejected too, but not abandoned by God.

Q. 23:23–30

With the exception of Sura 71, this account of Noah is longer and contains more details than any other account so far. It begins, again, with Noah calling on his people to worship God: '*We sent Noah to his people. He said, "My people, serve God, for He is your only god. Will you not heed Him?"*' (Q. 23:23). In their response, the disbelievers raise a number of objections (most of which are mentioned here for the first time): '*He is merely a mortal like you, trying to gain some superiority over you. God would have sent down angels if He had wished; besides, we never heard of anything like this from our forefathers. He is just a madman, so let's wait and see what happens to him*' (Q. 23:24–5).

This last statement is ominous. In response, Noah calls God to help him, at which God, in verse 27, inspires him to build the Ark '*under Our watchful eye and according to Our inspiration*' and instructs him to '*take pairs of every species on board, and your family*' and not to '*plead with Me for the evildoers: they will be drowned*' (Q. 23:27). The passage ends by recounting that, when Noah is settled in the Ark, he is taught, for the first and only time, how to thank God for saving him from the evil people ('*say, "Praise be to God, who delivered us from people who are unjust"*', Q. 23:28) and how to pray for a safe landing ('*say, "My Lord, let me land with Your blessing: it is You who provide the best landings"*', Q. 23:29). Note that, again, the punishment, although mentioned, takes a back seat, reduced to simply two words in Arabic, '*they will be drowned* (*innahum mughraqūn*)', in verse 27, while the account ends on the theme of God's mercy and generosity to Noah.

The placement of this passage within the sura as a whole would support a reading of this Noah account as primarily concerned with God's mercy to his prophets and the blessings He bestows on the believers. It comes, after verses enumerating manifestations of God's power and blessing, with the intention of persuading the disbelievers in Mecca, and is immediately preceded by Q. 23:21–2, '*There is a lesson for you in livestock: We produce milk for you to drink from their bellies. And they have many other benefits: you eat them and you ride on them, as you do in ships.*' By including the fact that livestock, like ships, carry people, these verses connect the lesson of livestock with that of the Ark in the following story of Noah, thereby implicitly presenting the account of the deliverance of Noah in the light of a blessing from God for which people should be grateful.[16]

Q. 21:76–7

This is the shortest of the Qur'anic Noah accounts and carries the bare minimum of the story:

Long before that, We answered Noah when he cried out to Us. We saved him and his people from the great distress and We helped him against the people who rejected Our signs: they were evil people, so We drowned them all.

As in Sura 37, the passage begins with Noah calling to God for help, and focuses on the generosity of God's response to his plea. Likewise, when a number of later prophets in the same sura, including Abraham, Job and Zachariah, call on God in their distress, He fulfils His promise to them, saving Abraham from the flames his people wanted to throw him into (Q. 21:69), removing Job's suffering and restoring his family to him (Q. 21:84) and curing Zachariah's wife of her barrenness (Q. 21:90). Rather than being a 'punishment story', this Noah account reflects the overarching focus of the sura; that is, God's aid of His prophets who call on Him in their distress, accounts of which are related in order to reassure the Prophet Muhammad and strengthen his heart against the accusations the disbelievers level at him in verses 3–5 and 112 of this sura.

Q. 11:25–49

This is the longest account in the Qur'an of the story of Noah and it is the first of a number of linked accounts relating stories of various prophets. The opening verses of the passage, Q. 11:25–6, set out what Noah is calling his people to: '*I have come to you to give a clear warning: worship no one but God. I fear for you that you may suffer on a painful Day* (*yawm alīm*).' This is followed by the reaction of the disbelievers (given at such length only here):

But the prominent disbelievers among his people said, 'We can see that you are nothing but a mortal like ourselves, and it is clear to see that only the vilest among us follow you. We cannot see how you are any better than we are. In fact, we think you are a liar.'

Q. 11:27

Verses 28–34 recount Noah's response to this rejection: if people are blind to his message, he cannot force them to believe; he is not asking for payment, nor is he going to drive away his followers; he does not claim to possess God's treasures, to know the unseen, or that he is an angel or that the people they despise will not be given anything good.[17] To these lengthy arguments, his opponents say, '*Noah! You have argued with us for too long. Bring down on us the punishment you threaten us with, if you are telling the truth*' (Q. 11:32). Noah's response to this is, '*It is God who will bring it down, if He wishes, and you will not be able to escape*' (Q. 11:33).

From verse 36 onwards, the second half of the Noah account in this sura moves on to tell the story of the flood, beginning with the building of the Ark, again '*under Our watchful eye*' (Q. 11:37). Noah is told that he should not plead for the disbelievers. As he builds the Ark, they laugh at him, but they will be shamed and punished (Q. 11:38–9). When the flood arrives, Noah is instructed, '*Place on board this Ark a pair of each species, and your own family – except those against whom the sentence has already been passed – and the believers*' (Q. 11:40), in response to which the prophet utters the following invocation, '*Board the Ark. In the name of God it shall sail and anchor. My God is most forgiving and merciful*' (Q. 11:41). Verses 42–44 describe the flood, with '*waves like mountains*', and tell of Noah's vain appeal to his son (who thought he would be saved by climbing a high mountain) to board the Ark. In verse 44, the statement, in very powerful Arabic, is given of God's order for the waters to subside: '*Earth, swallow up your water, and sky, hold back.*'[18] The account draws to a close with Noah asking God to fulfil His promise regarding his son to save his family from the flood, to which he receives the response: '*Noah, he was not one of your family. What he did was not right. Do not ask Me for things you know nothing about. I am warning you not to be foolish*' (Q. 11:46). When Noah finally lands in peace, the account concludes with the following words addressed to Muhammad: '*These accounts are part of what was beyond your knowledge [Muhammad]. We revealed them to you. Neither you nor your people knew them before now, so be patient: the future belongs to those who are aware of God*' (Q. 11:49). These sentiments are echoed at the end of the sura in verses 112–23 where Muhammad is ordered to persevere in worshipping God and trusting in Him: God is not unaware of what the disbelievers do.

Q. 29:14–15

The Noah account in Sura 29 is, like that in Sura 21, brief:

> *We sent Noah out to his people. He lived among them for fifty years short of a thousand and they were doing evil when the Flood overwhelmed them. We saved him and those with him on the Ark. We made this a sign for all people.*

In terms of its context in the sura from which it is drawn, it is given as an example to show the Prophet Muhammad and the believers that faith requires endurance and patience. It is clear from the Qur'an's discussion, later in the sura (Q. 29:56–60), of the possibility that Muhammad and his companions might emigrate and this must have been at a time when the Muslims were under severe and lengthy pressure in Mecca. The story of Noah, who continues, unfaltering, in his mission for '*fifty years short of a thousand*' (mentioned only here), in calling his people to God without giving up, is given as an example of long steadfastness. Although there is no denying that the account does indeed refer to the drowning of the evildoers and, implicitly, the fate of all evildoers, the narrative stress is on Noah's perseverance and the salvation of the people of the Ark, which remains as a sign for all. In line with this concept of the divine, the sura ends with an essentially benign promise: '*But We shall be sure to guide to Our ways those who strive hard for Our cause: God is with those who do good*' (Q. 29:69).

Q. 10:71–3

This three-verse account, which begins with the instruction, '*Tell them the story of Noah*' (Q. 10:71), deals with a moment clearly towards the end of Noah's mission, after his having long preached and argued with his people. The majority of the account is devoted to a challenge delivered by Noah to his people:

> *'My people, if my presence among you and my reminding you of God's signs is too much for you, then I put my trust in God. Agree on your course of action, you and your partner-gods, and do not be hesitant or secretive about it, then carry out your decision on me and give me no respite. But if you turn away, I have asked no reward from you; my reward is with God alone, and I am commanded to be one of those who devote themselves to Him.'*
>
> Q. 10:71–2

This is followed by a brief account of the rest of his story: '*But they rejected him. We saved him and those with him on the Ark and let them survive; and We drowned those who denied Our revelations*' (Q. 10:73).

The dominant theme of this passage is hence that of the prophet's challenge to the disbelievers, as is befitting the context of this passage within the sura. In the same sura, Muhammad is requested to say to his people, '*Wait and see; I too am waiting*' (Q. 10:20). And later: '*Do they say, "He has invented the Qur'an"? Say, "Bring a sura like it and call on everyone you can to help*"' (Q. 10:38). He is then told, '*If they do not believe you, say, "I act for myself and you for yourselves. You are not responsible for my actions nor am I responsible for yours*"' (Q. 10:41). Verse 69 declares that those who invent lies about God will not prosper. In a further challenge, at the end of the sura, Muhammad is instructed to say, '*Whoever follows the right path follows it for his own good and whoever strays does so to his own loss: I am not your guardian*' (Q. 10:108).

Q. 7:59–64

According to Nöldeke, this relatively short account is chronologically the last of the ten we are dealing with. In terms of its context within the sura, the opening verse of Sura 7 tells Muhammad, '*This book has been sent down to you – let there be no anxiety in your heart because of it – so that you may use it to give warning* (*li-tundhira bihi*) *and to remind the believers*' (Q. 7:2). The following verse tells the disbelievers to believe in the One God, as it is also stressed in the account of Noah. The use of the phrase *li-tundhira bihi* here is echoed in Noah's later usage of the words *li-yundhirakum* ('*to warn you*') in Q. 7:63. The lead verse of this passage, Q. 7:59, '*We sent Noah to his people. He said, "My people, serve God: you have no god other than Him. I fear for you the punishment of an awesome Day!"*', expresses the central tenets of Islam and the Qur'an: belief in God and the Judgement. This can also be found (with slightly variant wording) as the opening element of the Noah accounts in Suras 11 and 23.[19] The response, here given by the notables (*al-mala'*) among his people, whom we also see in the earlier Suras 26 and 11, is that they see Noah as being clearly astray: '*the prominent leaders of his people said, "We believe you are far astray*"' (Q. 7:60). In his answer, which makes up roughly half of the entire account, Noah retorts:

> *My people, there is nothing astray about me! On the contrary, I am a messenger from the Lord of all the worlds: I am delivering my Lord's messages to you and giving you sincere advice. I know things from God that you do not. Do you find it so strange that a message would come from your Lord – through a man in your midst – to warn you and make you aware of God so that you may be given mercy?*
>
> Q. 7:61–3

He stresses the message God has sent him with and his sincerity, but his message is rejected as lies by the disbelievers, who, having closed their ears to his warnings and refused to save themselves, are drowned in the flood. Again we see that, although the element of 'punishment' is undeniably present in the narrative, the main focus of the account is on Noah reasoning with the disbelievers in a gentle and rational way, with the disbelievers' watery fate being referred to only briefly at the end.

Immediately before this last account of the Noah story, in Q. 7:57–8, the Qur'an talks about the grace of God in sending water down from the sky and driving it to a dead land: '*Vegetation comes out of good land in abundance by the will of its Lord, but out of bad land only scantily. In this way we explain Our revelations in various ways to those who give thanks*' (Q. 7:58). The metaphorical rain of God's revelation, falling on both fertile and arid land through the preaching of His Messenger Noah, meets with a similar response: the good people believe and the bad do not benefit from it, and those who believed are saved from the physical flood, while the disbelievers drown in it. In the same vein, according to one Hadith, the Prophet Muhammad likened his revelation to abundant rain that falls on various types of land, some producing abundance and others, like rocky land, nothing.[20] At the end of the sura, Muhammad is instructed to say to his people that the revelation he has received brings them '*insights from [their] Lord, guidance and mercy to people who believe*' (Q. 7:203). Thus, here the account of Noah can be seen as providing an illustrative example of this natural phenomenon described by the Qur'an in Q. 7:57–8; the main theme here is, as with the Prophetic Hadith, the different responses to the revelation.

From the analysis given above, it is noteworthy that the accounts vary in size, content and tone according to the context each account has in its sura. Each account has details specific to it, and what is given in all of them is not the story of Noah as a person, or even a 'prophet of punishment', but of his prophethood, what he calls his people to do, their response and the result.

Who Drowned and for What Sins?

Bernhard Heller, in his *Encyclopaedia of Islam* chapter,[21] asserts that during the flood 'the waters drown everything', implying thereby that it is sent down by God as a universal punishment for all of humankind, a claim that is repeated by Marshall.[22] However, when one looks at the Qur'anic text itself (in the accounts of Suras 7, 11 and 23), it is only *al-mala'*, the prominent people in the society, who kept demanding that he drive away the '*worst kind of people*' amongst his followers, and those they have led astray (Q. 71:24–7), who will be punished, not everybody and everything. The Qur'anic usage of the term *al-mala'* is quite specific. It is used, for example, to describe Pharaoh's entourage in Q. 7:109 (*al-mala'u min qawmi fir'awna*, '*the leaders among Pharaoh's people*') and the Queen of Sheba Bilqīs' advisers in Q. 27:32 (*yā-ayyuhā'l-mala'ū 'aftūnī fī-amrī*, '*Counsellors, give me your counsel in the matter I now face*') and, in general, refers to the advisers around figures of significance, usually leaders of the disbelievers. These *mala'* are not punished simply, as Bell and Marshall allege, for their lack of belief. The Qur'an mentions other crimes: they are '*evil people*' (*qawm saw'*, Q. 21:77) who have threatened Noah with stoning (Q. 26:116), have '*schemed mightily*' (Q. 71:22), are '*doing evil*' (*ẓālimūn*, Q. 29:14), are '*sinful*' (*fāsiqūn*, Q. 51:46), are '*very unjust and insolent*' (*aẓlam wa-aṭghā*, Q. 53:52) and have committed sin to a great extent and led many astray (Q. 71:24 and 27).

In describing the final punishment of these evil people, the Qur'an is very brief: '*they were drowned*'. Normally, this occurs at the end of the whole account of Noah's mission, his attempts to persuade them of God's grace, his promises of rewards in this world and the next (Q. 71:4 and 10–20), his reasoning with them and his praying to God. It is, however, a different aspect that is much more prominent in all Qur'anic Noah accounts, as alluded to above. Before stating that *al-mala'* and their followers drowned, we frequently find God speaking in the plural of majesty: '*We saved him and those that were with him*' (*fa-anjaynāhu wa'lladhīna ma'ahu*, Q. 7:64); '*We saved him and the believers who were with him*' (*fa-najjaynāhu wa-man ma'ahu*, Q. 10:73); '*So We saved him and his followers*' (*fa-anjaynāhu wa-man ma'ahu*, Q. 26:119).[23] The Qur'anic stress is on how God saved Noah and his companions, not from drowning, but '*from the evil people*' and the great distress they suffered at the hand of these oppressors; they were carried on the Ark that sailed '*under Our watchful eye*' as '*a reward for one who has been rejected*' (Q. 54:14). Likewise, throughout these accounts, the good news of God's mercy is emphasised. On embarking, Noah says, '*Board the Ark. In the name of God it shall sail and anchor: my Lord is most forgiving and merciful*' (Q. 11:41). God says to Noah, '*When you and your companions are settled in the Ark say, "Praise be to God who has delivered us from a wicked people," and say, "My Lord, let me land with Your blessing: it is You who provide the best landings"*' (Q. 23:28–9). Finally, at the end of one account God says, '*We let him be praised by later generations: "Peace be upon Noah among all the nations!"*' (Q. 37:78–9).

A Punishment Story?

The Qur'anic and the Biblical Accounts

When comparing the Qur'anic with the biblical account of the Noah story, a number of striking differences become apparent. The biblical text, for example, uses a different style, presumably for a different purpose. The account begins with the story of Noah's father who begot Noah (Genesis 5, 26). After the flood, it continues for the whole of Chapter 9, including details such as the fact that he tilled the land, as well as anecdotes of his life, up to the point when Noah dies (Genesis 9, 36). The Bible provides a long list of detailed specifications about materials, dimensions, construction, windows, doors and waterproofing to explain how the Ark was built (Genesis 6, 12–16). The Qur'an on the other hand only mentions the *fulk* or *safīna* (Ark) itself and that Noah was instructed to build the Ark '*under Our watchful eye and according to Our inspiration*' (Q. 23:27). The Bible provides details such as the fact that the rain went on for 40 days and that, to check the level of water, Noah opened a window and sent the raven, which was hesitant, then he sent the dove, which came back because the water was still there. After seven more days he sent it out again and it came back with an olive leaf, and so on. In the Qur'an the flood is treated with much more brevity; the order is given for the water to recede and the Ark lands. Any other details have no connection to the purpose for which the story is used in the Qur'an.

Furthermore, in this regard, we have seen that, in harmony with the Qur'an's rational treatment of its teachings, dialogue marks the discussion. The disbelievers' views are given in full, and then answered in their context. It has also been shown that each account focuses on certain elements and contains material that is not found in other accounts. The conclusion of the story, that is, the flood and the downing of the unbelievers, is, however, mentioned or alluded to in all the accounts and it is presumably this that has led some to describe Noah as 'the first prophet of punishment'. As mentioned above, Heller regards the flood as universal, and says that the waters drowned everything. It has already been observed that in the Qur'anic accounts it is only *al-mala'* (the leaders among the evildoers) and their followers who were drowned. This view of the 'universal' flood has no basis in the Qur'an, which actually depicts it as being specific and localised, and is clearly inspired by other versions of the Noah story, such as those related in the Bible and popular religious legend.

For example, drawing again on the Bible for comparison, in the account in Genesis 6:5, God plans His punishment wrathfully:

> When the Lord saw that man had done much evil on earth and that his thoughts and inclinations were always evil, He was sorry that he had made man on earth, and he was grieved at heart. He said, 'This race of men whom I have created, I will

wipe them off the face of the earth – man and beast, reptiles and birds. I am sorry that I ever made them,' but Noah had won the Lord's favour.

Only one individual, Noah, wins God's favour. In Genesis 6:13 God says: 'The loathsomeness of all mankind has become plain to me, for through them the earth is full of violence. I intend to destroy them and the earth with them. Build yourself a ship'. Then He declares:

I intend to bring the waters of the flood over the earth to destroy every human being under heaven that has the spirit of life; everything on earth shall perish, but with you I will make a covenant, and you shall go into the ship, you and your sons, your wife and your sons' wives with you.

Genesis 6:17

In this account, only eight people survive and no one is given any chance to plead or give their view. There is no dialogue of any kind: 'In seven days' time, I will send rain over the earth for forty days and forty nights, and I will wipe off the face of the earth every living thing that I have made' (Genesis 7:4). And, in Genesis 7:20:

The waters increased and the mountains were covered to a depth of fifteen cubits. Every living creature that moves on earth perished, birds, cattle, wild animals, all reptiles and all mankind. Everything died that had the breath of life in its nostrils, everything on dry land. God wiped out every living thing that existed on earth, man and beast, reptile and bird; they were all wiped out over the whole earth, and only Noah and his company in the ship survived.

Such emphatic repetition within the same account is quite different from what has been seen in those given in the Qur'an where, whenever punishment is mentioned, it is with the two words '*they drowned*'. Although it could be argued that the very succinctness of the Qur'anic language in fact makes the Qur'anic account more powerful – and powerful language is among its most characteristic stylistic features, as Arabic grammarians have long pointed out – the backgrounding of the punishment of the flood in contrast to the foregrounding of Noah's statement of his message, the disbelievers long dialogue with Noah and his steadfast adherence to his prophetic mission and trust in God's mercy and reward, are all very noticeable elements of the Qur'an's presentation of the story of Noah.

This is, of course, not to say that the element of punishment does not exist. Even in Sura 29, where the focus is solely on Noah's perseverance in bringing God's message to his people over hundreds of years without giving up, so as to provide a lesson to the believers in Muhammad's time who were being tested, the account ends by showing that the evil actions of the disbelievers of Noah's time did not go unpunished. This is, as the exegete al-Rāzī observed, one of the *'ādāt* (habits, customs) of the Qur'an, that it passes comment on views and actions it does not agree with,[24] and, in keeping with this habit, the punishment of the evildoers is always stated, even if very briefly, to give a complete picture so that the lesson of the consequences of the unbelievers' actions would be drawn. This, however, does not necessarily mean that these consequences are the most important aspect of these passages, as, although present, they may not illustrate the predominant theme.

The nature of the Qur'an is such that each sura stands on its own and contains a complete, self-contained, independent message, which includes all of the fundamental elements of the Qur'anic message. The Qur'anic view of prophets is summed up in Q. 18:56, '*We only send messengers to bring good news and deliver warning*', and in Noah's case, he comes primarily '*to warn you and make you aware of God so that you may be given mercy*' (Q. 7:63). The Qur'an itself notes that it puts some of the prophets' stories together: '*We have caused Our word to come to them in a connected series* (*waṣṣalnā lahum al-qawla*) *so that they may reflect*' (Q. 28:51). One of the surest ways of conveying its message, as well as reassuring Muhammad and his community, was to tell the stories of earlier prophets, outlining their central message and explaining the rejection they faced and the suffering and frustration they experienced, as well as their perseverance until God's help came to them. Over the years, the disbelievers also needed to be warned more than once.

Are the Noah Accounts Repetitive?

People who are used to reading the story of Noah in the Bible are likely to feel that the story of Noah in the Qur'an is unnecessarily repeated. They approach the Qur'an with the expectation that it should be like the Bible. Yet, the Qur'an is different and uses the stories of previous prophets differently and for different purposes. We have seen that the story of Noah occurs ten times, but in various connections, one being as short as two lines, another spanning over 37 lines, and hence they cannot be the same. It is true that the basic element of them all is Noah being sent to his people who denied him and, in the end, God saving him and the believers and drowning the evildoers amongst the people of Noah. As we have said earlier, no story in the Qur'an is told in its entirety or for its own sake. The stories are sent to strengthen the Prophet Muhammad and his followers (compare Q. 11:120 which explicitly states: '*So [Muhammad], We tell you the stories of the prophets to make your heart firm and in these accounts truth has come to you, as well as a lesson a reminder for the believers.*'). We have seen that each telling of the story has something different to offer and fits its own context. There are statements in the various stories, mentioning the faith Noah is calling for, the responses of his own people and yet others are comments by God, each of which is similar to the situation Muhammad found himself in, what he was calling his people to, their reactions and responses and comments by God. We shall give a few examples from the stories of Noah to illustrate this (see Table 2).

As Table 2 shows, all this is an essential part and parcel of the function of the story of Noah in the Qur'an. It is not for entertainment and it is not popular literature; it is encouragement and reassurance of the Prophet and his followers, giving them comfort, reinforcing the message that that the Qur'an is all from God and Muhammad is '*nothing new among the prophets*' (Q. 46:9).

Each sura is a self-contained entity, which has the required elements to teach its lesson and make its impact. Each is like a sermon, delivered orally on a specific occasion in a specific context. So it would not say, as in an academic dissertation, 'This was dealt with on page 16' or 'this will be discussed in Chapter 5'. There is no repetition of the Noah story within any sura. Those who do not bear this in mind and expect the Qur'an to be composed like an academic dissertation will find problems that do not exist. In a number of suras in the Qur'an (see Q. 7, Q. 11, Q. 26 and Q. 54) there is a long list of many prophets, with the stories of how their people rejected them and the consequences for them. It is clear from such statements as, '*If they reject you, other people before them have rejected their messengers*' (Q. 6:33–6, Q. 22:42, Q. 35:4 and 25) that the Prophet was much troubled by their rejection, thinking that perhaps he should have done more. Many times he is told (see Q. 36:7–9 and Q. 2:6–7), '*God has sealed their hearts*' and '*your only duty is to convey the message* (*inna 'alayka illā'l-balāgh*)' (see Q. 13:40) and the Qur'an tried to show him that he was not alone or new among messengers (*bid'an mina'l-rusul*, Q. 46:9). There is a list of 14 instances under the word *kadhdhabat* ('they denied') in the concordance, in addition to other derived forms.[25] A full list was necessary to show that before Muhammad not one messenger escaped being rejected and not one rejecter of a messenger escaped punishment.

Table 2. Parallels between Noah and Muhammad

Noah	***Muhammad***
Serve God, you have no other god than Him (Q. 7:59)	*In matters of faith, He has laid down for you the same commandment that he gave to Noah* (Q. 42:13)
I am commanded to be one of those who devote themselves to Him (Q. 10:72)	*I am commanded to be one of those devoted to Him* (Q. 27:91)
If you turn away, I do not ask you for any reward (Q. 11:29)	*I ask no reward for this* (Q. 42:23; Q. 34:47)
You are clearly misguided (Q. 7:60)	*You must be deeply misguided* (Q. 36:47)
The leading disbelievers among the people of Noah said, 'He is merely a mortal like you' (Q. 23:24)	*'Is this man [Muhammad] anything but a mortal like yourselves?'* (Q. 21:3)
I am here to warn you plainly (Q. 71:1)	*I am only a plain warner to you* (Q. 46:9)
I will not drive away the believers (Q. 11:29)	*Do not drive away those who call upon their Lord morning and evening* (Q. 6:52)
I do not claim to have the treasures of God, nor do I know the unseen (Q. 11:31)	*If I had knowledge of what is hidden I would have abundant good things and no harm could touch me* (Q. 7:188)
Bring us the punishment you promise if you are telling the truth (Q. 11:32–33)	*When will this promise be fulfilled if what you say is true?* (Q. 36:48)
Every time I call them they […] cover their heads with their garments (Q. 71:7)	*See how [the disbelievers] wrap themselves up to hide their feelings from Him* (Q. 11:5)
It was revealed to Noah, 'None of your people will believe other than those who have already done so.' (Q. 11.36)	*Most of them […] refuse to believe* (Q. 36:7)

This was to support Muhammad's followers and warn those who rejected him. This rejection was over a period of 13 years, so it was necessary to make the point over and over again, orally, on different occasions, with varying lengths and content according to contexts.

So, when Muslims read or hear the various accounts of Noah's life and mission in the Qur'an, they do not see this as repetition, as they actually hear in his story about the teachings and history of their own religion and the efforts exerted by all the prophets, including Muhammad, in establishing devotion to God. In spite of all difficulties, there was the divine promise of encouragement and success:

Noah cried to Us and how excellent was Our response! We saved him and his people from great distress, We let his offspring remain on the earth, We let him be praised by later generations: 'Peace be upon Noah among all the nations!' This is how We reward those who do good: he was truly one of Our faithful servants. We drowned the others.

Q. 37:75–81

In reading about Noah and his followers being saved, Muhammad and his followers certainly found that this echoes God's declaration in the story of Jonah in Q. 10:103: '*In the end We shall save Our messengers and the believers. We take it upon Ourselves to save the believers.*'

Conclusion

Unlike some other accounts, such as that of the Bible cited in this chapter, which, as we have seen, gives details of the destruction caused by the flood, the Qur'an does not foreground the punishment element in the Noah story, merely saying '*they drowned*' ('they' being the prominent disbelievers and their followers), and implicitly reducing the physical scale of the flood and the extent of its destruction. Popular Islamic culture would seem to support this view, as the Qur'anic Noah does not seem to be conceived of as being linked with divine punishment or wrath, but rather with ideas of God's protection and blessings. In Egypt, for instance, lorries are seen decorated in fine calligraphy with *bi'smi'llāhi majrāhā wa-mursāhā* ('*In the name of God may it go, and in the name of God may it arrive*'), quoting Noah's invocation to God about the Ark in Q. 11:41. On getting away from a dangerous place, by plane or other means, many Muslims repeat what Noah was instructed to say in thanks for his deliverance in Sura 23, '*Praise be to God who has delivered us from people who are unjust*', and when arriving in any new place or country, they repeat his prayer of Q. 23:29, '*My Lord, let me land with Your blessing: it is You who provide the best landings*'.

Likewise, Arabic literature does not give attention to describing, analysing or showing any influence of the punishment in the Noah story. The famous grammarian 'Abd al-Qāhir al-Jurjānī was highly impressed by the power of language in God's command to the waters to recede.[26] The modern Arabic poet B. S. al-Sayāb was influenced again by the power of language, using Qur'anic expressions in his work.[27] Whereas, in the *Encyclopaedia of Islam*,[28] Noah is seen as the first prophet of punishment, many Muslim authors appear to see him as the first in a series of prophets bearing good news and warning of the Hereafter, in accordance with the following verses in which Muhammad is addressed:

We have sent revelation to you as we sent it to Noah and the prophets after him: to Abraham, Ishmael, Jacob, and the Tribes, to Jesus, Job, Jonah, Aaron, and Solomon – to David we gave the Psalms – [and] to other messengers [...] bearing good news and warning, so that mankind would have no excuse before God once the messengers had delivered their message.

Q. 4:163–5

Muslims also see Noah as the first of 'the messengers of firm resolve' who are given to Muhammad as an example to follow: '*Be steadfast [Muhammad], like those messengers of firm resolve (ulū'l-'azmi mina'l-rusuli)*' (Q. 46:35).

From the analysis and discussion above, it is clear that all prophets in the Qur'an were sent to promote the same fundamental beliefs. Although prophets in the Qur'an are sent to warn, they are not sent to predict doom. Their function is the same; they are bringers of good news and warning of the afterlife (*bashīr wa-nadhīr*). Likewise, their method of preaching is the same: '*Call people to the way of your Lord with wisdom and good teaching. Reason with them in the most courteous way, for your Lord knows best who has strayed from His way and who is rightly guided*' (Q. 16:125).

The function of prophetic stories is to reinforce the prophethood of Muhammad and reassure both him and the believers in their long struggle against persecution, which, they are promised, in the end they will win. God undertakes that '*We shall save Our messengers and the believers. We take it upon Ourselves to save the believers*' (Q. 10:103).[29] We have seen in Noah's case that the stories are not biographies, nor even histories of prophethood, but accounts of specific moments or events that are meant to give lessons. In Noah's case the ten accounts vary in size, form and tone according to the contexts, each one has information and objectives specific to its context and none of them can substitute the other in the same context. The distribution and recurrence are means by which to reinforce the message over the long period of preaching.

References to punishment are confined to two words, '*they drowned*', even in the longest accounts. Punishment is only for the prominent disbelievers who are out to suppress, oppress and lead others astray, and it is not universal in accordance with the Qur'anic principle, '*No soul shall bear the burden of another'* (Q. 53:38). The view that the story of Noah is one of punishment appears to be reductionist, in terms of its foundation in the Arabic text of the Qur'an: it is rather the teaching and exemplary steadfastness of Noah and his spiritual elevation that endure. As long as people read or hear the Qur'an, and declare the first part of the Islamic testimony of faith, *lā ilāha illā'llāh,* they will relive Noah's statement to his people, 'God *(Allāh), you have no other god than Him*' (Q. 7:59). And, as long as they travel, they will repeat his words, '*In the name of God may it go, and in His name may it arrive*' (Q. 11:41), '*My Lord, let me land with Your blessing: it is You who provide the best landings*' (Q. 23:29).

The fact that the Qur'an does not follow the biblical model of stating the full story in one place, but takes illustrative material from it to be used as required by the context of the suras, has the benefit of entrenching these stories from religious history, with its teachings and lessons, so that they are ever present in the minds of Muslims who hear and read the Qur'an.

The Qur'an often stresses that it confirms previous revelations from God, and this is also true when it continues the biblical teachings through the accounts of prophets, spreading these stories to a vastly wider audience, Muslims and non-Muslims who read the Qur'an: '*We have sent down the Qur'an to you with the Truth, confirming the Scripture that came before and protecting it*' (Q. 5:48).

8

Coherent Style: How to Read the Sura

Sūrat al-Jumuʿa (Q. 62)

Richard Bell[1] was the first English writer to undertake an analysis of the structure of suras in the whole text of the Qur'an. This was a useful approach with which many subsequent authors have engaged;[2] however, its usefulness was diminished, in Bell's hands, in a number of ways. First, the very high degree of speculation involved necessitated the use of words such as 'perhaps', 'maybe', 'probably', 'before' or 'after'. On p. 248 (vol. 1) of his *The Qur'an: translated with a Critical Rearrangement of the Surahs* in one single paragraph there are about 20 such vague expressions. While thus not hiding his sense of doubt, which could be expected in such a ground-breaking work, Bell at the same time shows a propensity to make unusual assertions without providing any support for them. Moreover, Bell often approached the text with his mind already made up, harbouring preconceptions about the origin of the Qur'an, the Prophet's character and career in dealing with his opponents.

Bell's readiness to dismiss parts of suras as being disconnected from the rest of the text, or to say that the text was confused, can be linked to a flawed understanding on his part of the language and style of the Qur'an. The discussion of *Sūrat al-Jumuʿa* will serve as an example.

Sūrat al-Jumuʿa is a Medinan sura, consisting of 11 verses after the *basmala*, that is, the opening of the sura with the words '*in the name of God*'. Bell asserts:

> This sura seems to consist of a number of disconnected pieces. Vv. 1, 2, 4 belong to the period shortly before the change of *qibla* when Muhammad is turning from

the People of the Book towards the Arabs. Into this, v. 3 has been inserted at some later stage. Verse 5 is little more than a scrap, noting down a simile [...] It shows the controversy with the Jews already fairly acute. Vv. 6–8 also belong to the controversy with the Jews [...] Vv. 9, 10 are quite unconnected and deal with the Friday prayer [...] verse 11 is evidently private and not really connected with the preceding verses unless it be that they are the public exhortation induced by such conduct as this verse takes note of.[3]

Let us now consider this in the light of a stylistic and contextual analysis of the sura. *Al-Jumu'a* is one of five suras known as *al-musabbiḥāt* (Suras 57, 59, 61, 62 and 64) each of which begins with the glorification of God. It is noted that in all the *musabbiḥāt* blame is directed at certain people later in the sura who did not live as the glorification of God requires:

Everything in the heavens and earth glorifies God, the Controller, the Holy One, the Almighty, the Wise [or: Judicious Decider].[4] *It is He who raised a messenger, among the people who had no Scripture, to recite His revelations to them, to make them grow spiritually and teach them the Scripture and wisdom – before that they were clearly astray – to them and others yet to join them. He is the Almighty, the Wise: such is God's favour that He grants it to whoever He will; God's favour is immense.*

Q. 62:1–4

Reminding the readers that all on earth and in heaven glorify God (Q. 62:1) in effect urges them to join the chorus of His worshippers; if they do not, the verse implies that they are in discord with the rest of creation. It highlights crucial attributes of God that make Him worthy of glorification and obedience, particularly the fact that He controls everything, that He is holy, mighty and the one who decides judiciously. Surprisingly, Bell thinks, without explaining why, that this sura belongs to the period shortly before the change of *qibla*.[5] Similar verses come at the beginning of Q. 57, 59, 61 and 64, none of which has anything to do with the change of *qibla*. Muhammad, moreover, did not 'turn' to the Arabs, as Bell suggested. He had been preaching to them from the beginning of his mission.

Q. 62:2 begins with an expression of *ḥaṣr* ('restriction'): '*It is He who...*'. *Ḥaṣr* is known in *balāgha* (Arabic rhetoric) to be a retort to someone who thought or claimed otherwise. This *ḥaṣr* in the first instance is a retort to those who begrudge the Arabs having a prophet. This is further corroborated by the expression *al-ummiyyīn* ('those who have no scripture'), mentioned in the same verse. Some Jews in and around Medina had expressed denial that the Arabs could have a prophet.[6] Q. 62:4 affirms,

'*Such is the favour* (*faḍl*) *of God,*[7] *who grants it to whoever He will*', that is, even to the *ummiyyīn*. Compare Q. 4:54 which makes the same point: '*Do they envy other people for the favour* (*faḍl*) *God has granted them? We gave the descendants of Abraham the Scripture and wisdom and we gave them a great kingdom.*' So the *ummiyyīn* are now given the *faḍl* of a messenger and scripture, just as the Jews were given similar *faḍl* before. God distributes His *faḍl* as He Himself chooses.

Recipients of *faḍl* should show gratitude by living according to the scripture, otherwise they are not benefiting from the teachings they have been given, rather it is a burden. This is stated plainly in Q. 62:5: '*those who have been charged to obey the Torah but do not do so are like asses carrying books.*' It is significant that the Qur'an does not say that 'Jews' are like asses, but only those who have been charged with the Torah and fail to carry it out.[8] It is clear from comparison with Q. 5:44 that it is rabbis in general who are entrusted with the preservation of the Torah and judging according to its teachings. The ones referred to in Sura 62 are the ones who restrict God's favour, denying Him the freedom to choose His Messengers and claiming that out of all people they are God's only friends. The use of the passive verb here, *ḥummilū al-Tawrāh*, reflects the passive in Q. 5:44, *istuḥfiẓū min kitābi'llāhi*, where the rabbis are rather praised for their obedience to the Torah:

We revealed the Torah with guidance and light, and the prophets, who had submitted to God, judged according to it for the Jews. So did the rabbis and the scholars in accordance with that part of God's scripture which they were entrusted to preserve and to which they were witnesses.

This careful discrimination between the Jews at large and the behaviour of some Jews is seen throughout the Qur'an. For example Q. 3:75 reads:

There are people of the Book [that is, Jews as shown by the context] who, if you [Prophet] entrust them with a heap of gold will return it to you intact but there are others of them who, if you entrust them with a single dinar, will not return it to unless you keep standing over them because they say, 'We are under no obligation towards the gentiles (al-ummiyyīn)'. They tell a lie against God and they know it. No indeed! God loves those who keep their pledges and are mindful of Him.

So, it is clear in *Sūrat al-Jumu'a* that those compared to asses are only those who refuse to carry out their duty and do not benefit from the Torah sent down to them by God with light and guidance. Likewise, Muslims call Muslim scholars who do not live according to the teachings of the Qur'an 'asses'. So they were branded in the past[9] and in the present day. In fact, the Qur'an also likens Arabs who run away from God's teachings to asses, as we will see later.

Bell appears not to have taken due note of the significance of *ḥaṣr* ('restriction' or 'confining') or of the use of *al-ummiyyīn*[10] and of *faḍl Allāh,* which He gives to whoever He chooses and which is so immense that it was not exhausted by granting prophethood to the Jews. Accordingly, Bell was bound to miss the connection between Q. 62:5 and the preceding verses when he declared that 'verse 5 is little more than a scrap noting down a simile [...] it shows the controversy with the Jews already fairly acute.'[11] Alan Jones[12] stated that 'the first four verses dwell on God's power, with verse 2 focusing on a specifically Arabian content. The middle section (verses 5 and 6) refers to Muhammad's Jewish opponents.' This again misses the point of *ḥaṣr* and the connection between the verses so far discussed. Bell states: 'Verses 6–8 also belong to the controversy with the Jews.'[13] In Q. 62:5 the Qur'an points out that some who have been granted the *faḍl* do not live up to it, here among the Jews, but this draws the attention to some Muslims as well, who will be shown in Q. 62:11 to be equally castigated.

Those who have been charged with to obey the Torah, but do not do so, are like asses carrying books: how base such people are who disobey God's revelations! God does not guide people who do wrong. Say [Prophet], 'You who follow the Jewish faith, if you truly claim that out of all people you alone are friends of God, then you should be hoping for death.' But because of what they have stored up for themselves with their own hands they would never hope for death – God knows the wrongdoers very well – so say, 'The death you run away from will come to meet you and you will be returned to the One who knows the unseen as well as the seen: He will tell you everything you have done.'

Q. 62:5–8

Those Jews who begrudged the Arabs their prophet and scripture claimed that they alone were 'friends (*awliyā'*) of God'.[14] The Qur'an challenges them, if, out of all people (*min dūni'l-nās*), Arabs included, they are truly God's friends, and recipients of His favour, they should wish for death to be joined with Him, but says they will not. They run away from death but it will catch them and they will be returned to God who will show them what they have been doing, including the fact that they did not carry out the instructions of the Torah.

So the text of Sura 62 up to verse 8 is directed in the first place[15] at those Jews who begrudged the *ummiyyīn* prophethood. But the *ḥaṣr* in verse 2, '*It is He who raised a messenger*', is also instructive for Muslims themselves, reminding them that, in spite of those Jews begrudging them God's favour, He and no one else, raised amongst them a messenger of their own when they had no scripture, to recite God's revelation to them, to make them grow spiritually and teach them the scripture and wisdom. It further reminds them that before this they were clearly astray. The Messenger was sent '*to them and to others yet to join them*'. At that time this was a reassurance from God that their faith would acquire future generations of believers, as part of the favour of God to those who had in the past been astray.[16] Having shown these believers the great favour they have been given, God immediately puts before them the example of those who have not lived up to His favour and refused to undertake their duty of living according to His teachings, so they should beware, listen to the teachings and obey.

The text then moves, in verse 9, to address '*you who have believed*' (coming after '*you who follow the Jewish faith*' in verse 6): '*When the call to prayer is made, on the Day of Congregation, hasten to remember God and leave off your trading.*' Bell[17] asserts that 'vv. 9–10 are quite unconnected and deal with the Friday prayer.' According to his assumption, the sura should have ended with verse 8, but this would mean that the sura was no more than a criticism of the Jews who did not obey and an allusion to the favour given to the Arabs in receiving a prophet. This, however, is not the pattern witnessed in the Qur'an. When God's favour is expressed, the Qur'an demands action on the part of the recipients to show gratitude. In *Sūrat al-Ḍuḥā* (Q. 93) the Qur'an reassures the Prophet that God has not forsaken him and that the future is better than the past, and gives evidence from his past experience: '*Did He not find you an orphan and sheltered you, lost and guided you, in need and made you well satisfied?*' (Q. 93:6–8). But then in Q. 93: 9–11 it goes on to say: '*So do not be harsh with the orphan and do not chide the one who asks for help, and talk about the blessing of your Lord.*' In *Sūrat al-Jumu'a*, having given the believers such favour, God now demands that they live up to these teachings and do not behave like those who fail to benefit from the teachings granted to them. The Prophet was sent to them to recite God's revelation, to make them grow spiritually and teach them the scripture and wisdom. All this is done in the Friday prayer and sermon. None of this is 'quite unconnected' as Bell claims.[18] The sura continues:

> *Believers! When the call to prayer is made on the day of congregation, go quickly to the prayer and leave off your trading – that is better for you, if only you knew – then when the prayer has ended, disperse in the land and seek out God's bounty. Remember God often so that you may prosper.*
>
> Q. 62:9–10

Friday in Arabic is called *yawm al-jumu'a* ('the day of gathering'). It has been suggested[19] that this particular day was the market day for Arabs and Jews, when the Jews in Medina bought what they needed for the Sabbath. This suggestion appears to be corroborated by the fact that, in the above verses, the Qur'an asks the believers to 'cease trading'. It does not say 'cease work' of any other kind or even 'cease staying at home'. They should cease trading in the market and come together to pray and remember God. It is at the mosque that they will glorify God (as in verse 1) and that the Prophet will recite the Qur'an to them, purify them, teach them the scripture and wisdom (as in verse 2).

Q. 62:10 uses two firm orders: *is'aw* ('hasten to') and *dharū'l-bay'a* ('leave trading'). In introducing regulations the Qur'an uses such orders, but they are couched in persuasive expressions such as 'you who believe', appealing to the fact that they have accepted the faith and joined the community of believers. Then, after the order it says in the same verse '*this is better (khayr) for you, if only you knew*', which suggests that God knows the benefit contained in this command and that, if they had such knowledge, they would eagerly obey the order. This persuasion continues in the same verse: '*When the prayer is ended, disperse (intashirū) in the land*'. This is another order, contrasting semantically with *al-jumu'a* ('getting together'), to show that the order to come together is only for a short while, after which they can go back to business. *Intashirū* is an order but is construed by jurists to be a permission (*li'l-ibāḥa*) and as being not as firm as the earlier orders to cease trading and hurry to the remembrance of God. It is interesting that the Qur'an says '*disperse in the land*' rather than 'go back to the market or your homes', thus suggesting that the whole earth (*al-arḍ*) is open to them. It goes on to say in the same verse, '*and seek the bounty (faḍl) of God*'. This *faḍl* connects to the earlier *faḍl* given to them in Q. 62:4. Before *al-jumu'a* ('gathering'), they were engaged in *al-bay'* ('trading'); after obeying God and going to prayer, their activity is called 'seeking the bounty of God'. Then they are reminded that while seeking His bounty they should remember Him much '*so that [they] may prosper*'. This ends the scheme of persuasion that runs through Q. 62:9–10. When asked to fulfil the obligation they were charged with, the believers are addressed by God in an endearing and persuasive manner in Q. 62:11: '*Yet they dash out towards trade or entertainment whenever they observe it, and leave you [Prophet] standing there. Say, "What God has is better than any entertainment or trade: God is the best provider."*' Q. 62:11 comes in sharp contrast to talk about – not talk *to* – those who have not completed the requirement. There is a shift (*iltifāt*) from being addressed to being talked about. In the language of the Qur'an this shows distancing and displeasure: '*Yet they dash out towards trade or entertainment whenever they observe it, and leave you [Prophet] standing there.*' Bell says, 'Verse 11 is evidently private and not really connected with the preceding verses'.[20] It is far from being unconnected; it is a contrast, referring to an actual event where the Prophet was delivering a sermon during the Friday prayer, a trade caravan arrived, accompanied as usual by some merriment, and a large number of people in the mosque dashed out to it except for about a dozen people.[21] The words *infaḍḍū ilayhā* ('dash out towards it') contrast sharply with *is'aw ilā* ('hurry to the remembrance of God') mentioned in Q. 62:9. They have not waited for the prayer to end (*quḍiyat al-ṣalāh*). The sermon is given *before* the prayer, which Bell does not seem to have realised. In addition, these people showed flagrant disregard to the Prophet; they left him standing there. He was facing them and addressing them, and yet they dashed out. If he had been sitting in the front line with his back to them and they had walked out surreptitiously, that would have been less flagrant. They are like asses who have been charged with bearing the teaching and who ignored it, as Q. 74:49–51 states. The symmetry with Q. 62.5 is very clear: '*What is the matter with them? They turn away from the Reminder (tadhkira) like frightened asses fleeing from a lion.*' In his sermon, the Prophet would be teaching them and reciting '*the revelations to them, to make them grow spiritually and teach them the Scripture and wisdom*' (Q. 62:2). The wisdom is for them to realise that what God has is better than trade and merriment, '*if only they knew*'.[22]

Finally, in Q. 62:12, the Prophet is instructed to remind them: '*What God has is better (khayr) than any entertainment or trade.*' Ending with the categorical statement: '*God is the best provider.*' It is significant that God Himself addresses the believers in verse 9 to instruct them but He asks the Prophet in verses 6 and 10 to address those Jews and Muslims who are violating the divine teaching given to them. The symmetry is balanced with reference to the two religions, Judaism and Islam and their followers. Both have been given some of God's favour (*min faḍli'llāh*), which is better for those who follow it; those who ignore this *faḍl* and do not live according to it are like asses. Both should remember that God is the best provider. Q. 62:4 ends with *wa'llāhu dhū'l-faḍli'l-'aẓīm* ('*God's favour is immense*') and verse 11 ends with *wa'llāhu khayru'l-rāziqīn* ('*God is the best provider*'), and who can provide better than '*the Controller, the Holy, the Mighty, the Decider, whose praise is celebrated by those in the heaven and the earth?*' (verse 1). Those who do not join in this praise and prove to be worthy of receiving His *faḍl* do not know what is best (*khayr*) for them. This symmetry connects the different parts of the sura.[23]

It is significant that crucial verbs in this sura have one common feature, which is speed. Thus *tafirrūna* ('*run away from*', verse 8), *is'aw* ('*rush towards*', verse 9), *intashirū fī'l-'arḍ* ('*disperse in the land*', verse 10) and *infaḍḍū ilayhā* ('*scatter towards it*', verse 11). In the first example, the speed is in running away from danger; in the other three in rushing to seek gain. This speed is an element that binds the parts of the sura together.

The title is very telling; one concise word, which gives the raison d'être of the sura. It brings the believers together to glorify God and gain knowledge of scripture and purification, leaving trading for a while and feeling sure of God's provision and *faḍl*. The believers who stay to the end of the gathering are observing and benefiting from the revelation with which they have been entrusted.

In order to appreciate the unity of *Sūrat al-Jumu'a* it was necessary to bear in mind characteristics of the Qur'an's language and style, free oneself of preconceived notions and attend to close examination of the text of the sura, analysing it according to the norms of the Qur'an. The sura does not, as Bell claimed, consist of a number of disconnected pieces. In fact, the text is tightly connected and balanced, both in form and content.

Sūrat al-Ḥadīd (Q. 57)

Richard Bell introduces his translation of *Sūrat al-Ḥadīd*, a Medinan sura consisting of 29 verses, with the statement that 'a series of passages of fairly early Medinan date forms the basis of this sura'.[24] He follows this with a short paragraph giving detailed analysis of presumed dates for the different passages and verses, full (as usual) of such conjectural words as 'probably', 'not too long after' and 'fairly closely'. Alan Jones introduces his translation of this sura by asserting, again after a statement on what he presumes to be the dates of different parts of the sura, that 'much of the sura stands as a creed, though there is some exhortation and some polemical material'.[25] In both translations, concern for dating verses is obviously seen as of great importance. This, however, is mere speculation, and it is difficult to see how they contribute in any way to understanding the sura.[26] In fact, it distracts from looking closely at the text of the Qur'an as we have it, which is the only certainty, and seeing the structure and purpose of the sura.

Bell's and Jones's references to the structure of the Qur'an follow a tradition that assumes that suras comprise a conglomeration of essentially disparate material and jump from one theme to another in a disjointed manner. Accordingly, in describing the structure of suras, Jones breaks them down into passages described in such terms as 'signs', 'stories', 'polemics' and 'perorations'. However, such labelling and listing, useful as they may be, does not contribute to understanding the structure or unity and purpose of suras and indeed may cloud the picture and distract the translator and the reader from seeing what the sura is actually about. It neglects the text and how it actually works. This section will present an analysis of *Sūrat al-Ḥadīd,* intended to show its organic structural and thematic unity, purpose and impact.

Sūrat al-Ḥadīd is the first in a group of five suras (Q. 57, Q. 59, Q. 61, Q. 62 and Q. 64), already mentioned in the previous section, which are referred to as *al-musabbiḥāt*: they are suras beginning with glorification of God using the verb *sabbaḥa/yusabbiḥu.* In all the *musabbiḥāt* blame is directed later in the sura at certain people who did not live as the glorification requires. In discussing this aspect of the beginning of Q. 57, Bell's and Jones's analyses do not examine the significance of such a beginning, the function of every section or verse in any given sura, and how it leads to what follows to build up an overall effect. The discussion below takes a different approach. Bell simply states that 'the passage extols Allah'[27] and Jones that 'the sura stands as a creed',[28] without any reference to the role of the initial section in the whole scheme of discourse in the sura.

In fact the first passage or group of verses that forms a discrete unit within *Sūrat al-Ḥadīd* comprises Q. 57:1–6:

> *In the name of God, the Lord of Mercy, the Giver of Mercy. Everything in the heavens and earth glorifies God – He is the Almighty, the Wise. Control of the heavens and earth belongs to Him; He gives life and death; He has power over all things. He is the First and the Last; the Outer and the Inner; He has knowledge of all things. It was He who created the heavens and earth in six Days and then established Himself on the throne. He knows what enters the earth and what comes out of it; what descends from the sky and what ascends to it. He is with you wherever you are; He sees all that you do; control of the heavens and earth belongs to Him. Everything is brought back to God. He makes night merge into day and day into night. He knows what is in every heart.*

By reminding the believers that all on earth and in heaven glorify God, these initial verses urge them to join the chorus of His worshippers and tell them that if they do not, they will be in discord with the rest of creation. The passage highlights crucial attributes of God that make Him truly worthy of glorification and obedience, particularly the fact that He controls everything and knows everything; His knowledge is emphasised in this passage about five times in different ways, so that anyone who tries to deceive himself or others into thinking that he has nothing to give (as requested in the following verse, Q. 57:7) knows that he cannot deceive God. This heralds the subsequent condemnation of the hypocrites in verses 13–15. Another important element of this passage is the fact that all will return to God to give account. As a piece of *targhīb* ('persuasion') to heed the orders of such a great Lord, and *tarhīb* ('instilling awe') to break down resistance to the instruction, this functions as a warm-up introduction to the instruction that is to follow.

This first passage leads on to a verse that is of fundamental importance to the sura as a whole in terms of its function. Q. 57:7 states: '*Believe in God and His Messenger, and give out of what He has made pass down to you: those of you who believe and give will have a great reward.*' The very core of this whole sura lies in the imperative *anfiqū* ('*give*') in this verse. This exhortation to the believers to give is characteristic of the way that the Qur'an does not simply throw out orders, but always aims to accompany the orders it gives with reasons and justifications in order to persuade people, psychologically and rationally, to do what it asks for, a technique termed *al-amr wa'l-targhīb* or *al-amr wa'l-tarhīb*. Such justifications can come before or after the imperative order, or both. In line with this, everything that comes before the imperative *anfiqū* in *Sūrat al-Ḥadīd* and everything that comes after it, to the very end of the sura, works to achieve this aim.

What is worthy of note in verse 7 is that before it asks the believers to give, it instructs them to believe in God and His Messenger, implying that anyone who does not give does not truly believe. Furthermore, when delivering this exhortation it does not say 'give some of your money' but rather '*give out of what He has made pass down to you*', reminding them that everything in life comes from God and that they will not have it forever, an element of persuasion designed to make its audience more inclined to give. In recompense for this the believers are promised '*a great reward*'.

Not only are they exhorted to give, if they believe, but they are then asked in verses 8–11 why they should not do so:

Why should you not believe in God when the Messenger calls you to believe in your Lord, and He has already made a pledge with you, if you have faith? It is He who has sent down clear revelations to His servant, so that He may bring you from the depths of darkness into light; God is truly kind and merciful to you. Why should you not give for God's cause when God alone will inherit what is in the heavens and earth? Those who gave and fought before the victory are not like others: they are greater in rank than those who gave and fought afterwards. But God has promised a good reward to all of them: God is fully aware of all that you do. Who will make God a good loan? He will double it for him and reward him generously.

As can be seen clearly here, the Qur'an does not give abstract, detached injunctions but speaks directly to its audience: '*Believe...*', and then asks, '*why should you not believe...?*', involving them in a dialogue. Then, in verse 9, it reminds them of God's kindness and mercy in sending the message to bring those who believe into the light, again to make them realise that those who do not heed are in darkness. Light is mentioned five times in this sura (from verse 9 to verse 28), helping, along with other repetitions, to cement the connections between its various parts. Verse 10 asks again, '*Why should you not give for God's cause when God alone will inherit what is in the heavens and earth?*', and affirms that those who hasten to give are better than those who hesitate, while still aiming to persuade even the hesitant by promising both '*a good reward*'. This idea of the giver being rewarded is then built on in verse 11 with the phrase, '*Who will make God a good loan?*', a powerful image in which God asks the faithful to render to Him a loan from the wealth He has given them, in return for which He promises double rewards and more on the Day when it will really count:

On the Day when you [Prophet] see the believers, both men and women, with their light streaming out ahead of them and to their right, [they will be told,] 'The good news for you today is that there are Gardens graced with flowing streams where you will stay: that is truly the supreme triumph!'

Q. 57:12

This promise of the great reward and supreme triumph awaiting the believers is then contrasted – another frequently used rhetorical technique – with the fate, not of the disbelievers (*al-kāfirūn*), but the hypocrites (*al-munāfiqūn*), those who pretend to be believers yet are not ready to give:

On the same Day, the hypocrites, both men and women, will say to the believers, 'Wait for us! Let us have some of your light!' They will be told, 'Go back and look for a light.' A wall with a door will be erected between them: inside it lies mercy, outside lies punishment. The hypocrites will call out to the believers, 'Were we not with you?' They will reply, 'Yes. But you allowed yourselves to be tempted, you were hesitant, doubtful, deceived by false hopes until God's command came – the Deceiver tricked you about God – today no ransom will be accepted from you or from the disbelievers. Your home is the Fire – that is where you belong – a miserable destination!'

Q. 57:13–15

All the verses up to this point are marshalled to soften the hearts of any true or even hesitant believer. This is why the hypocrites, who deprived themselves in this world from the light God sent down in the Revelation, will plead for some light but will be shut off. They are warned here that no ransom will be accepted from them on that day, they will be like the disbelievers. Then comes the question:

Is it not time for believers to humble their hearts to the remembrance of God and the Truth that has been revealed, and not to be like those who received the Scripture before them, whose time was extended but whose hearts hardened and many of whom were lawbreakers?

Q. 57:16

The hesitant are reminded, using the spectre of some who were given the scripture long ago and yet whose hearts did not soften but indeed hardened: '*Remember that God revives the earth after it dies; We have made Our revelation clear to you so that you may use your reason*' (Q. 57:17). Just as they see the dead land coming alive,[29] their hearts may still be revived in this life, if they use their reason. They are likewise reminded of the resurrection, judgement and fate they will all face:

Charitable men and women who make a good loan to God will have it doubled and have a generous reward. Those who believe in God and His Messengers are the truthful ones who will bear witness before their Lord: they will have their reward and their light. But those who disbelieve and deny Our revelations are the inhabitants of Hell.

Q. 57:18–19

Here, for the first time, the great honour and rewards of those who believe and give is contrasted explicitly with the fate of those who disbelieve and deny the revelation, suggesting that those who do not listen and obey put themselves in the second category, '*the inhabitants of Hell*'.

So far we have seen how the Qur'an marshals arguments to persuade the believers to give. From verses 20–4, the Qur'an moves on to tackle the subject from a different angle, aiming to break down two pretexts that might prevent believers from giving. The first is their perception that the life they enjoy now and the wealth they accumulate and covet are so important and long lasting that they are the be-all and end-all:

Bear in mind that the present life is just a game, a diversion, an attraction, a cause of boasting among you, of rivalry in wealth and children. It is like plants that spring up after the rain: their growth at first delights the sowers, but then you see them wither away, turn yellow, and become stubble. There is terrible punishment in the next life as well as forgiveness and approval from God; the life of this world is only an illusory pleasure.

Q. 57:20

Whatever they may have in this life is fleeting, therefore they should:

race one another for [their] Lord's forgiveness and a Garden as wide as the heavens and earth, prepared for those who believe in God and His Messengers: that is God's bounty, which He bestows on whoever He pleases. God's bounty is infinite.

Q. 57:21

This emphasises the generosity of God, mentioning '*a Garden as wide as the heavens and earth*', to which they should aspire by giving: *faḍl Allāh*, '*God's bounty*', occurs five times in the sura.

The second pretext is that, by giving for the cause of defence, which is the point in this sura, or even by participating in the defence, they expose themselves to poverty, physical harm or even death. In one Hadith, the Prophet said: '[Excessive concern for] children engender[s] cowardice and miserliness.'[30]

The Qur'an addresses people's fears by stating:

No misfortune can happen, either in the earth or in yourselves, that was not set down in writing before We brought it into being – that is easy for God – so you need not grieve for what you miss or be overjoyed by what you gain.

Q. 57:22–3

This is an explicit statement that everyone's term of life, fortune or misfortune, are ordained in the knowledge of God and there is no escape from them, so fear of death, poverty or misfortune should not be used as a pretext for disobeying God. Quite clearly there were some in the community who tried to dissuade others from giving:[31] '*God does not love the conceited, the boastful, those who are miserly and who tell other people to be miserly. If anyone turns away, remember that God is self-sufficient and worthy of praise*' (Q. 57:24). Their behaviour was particularly objectionable because giving, here, was for the benefit of the struggle to defend the Muslim cause, as is clear from

Q. 57:10 above ('*those who gave and fought before the victory are not like others: they are greater in rank than those who gave and fought afterwards*'). In particular, giving here refers to both material wealth and the self in support of the Muslim community in battle, which also follows from the general principle that *jihād* in the Qur'an is normally presented in the form of '*struggle [first] with your possessions and [then] yourselves*' (*bi-amwālikum wa-anfusikum*).[32] At the time of the revelation of these verses, there was no standing army per se and no defence budget as organised by any state to defend itself. It was expected that the believers would respond to the call to arms voluntarily, or if they could not fight themselves, provide the financial means for those who were physically able but financially embarrassed, hence the Prophetic Hadith, 'Anyone who equips someone going on the campaign will himself be considered as a campaigner'[33] (*man jahhaza ghāziyan fa-qad ghazā*).

Persuasion to give and contribute to the Muslim cause has, thus, in Q. 57, so far been conducted to appeal to those who believe in the message sent to Muhammad and the teachings within that message. This having been completed in the way we have seen, the sura moves on to widen the basis of its persuasion, this time by referring to the message of all previous prophets:

> *We sent Our messengers with clear signs, the Scripture and the Balance, so that people could uphold justice: We also sent iron, with its mighty strength and many uses for mankind, so that God could mark out those who would secretly help Him and His Messengers. Truly God is powerful, almighty.*
>
> Q. 57:25[34]

Thus, what the believers in Muhammad's message are required to do is brought into the realm of history. It is made clear that the preceding scriptures had the same objective, that is, the achievement of justice, and that iron '*with its mighty strength*' was sent down, like the Scripture and the Scale of Justice, so that God '*could mark out those who would secretly help Him and His Messengers*'.[35] Those who do not give and obey the teachings in the sura are shown to have abandoned the cause of God and His Messenger. Citing obligations brought by earlier messages is another technique by which the Qur'an presents and justifies its teachings,[36] and in this light the believers are now told that the message that was sent down to them through Muhammad is a continuation to a long line of prior messages:

> *We sent Noah and Abraham, and gave prophethood and scripture to their offspring: among them there were some who were rightly guided, but many were lawbreakers. We sent other*

messengers to follow in their footsteps. After those We sent Jesus, son of Mary: We gave him the Gospel and put compassion and mercy into the hearts of his followers. But monasticism was something they invented – We did not ordain it for them, only that they should seek God's pleasure – and even so, they did not observe it properly. So We gave a reward to those of them who believed, but many of them were lawbreakers.

Q. 57:26–7

All this reinforces the admonition addressed to the believers in Muhammad's message to listen and obey the request to give. If, as it says in verse 27, some Christians have opted for excessive spirituality, this is not the example to be followed because God has not ordained it; what He has ordained for all the messengers and their followers is made clear in verses 25 and 27, that they should uphold justice and seek God's pleasure. References to those who are '*rightly guided*' and the many '*who broke the law of earlier messages*' (verses 16 and 22) urge the believers in Muhammad's message to obey in order to be of the first category.

As the sura approaches its end we find verse 28 summarising:

Believers, be mindful of God and have faith in His Messenger: He will give you a double share of His mercy; He will provide a light to help you walk; He will forgive you – God is most forgiving, most merciful.

The believers are requested once again to believe truly in God and His Messenger and are again promised double rewards (as in verse 11), light (as in verses 12 and 19) and forgiveness. The final verse of the sura, Q. 57:29, '*The People of the Book should know that they have no power over any of God's bounty and that bounty is in the hand of God alone: He gives it to whoever He will. God's grace is truly immense*', emphasises to the believers that He has given them the grace of a prophet and a message (as in verse 9). Even if some People of the Book have claimed that prophethood and grace was confined to them, they do not control or limit God's bounty, rather He gives it to whoever He will and He has given it now to the believers in Muhammad's message.[37] Therefore they should listen, obey, give and contribute as they are instructed to do. By giving, they could hope to receive some of God's immense bounty.

Conclusion

From the brief reading undertaken in this section, it has hopefully been demonstrated that, from the first word, which glorifies God, to the last, which extols His bounty, the various verses which make up *Sūrat al-Ḥadīd* move logically from beginning to end in an organic flow, cemented, as has been seen, by repetition of many verbal elements reverberating in the sura. There is nothing alien or fragmented, irrelevant or forced. None of the constituent elements – be it glorification, argumentation, reference to the hereafter, rewards and punishments or prophetic history – stand in isolation. Rather, all are connected in an appeal to the heart and the mind, elsewhere expressed through '*a Scripture that is consistent and draws comparisons; that causes the skins of those in awe of their Lord to shiver [so that] their skins and hearts soften at the mention of God*' (Q. 20:23). It is this kind of appeal, with all its interconnected elements, that is the soul of the Qur'an, intended to move believers into action.

This analysis of *Sūrat al-Ḥadīd* has also made clear that Bell's and Jones's discussions on dating and labelling do not help readers to see the crucial point of this sura. Particularly, they do not take into account understanding the text on its own terms. This includes intratextuality and what al-Rāzī[38] calls *ādāt al-kitāb al-'azīz* ('the habits of the mighty book'), exemplified here in discussing the glorification passage in this sura and how it leads to the following material. The text must be read closely, without prior assumptions that it is disconnected, in order to understand its meaning.

It is, therefore, necessary to pay regard to certain highlights. For instance, in the glorification passage there is particular emphasis on God's knowledge (verse 4), which foreshadows His knowledge of those who will not obey the order to spend (verse 10) and also of those who are miserly and instruct others to be miserly (verse 24). It is also necessary to pay regard to the recurrence of other particular words and phrases in the sura, for example, those who '*lend God a good loan*' (verses 11 and 18). The word *nūr* ('light') occurs six times in the sura (verses 9, 12, 13 twice, 19 and 28) which helps bind the text together. There is also repetition of 'Why should you not...?' in verses 9 and 10, echoed in verse 16.

A very important principle in understanding the text is to realise that the Qur'an answers and comments on assumptions not stated: a whole book could be written on this. Verse 20 actually answers the assumption that people's enjoyment of this life is long lasting and therefore they should not part with their money. Verses 22 and 23 reply to the assumption that spending and participating in *jihād* may result in loss, and should therefore be discouraged: it states that every loss, if it happens, is already recorded in God's book and therefore unavoidable. Reference to the People of the Book (verses 25–7) answers the unspoken question, 'Why should Muslims only be tasked with this?' Similarly, when telling the believers, '*fasting is prescribed for you*' (Q. 2:183), the Qur'an says, '*as it was prescribed for those before you*'. Each of these answers is presented without actually stating the original assumptions. This is part of the Qur'an's well known feature of conciseness. Any such instance should be understood as a reply and as fitting into its allotted place in the structure of the sura.

Another important element is to understand the meaning of certain terms in the Qur'an and to cross reference them to other parts of the Qur'an. For example, *faḍl Allāh* ('God's bounty'), which occurs three times in the final verse (verse 29), here refers to the prophethood of Muhammad, as has been pointed out earlier. Stating that the People of the Book resented the notion of Muhammad being given prophethood, acts as a further incentive for the Muslims to obey the teachings he was sent with: '*It is He who has sent down clear revelations to His servant, so that He may bring you from the depths of darkness into light: God is clearly kind and merciful to you*' (Q. 57:9). This verse urges them to spend, which is the core of the sura. The intention of the Qur'an as a book of guidance leading to action should not be ignored when analysing or interpreting it. The text of the sura is vibrant. Note the dynamic exchange between the people of Paradise and those of Hell, and the image of the fleeting world in verse 20. Particularly powerful at the beginning of the sura is the long list of God's attributes (verses 1–6). The sura uses *jumal inshā'iyya* (initiation sentences) that address the audience and engage them, rather than speaking in the abstract or above their heads. It orders: '*believe*' and '*give*' (verse 7), '*bear in mind*' (verses 17 and 20) as well as '*race*' (verse 21). It questions: '*Why should you not...?*' (verses 8 and 10), '*Who will give God a loan?*' (verse 11) and '*Is it not time for the believers to...?*' (verse 16). It repeats certain phrases and words, speaking three times of '*doubling rewards*' (verses 11, 18 and 28) and '*light*' is mentioned five times (verses 9, 12, 13, 19 and 28). God's sending of prophets is referred to repeatedly: '*We have sent Our messengers...*', '*We sent Noah and Abraham*', '*We sent messengers to follow them*' and '*We sent Jesus*' (verses 25–7). God's '*great reward*' (verse 7) and '*generous rewards*' (verse 11) for those who follow the message appear alongside mentions of '*the great triumph*' (verse 12) and '*God's bounty*' (for example, verses 21 and 29). This whole array of linguistic and stylistic tools is used to impress the message on the hearts and minds of the audience.

Whatever Bell, Jones and others may surmise about dating and that a verse was originally somewhere else, the sura itself still stands inescapably as it is. This is the text of the Qur'an and it explains itself and its own structure.

Sūrat Yā Sīn (Q. 36): 'The Core of the Qur'an'

In the Muslim tradition there are certain parts of the Qur'an that are seen in popular Muslim culture to have particular potency when recited on specific occasions. Among these are the *Fātiḥa* (Q. 1), the 'Throne Verse' (Q. 2:255), *Sūrat Yā Sīn* (Q. 36) and the last three short suras of the Qur'an: *Sūrat al-Ikhlāṣ* (Q. 112), *Sūrat al-Falaq* (Q. 113) and *Sūrat al-Nās* (Q. 114). *Yā Sīn* is the longest of these, and the Prophet dubbed it 'the core of the Qur'an'.[39] In this section, we will study *Yā Sīn* in detail, concentrating on its theme, style and structure, all of which require close examination in the light of some controversial views expressed about this sura.[40] This section ends by addressing the significance of *Sūrat Yā Sīn* in Islamic society in general.

Theme

In the face of persistent denial by the disbelievers of Mecca that the Qur'an was a divine revelation warning them about the Resurrection and Judgement, and of their claim that Muhammad was merely a poet, in *Sūrat Yā Sīn* the Qur'an comforts the Prophet, affirms the divinity of the revelation and exonerates him of any responsibility for their continued disbelief after all his warnings. 'Warning' here means, above all, warning of resurrection and judgement after death (e.g. in Q. 5:51, Q. 4:30, Q. 19:39, Q. 39:71, Q. 40:15, Q. 42:7 and Q. 67:8–9). Following the initial introduction, *Sūrat Yā Sīn* affirms, in various ways, the Resurrection and Judgement. The key to this sura lies in its opening lines, beginning with the words '*By the decisive Qur'an, you [Muhammad] are truly one of the messengers*' (*wa'l-Qur'āni'l-ḥakīmi innaka la-mina'l-mursalīn*) (Q. 36:2–3),[41] where we have a divine oath, followed by a strongly emphatic structure (combining the particles '*inna*' and '*la*'), that 'you' (Muhammad) are one of the messengers. This is an example that illustrates the concise style of the Qur'an. It uses such linguistic tools as emphasis, negation and restriction to counter an unstated but implied claim, in this case that Muhammad is a poet and the Qur'an is poetry, not a divine revelation sent to the Messenger to warn of the Resurrection and Judgement. The implied claim here becomes explicit later in verses 69–70. It is essential to pay due regard to the significance of this beginning, countering an implied claim of the disbelievers, in order to appreciate the objective, structure and impact of *Sūrat Yā Sīn.*

The Meccan Qur'an deals repeatedly with the most fundamental beliefs of Islam – the unity of God, the prophethood of Muhammad and the Resurrection – all of which were difficult for the first Arab recipients to accept. The Resurrection in fact presented the greatest obstacle, as they found it the most difficult of these three claims to substantiate. Although the pre-Islamic Arabs were idolaters, they still believed that their idols were only intercessors for them with God, who they accepted as the only one who could create and provide for His creation.[42] It was possible to argue for the prophethood of Muhammad by referring to earlier prophets, such as Moses and Abraham, whom the Arabs knew of and did not seem to contest. The Resurrection, on the other hand, could not be proved on request. The Qur'an quotes them as repeatedly saying: '*What? When we are turned to bones and dust, shall we really be raised up in a new act of creation?*' (Q. 17:49). They also ask: '*Shall we show you a man who claims that when you have been utterly torn to pieces you will be raised in a new creation? Has he invented a lie about God? Is he mad?*' (Q. 34:7–8).

The words that keep recurring in their argument are *iẓām* ('*bones*'), *ramīm* ('*decayed*'), *rufāt* ('*small pieces*') and *turāb* ('*dust*'). They found the claim of resurrecting such substances '*a strange thing*' (*shay'un 'ajīb*, Q. 50:2). They saw difficulty in the scattered bones being put together again ('*Does man think We shall not put his bones back together?*', Q. 75:3). Another perceived difficulty was that these scattered remains would have disappeared into the earth ('*What? When we have disappeared into the earth, shall we really be created anew?*', Q. 32:10; '*To come back [to life] after we have died and become dust? That is too far-fetched*', Q. 50:3).[43] The claim that puzzled these non-believers even more related to the resurrection of the long-dead. Even if it were possible to raise the dead, their ancient forefathers had been buried so long that it would seem even more far-fetched to imagine they would be included in the Resurrection: '*When we have become dust and bones, shall we be raised up? And our earliest forefathers too?*' (Q. 56:47–8). They wanted a conclusive proof, evidence on the spot: '*Bring back our forefathers if what you say is true!*' (Q. 45:25). They wanted to know when the Resurrection would be and even challenged the Prophet to hasten it: '*They ask you to hasten the punishment*' (*yasta'jilūnaka bi'l-'adhāb*, Q. 29:53–4; see also Q. 36:48, Q. 51:12 and Q. 79:42).

The set of vocabulary used by the disbelievers in the verses cited above relate to the human body and its decay. The Qur'an, however, uses another set of vocabulary which relates to bodily resurrection. This includes *ba'th* ('raising of the dead'), *qiyāma* ('rising'), *nushūr* ('rising'), *khurūj* ('emerging from the grave'), *khalq jadīd* ('new creation'), *i'āda* ('bringing back'), *ma'ād* ('returning'), *al-nash'a al-ākhira* ('the second creation', as opposed to *al-nash'a al-ūlā*, 'the first creation'). This vocabulary is the direct opposite of the vocabulary of death and decay which made the Resurrection incredible to the disbelievers. As will be seen, in *Sūrat Yā Sīn* the Qur'an argues on different bases in order to counter the various arguments in the minds of the disbelievers. In fact, *Yā Sīn* brings together forcefully all the Qur'anic arguments for Resurrection. In essence it is the sum of Resurrection.

Structure

Richard Bell comments[44] that *Sūrat Yā Sīn* 'shows puzzling breaks in connection which render it difficult to give a satisfactory account of its composition'.[45] In his first short (11-line) paragraph, we find that he makes, as is his norm, five assumptions – expressed through 'maybe', 'perhaps', 'later this was displaced by' and on two occasions 'on the back of' – without giving any evidence or basis for these assumptions. However, examination of the functions of the initial oath and emphasis, as well as clear analysis of the actual arrangement of the subsequent material will give a different picture.

More recently, Alan Jones, after remarks about dating verses, states that 'some Muslim authorities take verse 12 [...] to be Medinan. The situation appears to be somewhat more complex with the sura having grown over a period.' Such speculation does not help in understanding the sura. He then remarks that 'the Sura divides into five main sections: a warning passage (1–12), a punishment parable (13–29), and a piece on God's signs (33–44), an eschatological passage (48–68) and a mixed narration (69–83). The sura contains two brief bridge-passages (30–32 and 45–47) which have been found troublesome by the commentators.'[46] Such analysis merely labels things, not always correctly, without exploring functions. Close analysis of the text will show that these remarks do not fully correspond to the actual structure of the sura or the functions of its various parts.

Yā Sīn is a Meccan sura, consisting of 83 verses. Its main theme is the Resurrection, while also providing confirmation of the prophethood of

Muhammad and a denunciation of the disbelievers' ingratitude to God. Structurally, it consists of seven sections as follows:

1. Verses 1–12 counter the unstated claim of disbelievers, confirm the divine origin of the Qur'an and the mission of Muhammad, clear him of blame for the disbelievers' obstinate rejection and give good news to the believers.[47] Verses 13–32 continue this by giving an example from past disbelievers to support the Prophet still further and warn the disbelievers who have derided their Prophet.
2. Verses 33–48 argue from natural phenomena for the reality of the Resurrection (evoking such images as the revival of the earth to bring forth grain), ending with God's mercy towards the disbelievers when they are in distress, whereas, if He wished, He could destroy them. Yet, they show ingratitude and mock the Resurrection, retorting, '*When will it come, if you are telling the truth?*'
3. Verses 49–65 reply to this question with a description of some of the rewards and punishments the Resurrection will bring.
4. Verses 66–8 come back to life in this world, resuming the warning, '*If we wish*' (in verse 44) with a series of warnings starting with '*If We wish*', including taking away their sight and paralysing them for their ingratitude. It highlights the effect of old age and thus acts as a real caution, not just a figure of speech as in verses 7–10.
5. Verses 69–70 deny the claim implied here and in verses 3–6, but made explicit elsewhere (for example, in Q. 21:5, Q. 26:192 and 224, Q. 51:30 and Q. 69:40–1), that what Muhammad is saying (i.e. the verses of the Qur'an he recites) is poetry.
6. Verses 71–6 provide another argument from nature, specifically animals, to show the disbelievers' ingratitude and the futility of their idols, asking the Prophet not to grieve at what they say: God knows and will deal with them.
7. Verses 77–83 are a detailed logical refutation (after previously having given 'signs' to ponder over), of the disbelievers' arguments against the Resurrection, ending with glorification of the all-powerful God to whom they will all return.

We will now deal with these sections in greater detail.

Verses 1–32

As mentioned earlier, the Qur'an exploits the linguistic tools of oath and emphasis at the beginning of the sura, in verses 2–3, to act as a retort to the disbelievers' implied denial of Muhammad's prophethood: '*By the decisive Qur'an, you are indeed one of the messengers.*' The Qur'an is mentioned as decisive proof of Muhammad's prophethood, thus the Qur'an is not the speech of a poet (see also Q. 69:38–41 where the same point is defended).[48] Such emphasis is employed to counteract denial, in which case one, two or three elements of emphasis are used in proportion to the degree of denial.[49] The Arabic language is recognised as the language of *ḥurūf al-ma'ānī*, that is, of articles and particles that express concepts. Thus, certainty is expressed by the particle '*inna*', rather than, as in English, using a word like 'certainly' or 'indeed'. Such features make the Qur'an concise, but to avoid misunderstanding it is essential to be aware of the full meaning of each particle and the implications of using it. The above examples are both retorts to implied assertions, just as the statement of faith, *lā ilāha illā'llāh,* is a retort to those who claim there are other deities.

This strong beginning reassures the Prophet, as God addresses him and affirms that he is on a straight path (*ṣirāṭ mustaqīm,* Q. 36:4 and 61). In verses 7–10 God affirms that the obduracy of the disbelievers is not the result of any failure on his part; he cannot do anything about it since they had not received any previous messenger, and God has sealed their vision so that they cannot see the straight path:

> *The verdict has been passed against most of them, for they refuse to believe. [It is as if] We have placed [iron] collars around their necks, right up to their chins, so that their heads are forced up, and set barriers before and behind them, blocking their vision: they cannot see. It is all the same to them whether you warn them or not: they will not believe.*
>
> Q. 36:7–10

This is not a warning, as Jones seems to take it,[50] but a figure of speech, exonerating the Prophet from any responsibility or blame on this count; the actual warning comes later (verses 65–8). Muhammad is told that he can only usefully warn those who believe and that he should give them good news.[51] This is similar to Q. 51:54–5, '*Turn away from them [Prophet] – you are not to blame – and go on reminding: reminding will benefit the believers.*' God then affirms, in the first person plural of majesty, that He will bring everyone back to life and is recording all their deeds (verse 11, '*Give such people the glad news of forgiveness and a noble reward*'; see also verses 49 ff.). This reward, we are told in the following verse, will be from God Himself, not from the Prophet: '*We shall certainly bring the dead back to life, and We record what they send ahead of them as well as what they leave behind: We keep an account of everything in a clear Record*' (Q. 36:12).

In verses 13–32 the Prophet is directed to cite an example of a town to whom not just one but three messengers had been sent, all of whom were rejected, mocked and threatened with stoning by the disbelieving populace. The townsfolk denied that God had sent these messengers just as the Meccans denied that Muhammad was sent. However, one man believed, and argued with his people:[52]

He said, 'My people, follow the messengers. Follow them: they are not asking you to reward them and they are rightly guided. Why should I not worship the One who created me. It is to Him that you shall be returned. How could I take beside Him any other gods, whose intercession will not help me and who would not be able to save me if the Lord of Mercy wished to harm me?'

Q. 36:20–3

They still did not believe and were punished for it, but the man who did believe was honoured by God (verse 27). This example supports Muhammad, and the closing comments also reassure him, confirming that human nature has always been the same, in the story of that town and in his own time; he is not to blame and should not grieve at what the Meccan disbelievers have been saying:

Alas, for human beings! Whenever a messenger comes to them, they ridicule him. Do they not see how many generations We have destroyed before them, none of whom will ever come back to them? [Yet] all of them will be brought before Us.

Q. 36:30–2

The phrase '*all of them will be brought before Us*' heralds the ensuing arguments for the Resurrection.

Verses 33:48

A series of three 'signs' shows the disbelievers God's power and grace and His ability to bring about life from the lifeless in this world and, consequently, His ability to bring about the Resurrection. The first (Q. 36:33–6; see also verse 73) is taken from agriculture, for which the disbelievers should be thankful:

There is a sign for them in the lifeless earth: We give it life and We produce grain from it for them to eat; We have put gardens of date-palms and grapes in the earth, and we have made springs of water gush out of it, so that they could eat its fruit. It was not their own hands that made all this. How can they not give thanks? Glory be to Him who created all the pairs of things that the earth produces, as well as themselves and other things they do not know about.

This type of sign recurs frequently in the Qur'an (e.g. in Q. 22:5–6 and Q. 50:7–11). It is noted that life comes from its opposite, the dead land.

The second sign is the phenomenon of night and day found in Q. 36:37–40:

The night is also a sign for them: We strip the daylight from it, and – lo and behold! – they are in darkness. The sun, too, runs its course: this is determined by the Almighty, the All Knowing and We have determined phases for the moon until finally it becomes like an old date-stalk. The sun cannot overtake the moon nor can the night outrun the day: each floats in [its own] orbit.

God's power created and continually manages these celestial objects in perfect order, alternating like life and death, and in phases like the phases of human life. Compare verse 39, about the phases of the moon, to verse 68, that says, '*If We extend anyone's life, We reverse his development. Do they not use their reason?*'[53] The perfect order of sun and moon, night and day, is also used as a sign, proof or image of the Resurrection in other parts of the Qur'an, for example in Q. 10:5–7 and Q. 13:2. Again it is noted that something comes from its opposite: night from day, darkness from light.

The third sign mentioned in this sura is that of Noah's ark, in which God '*carried their [human] seed*' (Q. 36:41). He also gives them similar ships to ride in. Again, we see opposites, here of something heavy that does not sink: '*If We wish, We can drown them, and there is no one to help them: they cannot be saved. Only by Our mercy can they be reprieved to enjoy life for a while*' (Q. 36:42–4).

The image of the ship recurs frequently in the Qur'an (e.g. see Q. 17:66–7, Q. 31:21–2 and Q. 42:32–4). Not only does this image illustrate God's power and grace in saving people (compare verse 23), but also His ability to drown them, if He wills. In the Qur'anic way of presenting its material, the grace of saving people should be met with gratitude, but some people may not show thanks (see Q. 10:23–4 and Q. 17:66–70). In *Yā Sīn*, the failure to show gratitude is mentioned as well: '*When they are told, "Beware of what lies before and behind you, so that you may be given mercy," they ignore [literally: turn their backs on] every single sign that comes to them from their Lord*' (Q. 36:45).

In verses 45–8 the disbelievers show their ingratitude by rejecting the call to beware of what is in store for them and by deriding the call to give in charity from what God has given them (compare verse 21), saying, '*Why should we feed those that God could feed if He wanted? You must be deeply misguided.*' In verse 48, they also show ingratitude by mocking the Resurrection, asking, '*When will this promise be fulfilled, if what you say is true?*'

Verses 49–65

The answer comes immediately: '*But all they are waiting for is a single blast that will overtake them while they are still arguing with each other*' (verses 49–50). As they ask, 'When will this promise be fulfilled?', the original pattern of signs used as arguments is suspended to show them what will happen to them when the Judgement comes.

Verses 51–65 comprise a lengthy passage describing the Resurrection, the Judgement and the fates of the believers and the disbelievers,[54] ending with the disbelievers being told:

> *'Children of Adam, did I not command you not to serve Satan, for he was your sworn enemy, but to serve Me. This is the straight path. He has led great numbers of you astray. Did you not use your reason? So this is the Fire that you were warned against. Suffer it today because you went on ignoring [My commands].' Today We seal up their mouths, but their hands speak to Us and their feet bear witness to everything they have done.*
>
> Q. 36:60–5

The reply to the disbelievers' question about the time of the Resurrection suspends the expected arrangement of Qur'anic material. Deliverance from peril at sea should be met with gratitude. When this does not come, the disbelievers are sternly threatened that God could, if He wished, expose them to other dangers (Q. 17:66–9, Q. 10:22–4 and Q. 31:31–2).[55]

Verses 66–8

The Qur'an resumes the subject that was suspended by the description of the Resurrection and threatens that in return for the disbelievers' ingratitude, God could, even in this world, take away their sight and paralyse them:[56]

> *If We will, We take away their sight. They struggle to find the path, but how can they see it? If We will, We paralyse them where they stand, so that they cannot move forward or backward. If We extend anyone's life, We reverse his development. Do they not use their reason?*

This is the real caution, as opposed to the figure of speech in verses 7–10, a passage which describes the disbelievers' state of denial. What we have here is not an immediate threat; the clause *wa-law nashā'u* ('*if We will*') at the beginning of the passage is introduced by '*law*', which the grammarians call *ḥarf imtināʿ li-imtināʿ* ('a particle of one thing not happening because another thing has not happened'): these things have not happened (to them) because God has not willed it. This echoes the description, in verse 5, of God, who sent the Qur'an, as being the Almighty, the Merciful. The disbelievers can see for themselves how God is able to reverse human development in old age, so He can take their sight or paralyse them, though in His mercy He does not.

Verses 69–70

These verses confirm that the Qur'an is not mere poetic illustration on the part of the Prophet, as alleged by the disbelievers who claimed he was a poet,[57] but '*a revelation, an illuminating Qur'an to warn anyone who is truly alive, so that God's verdict may be passed against the disbelievers*' (Q. 36:70). This echoes verses 7 ('*The verdict has been passed...*') and 11 ('*You can warn only those who follow the Qur'an and hold the Merciful One in awe...*').

Verses 71–6

This next section returns to recounting the signs of God's power and grace to be found in nature, this time in His creation of animals and domesticating them for the benefit of humans: '*among the things made by Our hands, We have created livestock they control, and made them [the animals] obedient, so that some can be used for riding, some for food, some for other benefits, and some for drink. Will they not give thanks?*' (Q. 36:71–3). The mention of '*Our hands*' here echoes verse 35, '*It was not their own hands that made all this. How can they not give thanks?*' In verses 33, 37 and 41, the introductory expression '*There is a sign for them in...*' is used, and in 46, '*They turn their backs to every sign that comes to them*'. In this section, in verses 71 and 77, the introductory phrases are '*Can they not see?*' and '*Can man not see?*', which echo verses 9 ('*...they cannot see*') and 66 ('*If We will, We take away their sight...*'). Instead of thanking God for these gifts, however, the disbelievers worship false gods that have no power to help them: '*Yet they have taken other gods beside God to help them, though these could not do so even if they called a whole army of them together!*' (Q. 36:74–5). Here the disbelievers are shown to be ungrateful and senseless.[58]

The link here between animals and idolatry is clarified by reference to Q. 6:136, in which the idolaters allocate some of the animals God has given them to other gods. They worship these gods, thinking they will help them, but they cannot, and will indeed be used against them on the Day of

Resurrection. The sura next returns to consoling the Prophet in verse 76, '*So [Prophet], do not be distressed at what they say: We know what they conceal and what they reveal.*' In the style of the Qur'an, this 'knowledge' entails judgement in the future (e.g. Q. 6:59–60, Q. 31:24 and Q. 34:2–5). Here again we find opposites: God's grace is met with ingratitude, while the disbelievers worship idols that cannot benefit or harm them and will be witnesses against them.

Verses 77–83

This final section contains a series of arguments, based not on signs but on logical answers to man's arguments, that prove God's ability to raise the dead. It begins, echoing the 'sight/blindness' metaphor used earlier in the sura:

Can man not see that We created him from a drop of fluid? Yet – lo and behold! – he disputes openly, producing arguments against Us, forgetting his own creation. He says, 'Who can give life back to bones after they have decayed?' Say, 'He who created them in the first place will give them life again: He has full knowledge of every act of creation'.

Q. 36:77–9

So, having done something once will make it less difficult to do it again: '*It is He who produces fire for you out of the green tree – lo and behold! – and from this you kindle fire*' (Q. 36:80–1). Creating something from its opposite, such as fire from green trees, is possible and can be perceived by the senses. It is possible, therefore, that life will pulsate again in a body that is disintegrated and lifeless.[59] Here again things are made from their opposites:

Is He who created the heavens and earth not able to create the likes of these people? Of course He is! He is the All Knowing Creator: when He wills something to be, His way is to say, 'Be' – and it is!

Q. 36:81–2

The creation of man, or bringing him to life again after death, is easier than creating the universe (which is far greater than a human being), when it was not there in the first instance.[60] This argument challenges the disbelievers of Muhammad's time who did acknowledge that God created the heavens and the earth, but could not conceive how He could 'create humans anew' after their death. Creation (or any other form of activity, however great the object may be) does not require any substance or time on the part of God, the Originator. Herein lies a contrast with the activity of human beings, which takes time for fulfilment and requires a given substance that can be worked on.[61]

The final verse of the sura, '*So glory be to Him in whose Hand lies control over all things. It is to Him that you will all be brought back*' (Q. 36:83), glorifies God above any notions the disbelievers might have about Him that He is unable to bring about the Resurrection. It puts all power in His hand and confirms that they will be taken back to Him (compare verse 22).

Alan Jones considers these verses 69–83 to be a 'mixed peroration about Muhammad to Muhammad also including sign passages that might originally have formed part of the third section.'[62] However, the disbelievers' claim that Muhammad was a poet is not a peroration, but the central claim, which the Qur'an refutes right from the beginning of *Yā Sīn*. The only part that could mistakenly be seen as a peroration is the final verse of the sura; however, the whole of *Sūrat Yā Sīn* addresses the Resurrection. It begins with God sending the Prophet to warn about the Resurrection and ends with the return to God on the Day of Resurrection. Jones's claim that the signs at the end might originally have been part of the third section does not fit with the overall structure, nor with the functions of the different sections. The pattern was suspended after the ship to show their ingratitude and their audacity at mocking the Resurrection with their questions. The answer entails description of what will happen when it comes. Verses 70–6 are a rebuttal of their *shirk* (polytheism) and is different from the material in what we have here identified as the third section. Verses 76–82 are a final, logical, silencing conclusion to the sura, ending with '*To Him you will be brought back*'. This is the whole point of *Yā Sīn* and could not originally have been part of the third section.

From the above discussion, the structure can be seen to be well-knit and the different sections follow each other in a clear way. This is made even more cohesive by a number of verbal connections. Some of these have already been mentioned, but more are listed here:

1. *Nuḥyi'l-mawtā* ('*We give life to the dead*') in verse 12 can be seen to be mirrored in verse 78, *yuḥyi'l-'iẓām* ('*who can give life to the bones?*').
2. Repetition of 'other gods', in verses 23–4, '*How could I take besides Him any other gods whose intercession would not help me and who would not be able to save me if the Lord of Mercy wished to harm me? Then I would clearly be in the wrong*', and in verses 74–5, '*Yet they have taken other gods beside God to*

help them, though these could not do so, even if they called a whole army of them together'.

3. Repetition of words from the root *ḍ-l-l*: in verse 24, the believer says, '*Then I would clearly be in the wrong*' (*innī idhan la-fī ḍalālin mubīn*); in verse 47, the disbelievers address the believers saying, '*You are clearly deeply misguided*' (*fī ḍalālin mubīn*); and in verse 62, God says, '*[Satan] has led astray (aḍalla) great numbers of you. Did you not use your reason?*'.
4. Repetition of the word 'blast' (*ṣayḥa*): in verse 29, '*there was just one blast (ṣayḥatan wāḥidatan), and [the people of the town] fell down lifeless*'; in verse 49, '*But all they are waiting for is a single blast (ṣayḥatan wāḥidatan) that will overtake them while they are still arguing with each other [...] They will say, "Alas for us! Who has resurrected us from our resting places?"*'; in verse 53, '*It was just one single blast (ṣayḥatan wāḥidatan) and then – lo and behold! – they were all brought before Us.*'.
5. Another kind of non-verbal, thematic echo can be seen in verse 30, '*Alas for human beings! Whenever a messenger comes to them they ridicule him*', and in verse 46, '*they ignore every single sign that comes to them from their Lord*'.

Such echoes contribute to the cohesion of the whole sura in words, structure and meaning, making it all the more surprising that Bell thought it 'difficult to give a satisfactory account of its composition'.[63]

Style

Sūrat Yā Sīn displays a number of stylistic elements characteristic of the Qur'an. One such feature is the omission of details that are not necessary for the particular context in favour of concentrating on the message. Hence in Q. 36:13–14, '*Give them the example of the people to whose town messengers came. We sent two messengers but they rejected both. Then We reinforced them with a third*', the town is not named, nor are the three messengers, nor the believing man (mentioned later in the account, in verse 20) who came from the other side of the town to support the messengers.[64] The Qur'an is only interested in the lessons that can be drawn, and this is clear from the way the story is told here, without loading them with extra details. This is the normal practice of the Qur'an.[65] Akin to this is the fact that the sura does not begin by stating the disbelievers' claim that Muhammad was a poet, but goes straight in to refute this claim using an oath and emphasis, as explained earlier.

The Qur'an's central aim is to guide (stated, for example, in Q. 2:2 and Q. 17:9–10). It is a passionate text that seeks to win people over. As we will now discuss, it argues from history, the future, nature and logic for *targhīb* and *tarhīb* ('persuasion' and 'dissuasion').

The Qur'an's use of logic to argue its case has been addressed above during the discussion of Q. 36:77–83. *Sūrat Yā Sīn* can also clearly be seen to argue from history in the initial section, in which it tells the Prophet to remind the disbelievers about the people of a town who mocked their messengers, denied the message and killed the one man who argued on the side of the messengers. It also brings to the attention of the Prophet that here was a town to which three messengers were sent, plus a supporter. So, given that the people of this town rejected them all, it is not surprising if the people of Mecca reject a single messenger like himself. The mention of three messengers at this time suggests that the Prophet must have been saddened at being rejected by his own people. (Other references to the Prophet's sadness at being rejected can be found in *Sūrat al-An'ām* (Q. 6:35–6), *Sūrat al-Kahf* (Q. 18:6), *Sūrat Ṭa Ha* (Q. 20:2 ff.) and in *Sūrat Yā Sīn* in verse 76.)

Likewise, in the description of the Resurrection, Judgement and the abodes of the believers and disbelievers in verses 49–83 the Qur'an argues through its depiction of the future.

In verses 33–6, the Qur'an argues from nature when it uses the example of agriculture and the regeneration of life to show God's power and urges the disbelievers to be thankful for His bounty.

In verses 37–40, the Qur'an shows God's power to order the universe and also to move such important celestial bodies from one stage to another:

The night is also a sign for them: We strip the daylight from it, and – lo and behold! – they are in darkness. The sun, too, runs its determined course laid down for it by the Almighty, the All Knowing. We have determined phases for the moon until finally it becomes like an old date-stalk. The sun cannot overtake the moon, nor can the night outrun the day: each floats in [its own] orbit.

Ships, in this sura, are also shown to be under God's control, His being the power to keep them afloat, to move them or to sink them. This is an idea which is repeated many times in the Qur'an:[66]

Another sign for them is that We carried their seed in the laden Ark, and We have made similar things for them to ride in. If We wish, We can drown them, and there is no one to help them: they cannot be saved. Only by Our mercy can they be reprieved to enjoy life for a while.

Q. 36:41–4

As has been seen earlier, an essential feature of style in *Yā Sīn* is that in the deep structure of the sura runs the creation of things from their opposites, which is very fitting for a sura that came to counteract disbelievers' incredulity that life could come again to bones after they have decayed.

The Core of the Qur'an

We can now ask why the Prophet called *Sūrat Yā Sīn* 'the core of the Qur'an'. This undoubtedly relates to the fact that it focuses on the heart of the Islamic faith, that is, belief in the One God, the sole Creator and Controller of everything, who sends scriptures to messengers He chooses and to warn of the Resurrection when everyone will return for Judgement.

The unity of God is made clear in the sura using descriptions of all His signs and actions, which demonstrate His power, contrasted with the total lack of power of those they take as gods beside Him (verses 74–5). However, *Sūrat Yā Sīn* focuses on the Resurrection because this is what the disbelievers rejected in particular and, because of this, rejected the Prophet who warned about it, calling him a poet and claiming that the Qur'an was mere poetry. This focus is made clear at both the beginning of the sura when Muhammad is told that he has been sent *li-tundhira qawman* ('*to warn a people*'), in verse 6, and in the reminder of the Resurrection in the final words of the sura, in verse 83, *wa-ilayhi turja'ūn* ('*to Him you will be brought back*').

Other suras mention all these things (e.g. *Sūrat al-Qiyāma* (Q. 75) to mention only one), yet they were not called 'the core of the Qur'an'. In *Yā Sīn* the description of the Resurrection – the longest in any one sura – is surrounded by a condensed collection of all the arguments found elsewhere in the Qur'an. *Yā Sīn* is about argument and counter-argument. The disbelievers argue and ask sarcastic questions: '*Why should we feed those that God could feed if He wanted?*' (verse 47), '*When will the Resurrection be if what you say is true?*' (verse 48), to which God retorts, finally, '*Today We seal up their mouths, but their hands speak to Us and their feet bear witness to everything they have done [...] Can they not use their reason?*' (Q. 36:65–7). From then on, it is God who asks the questions, until verses 77–8 that return to sum up the argument:

Can man not see that We created him from a drop of fluid? Yet – lo and behold! – he disputes openly, producing arguments against Us, forgetting his own creation. He says, 'Who can give life back to bones after they have decayed?'

The rest of the sura consists of God's logical answers to this question.

A marked feature of the Qur'an is the way it listens to all the arguments, accusations and abusive remarks about God, the Qur'an and the Prophet. It records them all and then deals with them. *Sūrat Yā Sīn* provides a good example of this feature.

The Prophet clearly loved *Yā Sīn,* as mentioned earlier, because it was a direct address to him from the beginning, emphasising his prophethood and the straight path sent from God, which he followed. His opponents are blind to this path, but it is not his fault. His situation is corroborated by the story of the previous messengers who preached the same ideas, to which good people testified. Then come the strong arguments for the Resurrection, which show the power and grace of God in His creation and the description of the rewards of those who follow the straight path, compared to the torment of the disbelievers. (It should be pointed out that the torment occupies no more than seven lines out of the 70 in the sura, and that the caution given by God in verses 66–7 is entirely hypothetical.) The Qur'an is confirmed, in *Yā Sīn,* to be truly a revelation from God and not poetry made up by the Prophet; therefore, he should not be saddened by what the disbelievers say. Idolatry is shown to be baseless, and idols, far from helping those who worship them, will indeed be a source of torment for them. The sura ends with logical arguments against the doubts in the minds of the disbelievers, glorifying God who is in control of all and to whom all will be returned.

Special Importance

As previously noted, the Prophet is reported to have said: 'Everything has a core and the core of the Qur'an is *Yā Sīn.*'[67] Because the Prophet dubbed *Yā Sīn* 'the core of the Qur'an', and because of its contents, outlined above, it appeals to the hearts of Muslims, both as individuals and communities. Throughout the Muslim world it has particular importance, both for the living and the dead. The living resort to it especially in times of distress and urgent need, in difficult circumstances and against oppressors, since it shows God's great power and grace, which they seek to invoke. I recall being told in my home village in Egypt about a teacher who feared one day that he was going to be sacked. The job was crucial to him and his family, so he sat for the whole weekend reading *Sūrat Yā Sīn,* and when he returned to work the situation had changed, and the threat dematerialised.

Numerous stories like this keep alive the potency attributed to the sura and the frequent resort to it. When going to meet someone you fear, it is customary for many to read verses 8–10, which refer to the caution that God could block their sight[68] and freeze them where they stand (verses 66–8) and the final affirmation in verse 82 that God is in control of everything: '*When He wills something to be, His way is to say, "Be" and it is.*' In this, as well as the examples of God's power shown in the 'sign passages' lies the potency attributed to *Yā Sīn*.

In Muslim countries there is a traditional practice called *'iddīyat Yā Sīn*: reading the sura 40 times. Forty is a significant number and the reading can be done by one individual or, more often, a group of people sharing the readings.[69] This is done in memory of the dead and to bless a house. When I visited Malaysia in 2006, I arrived at the house of an important official who had gathered a group of his friends to read *Yā Sīn* and I immediately joined in, as I recognised straight away what they were doing and why, from my experience in the Middle East. *'Iddīyat Yā Sīn* is also read in times of distress against oppressive leaders.

The Prophet is also reported to have said, 'Read *Yā Sīn* over your dead.'[70] Al-Rāzī suggests that for this reason it was recommended to read it for the dying person, at his head: 'At the time when his concentration is only on God, reading *Yā Sīn* will strengthen the person's heart and confirm the three Islamic beliefs: God, prophethood and the Resurrection.'[71] It will allow him to hope for the rewards that await the believers. In Egypt, for instance, Muslims read *Yā Sīn* at the grave after burial and, during seasonal visits to the grave after that, family and friends will bring a Qur'an reciter who will sit and read the sura at the graveside. Then the family will distribute food in charity. Because people are so grieved at death and feel that the deceased is lonely, facing God and the results of their past deeds in the world, and is thus in need of help and mercy, they resort to reading *Yā Sīn*, hoping it will bring comfort to the deceased. In Egyptian villages, the 40th day after burial is an important occasion and people gather and read *Yā Sīn*, preferably 40 people each reading it once so that the *'iddiyat Yā Sīn* is achieved in a short time.

Around this respect for *Sūrat Yā Sīn* more elaborate traditions have built up, such as those reported by al-Bayḍāwī in his statement of the merits of *Sūrat Yā Sīn* at the end of his exegesis of the sura.[72] These promise extravagant rewards for its recitation, including great numbers of angels attending the death, washing and burial of the deceased, and relief during the process of dying and afterwards.[73]

In short this sura is a mainstay for Muslims, for those living in need and for the deceased. In normal circumstances it is good to read and hear *Yā Sīn* because it confirms the core beliefs in a powerful and condensed form that is easy to read in a limited time. *Sūrat Yā Sīn* is also frequently printed in a small pamphlet form on its own, or along with a few other passages, as mentioned earlier. The pamphlet will be carried and read for protection and blessing.

Conclusion

Warning of the Resurrection was a fundamental function of the Prophet. Resurrection and Judgement are the pinnacle of the Islamic belief in the One God who creates, sends scriptures and will call people to account in the end. Without the Resurrection, the creation of people would be in vain (*'abath*) and contrary to the attributes of God as *al-malik al-ḥaqq* ('*the true King*', Q. 23:115–16) and *aḥkam al-ḥākimīn* ('*the fairest of judges*', Q. 95:8), who would not treat in the same way those who believe and do righteous deeds and those who corrupt the earth (Q. 38:28 and Q. 68:35–6). For this reason, the Resurrection and Judgement are referred to directly or indirectly in every page of the Qur'an.

Most of the Arabs first addressed by the Qur'an could not accept the Resurrection and fiercely argued against it. As stated earlier, their arguments were based on the decay of the human body, which they thought could not be brought together and revived again. This was their sole argument for the Resurrection being *'ajīb* ('*strange*'). The Prophet who warned about it was seen as either a poet or a madman or someone who invented lies about God. Against this the Qur'an marshalled the numerous arguments we have seen in *Sūrat Yā Sīn*, which give strong refutations of the disbelievers' own arguments. The Qur'an notes the disbelievers accepted that it was God who created the heavens and earth and who created them in the first place. With this in mind, it argues that recreating the human being is an easy task for the one who created what is greater and more complex than a human being. Indeed, God is capable of creating things from their opposite. This shows the Meccan disbelievers' logic to be weak and inconsistent. Had they not believed in God's creation, they would have been harder to convince. It is true that they asked the Prophet to prove the Resurrection on the spot by bringing back some of their ancestors:

They say, 'There is only our life in this world: we die, we live, nothing but time destroys us.' They have no knowledge of this; they only follow guesswork. Their only argument, when

Our clear revelations are recited to them, is to say, 'Bring back our forefathers if what you say is true.'

Q. 45:25

From the Prophet's point of view the answer was easy; it was not he who could do this but God, who created them: '*[Prophet,] say, "It is God who gives you life, then causes you to die, and then He gathers you all to the Day of Resurrection of which there is no doubt, though most people do not comprehend*"' (Q. 45:25–6). The Resurrection comes only at the appointed time (*al-ajal al-musammā*), known only to God.

The disbelievers, in spite of all their obduracy, were aware that they were not in a very strong position. The Qur'an produces arguments for the Resurrection from two areas: first, what people can see and feel around them in the realm of plants, astronomical phenomena and ships at sea; and second, logical deduction from axioms obvious to everyone. This may explain the fact that those who accepted Islam eventually gave up their objections about the impossibility of the Resurrection willingly. They also gave up the claim that the Qur'an and what it said about the Resurrection was poetry, and that the Prophet was a poet. After all, they themselves did not stick to this explanation and wavered, claiming that he was possessed, a sorcerer or was inventing things about God (e.g. compare Q. 21:3–5, Q. 46:7–8 and Q. 52:29–34). It is notable that in the later Medinan suras and in the Hadiths there was no need to argue any longer for the possibility of Resurrection. Rather, what the Qur'an does when speaking to Muslims in these verses is to remind them, saying that if they truly believe in God and the Last Day, they should do such and such (e.g. as in Q. 2:232, Q. 8:41 and Q. 65:2).

Sūrat Yā Sīn presents the Resurrection not as the mere musings of a poet, as indicated in verse 69, but as a well-argued reality. The implications of belief in the Resurrection are far-reaching in terms of behaviour and personal responsibility; it demands that people undertake difficult and challenging tasks or refrain from highly desirable things. That is why it figures so prominently throughout the Qur'an. *Sūrat Yā Sīn* is the Qur'an's longest and most powerful argument for this belief.

9

Evidential Style: Divine Oaths in the Qur'an

This chapter will examine the divine oaths, those made by God and which constitute the great majority of oaths in the Qur'an. They occur in 33 instances and in 30 suras, which is just over a quarter of the total number of suras. This volume indicates the importance of this feature in the Qur'an, and Qur'anic oaths have accordingly attracted much discussion both in the Islamic tradition and in Western scholarship[1] on the Qur'an. In the Islamic tradition the oath (*qasam*) is normally discussed in Arabic grammar texts and in Qur'anic studies.

Grammar textbooks discuss the elements of oaths as follows:

1. *Adāt al-qasam*, the particle of the oath. Oaths are introduced either by a particle (such as '*wa*', '*bi*' or '*ta*', in descending order of frequency) or by a verb (such as '*uqsim*', '*I swear*' or '*la-uqsim*', '*indeed I swear*').
2. *Al-muqsam bihi*, the object of the oath, appearing in Arabic in the genitive case.
3. *Al-muqsam 'alayhi*, known also as *jawāb al-qasam*, what is being sworn about, introduced by the emphatic particle *'inna'*, with its predicate introduced by the emphatic '*la*' or by '*laqad*' or with the negative particle '*mā*'. In many cases the thing sworn about is omitted (*maḥdhūf*) but can be deduced from the following text in which case it has a more rhetorical effect.

This study deals only with divine oaths, so we should bear in mind the identity of the person who is swearing (*al-muqsim*). This will help keep the function of the oath clear.

In Qur'anic studies, the best-known text that deals with the subject of oaths in the Qur'an is *al-Tibyān fī aqsām al-qur'ān* by Ibn al-Qayyim al-Jawziyya (d. 751/1350). It has remained the first point of reference for the study of oaths. It covers the subject extensively but does not seem to have a well-defined system or theoretical base. It also digresses from the topic, for instance in dealing with the oaths '*by the pen and what they write*' in Q. 68:2, the author talks about the varieties of pens.[2] In dealing with '*and in yourselves (there are signs)*' in Q. 51:21, he digresses for some 80 pages about signs in the human body.[3]

Ibn al-Qayyim generally follows the tradition of atomistic Qur'anic exegesis (*tafsīr*) which includes varieties of meanings for single words without due regard to the context or the relationship between the *muqsam bihi* and the *muqsam 'alayhi*; however, the book gives very useful insights on the oaths. Badr al-Dīn al-Zarkashī (d. 794/1391), in his book *al-Burhān fī 'ulūm al-qur'ān*,[4] and Jalāl al-Dīn al-Suyūṭī (d. 909/1515), in his famous book *al-Itqān fī 'ulūm al-qur'ān*,[5] discuss Qur'anic oaths, but rely mainly on what Ibn al-Qayyim said. These three have remained the most quoted sources in Arabic on the subject.

In English, in recent years, a number of studies have dealt with oaths in the Qur'an, including in particular the following:

1. G. R. Smith (1970)[6] presented a very useful survey of the material, but focused on grammatical analysis and artistic merit. He defined his task as follows:

   > In this article, these oaths, together with their *jawābs,* are isolated, categorised and translated. An attempt is made in each case to look into the semantic problems and to examine the role of each oath in the particular passage. The various linguistic 'aids' employed to strengthen the effect of each oath or group of oaths are discussed.[7]

   An example of his analysis will be given in the Appendix at the end of this chapter.

2. Mustansir Mir (1990) made a valuable contribution by presenting in English[8] the views of Ḥamīd al-Dīn 'Abd al-Ḥamīd Farāhī (1883–1930), which offered a new interpretation of some Qur'anic oaths. Farāhī dealt with six instances of oaths. He viewed these oaths not as a mere literary device but as providing arguments for what is being sworn about. This was a valuable interpretation in modern *tafsīr* but his remarks were written in Urdu and, even when Mir summarised them,

in a publication not much known, they seem to have been missed by subsequent Qur'anic scholars.[9] An example of Mir's analysis will be given in the Appendix.

3. Angelika Neuwirth's study[10] (2004) gives a fine example of structural and literary analysis of the material, dealing as it does with images and metaphors:

> It [concentrates] on those groups of introductory sections that in Western scholarship usually are treated as the most evident example of *kāhin* influence[11] on Qur'anic speech and therefore are considered to be dark, obscure, enigmatic, namely the introductory oaths of a series of early Meccan suras.[12]

Neuwirth's article presents an impressive survey, listing, labelling and classifying material, but the concentration is on the elements used for the oath, that is, on the *muqsam bihi.* Neuwirth states:

> In the present study all *sūras* starting with oath clusters will be surveyed. With one exception (*sūra* 37) these *sūras* belong to the first Makkan period according to Nöldeke's chronology.[13]

She classifies them as follows:

a. oath clusters of the type *wa'l-fā'ilāt*;
b. oath clusters alluding to particular sacred localities;
c. oath clusters resorting to cosmic phenomena and certain time periods of the day and the night. Oath clusters of this particular type, appearing in a few instances, without prominent introductory function, in the interior sections of early Makkan suras will also be considered.

An example of her analysis will be given in the Appendix.

4. G. R. Hawting,[14] in the *Encyclopaedia of the Qur'ān*, refers very briefly to the oaths dealt with here, even though they comprise the vast majority of oaths in the Qur'an, saying that 'their compressed grammar and unusual vocabulary[15] pose difficulties of interpretation' and that stylistically they have been understood to be akin to the rhymed prose of the pre-Islamic soothsayers. He then turns to concentrate on what he calls 'binding oaths', referring to cases of pre-Islamic oaths of abstinence from marital relations which were superseded by the Qur'an. He also deals with oaths by historic figures such as Abraham and Joseph, and deals with vocabulary of oaths, breaking oaths and so on. An example of Hawting's analysis will be given in the Appendix.

This chapter proposes a reclassification of the oaths in the Qur'an, not according to the *muqsam bihi* (what the oath swears by), as has been the focus of previous studies (Smith, 1970; Neuwirth, 1993), but according to the *muqsam 'alayhi* (what the oath asserts). A classification on these new terms, combined with a conscious awareness of the relevance of the *muqsim* (the giver of the oath) should yield a fresh interpretation and appreciation of the function and relevance of the oath as a whole and indeed of the *muqsam bihi* (what is sworn by). Our study will be based on three principles: a holistic, rather than an atomistic interpretation of the Qur'anic text; contextual interpretation; and intertextuality of the text of the Qur'an,[16] which shows how oaths resonate in other parts of the Qur'an.

Our discussion will also seek to establish that all the oaths discussed are in fact evidential, producing arguments for what the oaths assert. In some instances our analysis will correct traditionally held views as to what exactly is the *muqsam 'alayhi.* The three principles just mentioned will help establish and clarify this.

In some isolated rare instances in traditional *tafsīr* we come across suggestions that God swears by certain objects perhaps because the message in them is proof for what the oath asserts.[17] It was perhaps al-Rāzī who put this idea in its clearest form. Commenting on the oath in Sura 51, he states as one of the possible interpretations:

> The oaths which God Almighty swore are all evidence which He introduced in the form of oaths (dalā'il akhrajahā fī ṣūrat al-aymān), just as someone says to his benefactor, 'I swear, by the many favours you gave me, that I continue to thank you', mentioning the favours which are a suitable cause for continued thanks.[18]

However, this important view does not seem to have had much influence in classical exegesis, where discussion of oaths concentrated on the items sworn by as showing the greatness of God, rather than providing arguments for what the oaths assert.

As mentioned above, Farāhī followed a view similar to that of al-Rāzī when discussing six oaths in the Qur'an.[19] It will be seen in the ensuing discussion that our analysis of the oath differs in important respects from that given by Farāhī.

On the basis of the proposed reclassification and the principles set out above, we now proceed to deal with the oaths.

Quantity and Location in the Qur'an

Divine oaths occur mainly at the beginnings of the following suras: Q. 36, Q. 37, Q. 38, Q. 43, Q. 44, Q. 50, Q. 51, Q. 52, Q. 53, Q. 68, Q. 75, Q. 77, Q. 79, Q. 84, Q. 85, Q. 86, Q. 89, Q. 90, Q. 91, Q. 92, Q. 93, Q. 95, Q. 100 and Q. 103. In addition, others occur inside the following suras: Q. 15, Q. 51, Q. 56, Q. 69, Q. 70, Q. 74, Q. 81, Q. 84 and Q. 86. This volume indicates the importance of the feature in the Qur'an. It will become clear that isolating divine oaths for discussion will give a focused and clear picture of their nature and crucial function in Qur'anic discourse. The oaths listed here will be discussed below under our new classification.

The Function of Oaths in Arabic

We should first give the general function of an oath in Arabic, then move to its function in the Qur'an. The general function of an oath is to highlight a statement that requires emphasis. Books on rhetoric (*balāgha*) include discussions on *aḍrub al-khabar* (the modes of presenting a statement to the addressee) and identify three modes:

1. *ibtidā'ī* (initial): if there is no reason to expect the addressee will doubt or deny a statement, then there is no need to use any particle of emphasis with the statement;
2. *ṭalabī* (the addressee demands some assurance): if the speaker thinks that the addressee may doubt what is being said, then they should give some emphasis;
3. *inkārī* (the addressee denies the statement presented to him): if the speaker considers that the addressee will reject the statement, then more particles of emphasis should be employed, such as through '*inna*', with an added '*lām*' of emphasis (e.g. *inna'llāha la-ufuwwun ghafūr*, Q. 22:60) or an oath.[20]

Scholars of *balāgha* have also established the following principle: *li-kulli maqām maqāl*,[21] that is, every context requires its specific, suitable form of speech. An oath provides a powerful emphasis to statements in Arabic and not surprisingly the Qur'an uses oaths to underline statements relating to the basic beliefs of Islam. Throughout the Meccan period, the Qur'an concentrated on establishing the three fundamental beliefs of Islam: the unity of God, the prophethood of Muhammad, as well as the Resurrection of the dead and Judgement. These proved to be very difficult for the

Meccans to accept, as discussed in the previous chapter. The Qur'an uses various means to persuade and convince them of the truth of these beliefs.

Instead of believing in God alone (*tawḥīd*), most of the Arabs to whom the Qur'an was originally addressed were polytheists (*mushrikūn*) (Q. 12:106). Also, they had no previous experience of a human being from among themselves asserting that he was a prophet of God. They expected a prophet to be an angel (Q. 17:94–5). The most difficult hurdle for them, however, was to believe in the resurrection of the body (Q. 34:7–8, Q. 47:16–17 and Q. 56:47–8). It was natural in such a situation that the Qur'an would use the strongest form of emphasis, which is an oath made by God Himself, no less. This situation continued throughout the Meccan period. In Medina, the addressees were mainly the believers who did not need an oath to convince them about basic tenets of the faith.[22] We shall see in the following discussion how the Qur'an goes beyond this general function of mere emphasis in its employment of divine oaths.

Categories of Divine Oaths in the Qur'an

I will not be discussing the oaths according to serial occurrence in the Qur'an as appears to have been followed by Farāhī, for instance.[23] Nor will they be discussed here under the form of the *muqsam bihi* (what is sworn by), as followed by Ibn al-Qayyim, al-Suyūṭī and others, or under oaths alluding to particular sacred localities or cosmic phenomena and certain times or celestial phenomena, as followed by Neuwirth.[24] Such studies are concerned above all with the *muqsam bihi*. The present study considers that classifying the material according to the *muqsam 'alayhi* (what an oath asserts), while keeping in mind the giver of the oath and the addressee, is more likely to lead to an accurate interpretation and appreciation of their functions and indeed of the relevance of the *muqsam bihi* and the oath as a whole. Accordingly, the oaths will be discussed under three categories on the basis of what they seek to establish: the oneness of God, the prophethood of Muhammad and the Resurrection in this ascending order of frequency. The discussion will also examine how the oaths function in their contexts in the Qur'an.

Oneness of God

Concerning the oneness of God (*tawḥīd*), there is one oath in Q. 37:1–5: '*By those ranged in rows, who chide forcefully and recite God's word, truly your god is One, Lord of the heavens and the earth and everything between them*'. The Qur'an swears here by the angels, showing what they actually do, being ranged in rows (Q. 37:1 and Q. 78:38), rebuking those who make false claims about them (Q. 37:161–7)[25] and reciting God's word and praising Him. The angels in the sura describe their own true status (Q. 37:164–6), '*Everyone of us has his appointed place: we are ranged in ranks, we glorify God.*' This is a powerful retort, making the angels themselves denounce the pagans' claims that the angels were God's daughters and could bring them nearer to Him,[26] and show themselves to be servants to the One God. The angels are described at the beginning of the sura with three attributes: they are ranged in rows, chiding and reciting. The particle of the oath is '*wa*', followed by these three descriptions given in short, powerful adjectives, which makes the statement all the more forceful, before giving the *jawāb al-qasam* or *al-muqsam 'alayhi,* the complement of the oath, introduced by the emphatic '*inna*' and containing the further emphasis of '*la*': *inna ilāhakum la-wāḥid,* 'your god is certainly one'.

On the basis of the above analysis it may be seen that the first three verses refer to one entity: the angels. In the *tafsīr* tradition, however, there are other views: first, they question whether the three adjectives refer to one or multiple entities and, second, when they are taken to refer to one entity, which that is exactly. Taking them as referring to one entity, al-Bayḍāwī gives a summary of what other exegetes have given in a list of four:

1. angels in rows;
2. planets and stars in rows;
3. souls of scholars (*'ulamā'*) in worship;
4. souls of fighters in *jihād.*

There are three reasons for such variations:

1. The adjectives do not specify exactly the nouns they qualify. This is *maḥdhūf* (omitted), as is common in Arabic.
2. There is the tendency of many exegetes towards atomistic interpretation; that is, dealing with individual words on their own and what each could possibly or even remotely mean without regard to the historical or textual context.
3. This tendency normally does not pay regard to what the Qur'an says in other parts, contrary to the well-established principle that *al-qur'ān yufassir ba'ḍuhu ba'ḍan* (different parts of the Qur'an explain each other).[27]

Historical context would not support the notion of fighters in *jihād* in rows. The sura is Meccan, addressed to disbelievers of Mecca who had no notion at that time of Muslim fighters in rows in *jihād*, nor of rows of *'ulamā'* preaching. Similarly, the context would not support the notion of rows of planets (even if they can be seen in rows), rebuking and reciting God's word. All this shows how strange the atomistic approach can be. The context supports the reference to the angels and this is confirmed by later reference in the sura (verses 149–60).

As regards the reference of the first three verses of the sura to multiple entities, al-Rāzī lists views of other exegetes that verse 1 refers to birds because birds are described elsewhere in the Qur'an as *ṣaffāt* (Q. 67:19, '*spreading their wings*'). This is the term mentioned at the beginning of Sura 37, and verse 2 refers to everything that rebukes disobedience to God, while verse 3 refers to everything that is recited from God's book.[28]

Apparently exegetes such as al-Rāzī, al-Bayḍāwī and al-Suyūṭī felt it was part of modesty and intellectual honesty to list any view that had been expressed even if it totally disregarded the context. This perhaps led to the view that these oaths were 'dark, enigmatic and obscure'[29] when, properly seen, they are not.

Prophethood of Muhammad

Oaths from eight suras come under this section, to be found in Q. 93, Q. 68, Q. 53, Q. 89, Q. 85, Q. 38, Q. 50 and Q. 36. Following the discussion of their functions, a summary will be given at the end of this section.

Sūrat al-Ḍuḥā (Q. 93)

By the morning brightness and by the night when it grows still, your Lord has not forsaken you [Prophet] nor does He hate you, and the future will be better for you than the past. Your Lord is sure to give you so much that you will be well satisfied. Did He not find you orphaned and shelter you? Did He not find you lost and guide you? Did He not find you in need and satisfy your need?

Q. 93:1–8

Early in his mission the Prophet experienced a period of cessation of the revelation which saddened him and made some opponents say that Muhammad's Lord had forsaken him and now hated him.[30] This sura gives the Prophet a calm but powerful assurance. What are invoked for the oath are natural phenomena. The Prophet is reminded first of the morning brightness. Verses 1 and 2 in this oath herald the relief that cannot be far behind. God gives darkness to the night, then brings out the morning brightness (Q. 79:29), '*That is His sunna (practice) and you will find no change in God's practice*' (Q. 48:24). This is an evidential oath; the *muqsam 'alayhi,* the thing enforced through the oath, comes with two negations: '*your Lord has not forsaken you [Prophet] nor does He hate you*' (*mā wadda'ka rabbuka wa-mā qalā*). The subject of the two verbs is the reassuring *rabbuka* ('*your Lord*'). The rhythm and rhyme at the end are also calm and reassuring. In one line of Arabic, any thought of being forsaken or hated is dispelled. After the claims of the Prophet's opponents have been negated, verses 4 and 5 begin with the '*la*' of the oath for further emphasis, which further strengthen the statement. Just as the morning brightness is coming soon, the future will be better for the Prophet than the past and his Lord will give him so much that he will be well satisfied. The omission of the object of giving makes it open to endless giving.

Having assured the Prophet of the future, the sura goes on to make him admit (*istifhām taqrīrī*) how much his Lord has given him before – '*Did He not find you an orphan*' (*a-lam yajidka yatīman*) – referring to three vulnerable states in his earlier life that God put right for him, states that the Prophet could not deny. This sura reassures the Prophet, but it also gives reassurance to the believers in general. Verses 5 ('*your Lord is sure to give you [so much] that you will be well pleased*') and 11 ('*talk about the blessings of your Lord*') are among the most quoted verses of the Qur'an, isolated and framed in beautiful calligraphy and hung by Muslims in their homes and offices.

Sūrat al-Qalam (Q. 68)

Using a strong oath, the sura refutes the Prophet's opponents' claim that he was mad:

By the pen, by what they write, you [Prophet] are not, by receiving your Lord's grace, a madman: you will have a never-ending reward – truly you have a strong character – and soon you will see, as will they, which of you is afflicted with madness. Your Lord knows best who strays from His path and who is rightly guided.

Q. 68:1–7

God swears by the pen that the Prophet is not mad as his opponents claim. Swearing by the pen is a striking oath. God has been described as '*the most generous, who taught by the pen, who taught man what he did not know*'

(Q. 96:4–5). So the Qur'anic revelation, sent as a grace from God to the Prophet, bringing learning and the instruction to learn, cannot be a sign of madness. '*What they write*' refers to angels writing down revelation. The Qur'an is described as '*inscribed in honoured scrolls, exalted, pure, by the hands of noble and virtuous scribes*' (Q. 80:13–16). Even if we take 'they' to refer to scribes in general, still learning to write is a mark of God's blessing and the revelation that stressed this cannot be a sign of madness.

The oath goes on with the emphatic '*inna*' and '*la*' to confirm that the Prophet will have an unending reward from God. He does not ask for rewards from the disbelievers (verse 46). The oath further confirms that he is *'alā khuluqin 'aẓīm*, which could refer to his strong constitution and character, negating any madness. It could also be praising him for his moral character, which is the opposite of the description of his opponent as being a '*contemptible swearer, [...] backbiter, slander monger, [...] hinderer of good, [...] sinful, aggressive, coarse and on top of all that, an imposter*' (Q. 68:10–13). The Prophet's opponents' accusation that he was mad is reiterated at the end of the sura, in verse 51, with a rebuttal, confirming that the Qur'an is nothing other than *dhikrun li'l-'ālamīn*, '*a reminder for all*'.

Sūrat al-Najm (Q. 53)

By the star when it descends, your companion has not strayed; he is not deluded; he does not speak from his own desire. The Qur'an is nothing less than a revelation that was sent to him. It was taught to him by an angel with mighty power and great strength, who stood on the highest horizon and then approached – coming down until it was two bow-lengths away or even closer – he revealed to God's servant what he revealed. The Prophet's own heart did not distort what he saw.

Q. 53:1–11

The Qur'an rejects the assertion of the Prophet's opponents that he was astray, deluded and speaking from his own fancy, not revelation. It is stressed that it is no less than a revelation and shows the angel of the revelation imparting the Qur'an in an undoubted way as coming so close to the Prophet, and his '*heart did not distort what he saw*'. Before this affirmation comes the oath, '*by the star when it descends*' (*wa'l-najm idhā hawā*). Descending makes it easier to see and be guided by than when it is too high up in the sky. Al-Rāzī explains that when the star descends it is easier to determine from it the four directions (east, west, north, south) than when the star is in the middle of the sky.[31] The stars in the Qur'an give guidance during the night so that people do not lose their way: '*It is He who made the stars so that you can be guided by them in the dark, on land or sea*' (Q. 6:97, see also Q. 16:16). So to deny that the Prophet has strayed, the oath invokes the star, an image well known to the Arabs in their travel by night guided by the stars. The star is not astray and the Prophet is addressed in the Qur'an, stressing his task of guiding people: '*Truly you guide to a straight path*' (Q. 42:52). The image is integral to the argument and not a mere ornament or formula. The star guides, and revelation (*waḥī*) mentioned in verse 4 is the star that guides the Prophet: '*I only follow what is revealed (yuḥyi) to me*' (Q. 46:9). The oath in Sura 53 encourages the Prophet and affirms the genuineness of the revelation of the Qur'an in a powerful way, as we have seen earlier in discussing Sura 37.[32]

Sūrat al-Fajr (Q. 89)

By the daybreak, and ten nights, by the even and the odd, by the night as it passes…

Q. 89:1–4

This sura enlists the daybreak to give an immediate reassurance of relief as dawn breaks through the long darkness of the night. Verse 4, '*by the night as it passes*', contrasts with the brightness of daybreak but again reassures the Prophet that the darkness is passing, as in Q. 93:1–2, '*by the morning brightness and the night*'.

Between these lie verses 2–3, '*by ten nights, by the even and the odd*'. Much has been said about the meaning of these two verses by both Muslim exegetes and non-Muslim scholars.[33] It was suggested they refer to the last ten nights of Ramadan or the first ten nights of the month Dhū'l-Ḥijja. Ramadan is unlikely as the fasting and night devotion were introduced in Medina, long after the present sura was revealed. Moreover, neither of these fits the context of the coming punishment, mentioned in the verses to follow. Unlike in Sura 52, for instance, where the punishment is eschatological, in this sura the punishment is temporal, similar to what happened to Pharaoh and the people of 'Ād and Thamūd. Likewise, the first ten nights of Dhū'l-Ḥijja are nights for increased devotion, occurring in a forbidden month, where no fighting or infliction of harm even on animals and plants in Mecca is allowed. It is unlikely they are invoked to confirm the coming of punishment for the Meccan disbelievers. Moreover, *Sūrat al-Fajr* is Meccan and was revealed years before the obligation of the fast of Ramadan. Although it is the Prophet who is being addressed, his opponents are also intended to receive warning of punishment. It is unlikely they could have been persuaded by an oath referring to ten nights in Ramadan or Dhū'l-Ḥijja. It can, however, be assumed the ten nights refer to the first ten nights of the month Muḥarram, which can be seen as the dawn of the new year, promising change from the ending year and thus carrying some reassurance. The nights mentioned in verse 2 contrast with daybreak mentioned in verse 1, and what we have here is perhaps an intimation that the punishment will not be coming very soon but it is coming, even if one has to wait for it. The figure ten is frequently shown in the Qur'an to indicate a high maximum.[34] The point is, however, that even if they are a full ten nights, they will still pass.

The following oath is by the even and the odd. The figure ten consists of even and odd and they follow each other in swift succession.[35] Here, then, the Prophet is assured that although there is a period of waiting it will all pass: '*by the night as it passes*'. This powerful, solemn oath is emphatically followed by the question, addressed to the Prophet (or 'you' in general as the Prophet is the first addressee but the Qur'an is guidance for all): '*is this a strong enough oath for a sensible*[36] *person?*' (Q. 89:5). He would naturally accept this as an assurance. To confirm this further, he is asked:

> *Have you not seen how your Lord dealt with the people of 'Ād, of Iram, [the city] of lofty pillars, whose like has never been made in the land, and the Thamūd, who hewed into the rocks in the valley, and the mighty and powerful Pharaoh, all of whom committed excesses in their land and spread corruption there, so your Lord let loose a scourge of punishment upon them?*
>
> Q. 89:6–13

The complement of the oath at the end of verse 5 is left unstated, which arouses the expectation of the reader, and when they have read the following verses, they will confirm that the unstated complement must be, 'Your Lord's punishment is certainly coming for your opponents'.

Sūrat al-Burūj (Q. 85)

> *By the sky with its towers, by the promised Day, by the witness and the witnessed! Perish the makers of the Trench, with the fuel-stoked fire! They sat and witnessed what they were doing to the believers. Their only grievance against them was their faith in God, the Mighty, the Praiseworthy, to whom all control over heavens and earth belong: God is witness over all things.*
>
> Q. 85:1–9

By referring to the torture suffered by believers in an earlier religion, for no other reason than their belief in God, this sura must have given some encouragement to the believers who were suffering in Mecca. God swears by the sky with its tremendous towers (or, towering constellations) as it was above the heads of the oppressors and their terrible act, intended to terrify the oppressors with the power in the sky which could bring disaster to them,[37] and by the promised Day which refers to when they will meet their final punishment. He swears by the witness (*shāhid*): this can be God (mentioned as witness in verse 9) or the criminals themselves (Q. 4:87) or their own tongues, hands and feet (Q. 24:24; see also Q. 41:20–1), that is, everything that will come and give testimony on the Day of Judgement, including the tortured believers and the torturers themselves, who will not be able to deny their own actions that day. Then He swears by the witnessed (*mashhūd*): the tortured believers watched by their torturers, who were also witnessed by God.

What is sworn about is left unstated, because of the terrible act that is described, and so that the expectation of the reader is heightened. 'Perish the makers of the trench' may be assumed to be what is sworn about (*muqsam 'alayhi*), but it is not suitable for this, being an invocation (*du'ā'*), while the oath is for strong emphasis. Besides, if it were the *muqsam 'alayhi* it would have been introduced by a particle of emphasis.

The verses continue with condemnation, depicting the scene. Later in the sura come '*Prophet, your Lord's punishment is truly stern – it is He who brings people to life and will restore them to life again*' (Q. 85:12–13) and '*Have you not heard the stories of the forces of Pharaoh and Thamūd?*' (Q. 85:17–18). From this we can deduce that the *muqsam 'alayhi* encouraged the Prophet and the believers in Mecca and gave warning to their oppressors.

Sūrat Ṣād (Q. 38)

By the Qur'an with its message [dhikr]...! Yet, the disbelievers are steeped in arrogance and hostility.

Q. 38:1–2

The particle of the oath '*wa*' is followed by the *muqsam bihi* (what is sworn by), in this case the Qur'an, described as *dhī'l-dhikr*, '*containing a message (or: reminder)*'. But unlike Sura 37 where the complement of the oath is stated (*madhkūr*), in Sura 38 the complement is only implied (*maṭwī*). Where the complement is stated, it begins with '*inna*', as in Q. 37:4 ('*By those [angels] ranged in rows ... truly your god is one*'), or with the negative particle '*mā*' as in *mā wadda'ka rabbuka*, '*your Lord has not forsaken you*', as in Q. 93:3. When the complement is implied, it makes the oath more striking, raising the expectation of the listener or reader. When the listeners have heard the following statements, containing the allegations of the disbelievers, they will see that the complement is something that negates what they have claimed. In this sura, what the disbelievers doubted was the prophethood of Muhammad, whom they called a lying sorcerer, especially as he asserted the oneness and uniqueness of God and the Resurrection:

> *Yet the disbelievers are steeped in arrogance and hostility. How many generations We have destroyed before them! They all cried out, once it was too late to escape. The disbelievers think it strange that a prophet from among their own people has come to warn them: they say, 'He is just a lying sorcerer. How can he claim that all the gods are but one god? What an astonishing thing to claim!' Their leaders depart, saying, 'Walk away! Stay faithful to your gods, that is what you must do. We did not hear any such claim in the last religion. It is all an invention. Was the message [dhikr] sent only to him out of all of us?' In fact they doubt My warning; in fact they have not tasted My punishment yet. Do they possess the stores of the blessings of your Lord, the Mighty, the All-Giving?*
>
> Q. 38:2–8

The disbelievers were arrogant and resented that the Prophet was given prophethood out of all of them (see also Q. 43:31–2).

The complement of the oath therefore would be something like, 'all their claims that you are a lying sorcerer has no basis'. The *muqsam bihi* (the thing sworn by) in this sura is the Qur'an, which contains *dhikr*, thus proving Muhammad's prophethood and encouraging him to bear patiently with what they claim.

Sūrat Qāf (Q. 50)

This sura is similar to Sura 38 which we have just discussed. The disbelievers denied Muhammad's prophethood and the oath is given '*by the glorious Qur'an*' (*wa'l-qur'āni'l-majīd*), as evidence to confirm his prophethood.

Sūrat Yā Sīn (Q. 36)

Likewise in *Sūrat Yā Sīn*, the disbelievers asserted Muhammad was a poet (Q. 36:69) and the oath in verses 1–3 is given '*by the decisive Qur'an*' (*wa'l-qur'āni'l-ḥakīm*), as evidence to confirm his prophethood.

Summary Classification of Oaths on the Prophethood of Muhammad

To sum up this section on the prophethood of Muhammad, we note the following:

- Sura 93 denies that God hates the Prophet or has forsaken him.
- Sura 53 denies the claim that he strayed.
- Sura 68 denies the claim that he was mad.
- Sura 38 denies the claim that he was a lying sorcerer.
- Sura 50 denies the claim that he was lying.
- Sura 36 denies the claim that he was a poet.
- Sura 89 and Sura 85 affirm that the punishment of his opponents is coming.

We now come to the third Islamic belief which, judging by the space it occupies, seems to have been even more difficult for Arabs to accept and required more emphasis by evidential oaths: the Resurrection.

The Resurrection

Oaths from 16 suras come under this category: Q. 51, Q. 52, Q. 56, Q. 69, Q. 74, Q. 77, Q. 79, Q. 81, Q. 84, Q. 86, Q. 90, Q. 91, Q. 92, Q. 95, Q. 100 and Q. 103. A classification of the functions of these oaths will be given at the end of the section.

Sūrat al-Ṭāriq (Q. 86)

By the sky and the night – comer – What will explain to you what the night – comer is? The piercing star – there is a watcher over every soul. Man should reflect on what he was created from. He is created from spurting fluid, then he emerges from between the backbone and breastbone: God is certainly able to bring him back to life. On the day when secrets are laid bare he will have no power and no one to help him.

By the sky and its recurring rain, by the earth that bursts forth! This is truly a decisive statement; it is not something to be taken lightly. They plot and scheme, but so do I: [Prophet,] let the disbelievers be for their short while.

Q. 86:1–17

A consistent argument for the Resurrection runs through this sura and explains the *muqsam 'alayhi* (the claim supported by the oath). God swears by the sky which is above everybody, as if watching them all, and by *al-ṭāriq*, '*the night-comer*', that emerges in the darkness of the night, a significant entity made more intriguing by the question, '*What would explain to you…*', followed by the explanation, '*the piercing star*' (*al-thāqib*), which again is watching everyone below. *Ṭāriq* and *thāqib* are two piercing words that will reverberate throughout the sura. What is asserted by the oaths, introduced by the emphatic '*in*', tells us that every soul has a watcher over it, recording everything it does. The emphatic '*lamma*' in '*there is a watcher over every soul*' comes to complete the emphasis in this statement which is the heart of the sura. Since they are all watched and everything is recorded, they will be judged (Q. 6:61–2).

Then follow two arguments for the Resurrection. The first is embryological, telling us that man was created from a spurting fluid, gushing forth. This is the beginning of a long series of developments in the womb explained in great detail in Q. 22:4 and in Q. 23:12–16, given as an argument for the Resurrection. Because of *Sūrat al-Ṭāriq* being so condensed, the argument goes from this fact straight to his emerging (*yakhruj*) from between the backbone and the breast bone, again coming out, reinforcing the earlier image. Traditional exegetes (and translators) take this *yakhruj* to refer to the fluid, claiming that it comes from the loin of the man and the breastbone of the woman. They are led to this by thinking that, since the word *yakhruj* is close to the word denoting fluid, it should refer to it, according to the grammar rule that the pronoun refers to the closest preceding noun;[38] however, in fact this is not a universal rule in the Qur'an (see Q. 12:7–8 and Q. 48:9). No basis is given for the claim that the fluid comes from the woman's breastbone. This explanation also disturbs the consistent imagery witnessed in this sura. More consistent with the structure of the images is to say that the foetus, which is contained between the breastbone and loin of the woman, will emerge from her at birth, just as a dead person, contained in the grave, will emerge at the Resurrection. Thus the images reinforce each other. *Yakhruj* and the noun *khurūj* are used in the Qur'an to express the emergence of a plant from the ground (Q. 78:15), of the foetus from the womb (Q. 40:67) and of the dead from the grave: *kadhālika'l-khurūj* ('*such is the resurrection*') (Q. 50:11 and Q. 71:18). This very image of God's creating the foetus that emerges from the womb is used to show that God is also able to bring humans back from death to life. The Qur'an categorically asserts: '*He [God] is certainly able to bring him back to life*'[39] (Q. 86:8). He will be brought back to face the Judgement: '*On the Day when secrets are laid bare he will have no power and no one to help him*' (Q. 86:9–10).

Then comes the second oath, again by the sky, this time giving life through rain that causes the production of plants: '*By the sky and its recurring rain* (*al-raj'*)[40]...' This recalls the earlier occurrence of *raj'* in verse 8, '*He is certainly able to bring him back (raj'ihi) to life*'. The Resurrection is referred to as *raj'*[41] and so is the rain.

Then comes the next oath: '*by the earth that cracks open* (*dhāt al-ṣad'*)*!*' This refers to the bursting of a plant up through the ground (compare Q. 80:26), again reinforcing every image that has gone before of 'piercing', 'breaking through', 'coming out' and 'laying bare', all to confirm the idea of people breaking out of their graves at Resurrection to face the Judgement: '*This [God's ability to resurrect for judgement] is truly a decisive statement, it is not something to be taken lightly*' (Q. 86:13).

The sura ends with warning to the disbelievers that their schemes against the Prophet and his message are futile: '*...let them be for a while*' (Q. 86:17). Their life on earth and in the grave is only a short time before they face Resurrection and Judgement (see also Q. 23:114 and Q. 46:35).

Serial Oaths

Under this classification of oaths on resurrection come four examples in Suras 51, 77, 79 and 100. In each there is one unit that develops in a series of stages or actions, working together as a complete entity, intended in Q. 51 and Q. 77 as an argument for the Resurrection and in Q. 99 and Q. 100 as a representation of its initial impact.

Sura 51:1–6

By those [winds] that scatter far and wide, that are heavily laden, that speed freely, that distribute [rain] as ordained! What you people are promised is true: the Judgement will come.

The scatterer moves and carries rain that falls on the land, producing life in plants, and in the same way, life will emerge from the earth at the Resurrection. Many Qur'anic verses, among them Q. 7:57, Q. 35:9, Q. 41:39 and Q. 50:11, deal with this. All the elements here refer to one and the same thing, the wind.

The traditional view of many exegetes (followed by translators) was atomistic, taking each element on its own and in isolation of the others in the series, which obscures the links between them and what the oaths assert, stripping them of their force as arguments. Al-Suyūṭī,[42] for example, takes verse 1 to refer to wind and verse 2 to refer to rainclouds, but he then shifts, in verse 3, to boats moving on water and declares verse 4 to refer to the angels distributing provisions and grain. Al-Bayḍāwī[43] takes verse 1 to refer to the wind, fertile women who give birth to children, or the causes, angels and others, that spread human beings (simply because any of these can be said to spread one thing or another). Verse 2, he states, refers to rainclouds, winds carrying clouds, pregnant women carrying children or the causes of all those. Verse 3 refers to boats moving easily on water, wind blowing at speed or stars that run in their orbits (simply because any of these can be said to run or move at speed). Verse 4 is taken to refer to the angels, or angels and others, that apportion things or the wind that apportions rain. This jumble of diverse things pays no regard to the context and what the verses are leading to. It merely explains every word and what it could conceivably mean, which obscures the whole picture and does not clarify what each word means in this particular context. In all cases the *mufassirūn* (exegetes) included the word that fits the context, but buried it in a list without any differentiation. What led to this all-inclusive approach is the fact that a noun like *al-dhāriyāt* (in verse 1, '*those [winds] that ascatter far and wide*') appearing in the form or pattern of *fā'ilāt* is originally an adjective. The noun it refers to and describes (i.e. 'winds') is omitted because the usage in Arabic and elsewhere in the Qur'an (Q. 18:45) makes it clear that it means, even on its own, nothing other than the winds. Exegetes of the atomistic approach pay no regard to the context that should determine which particular meaning of the word should be selected and is supported by usage somewhere else in the Qur'an. They take '*are heavily laden*' in verse 2 to refer to boats with heavy cargo, but here it refers to clouds heavily laden with rain, as in '*He builds up the clouds heavy with rain*' (Q. 13:12). They take '*that speed freely*' in verse 3 to refer to boats, but it applies here to wind (see also Q. 21:81). They take '*distributing*' in verse 4 to refer to angels, but here it refers to the winds that distribute rain as God plans, pouring it on whatever He wishes and diverting it from whatever He wishes (see also Q. 24:43 and Q. 30:48–50). The fact is that the series of actions through which the wind goes is used in the Qur'an as an argument for the Resurrection (as in Q. 30:48, Q. 35:9 and Q. 7:57). Thus the meanings we opt for here are corroborated in the Qur'an and it is they that fit the context of the oaths. The oath employs the wind in its successive stages, leading to the production of plants from dead land, to show God's power to resurrect the dead. The same series, leading to the same result, is used in the Qur'an without the oath, but decisively explains the evidential function of the oath as we have outlined:

It is God who sends out the winds; they stir up the clouds; He spreads them over the skies as He pleases; He makes them break up and you see the rain falling from them. See how they rejoice when He makes it fall upon whichever of His servants He wishes, though before it is sent they may have lost all hope. Look, then, at the imprints of God's mercy, how He restores the earth to life after death: this same God is the one who will return people to life after death – He has power over all things.

Q. 30:48–50

Similarly:

It is God who sends the winds, bearing good news of His coming grace, and when they have gathered up the heavy clouds, We drive them to a dead land where We cause rain to fall, bringing out all kinds of fruit, just as We shall bring out the dead. Will you not reflect?

Q. 7:57

This shows that the oath is not as dark, enigmatic or obscure as some have claimed, nor does it allow for the jumble of things listed by al-Bayḍāwī and al-Suyūṭī.

It should be pointed out that the clouds laden with rain in verse 2, which speed easily and bring vegetation to a dead land, as is clear in parts of the Qur'an cited above, are a sign of God's mercy who brings life to a dead land and is thus, in the same manner, able to bring life to dead bodies. This has nothing to do with a retributional storm as suggested by Neuwirth.[44] The oath cluster is not linked with the 'retributional legends' that come later in the sura. The same can be said of the reference by Farāhī to rain wiping out many a rebellious nation.[45] When water is used for destruction, as in the case of Noah, God says, '*We opened the gates of the sky with torrential rain, burst the earth with gushing springs, the waters met for a pre-ordained purpose*' (Q. 54:11–12). The vocabulary is markedly different from the image of 'speeding easily to water a dead land' and is not intended to threaten drowning or destruction.

Sura 77:1–7 (al-Mursalāt)

By those sent forth in swift succession, violently storming, spreading far and wide, separating forcefully, delivering a reminder, to excuse or to warn: what you are promised will come to pass.

The term *mursalāt* (*'sent forth'*), appearing as the title of the sura and in verse 1, relates to the verb *arsala, yursilu,* frequently used in the Qur'an with the wind (see Q. 7:57, Q. 30:46 and Q. 35:9). It is about violent winds that are meant to separate the disbelievers from the believers for destruction (see Q. 24:43 and Q. 46:24–5). Again, this is a reminder that, as this happens in the world, so at the Resurrection (Q. 30:14) there will also be destruction for disbelievers and separation between them and the believers. This sura shares with Sura 79 and Sura 100 in giving an image to evoke what will happen at the Resurrection. God, who is capable of letting lose violent winds in this world, is capable of bringing about the Hour of Doom and Resurrection. Typically, some classical commentators produce various possibilities. Al-Suyūṭī, who takes the first part as referring to wind, interprets verse 4 (*'separating forcefully'*) as 'the verses of the Qur'an that separate between right and wrong; lawful and forbidden', while verse 5 (*'delivering a reminder'*) means to him the angels bringing revelation to prophets.[46] Al-Bayḍāwī gives still more possibilities, including angels and good souls, and ending with the punishing, destructive winds.[47] Such is the result of the atomistic approach in *tafsīr*; the commentators have explained the different meanings a word can have, but have not established what a word means in the particular context in which it appears.

Sura 79 (al-Nāzi'āt) and Sura 100 (al-'Ādiyāt)

Connected to the Resurrection are the oaths in the two scenes at the beginning of Suras 79 and 100. Sura 79 begins:

> *By the forceful chargers, speeding across lands, sweeping ahead at full stretch, overtaking swiftly to sort a matter out, on the day when the blast reverberates and the second blast follows, hearts will tremble and eyes will be downcast.*
>
> Q. 79:1–9

Al-Suyūṭī takes these to refer to the angels and al-Bayḍāwī takes them to refer to the angels of death who pull out the souls of the believers from their bodies, or the stars that go from east to west, or the descriptions of virtuous souls when they leave the body, or the souls of the people going on a raid, or their hands pulling the bows or (at last!) a description of their horses. Again, this shows the atomistic approach of *tafsīr* that pays no regard to context or usage in Arabic generally.[48] The last suggestion about horses is really the only relevant one. There are five adjectives used in the Arabic verses: *nāzi'āt* (verse 1), *nāshiṭāt* (verse 2), *sābiḥāt* (verse 3) and *sābiqāt* (verse 4), which are used in Arabic dictionaries and poetry to refer to horses going at different speeds. The final adjective, *mudabbirāt* (verse 5, 'to arrange or settle an issue') obviously refers to the result of the raid. Other suggestions given by Bayḍawī obscure the image, well-known to the Arabs in relation to horses, arriving unexpectedly on a raid and casting terror into the hearts of an encampment. It is used to help the audience imagine the fear that will make their hearts tremble and their eyes downcast at the sudden arrival of the Hour of Doom and Resurrection. This is confirmed by the following verses:

They say, 'What? Shall we be brought back to life after we have turned into decayed bones?' and they say, 'Such a return is impossible!' But all it will take is a single blast, and see! They will be back above ground.

Q. 79:10–14

Literal translation into English of the condensed Arabic statements, whose words readily have their associations with horses, which is not the case in English, renders the English unintelligible.[49] Arberry, for instance, produces this beautiful version with rhythm and rhyme that echo the original Arabic rhythm and rhyme and show great ability:

By those that pluck out vehemently
And those that draw out violently,
By those that swim serenely
And those that strip out suddenly
By those that direct an affair[50]

But the original meaning is lost in English for two reasons: first, the words do not readily refer to horses in English dictionaries and literature as they do in Arabic; and, second, the nouns that qualify the adjectives are omitted in Arabic (a common feature, as mentioned above), but the adjectives still refer to horses.

Sūrat al-ʿĀdiyāt (Q. 100) starts with the following oath:

By the charging steeds that pant, and strike sparks with their hooves, that make dawn raids, raising clouds of dust, and plunging into the midst of the enemy...

Q. 100:1–5

The image here is obviously one of horses raiding suddenly in the morning, with the same intention of explaining the fear that will strike people at the Resurrection that will come suddenly.[51] *Al-mughīrāt ṣubḥan* (verse 3) is reminiscent of a term still known in Arabia for a morning raid, *taṣbiḥa* coming from the same root *ṣ-b-ḥ*.

Suras 79 and 100 use one and the same image with the same intention. The difference is that in Sura 79 the concentration is on the increasing speed of the horses as they reach their destination. This is fitting in view of the fact that in the same sura the disbelievers are described as eagerly waiting for the arrival of the Day of Judgement: '*They ask you [Prophet] about the Hour, saying, "When will it arrive?"*' (Q. 79:42–3).

In Sura 100, in addition to the speed, the drama of '*striking sparks with their hooves*' and '*plunging into the midst of the enemy*' is maintained in the following verses 9–10, '*when the contents of graves are thrown out and when the secrets of hearts are uncovered.*'

The imagery in the oath aims to elicit, in the unbelievers, a sense of urgency and fear of the sudden Resurrection and Judgement that will overtake them. This suggests the *muqsam 'alayhi*, which is left unstated in this oath. The fact that man is ungrateful to his Lord and loves wealth excessively, as mentioned in verses 6–8, is not the *muqsam 'alayhi*, but a separate idea consequent on how God subjected horses to man for which he should be grateful (see Q. 36:71–2).

Sura 76 (al-Qiyāma)

I swear by the Day of Resurrection and by the self-reproaching soul! Does man think We will not put his bones back together? Yes, indeed, we can reshape his very fingertips.

Q. 76:1–4

Verse 1 causes a number of problems to interpreters. It starts with the particle '*lā*' which may be a negative particle, in which case the meaning would be 'I will not swear by the Day of Resurrection', in the sense that it is so obvious and needs no oath. Or, the negative '*lā*' stands on its own, meaning 'the situation is not as those who deny the Resurrection say'. Then comes '*I swear...*'. In another opinion, '*lā*' is not a negative particle, but the emphatic '*la*' extended in length by the *madda* before *uqsimu* ('*I swear*').

There is a further question: how does God swear about the Resurrection by the Resurrection? In fact, the oath is about His ability to bring the bones back together. This is in answer to those[52] who thought that having been scattered and dispersed in the earth the bones could not possibly be collected together (see Q. 32:10). In Q. 50:4, the answer is: '*We know very well what the earth takes away from them: We keep a comprehensive record.*' He who can bring about the Day of Resurrection with all that it contains, is well able to collect the bones together as he created them in the first place, complete with their fingertips, and develop them into human beings. The basis of the argument, then, is that He who can do a great act is able to do a smaller one.

The four serial oaths in Q. 51, Q. 77, Q. 79 and Q. 100, together with that in Q. 37, share a common feature as all are in the form or pattern of *fā'ilāt*. Many writers on oaths and translators of the Qur'an deal with them summarily as *kāhin* style, that is, the style employed by the soothsayers of pre-Islamic Arabia, as if this says everything about the sections of the suras in which the oaths occur.[53] This does not help much and avoids the required analysis. G. R. Smith asserts:

> It should be stated that there are no apparent resemblances between the feminine plural participle oaths [that is, the pattern *fā'ilāt*] and anything in pre-Islamic literature or in the quoted utterances of the *kāhins*.[54]

I agree with his view about the *kāhins*, but am not going to discuss them in this chapter. My discussion will show that the Qur'anic oaths are quite different from *kāhin* oaths.[55]

Moreover, atomistic exegetes do not consider the oaths 'dark, enigmatic or obscure', but capable of more than one meaning, each of which is suitable on its own as an object of an oath, since each is created by God and shows His power and care.[56] As we have seen, the holistic rather than the atomistic approach is corroborated by the Qur'an and fits the context.

Sura 90 (al-Balad)

> *I swear by this city – and you [Prophet] are an inhabitant of this city – I swear by parent and offspring that We have created man for toil and trial (kabad).*
>
> Q. 90:1–4

Mecca was the city that received revelation and the recipient of that revelation lived there. The imagery used in this chapter indicates hardship. Mecca is referred to in the Qur'an as being in an uncultivated valley (Q. 14:37). The Prophet is later told, in Q. 47:13, '*We have destroyed many a town stronger than your own [Prophet] – the town which expelled you.*'

He is repeatedly reminded that people in times of earlier prophets also rejected them (e.g. see Q. 22:43–5).

The second oath is by parent and offspring. This relationship involves weakness at the beginning and end of life for both parent and offspring (see Q. 22:5 and Q. 30:54). The oath here also recalls that mothers struggle to carry their children and struggle to give birth to them (Q. 46:15). What makes parents and offspring worthy of being used in an oath is that it demonstrates God's power. Q. 25:54 stresses: '*It is He who creates human beings from fluid and makes them kin by blood and marriage: your Lord is most powerful.*' The weakness involved is a reminder to the arrogant person referred to in the following verses.

What is asserted, the *muqsam 'alayhi*, is: '*We have created man for toil and trial (kabad).*' *Kabad* can be interpreted as the burden of trust and responsibility (*amāna*) (see Q. 33:72) or of struggling on the way to meet one's Lord (see Q. 84:6). *Kabad* also reminds the Prophet that difficulty is a normal part of man's life, which should be met with patience. Indeed, it is a reminder to all, not just the Prophet and is quoted by, and to, individual believers counselling fortitude.

The rest of the sura reminds the ungrateful, arrogant human being and challenges him:

> *Yet he has not attempted the steep path. What will explain to you what the steep path is? It is to free a slave, to feed at a time of hunger an orphaned relative or a poor person in distress, and to be one of those who believe and urge one another to steadfastness and compassion. Those who do this will be on the right hand side but those who disbelieve in Our revelations will be on the left hand side, and the Fire will close in on them.*
>
> Q. 90:11–20

Sura 91 (al-Shams)

> *By the sun in its morning brightness and by the moon as it follows it, by the day as it displays the sun's glory and by the night as it covers it, by the sky and how He built it, and by the earth and how He spread it, by the soul and how He formed it and inspired it to know its own rebellion and piety! The one who purifies his soul succeeds and the one who corrupts it fails.*
>
> Q. 91:1–10

Here we have a series of contrasted astronomical phenomena to emphasise the contrast within the human soul, with its rebellion and piety. The oath leads to the *muqsam 'alayhi*: final success of those who purify their souls and failure of those who corrupt them. It is God who created all the contrasting elements. The contrast in His creation is well established, providing an argument for contrasting fates.

Sura 92 (al-Layl)

By the covering night, by the radiant day, by the male and female He created, the ways you take differ greatly. There is the one who gives, who is mindful of God, who testifies to goodness – We shall smooth his way towards ease. There is the one who is miserly, who is self-satisfied, who denies goodness – We shall smooth his way towards hardship.

Q. 92:1–10

Here again, God swears by great phenomena of His creation, contrasting night and day, male and female and the differences between people to emphasise the contrast between people who do good and those who do not, and the differences in their destinies at the Judgement.

Sura 95 (al-Tīn)

By the fig, by the olive, by Mount Sinai, by this safe city! We created man in the finest form, then We reduced him to the lowest of the low but those who believe and do good deeds will have an unending reward. After this, what makes you [man] deny the Judgement? Is God not the fairest of judges?

Q. 95:1–8

Most interpreters take the fig and the olive to mean the actual fruit. Both show the power of God who creates various fruits, all watered by the same water, but some are better in taste than others, as Q. 13:4 states. The same verse ends with, '*In this there are signs for those who reason*', followed by an expression of surprise at those who deny the Resurrection (Q. 13:5). In Q. 23:20, the Qur'an mentions a tree growing out of Mount Sinai that '*produces oil and seasoning for your food*', used, among other things mentioned before and after it, as a sign of God's power to resurrect the dead. In connection with the '*safe city*', Abraham prays to God (Q. 2:126 and Q. 14:37) to provide fruit for the people of Mecca. On the other hand, some interpreters see all the oaths as symbolic of the sites of prophets:[57] the fig referring to the area where Noah's Ark landed or to a temple there, the olive to the Holy Land where Jesus received his message and Mount Sinai, where Moses received his, while '*this safe city*' refers to Mecca where

Muhammad received his. It was Abraham who first prayed to God to make this land safe (Q. 2:121 and Q. 14:35), safety for the Sanctuary of Mecca is also emphasised in Q. 29:67 and Q. 106:4.

According to this interpretation, the oaths provide an argument that the *muqsam 'alayhi,* man's destiny, resurrection and judgement, were established in earlier religions before Islam, just as the Qur'an said to the Muslims in Medina, '*Fasting has been made obligatory for you as it was for those before you*' (Q. 2:183), a separate argument to persuade them to accept the obligation. So what Muhammad was calling them to believe in was '*not a new thing amongst prophets*' (Q. 46:9). Judgement was recognised in earlier religions, too.

Traditional interpreters and modern authors, such as Farāḥī, Smith and Neuwirth, take the *muqsam 'alayhi* to be that God made man in the best form, but then '*reduces him to the lowest of the low*'. I have come to believe that the *muqsam 'alayhi* is actually omitted after verse 4 (just as it was omitted in other oaths at the beginning of Suras 38, 50, 79 and 100). It is, however, understood in the light of verse 7, '*What makes you deny the Judgement?*' So the oath is 'I swear by the fig [...] that the Judgement is coming'. '*We created man in the finest form, then we reduced him to the lowest of the low*' refers to the decay of old age, mentioned in Q. 22:5, when a person will forget everything they once knew. Note the parallel between *yuraddu ilā* (Q. 22:5, '*some are left to live on*') and *radadnāhu* (Q. 95:5, '*[We] reduced him*') followed by the superlatives *ardhal al-'umur* and *asfal,* respectively. The effect of old age is emphasised in Q. 36:68: '*If We extend anyone's life, We reverse his development.*' This process is used as an argument for the Resurrection in Q. 22:5. So '*We created man in the best form*' is not the *muqsam 'alayhi* for '*by the fig*' since degeneration after strength is a very obvious fact to everybody and does not need an oath to establish it. It is true that it begins with *laqad khalaqnā,* containing the particle '*la*' we find in oaths, but so do identical statements like Q. 15:26 and Q. 32:12 which have no oaths. Ibn al-Qayyim makes the salient observation that the *muqsam 'alayhi*:

> is intended to be emphasised and established, so it must be suitable to be the *muqsam bihi* [...] while obvious things like the sun, the moon [...] are to suitable to be the *muqsam bihi,* but not the *muqsam 'alayhi.*[58]

Sūrat al-Tīn goes on to announce that faith and good deeds are the way to salvation and lasting life with good rewards.

Sura 103 (al-'Aṣr)

By the declining day, man is in loss, except for those who believe, do good deeds, urge one another to the truth, and urge one another to steadfastness.

Q. 103:1–3

Here God swears by the mid-afternoon time, when the daylight declines, or by time in general, both of which fade for any individual human. The amount of time available to any person is his only chance and unless he uses it to believe and do good deeds, he is deep in loss. Because of this the Qur'an urges people to '*race*' (*sābiqū*) for forgiveness (Q. 57:21) and 'hasten' (*sāri'ū*) to do good deeds (Q. 3:133) before:

death comes to one of you and he says, 'My Lord, if You would only reprieve me for a little while, I would give in charity and become one of the righteous.' God does not reprieve a soul when its term comes.

Q. 63:10–11

The argument in *Sūrat al-'Aṣr* is that the very thing God is swearing by is a proof of man's loss and he should use it in the way suggested. The '*declining day*' also carries the connotation of something coming to an end, such as the lives of humans, and this therefore places even greater emphasis on the idea of 'urging' one another to act righteously, before it is too late.

Sura 52 (al-Ṭūr)

By the mountain, by writing inscribed in unrolled parchment, by the much-visited House, by the raised canopy, by the ocean, ever-filled, your Lord's punishment is coming – it cannot be put off – on the Day when the sky sways back and forth and the mountains float away.

Q. 52:1–10

The *muqsam 'alayhi* is the punishment following the Resurrection and Judgement, and the oath is made by five elements: first is the mountain, taken to refer to Mount Sinai, where Moses received his message. It can also mean 'a mountain' that seems so firm and solid (*awtād*, Q. 78:7), yet on the Last Day it will float away.[59] The second element is writing inscribed on unrolled parchment. Here again, it is solid, unalterable and spread out for all to see. Suyūṭī takes this to refer to the Torah or the Qur'an. Some say it refers to where the angels write down the deeds of human beings. This last meaning is more suitable for Judgement and is corroborated by Q. 17:13–14:

'On the Day of Resurrection, We shall bring out a record for each of them, which they will find spread wide open, "Read your record".' According to the deeds recorded, in this context, the punishment will follow inevitably. The third element is '*the much-visited House*'. Some say it is the home in heaven, but this is inconsequential and more likely it is the Ka'ba, described in the Qur'an as '*the first house [of worship] to be established for people*' (Q. 3:96), which was the centre of Mecca, much visited and much venerated by the Arabs, even before Islam. So far the oath refers to two messages (both of which confirm the Resurrection and Judgement). The Qur'an refers to earlier messages and particularly that of Moses, in support of its teaching (see also Q. 2:184 and Q. 28:48). The fourth element of the oath is the canopy raised high, the sky, which shows God's power and care in many other places in the Qur'an, but the falling of the sky is also used as a threat (e.g. in Q. 22:65 and Q. 17:92): on the Day of Judgement it will split or break (Q. 82:1 and Q. 84:1). The fifth and final element of the oath is *al-baḥr al-masjūr*, also used as a threat in Q. 10:22, Q. 17:67–9 and Q. 24:40, even though it is normally a sign of God's care (Q. 16:14 and Q. 45:12). So the oaths could be referring to two divine messages that warn of punishment for wrongdoers, and then two stark entities which can be instruments of punishment – the sky and the sea – even though they are normally a blessing.

Internal Oaths

So far we have dealt with oaths occurring at the beginning of suras. This was for ease of handling the material. We now turn to oaths internal to the suras. It is not that they are different or will change the classification we adopted according to the *muqsam 'alayhi* (the thing to be confirmed by the oath). The only possible difference is that placing the oath at the start of the sura puts the focus on the issue at stake, for example resurrection, right at the beginning, which can affect the name of the sura (compare *Sūrat al-Qiyāma*, 'Resurrection'). There are a number of such cases where the oath occurs inside the sura (Suras 51, 56, 69, 74, 81, 84 and 86).

Sūrat al-Dhāriyāt (Q. 51:23)

On the earth there are signs for those with sure faith – and in yourselves too. Do you not see? – In the sky is your sustenance and all that you are promised. By the Lord of the heavens and the earth! All this is as real as your speaking.

Q. 51:20–23

As can be seen from the examples given here, God does not normally swear by Himself, that is, saying by Allah, as the oath is meant as evidence of the Resurrection. Here He is swearing by His lordship of the heavens and the earth with all the signs they contain. The disbelievers are seen in the Qur'an to admit that God created the heavens and the earth (Q. 39:38). They would also not deny that their sustenance (*rizq*), such as rain, comes from the sky and that there are signs on earth. Thus God's lordship of the heavens and the earth and the signs they contain are given as evidence for the statement of the oath. Since God is already acknowledged as creator, His ability to resurrect people should likewise be acknowledged; thus the function of the oath.

Sūrat al-Wāqiʿa (Q. 56:75–80)

I swear by the positions of the stars – a mighty oath, if you only knew – this is truly a noble Qur'an, in a protected Record that only the purified can touch, sent down from the Lord of all the worlds.[60]

The discussion above on Q. 74:1–2 applies here. The context of the oath in Sura 56 is the confirmation of the Resurrection, contrary to what the disbelievers argued in Q. 56:47–8, followed by confirmation and a strong, four-pronged argument. The oath comes to say that this is not just fanciful talk, but a noble Qur'an (*qur'ān* also meaning 'recitation'), not composed by Muhammad, but coming from high above in a protected record, touched only by the purified. Swearing the mighty oath of the positions of the stars, again far above and beyond anyone's reach, yet giving light and guidance to those below (see Q. 16:16). The Qur'an comes from an even higher level and it too is sent down to give light and guidance. The oath reinforces the foregoing argument for the Resurrection by asserting the supremacy of what the Qur'an says about it, coming as it does from the Lord of all the worlds and not from any level within reach of human beings.

Sūrat al-Ḥāqqa (Q. 69:38–40)

I swear by what you can see and what you cannot see: this [Qur'an] is the word [spoken by] an honourable messenger, not the word of a poet – how little you believe – nor the word of a soothsayer – how little you reflect! This [Qur'an] is a message sent down from the Lord of the worlds.

Q. 69:38–43

Again, this comes in the context of the Resurrection and Judgement (verses 13–27), followed by the oath to confirm that the discussion of Resurrection and Judgement is not fanciful talk, but revelation. Al-Rāzī suggests that '*what you can see and what you cannot see*' covers all, including the Creator, this life and the next, bodies and souls, humans and jinn, blessings both obvious and hidden.[61] The point of the oath is to remind humans they are not able to see everything. They cannot see the angel (the '*honourable messenger*', mentioned in Q. 81:19–20) who reveals the Qur'an to the Prophet.

Sūrat al-Takwīr (Q. 81:15–23)

This is similar in that it deals with the Resurrection. The oath comes after the description of the Day of Judgement:

I swear by the planets that recede, move and hide, by the night that descends, by the dawn that softly breathes: this is the word [spoken by] a noble messenger, who possesses great strength and is held in honour by the Lord of the Throne, obeyed there and worthy of trust. Your companion is not mad: he did see him on the clear horizon.

The oath is by planets, high in the sky that move and hide, by night and dawn when it breathes; all cannot be denied by the disbelievers, even though they are not always seen by humans. Although they cannot see the angel of revelation, referred to as the '*noble messenger*', this does not negate his existence and transmission of the Qur'an. In Sura 69 above, the verses make a clear distinction between the revelation received through the angel and poetry, here between revelation and the results of being possessed by a jinn or madness.

Sūrat al-Inshiqāq (Q. 84:16–19)

I swear by the twilight, by the night and what it covers, by the full moon: you will progress from stage to stage.

Again, the context is the Resurrection and Judgement. The oath covers a series of stages of the time of day: twilight, night and full moon. The progression is natural and inevitable, just as the progression of these people who deny the Resurrection will be from the end of their lives, to the grave, to the Resurrection when they will see the full light of what they have denied. They can see the stages of life and death, but not the stage beyond. The oath confronts the disbelievers with a phenomenon of progression they witness and experience regularly. The One who causes this progression in the life of this world is the One who will continue it in the next, and He is well able to do so.

Sūrat al-Muddaththir (Q. 74:32–7)

By the moon! By the departing night! By the shining dawn! It [the Fire, saqar[62]] is one of the mightiest things, a warning to mortals, to those of you who choose to heed and those who lag behind.

Again the oath is by a series of stages of the time of night, leading to the shining dawn, coming from darkness into light, a phenomenon occurring nightly, but which is great and shows God's great power, just like the Fire which the disbelievers deny now, but will not be able to deny when they come to it. The coverings will be removed from their eyes and they will be able to see (compare Q. 50:22 and Q. 52:14–15) as clearly as they see the dawn. The pronoun '*-hā*' in '*innahā iḥdā al-kubar*' in verse 35 is feminine and therefore refers to the Fire: it comes between two passages describing Hell, using the female noun *saqar*, which the disbelievers will suffer, but not the companions of the right hand, who will be in Paradise (verses 39–40).

This completes all the divine oaths in the Qur'an, dealing with the Resurrection. We will now give a summary classification of all the oaths on the Resurrection.

The oath(s) in:

- Sura 51 gives an argument from nature for the Resurrection.
- Sura 52 confirms the Resurrection and the punishment of the disbelievers.
- Suras 56 and 81 confirm the veracity of the Qur'an that speaks about Resurrection and Judgement.
- Suras 77, 79 and 100 warn of the suddenness and awesomeness of the Resurrection.
- Sura 75 establishes God's ability to bring about the Resurrection.
- Suras 74 and 84 use natural phenomena to show the progression towards Resurrection.
- Sura 95 confirms the Resurrection and Judgement as evidenced in successive revelations, and provides arguments from human development.
- Sura 86 concerns the recording of human deeds for Judgement and embryological and agricultural arguments for the Resurrection.
- Suras 90, 91, 92 and 103 confirm the human situation and destiny in Judgement.

Conclusion

In Arabic grammar and rhetoric, oaths are meant to emphasise a point for those who doubt or deny it. This function is well implemented in the Qur'an, especially as the doubt of the unbelievers was about the fundamental beliefs in the unity of God, the prophethood of Muhammad and above all the Resurrection and Judgement. The Qur'an was clearly very much interested in having its message listened to by those who doubted or denied it. It did not state its message with no interest in how it is received, but tried hard to convince those who rejected it by using oaths,[63] other arguments and by persuasion and dissuasion, known as *targhīb* and *tarhīb*.

Divine oaths in the Qur'an, moreover, are not merely for emphasis; they serve, in addition to the general function of oaths in Arabic, another important function that makes them stand in a class of their own: they are evidential oaths; they furnish an argument or evidence for the statement of the oath. This was more fitting for the Qur'an. A simple oath may be readily ignored; an evidential oath has more chance of being listened to and is more likely to convince. In divine oaths, as seen earlier, the Qur'an employs obvious, tangible elements such as the following:

- astronomical: the sun, the moon, the stars, sky and earth;
- physical: the wind;
- time: dawn, mid-morning, mid-afternoon, twilight, night, ten nights, the Promised Day and the Day of Resurrection;
- places: Mount Sinai and Mecca;
- gender and reproduction: male and female;
- relationships: parent and offspring;
- animals: horses;
- plants: figs and olives;
- others: the Qur'an, angels, the pen and what they write, the Lord and life.

In using such elements, the oaths echo other references in the Qur'an that give further explanation and make the oaths all the more effective. For example, Q. 91:3–4, '*By the day as it displays the sun's glory, by night as it covers it*', recalls Q. 28:71–3:

Say, 'Just think: if God were to cast perpetual night over you until the Day of Resurrection, what god other than He could bring you light? Do you not listen?' Say, 'Just think, if God were to cast perpetual day over you until the Day of Resurrection, what god other than He could give you night in which to rest? Do you not see? In His mercy He has given you night and day, so that you may rest and seek His bounty and be grateful.'

The oath by the pen in Q. 68:1 recalls '*Your Lord is the most generous, who taught by the pen*' in Q. 96:3–4 and '*If all the trees were pens and all the seas, with seven more seas besides, [were ink,] still God's words would not run out*' in Q. 31:27.

An important point about divine oaths in the Qur'an is that although they were introduced to convince, in the first instance, the disbelievers in Mecca at that time (but still seek to persuade all disbelievers), they have remained a source of awe, reflection and certainty for the believers: '*They reflect on the creation of the heavens and earth: Our Lord, You have not created all this without purpose – You are far above that*' (Q. 3:191). The elements of the oaths inspire glorification of God and provide confirmation of the fundamental beliefs, through which '*the faithful grow in faith*' (*yazdāda'lladhīna āmanū īmānan*, Q. 74:31). The proper study of the oath should therefore not stop at classifying and discussing their forms. Studying the oaths according to their functions and objectives, as shown in this chapter, brings us closer to the meaning of the Qur'an than any classification according to form or style.

Appendix

Here are the opinions of three scholars cited above on Sura 51 (*Sūrat al-Dhāriyāt*) for comparison with my explanations.

Smith

By those winds carrying away, those which bear a load, those which run easily, and those which distribute according to command! That which you are promised is indeed true. The judgement is indeed about to happen. By heaven with its tracks! You are sure of varying words and he who is turned away will turn away from it.

Having accepted all the participles as referring to the winds, we are back again with the natural phenomena of the universe. The same remarks in this connection, therefore, apply here as those above under LXX, 40–41. Again we have a series of very well balanced oaths, made up of the feminine plural participles and an indefinite noun in the form of the *manṣūb*, that in verse 1 being the *maf'ūl muṭlaq*. These oaths have a rhyming pattern, *-wan/-ran/-ran/-ran*. Both *jawābs* are nominal sentences with the *lām al-ta'kīd* prefixed to the predicates, and form their own rhyming scheme, *-qun/-'un*. It is the balance and the rhyme, in particular, in this first part of the passage under discussion which round off a successful string of oaths emphasising brilliantly the ideas expressed in the *jawābs*, namely that the promises made to the people of Mecca are not idle promises and that the judgement will inevitably fall on them.[64]

Farāhī

In S. 51, verses 5–6 (MA [*muqsam alayhi*]) assert that human actions shall be recompensed in the hereafter. Verses 1–4, 7 (MB [*muqsam bihi*]) produce the requisite evidence. As agents of divine mercy, the winds and rains have wiped out many a rebellious nation. But the same elements of nature which destroyed Noah's opponents and Pharaoh's troops also delivered Noah and Moses and their followers. This shows that God is not indifferent to man's conduct on earth. He rewards and punishes in this world, and He will do so in the next life as well.[65]

Neuwirth

The oath cluster again presents a tableau of clouds signalling a rain-storm. Again there is a continuous movement followed up until it reaches its destination, the clouds again being prototypes of particular eschatological features. In the end something still unexperienced is announced to come down: *inna-l-dīna la-wāqi'*. Here the element to fall down is named explicitly, a deviation from the treatment of oaths observed in the previous cases, where the tension aroused by the tableau was upheld for some time. On the other hand, the matrix of images proves very efficient: throughout the long *sūra* the examples of retributional catastrophes are taken from among phenomena that are imagined to fall down from heaven; thus the people of Lūṭ are punished by *ḥijāra min ṭīn* (v. 33), the people of 'Ād are seized by a suffocating wind, *rīḥ 'aqīm* (v. 41), those of Thamūd by a thunderstorm, *ṣā'iqa* (v. 44); the well-known fact that the people of Nūḥ are extinguished by a rain flood does not deserve explicit mention (v. 46). The entire section of retributional legends constantly refers to the prototype of phenomena involving catastrophes 'raining down from the sky', introduced in the oath cluster. [...] It is evident from this *sūra*, which is counted among the later pieces within the first Makkan period, that the structural function of the introductory oath clusters has changed during the Makkan development: it still introduces a prototypical tableau of the imminent eschatological incidents, but the sensation of an 'enigma' which used to be involved in the early cases has now disappeared; the anticipation of the explicit mentioning of the eschatological phenomena, therefore need not be withheld for long – it is immediately dissolved. The second role of the oath cluster now emerges as all the more efficient in its function of a 'matrix of images' for diverse, but psychologically related – in the listener's mind – signs of divine omnipotence which we found dispersed over the whole *sūra*.[66]

10

Rhetorical Style: Arabic of the Qur'an

The Qur'an uses the fact that it was revealed in Arabic to argue that the Arabs who heard it had no excuse for not understanding:

> *We have sent it down as an Arabic Qur'an so that you [people] may understand.*
>
> Q. 12:2

The first objective of the Qur'an is to guide and it uses effective language (*qawlan balīghan*, Q. 4:62). That is why it uses persuasion and dissuasion (*targhīb* and *tarhīb*). After all it came to change people's beliefs and practices, so the rhetorical effect is intended throughout and overrides formal grammar. European scholars who approached it within a framework of formal grammar in their own languages found problems, for example the great Theodor Nöldeke with his comments on the rhetorical devise called *iltifāt* (shift) as will be discussed later. John Burton wrote about the 'Linguistic errors in the Qur'an'.[1] Similarly John Wansbrough[2] saw grammatical error where in fact stylistic considerations overrode formal grammar. These scholars neglected the consideration of Qur'anic rhetorical style which was already part of the Arabic language. This is what will be discussed in this chapter.

As Abū 'Ubayda stated:

> Since the Qur'an was revealed in the language of the people of the Prophet, the early generations and those who were present at the time of the Prophet did not ask about its meanings because they were Arabs and Arabic was their language

and their knowledge gave them no need to ask about its meanings. The ways of expression and conciseness were similar to what the Arabs had in their tongue. The Qur'an did include such ways of *i'rab, gharīb* and *ma'ānī* as were present in the Arabic language.[3]

So, the Qur'an conformed to Arabic speech: it provided the reason for codifying Arabic grammar and stylistics and was used as a criterion for these disciplines. It was in order to make sure that all Muslims, especially non-Arabs, could read the Qur'an accurately that Muslims began to think of writing down a grammar of their language, based on the text of the Qur'an, on Arabic poetry and speech. Arabic phonetics originated in the quest to describe exactly the proper pronunciation and articulation of the Qur'an and developed into the science of *tajwīd* and the art of reciting the Qur'an. Similarly, the study of Arabic rhetoric flourished for the service of the Qur'an, culminating in the works of the outstanding scholar 'Abd al-Qāhir al-Jurjānī (d. 474/1078), particularly his *Dalā'il al-i'jāz* and *Asrār al-balāgha* (see bibliography), which investigate the style and rhetoric of the Qur'an in an attempt to identify the reasons for the inimitability (*i'jāz*) of its language. In his opinion, the central issue of Arabic grammar is *ta'līq* or 'syntactic relations', which is closely bound up with stylistics. In fact, it is only by studying these two disciplines together in the Qur'an that one gains a true understanding of how they work.

Even in their study of the principles of literary criticism, Arab critics drew heavily on the text of the Qur'an, as can be seen, for example, in the celebrated work of the critic Ibn al-Athīr (d. 630/1233)[4] in his *al-Mathal as-sā'ir fī 'adab al-kātib wa'l-shā'ir* on the criticism of prose and poetry. As al-Suyūṭī (d. 911/1505), a writer on many subjects including Qur'anic studies and linguistics, states, the Qur'an was in fact the source for all branches of Arab knowledge.[5] In the Islamic educational system, learning grammar is connected with the Qur'an. In the first grammar lessons at the primary school of al-Azhar in Cairo (which opened in 972 CE), students are introduced to *al-mabādi' al-'ashara*, 'the ten introductory aspects', with which the grammar textbook begins and which are necessary when embarking on the study of any branch of knowledge. They include the definition of that particular discipline, its name, the issues it deals with, its founder, its relation to other subjects, its status among other subjects and how the Qur'an views the learning of that subject. The status of grammar, students are told, is foremost because it ensures correct understanding and reading of the Arabic text of the Qur'an, and as such, its study is incumbent on the Muslim community. In addition to any educational or secular purpose, learning grammar and linguistics in general is a religious duty in al-Azhar and similar traditional institutions of learning in the Muslim world.

Thus, in the Muslim world, the Qur'an is the starting point of Arabic linguistic scholarship. Outside the Muslim world, another vigorous tradition of Arabic linguistic scholarship has developed in Western universities (especially since the seventeenth century), which from the beginning was driven in no small measure by its relevance to the Qur'an and Islam (Arabic studies in Europe). This has led to the production of monumental works in the study of Arabic and Islam in leading European centres of learning, in various languages, including Dutch, English, French, German, Italian, Russian and Spanish.

Grammar and Rhetoric

It would be incorrect to talk about the grammar of the Arabic Qur'an as being different from general Arabic grammar; no scholar, neither Arab nor non-Arab, has written as a separate study a comprehensive grammar of the Qur'an. The Qur'an conforms to the grammatical norms of Arabic and includes some dialectal features in the different readings, all of which were understood by the Arabs who first heard the revelation. Around the Prophet, there were Muslims from all parts of Arabia, and there are no comments on record that any of the Qur'an's grammatical features were found to be foreign to the Arabic language people were used to.[6]

When grammarians devised their rules, based on what is general and regular in Arabic (*muttarid*, see section below on 'Declension (*i'rāb*)'), and found that certain instances in the Qur'an, notably various dialectal features, did not conform to the general pattern, they still recognised that these do conform to other recognised grammatical or stylistic patterns in the language, and thus, even if they were not included as part of the *muttarid* rules of grammar[7] and were considered abnormal (*shādhdh*), they were still correct (*faṣīḥ*) since they belonged to the language of the age of normative Arabic (*ihtijāj*). This age is normally considered to be the period up to the middle of the second century AH in urban centres and the mid-fourth century AH in Bedouin localities. The language of this era is regarded as correct and fit to be used as a linguistic model.

The Arabic language is broader than the *muttarid* rules and irregularity does not preclude correctness (*al-shudhūdh lā yunāfī al-faṣāḥa*). Rather than speaking of the grammar of the Qur'an, then, it would be more accurate to speak of the Qur'an's ways of using Arabic grammatical patterns in expressing its message and how these work in tandem with rhetorical considerations. In this chapter, various grammatical features in the Qur'an will be dealt with. A scheme that may help the discussion to be more inclusive and systematic and that concentrates on the central issue of Arabic grammar (the *ta'līq* or 'syntactic relations') is to look at the cues of syntactic relations and how the Qur'an deals with them, and then, to look at some frequently used rhetorical features in the Qur'an.

Syntactic Relations and Their Cues

Like all other languages, Arabic has a set of 'cues' for determining syntactic relations between the different parts of a sentence. These can either be morpho-syntactic or semantic. In Arabic, morpho-syntactic cues have been categorised as follows:[8]

1. morphological structure (*binya*) of a word;
2. declension (*i'rāb*);
3. binding (*rabṭ*);
4. order (*ruṭba*);
5. syntagmatic requirement (*taḍāmm*);
6. verbal context (*siyāq*).

Semantic cues include such categories as predication, transitivity and purpose, which will not be dealt with here. These cues determine the grammatical function of words and make the meaning of the sentence clear. They act together in what is known in Arabic as *tadāfur al-qarā'in*, 'interrelatedness of links'. This makes it sometimes possible to dispense with a given cue because other cues still make the grammatical function and meaning of the statement clear. The language of the Qur'an, and Arabic in general, has norms for observing verbal cues or dispensing with them for stylistic purposes in order to achieve certain effects that serve the intended message in any given situation.

Morphology

The Morphological Unit

A morphological unit can have multiple meanings. The definite article '*al-*' can refer to a class (*jinsiyya*), such as in *al-insān*, 'mankind' or 'the human being' (Q. 70:19), or it can refer to something already mentioned or understood from the context (*'ahdiyya*), such as in *al-nās*, 'the people of Mecca [mentioned earlier]' (Q. 17:93) or *al-kitāb*, 'the book [referring to the Qur'an]' (Q. 5:48). '*Al-*' can also be used as a resumptive pronoun, as in Q. 9.26 saying, '*He punished the disbelievers – this is what the disbelievers [al-kāfirīna, instead of 'they'] deserve*', or it can be used for binding (*rabṭ*), as in Q. 79:39 saying, '*As for anyone who has transgressed and preferred the present life, Hell will be home* [*al-ma'wā*, meaning 'his home']'.

This last usage serves to maintain rhythm and rhyme, an important consideration in the Qur'an, and gives the statement a generality that will include this person and any of his type. Generality of meaning (*ta'mīm*), as will be seen, often has an important place in the Qur'an.

Departure from Regular Morphology

Departure by omission: An instance of omission is that of the letter *yā'* (long i-vowel), indicating the first person singular, at the end of *da'āni* in '*When My servants ask you [Prophet] about Me, I am near, I respond to those who call me (da'āni)*' (Q. 2:186), leaving only the *kasra* (short i-vowel). Rhetorically, this serves the function of shortening the statement to express how close God is to anyone who calls Him, which is the point of this verse. This is enhanced by omitting the words 'Say to them' following 'When My servants ask you' earlier in the sentence, as well as stated expressly in the words 'I am near'. The omission for stylistic effect does not impair the sense, as the *kasra* at the end of the two words indicates the original form of the word (the *yā'* is also omitted in *al-dā'i* in the same verse). Again, in *rabbanā wa-taqabbal du'ā'i, 'Our Lord, accept my request'* (Q. 14:40), the final *yā'* is omitted in order to maintain the rhythm and rhyme (see also Q. 18:64 and 66; Q. 22:54; Q. 40:15 and Q. 67:17).

Departure by addition: Addition takes place, for instance, in Q. 37:130, '*Peace be to Ilyāsīn*' instead of '*Ilyās*' (although al-Rāzī suggests that he is Ilyās b. Yāsīn), where the addition of '*-īn*' maintains the rhythm and rhyme for effect.

Declension (i'rāb)

I'rāb has occupied Arab grammarians to a great extent, even though in many situations it is not necessary as a cue for syntactic relations, as in pronouns and indeclinable nouns, in weak *lam* verbs and in nouns that do not allow for final vowels to appear, which are frequent in Arabic. The Qur'an conforms to the general rules of *i'rāb,* but there are notable examples where the general rules are set aside, and less common dialectal patterns are used for stylistic purposes. One well-known case is the occurrence of a sound masculine plural in a list of entities, where there is a departure from co-ordination for rhetorical purposes. In Q. 5:69, '*The believers, the Jews, the Christians and the Sabians – all those who believe in God and the Last Day – there is no fear for them, nor will they grieve*', all the nouns are governed by the accusative ending '*-īna*', but the Sabians appear in the nominative, ending in '*-ūna*'. This has been taken to be an example of *iltifāt,* that is, a departure from the general rule for the purpose of highlighting, in this case the Sabians, in order to emphasise that even they, who are less close to the scriptural tradition, will have no fear or cause to grieve.[9] Another example of shift can be seen in Q. 2:177, in this case from the expected nominative *al-ṣābirūn,* '*those who are steadfast*', which would be in coordination with the other nouns, to the accusative *al-ṣābirīn,* so as to highlight the importance of this particular quality in the situation.

A number of occurrences of *iltifāt* have been described as 'linguistic errors'[10] by John Burton. He regards, for instance, the occurrence of *al-muqīmīna'l-ṣalāt,* '*those who perform the prayers*', instead of *al-muqīmūna'l-ṣalāt* in the middle of a list of types in Q. 4:162 as a linguistic error, although this is recognised as an admissible, familiar pattern in Arabic[11] and as a form of *iltifāt.*[12] Another example which Burton considers to be an error is Q. 20:63, saying '*inna hādhāni la-sāḥirāni*', 'These are certainly two sorcerers', said about Moses and Aaron by Pharaoh's sorcerers. Normally, *hādhāni* is governed by *inna* and should have been rendered as *hādhayni* (i.e. in the accusative instead of the nominative it appears in); however, there is an Arabic dialect known as *lugha man yulzimu al-muthannā al-alif* (a dialect in which the dual invariably has the nominative ending), rendering the word *hādhāni* for all cases).[13] The reason for this departure from the normal rules is therefore the observance of *hikāya* (quoting what someone has said), regardless of the normal rules of inflection, a dialectal feature that has been used here for rhetorical effect. The statement quoted is made by sorcerers, and in sorcery, as observed even now in Arabic, sound effect is important as part of the incantation. Here, we have three successive words all with *alif* (long a-vowel), followed by *nūn* (consonant n): *hādhāni, sāḥirāni* and *yurīdāni,* so to change *hādhāni* into *hādhayni* would break the pattern. The general grammatical rule has been suspended here for a rhetorical purpose, and as in all these examples, the suspension of *i'rāb* has not impaired the meaning, because other cues determine the grammatical functions of the individual words. Cues cooperate in the sense that the structure, word order, syntagmatic requirement, and so on, all indicate the grammatical function, even if the general rule of *i'rāb* is suspended. Another occurrence of suspension of *i'rāb* occurs in Q. 12:11 when Joseph's brothers say to their father, '*Why do you not trust us (lā ta'mannā) with Joseph?*' The verb should have been in the indicative mood, *ta'manunā*, but this rule was set aside for the purpose of *idghām* (gemination), in this case of the two *nūns* close together, which makes the pronunciation lighter (*akhaff*) in Arabic, an intended phonetic effect.

Binding (rabṭ)

Binding is achieved by reference, concordance and particles.

Reference (ihāla)

Ihāla can be achieved through the use of the following devices: repetition of the same word or phrase; personal, demonstrative or relative pronouns; the definite article '*al-*'; and, sometimes, the binding element may be omitted.

Repetition: There are numerous examples of this in the Qur'an:

Do they not see that God brings life into being and reproduces it. Truly this is easy for God.

Q. 29:19

It was not without purpose that We created the heavens and earth and everything in between. That may be what the disbelievers assume. Woe to the disbelievers from Hellfire!

Q. 38:27

This type is known in *balāgha* as *wad' al-ẓāhir mawdi' al-ḍamīr* (using a noun in place of a pronoun). Repetition of the name of God, as above, in an independent statement to indicate His capabilities or qualities, in contrast to the other gods of the polytheists, is especially common. Repeating 'the disbelievers' instead of using the pronoun 'them' indicates that their disbelief was the cause of their opinion and their doom.[14] It also creates, as in the first case, an independent statement, quotable on its own and effective in religious discourse.

Repetition may also be used to recapitulate and refresh the memory when a sentence has become long. Again, this type of binding is quite common in the Qur'an:

When there came to them a scripture confirming what they already had; when [...]; when [...]; when there came to them [...], they disbelieved.

Q. 2:89

Why, when the soul of a dying man comes up to his throat, while you merely gaze on – We are nearer to him than you, though you do not see Us – why, if you are not subjected, do you not restore his soul to him?

Q. 56:83–7

Pronouns: The personal pronoun must refer to a referent, normally the nearest suitable preceding referent, and it must agree with this both in form and in meaning. Sometimes, the referent is not stated but deduced (*mutaṣayyad*). For example, in Q. 2:182, '*But if anyone knows that the testator has made a mistake, or done wrong, and so puts things right between them, he will incur no sin*', 'them' stands here for the parties involved. Also, in '*If God were to punish people [at once] for the wrong they have done, there would not be a single creature left on its surface*' (Q. 35:45) and in '*everyone on it perishes*' (Q. 55:26), 'its' and 'it' are generally understood to mean 'the earth'. This is in accordance with the rule according to which 'it is permissible to omit what is understood', and it has the benefit of conciseness.

The principle of proximity of the referent can be dispensed with if the relationship is understood without ambiguity. For example, in '*There are lessons in the story of Joseph and his brothers for those who seek them. They said, "Although we are many, Joseph and his brother are dear"*' (Q. 12:7–8), 'they said' does not refer to the closest referent ('those who seek') but to 'his brothers'.

As regards agreement between the pronoun and its referent, the Qur'an departs from this in numerous situations. First and foremost, this is the case of *iltifāt*, 'grammatical shift' for rhetorical purposes, a widespread feature of Qur'anic style, of which hundreds of examples can be cited. In discussing some examples of this feature Nöldeke remarks, without referring to the Arabic term, that 'the grammatical persons change from time to time in the Qur'an in an unusual and not beautiful way'.[15] Arab writers, in contrast, see the matter differently. The critic, Ibn al-Athīr, for instance, after studying this stylistic feature, classes it among the 'remarkable things and exquisite subtleties we have found in the glorious Qur'an'.[16] Rhetoricians have called this stylistic feature *shajāʿat al-ʿarabiyya* because in their opinion it demonstrates the daring nature of the Arabic language. If any daring is to be attached to *iltifāt*, it should, above all, be the daring of the language of the Qur'an, since it employs this feature according to effective patterns and for stylistic reasons, more extensively and in more variations than does Arabic poetry. Ibn al-Athīr, writing about rhetoric in prose and poetry, derives most of his examples from the Qur'an. The hundreds of examples in the Qur'an clearly show that stylistic considerations can overrule grammar, but always for a rhetorical purpose, without impairing the sense or causing any ambiguity.

Six types of *iltifāt* have been identified, but only those relating to shifts in person as reflected in the pronoun and its referent will be discussed here. The other types of *iltifāt* are change in number, between singular, dual and plural; change in addressee; change in the tense of the verb; change in case-marker; and use of nouns in place of pronouns.[17] Change in person, between first, second and third, is the most common occurrence of this type. For example, in '*Who created the heavens and earth? Who sends down water from the sky for you – with which We cause gardens of delight to grow: you have no power to make the trees grow in them – is it another god beside God?*' (Q. 27:60), the Qur'an shifts to the first person plural of majesty ('We'), which occurs at a crucial point for the listeners (see also Q. 14:4). There is a shift from first to third person in '*Give, out of what We have provided for you, before death comes to one of you and he says, "Reprieve me Lord", but God reprieves no soul when its time comes*' (Q. 63:10–11). This shift makes the final statement independent and absolute. It also indicates the contrast with other gods who do not have such power.

An example of a shift from third to second person is '*Praise be to God [...] You alone we worship, You alone we ask for help*' (Q. 1:1–4). After establishing that praise is only due to the Creator who has such attributes to make Him truly worthy of praise and the only true source of help, the worshipper turns to address God directly for the rest of the sura to ask for His help. A further example, this one from second to third person, can be found in '*It is God who has given you spouses [...] and from them He has given you children and grandchildren. How can they believe in falsehood and deny God's favours!*' (Q. 16:72). In this shift from 'you' to 'they', God turns to call everyone to witness the ingratitude of the people in question.

Similarly, in examples of other types, we witness departure from grammatical rules for specific rhetorical purposes. Without such rhetorical purpose, departure from the normal rules would be *mumtani'*, 'inadmissible', according to the rules of rhetoric, and there is always a proviso that the departure does not cause any *labs*, 'confusion, obscurity'.

On some occasions, there are two preceding referents and only one is selected, as in *arākum qawman tajhalūna*, '*I can see you are people who behave foolishly*' (Q. 11:29), in which the verb is in the second person (literally 'you behave foolishly'), rather than the third ('they behave foolishly', *yajhalūna*). The person in the verb is therefore in agreement with *arākum* ('I see you', second person) rather than with *qawman* ('a group') which is third person. In certain cases, the departure can also be in agreement in number, for example in '*They swear by God in order to please you [believers]. But God and His Messenger have more right that they should please Him*' (Q. 9:62), in which use of the singular pronoun avoids referring to God and His Messenger with a single pronoun ('Him' instead of 'them'), which would detract from *tawḥīd*, 'monotheism', and pleasing God would in any case please the Prophet.

Agreement in definite/indefinite status can also sometimes be departed from when the indefinite has been defined by an adjective, which brings it closer to being definite, as, for example, in *waylun li-kulli humazatin lumazatin alladhī jama'a mālan*, '*Woe to every fault-finding backbiter, who amasses wealth*' (Q. 104:1–2; see also Q. 50:32–3 and Q. 57:23–4). Here, one would expect not to find a relative pronoun in accordance with Arabic grammar as the relative clause refers to an indefinite noun.

Departure can also be from expected gender agreement, as in '*If We had wished, We could have sent them down a sign from heaven at which their necks would have stayed bowed down in utter humility*' (Q. 26:4), where *khāḍi'īna*, 'in humility', is masculine plural, but should be feminine singular as it refers to their necks (treated in Arabic as feminine singular). The use of the masculine plural shows more humility by implicitly including not just the necks of the disbelievers, but the rest of their persons which would indeed require the masculine plural form, and also maintains the rhyme which is an important consideration. Nor is the sense marred. Another example is '*On the day when you [Prophet] see the believers, both men and women, with their light streaming out before them*' (Q. 57:12), in which *yas'ā nūruhum*, 'their light streaming out', takes the masculine pronoun which includes both men and women according to the principle of *taghlīb*, 'grammatical preponderance' (see also Q. 57:13 and Q. 64:14). Finally, a construction known as *murāwaha*, 'alternation' between genders for a specific consideration can be seen in Q. 33:31, '*whoever of you [wives of the Prophet] is obedient (wa-man yaqnut) to God and his Messenger and does good (ta'mal ṣāliḥan), We will give her a double reward*. Here, the first verb *yaqnut* is masculine in agreement with the adjacent pronoun *man* ('whoever'), while the second verb *ta'mal* is feminine in agreement with the wife.

The demonstrative pronoun (such as *dhālika* and *ūlā'ika*) is frequently used as a binder in the Qur'an, for example in '*Whoever does good and believes, be it a man or a woman, these will enter paradise and be provided for without measure*' (Q. 40:40) and in '*The ones who lower their voices in the presence of God's Messenger, these are the ones whose hearts God has proved to be aware*' (Q. 49:3). The rhetorical purpose of using the demonstrative pronoun is to emphasise and highlight the class of persons who are being talked about. Similarly, the relative pronoun highlights, emphasises and singles out for either praise as in *alladhīna āmanū*, 'those who believe' in '*Those who believe and do good deeds, We do not let the reward of those who do good go to waste*' (Q. 18:30), or disparagement as in *alladhīna kafarū*, 'those who disbelieve' in '*When Our revelations are recited to them, you [Prophet] will recognise the denial in the faces of those who disbelieve*' (Q. 22:72). Again, this usage can make the final clause independently quotable.

The definite article 'al-' used as a binder

God is the light of the heavens and the earth. His light is like a niche in which there is a lamp, the lamp inside a glass, the glass is like a glittering star.

Q. 23:35

The repetition (using '*al-*' here rather than a pronoun), is particularly effective for the image and the way it is built up one layer inside the other (see also Q. 33:10). Another example is '*For him who feared the meeting with his Lord and restrained the soul [that is, his soul] (wa-nahā al-nafsa) from base desires, Paradise will be the home [that is, his home]*' (Q. 79:40–1). This latter example is one of several in which the use of '*al-*' instead of the pronoun helps maintain rhyme.

Omission of the binding element: In cases where there is no ambiguity, a binding element can be omitted in accordance to the general rule that 'there is no omission without an indicator to what is omitted' (*lā hadhfa illā bi-dalīl*). Pronouns in the third person in particular provide many examples of this in the Qur'an. For example, in Q. 2:75, '*God is not unaware of what you do*' is rendered as *mā ya'malūna rather than ya'malūnahu*. The omitted pronoun is clear from the context, and in many cases its omission preserves the rhyme. In the following case the rhyme is not involved: '*If you do not do, and you will not do...*' (Q. 2:24), meaning 'If you do not do that', where the pronoun 'that' is omitted.

Concordance

Binding is also realised by concordance (*mutābaqa*) in gender, number, case-ending, definiteness/indefiniteness and person (first, second or third). Concordance in these various elements binds words together and helps determine their grammatical functions. Concordance in number still pertains when a noun is singular in form but has the sense of plural, as in *wa-naḥnu ʿuṣbatun*, '*while we are a group*' (Q. 12:8), where *ʿuṣbatun* in the singular has a plural meaning and agrees with the plural pronoun *naḥnu*, 'we'. Likewise, *antum qalīlun*, '*You were few*' (Q. 8:26) and *naḥnu jamīʿun*, '*we together*' (Q. 54:44).

The relative pronoun *man* is grammatically singular and should, therefore, be followed by a singular pronoun even when the plural is intended, as in '*Did he not know that God had destroyed many generations before him, who had greater power than him (man huwa ashaddu minhu)?*', where *huwa* is a singular pronoun meaning 'many'.

Particles (*adāh*)

Particles are very important in binding Arabic sentences. The Arabic sentence, whether declarative, conditional or affective, with its numerous subdivisions, relies, in the overwhelming majority of cases, on the particle to bind its parts and express its grammatical category.[18] In Q. 6:107, *law shā'a'llāhu mā ashrakū*, 'If it had been God's will they would not have joined other gods with Him', without the conditional particle '*law*', the negative particle '*mā*' would have become *maṣdariyya* (an infinitive particle) to turn the meaning of the statement to 'God willed their joining others with Him'. Even when particles introduce nouns, as in the case of prepositions, conjunctions, exceptions and others, the particle still acts as a binder. As is amply illustrated in works like Ibn Hishām's *Mughnī al-labīb*,[19] the Qur'an employs particles extensively in its discourse for various stylistic purposes, such as the achievement of conciseness, cohesion and various other stylistic purposes.

Word Order

There are some instances in which the order of various lexical items in the Arabic sentence is fixed, as is the case in the positioning of prepositions and the nouns they govern, and of the various particles denoting exception, conjunction and interrogation, all of which must precede the noun.

An example from the Qur'an of another type of fixed-order sentence is *la'anahu'llāhu, 'God rejected him [Satan]'* (Q. 4:118), where the object is an inseparable pronoun ('*-hu*'), and so has to be attached to the verb and come before the subject. But there are also cases where the order is not fixed, such as the positioning of the object in relation to the verb and its subject, or that of the predicate of the subject of a nominal sentence. In a non-fixed order sentence, the object may be introduced first to serve a stylistic purpose of restriction (*hasr*) as in *iyyāka na'budu, 'You alone we worship'* (Q. 1:5). Departure from original word order for rhetorical purpose is very common in the Qur'an. Take, for example, Q. 37:86, *a-'ifkan ālihatan dūna'llāhi turīdūna, 'How can you choose false gods below God?'* The rhetorical question, put by Abraham to his people, shows objection to their worship of false gods, and the level of objection is reflected in the arrangement of the word order of the question itself, in diminishing strength. The strongest objection is that they are false; the fact that they are worshipping false gods comes second, especially as these false gods are inferior to God, and the final cause for objection is the fact that this has all been done on their own volition. In this case, an alternative word order such as *a-turīdūna ālihatan dūna'llāhi ifkan* would weaken the impact of both the statement and the objection being made.[20] Finally, in certain circumstances, the usually unfixed order has to be fixed, as in the verbal sentence *ḍaraba Mūsā 'Īsā*, 'Mūsā hit 'Īsā', in which, if the order were unfixed, the lack of *i'rāb* would leave the statement open to ambiguity, hence the first noun has to be the subject.

In a sentence where a number of adjectives of various kinds occur, the Qur'an tends to arrange them in order of length with the shortest first. For example, in Q. 40:28, *wa-qāla rajulun mu'minun min āli fir'awna yaktumu īmānahu, 'A secret believer from Pharaoh's family said'*, we have a single adjective (*mu'minun*, 'believing') coming before a prepositional phrase (*min āli fir'awna*, 'from Pharaoh's family') and then we have the adjectival clause (*yaktumu īmānahu*, 'who kept secret his faith'). This particular order serves to balance the sentence and maintain a good, effective rhythm (see also Q. 2:68–9 and Q. 23:117).

Syntagmatic Requirement (taḍāmm)

This is another wide area where grammar and rhetoric work together to serve the text of the Qur'an, including such features as omission, addition, separation, parenthesis and abnormal syntax.

Omission

Omission is a huge area in the Qur'an as can be seen from such books as *Majāz al-qur'ān* by 'Izzedīn Ibn 'Abd as-Salām.[21] It serves conciseness, an important stylistic feature of the Qur'an. As always with the principle of *lā hadhfa illā bi-dalīl,* there has to be something to indicate the omitted part, such as a well-recognised pattern of the word, a cue or the context. Here are a few examples:

1. Omission of the first member of the construct phrase (*iḍāfa*), in particular, occupies the largest space in *Majāz al-qur'ān.* For example: '*Ask the town'* meaning 'ask the people of the town' (Q. 12:83).
2. Omission of the final radical of the active participle as in *al-dā'i* instead of *al-dā'ī* (Q. 2:186), as explained earlier, or *hādi* instead of *hādī* (Q. 22:54).
3. Omission of the interrogative particle, as when Moses asks Pharaoh, *wa-tilka ni'matun tamunnuhā 'alayya, 'Is this a favour you reproach me for?'* (Q. 26:22), without the interrogative '*a*' since the intonation suffices.
4. Omission of a clause, as in '*If one of you is sick or on a journey, then [fast] on other days later*' (Q. 2:184) where 'and breaks the fast' is omitted (see also Q. 23:10 and 20).
5. Sometimes multiple sentences may be omitted, and there are many examples of this in the story of Joseph. For example, the king's cupbearer says, '*I can tell you the meaning of this dream. Give me leave to go.*' (Q. 12:45), and here the scene cuts immediately to his interview with Joseph, omitting all the possible narrative in between.

Addition

In Q. 27:5, *wa-hum fī'l-akhirati humu'l-akhsarūna,* '*and they, in the life to come, they will be the ones who will lose most*', the pronoun '*hum*', 'they' is added and repeated before the end for further emphasis.

Separation (Grammatical)

In Q. 62:1, *yusabbihu li'llahi mā fī'l-samāwāti wa-mā fī'l-arḍi'l-maliki'l-quddūsi'l-'azīzi'l-ḥakīm,* '*Everything in the heavens and the earth glorifies God, the Controller, the Holy One, the Almighty, the Wise*', the subject is placed between God and the nouns that qualify Him, to give the sentence rhythm, rhyme and balance and keep the emphasis on the nouns at the end.

Parenthesis

Parenthesis is a very widespread feature of the Qur'an. Many examples of separation are brought about by the insertion of parenthetical statements, for example, '*And those who implore God's forgiveness for their sin when they do wrong – and who forgives sins but God? – and never knowingly persist in doing wrong*' (Q. 3:136). Normally, when the Qur'an mentions a view or a statement with which it does not agree, it interrupts the flow of the sentence with a comment,[22] as in the following verse, '*They apportion to God a share of the produce and the livestock He created, saying, "This is for God" – so they claim! – "and this is for our idols*"' (Q. 60:136).

Abnormal Syntax

For example, in *wa-inna kullan lammā la-yuwaffiyannahum rabbuka a'mālahum, 'To each your Lord has not yet – He certainly will repay them for their deeds*' (Q. 11/111), the particle '*lammā*', 'not yet' should, grammatically speaking, introduce an imperfect verb in the jussive mood (*yuwaffihim*), but instead it comes before 'He will certainly', which indicates what has been omitted: 'He has not yet, but certainly will, repay them'. The omission is obvious; it avoids the unnecessary repetition that would weaken the statement, and the unusual syntax makes the statement more powerful and the threat more potent.

Context (siyāq)

Context is of crucial importance in determining meaning and syntactic relations. When other cues are departed from, which may result in ambiguity, context resolves this, and thus it has been rightly considered one of the key instruments in exegesis.[23] There are numerous examples in the Qur'an, of which only three will be cited here. In Q. 16:5, *wa'l-an'āma khalaqahā lakum fīhā dif'un wa-manāfi'u*, '*And livestock – He created them for you too. You derive warmth and other benefits from them*', grammatically, the phrase *lakum* may be governed by the verb *khalaqa*, where the meaning would be 'He created the cattle for you, in them there is warmth and…', or it could be the predicate of *dif'un*: 'there is warmth […] in them for you'. The context resolves this ambiguity, because the following verse has '*and there is beauty in them for you*', which parallels 'there is warmth in them for you'.

In Q. 13:11, *lahu mu'aqqibātun min bayni yadayhi wa-min khalfihi yaḥfaẓūnahu min amri'llāhi, 'Each person has guardian angels before him and behind, watching over him, by God's command*', the phrase *min amri'llāhi* ('by God's command') follows the verb *yaḥfaẓūnahu* ('they watch him') and could be interpreted as grammatically governed by it, meaning 'they protect him from God's command', but the correct reading is to see it as relating to *mu'aqqibātun* ('angels following [him]'), even though it is distant from it, as becomes clear from the context at the end of the verse: '*when God wills harm on a people, no one can ward it off*'.

The above two examples work in a local context, but an example of the importance of global context can be seen in Q. 6:37–8 where the disbelievers have demanded that the Prophet should produce a miraculous sign, and he is instructed to say, '*God is able to send down a sign*'. Then comes the comment, '*All the creatures that crawl on the earth and those that fly with their wings are communities like yourselves. We missed nothing out in the book (al-kitāb) and in the end they will be gathered to their Lord*'. Here, many exegetes have understood the word *al-kitāb* to refer to the Qur'an, which it in fact often does, and relate this to the preceding statement. They argue that this means that the Qur'an contains knowledge of everything, including all the animals and birds, and go on to say that these will be gathered before God, which is irrelevant to the context. Clearly there is a misreading here. The statement should stop at 'communities like yourselves'. Here they are reminded that all the creatures God created are miraculous signs. The rest of the verse is actually a retort by God, addressed to the intransigent disbelievers, and the book (*al-kitāb*) means the records of deeds. He warns that all that the disbelievers say is recorded against them and they will eventually come up for judgement.

Enhancing the Impact: Frequently Used Rhetorical Features in the Qur'an

These serve to enhance the rhetorical effect and the impact of the languages of the Qur'an. A few are given here.

Affective Sentences (jumal inshā'iyya)

In addition to the declarative sentence (*khabariyya*), the Qur'an frequently uses affective sentences. This serves to involve the reader or listener, a very important consideration in Qur'anic discourse. This explains the frequent occurrence of imperative, prohibition, interrogative, proposition, exhortation, wishing, hoping, supplication, exclamation and oaths.

Verbal Sentences

The Qur'an employs the power of the verbal sentence, using the past tense for historical accounts in its argumentation and also when discussing the afterlife. This is effective in making such momentous events of the afterlife (mentioned directly or indirectly on almost every page of the Qur'an) seem as if they are already here, a device crucial for Qur'anic discourse and techniques of persuasion. This may involve *iltifāt,* shift in tense as, for example, in Q. 20:125–6 and Q. 40:48–50.

Generalisation

The Qur'an frequently uses generalisation since it maintains that it is for all people. It classifies people, using such plurals as *al-mu'minūn,* 'the believers', *al-muttaqūn,* 'those who are mindful of God', *al-kāfirūn,* 'the non-believers', *al-ẓālimūn,* 'the evildoers' and so on, and employs conditional sentences with grammatical particles such as '*man*', 'whoever'; '*mā*' 'whatever'; '*ayy*', 'whichever'; *haythumā* and *aynamā,* 'wherever', and also the indefinite noun.

Frequent Use of Adjectives

This is an important means of Qur'anic persuasion and argument, noticeable from the very beginning: '*Praise be to God, Lord of the worlds, the Lord of Mercy, the Giver of Mercy*' (Q. 1:2–3). Because He has such attributes, He is worthy of praise and worship. The required path is the '*straight*' one (verse 6), the one '*whose followers are blessed and not the object of anger*', nor '*those who are astray*' (verse 7), so qualified it is worthy of asking God's guidance to it. The believers are described in many ways (e.g. see Q. 23:1–10 and Q. 70:22–9).

Emphasis

Because the Qur'an first addressed people who doubted or denied its messages, it frequently employs emphasis, using particles such as '*inna*' and '*la-*', and the suffix '*-anna*' with the imperfect verb is widely used.

Contrast

Contrast occurs naturally in a book that declares, in Q. 18:29, '*Say [Prophet], "Now the truth has come from your Lord. Let those who wish to believe in it do so and let those who wish to reject it do so*'' and it is a central feature of Qur'anic style. One of the linguistic habits of the Qur'an is to contrast two classes of beings or things and their respective destinies. Thus, the Qur'an contrasts this world and the next (each occurring, normally together, exactly 115 times); believers and disbelievers; Paradise and Hell; angels and devils; life and death; secrecy and openness, and so on, all found to occur the same number of times.[24] Grammatically, contrast is achieved by such linguistic structures as 'those who [...] and those who' (*man [...] wa-man*), as found in Q. 4:123–4 and Q. 92:5–8. Another frequently used device is 'as for [...] and as for' (*amma [...] wa-amma*) as in '*On the day when some faces brighten and others darken, as for those with darkened faces it will be said [...] and as for those with brightened faces*' in Q. 3:106–7. Sometimes the contrasted elements follow each other without any conjunction, which shows the contrast even more powerfully, as in Q. 89:25–7, '*On that Day, no one will punish as He punishes, and no one will bind as He binds. You soul at peace, return to your Lord, well pleased and well pleasing, go in among my servants and into my Garden.*'

Stories and Parables

The Qur'an makes frequent use of stories and parables. Some of the best known of these are the stories of earlier prophets, such as Noah, Moses and Jesus, scattered throughout the text. Other examples of stories are those of the People of the Cave and others in Sura 18; the story of Corah (Q. 28:76–83); the Companions of the Garden (Q. 68:17–32); the man with two gardens (Q. 18:32–43); Solomon and the ant, Solomon and Sheba (Q. 27:20–44) and the People of Sheba (Q. 34:15–21). These are always used to illustrate arguments and ideas.

Dialogue and Direct Speech

The Qur'an frequently uses direct speech to bind each person by what they utter, rather than claiming in reported speech. Arabic grammar allows shifts between direct and reported speech within a sentence after such verbs as *qāla*, 'he said'. The fact that this verb occurs in the Qur'an more than 300 times is some indication of how frequently direct speech and dialogue are used.

For example, the Qur'an depicts Moses speaking with God and Pharaoh (Q. 26:11–51),[25] God speaking to the angels and Satan (Iblīs) (Q. 2:30–3,

Q. 38:71–85 and *passim*). Dialogue is also used in descriptions of the hereafter; the people in bliss express their joy and gratitude, while those in torment argue and blame one another, and sometimes the people in Paradise speak to those in Hell (Q. 7:44–50, Q. 34:30–3, Q. 37:50–62 and Q. 40:47–50). Part of the reason that this narrative device is used in the Qur'anic discourse is that direct speech is more lively, dramatic and easier to understand than reported speech. It also allows listeners to form their own judgement of character and events from an impartial standpoint as each personality emerges through what they utter, rather than through an indirect claim or report that this is what they said.

Conciseness (ījāz)

The Qur'an is well-known for its short, proverbial statements, as Draz rightly affirms.[26] It frames its statements in such a way as to make them proverbial and capable of multiple meanings, such as in Q. 2:212, *wa'llāhu yarzuq man yashā'u bi-ghayri ḥisāb.* In Arabic this can mean 'God provides for whoever He will without counting or being grudging' or 'without calling him to judgement in the hereafter' or 'without anyone there to criticise or suggest to Him why He should give to this one or that, or this much or that' or 'without the recipient expecting to get that much'. Since the context is God's power and generosity, the multiplicity of possible meanings enrich the statement and are all appropriate. This feature makes the Qur'an quotable for all sorts of situations. If we remember that the Prophet dealt with believers and non-believers of his time and that he lived during his mission for 23 years and went through various stages from being persecuted to being a head of state, one can understand why the Qur'anic text contains quotable statements for a great range of situations. This is one of the ways Muslims encounter the language of the Qur'an in everyday life.[27]

Imagery

The use of imagery has been recognised as one of the most frequent, marked and effective literary and rhetorical devices in the Qur'an.[28] One of the most famous aggregations of images is to be found in the Verse of Light (Q. 24:35):

God is the Light of the heavens and earth. His Light is like this: there is a niche, and in it a lamp, the lamp inside a glass, a glass like a glittering star, fuelled from a blessed olive tree from neither East nor West, whose oil almost gives light even when no fire touches it – light upon light! […] shining out in houses of worship.

Comparison is made between the deeds of good people and those of people who disbelieve:

But the deeds of disbelievers are like a mirage in a desert: the thirsty person thinks there will be water, but when he gets there, he finds it is nothing. There he finds only God, who pays him his account in full […] Or like shadows in a deep sea covered by wave upon wave, with clouds above – layer upon layer of darkness – if he holds out his hand, he is scarcely able to see it. The one to whom God gives no light has no light at all.

Q. 24:39–40

To give but one more example: '*On that Day [Judgement Day] We shall roll up the skies as a writer rolls up his scrolls*' (Q. 21:104).

Rhyme

Rhyme at the end of verses is a consistent stylistic feature in the Qur'an which has an aesthetic effect. It also gives finality to statements and accords with the general feature of classification and generalisation, frequently using the plural endings *-ūn* and *-īn*. The ending of the verse can be an integral part of it (as in Sura 1 where all verses end in *-īn* and *-īm*) or a related comment, such as in Q. 4:34–5, 'God is most high and great (*'aliyan kabīr*) […] He is all knowing, all aware (*'alīman khabīr*)', but it is not just for embellishment.[29]

Rhythm

Rhythm is a very obvious feature of the language of the Qur'an, not only in the early, short suras, such as Q. 79, Q. 92, Q. 99 and Q. 100, but even in the longest sura (Q. 2). Here is one example from Sura 79:

Wa'l-nāzi'āti gharqā, wa'l-nāshiṭāti nashṭā, wa'l-sābiḥāti sabḥā, fa'l-sābiqāti sabqā, fa'l-mudabbirāti amrā.

Q. 79:1–5

Tammām Ḥassan analysed the stress patterns in the Qur'an and showed that the distances between each two successive major stresses is equal or nearly so, and this produces a marked rhythm.[30] So for instance in the following verse:

Aw kaṣayyibin mina'l-samā'i fīhi ẓulumātun wa-ra'dun wa-barqun yaj'alūna aṣābi'ahum fī adhānihim mina'l-ṣawā'iqi ḥadhara'l-mawti wa'llāhu muḥīṭun bi'l-kāfirīn.

Q. 2:19

Memorability

One objective of the language of the Qur'an and how it is presented is to make it easy to remember. Linguistically, this is seen in such features as conciseness, quotable statements, stories, imagery, balance and contrast as well as rhythm and rhyme. It is not surprising that a vast number of Muslim Arabs and non-Arabs, eager to learn the divine speech, are enabled by such features as those listed above to learn all the Qur'an, or parts of it, by heart.

Conclusion

It is clear from the foregoing that the Qur'an uses Arabic grammar and rhetoric together to serve its own purposes. Grammar may follow the normal rule (a process known as *istishhāb al-aṣl*). Rhetorical considerations, however, can give priority to *al-'udūl 'an al-aṣl*, 'departure from the original norm' or, as the scholars of *balāgha* say, *al-khurūj 'alā muqtaḍā al-ẓāhir*, 'departure from what is normally expected', but only 'for considerations required by the situation in certain contexts'.[31] We have seen how the Qur'an employs a feature like *iltifāt* (shift) more frequently than Arabic literature in general and how this was termed 'the boldness of the language of the Qur'an'. Rhetoric can override grammar. The Qur'an instructs the Prophet, '*Speak to them about themselves, using penetrating words (qawlan balīghan)*' (Q. 4:63).

The linguistic and stylistic qualities that mark the language of the Qur'an have been seen as marks of high eloquence and used in Arabic literature throughout the ages. As noted above, the Qur'an was the starting-point for all the branches of Arabic language scholarship. It was seen as a main source of literary language and style. All books on rhetoric (*balāgha*) take their examples mainly from the Qur'an. Oratory in Arabic relies for its effective quotations on the Qur'an. Not only classical writers but also the Nobel Prize winner, Najib Mahfouz, who learned the Qur'an as a child and continued to read it throughout his life, employed Qur'anic words and phrases in his novels verbatim in the early years, where scores, and even hundreds can occur, and continued to do so, if more subtly, to the end of his career.[32]

Having covered the style of the Qur'an up to Chapter 10 we now move to the third part of this book which deals with the impact of the Qur'an within the Muslim world in Chapter 11 and outside the Muslim world in Chapters 12 and 13.

PART III
Impact

11

The Arabic Qur'an in the Muslim World

As we have seen in this book so far, right from Chapter 1, the perception of the Qur'an's teachings by those Western scholars we have discussed was taken from English translations and not the Arabic text, and this has been a crucial factor in misunderstanding and misinterpretation of the Qur'an. It is the Arabic Qur'an that must be the starting point for all discussions.

The Qur'an in the original Arabic has had a profound and lasting effect on the theology, language and culture of the Arab and non-Arab Islamic peoples in their various countries. Theologically, it is the Arabic text, seen as the direct word of God that is considered to be the true Qur'an and which is read in acts of worship. Translations of the Qur'an are deemed to be merely renderings of the meanings of the Qur'an; no translation can be taken to be the Word of God in the same way as the Arabic, and thus none has the same status. In many Muslim countries, translations of the Qur'an are not accepted for publication or sale unless they are accompanied by the Arabic text. All Muslims, Arab and non-Arab, learn and read the Qur'an, or parts of it, in Arabic, in order to have the satisfaction and blessing of reciting the holy speech, the very same words that were uttered from the mouth of the Prophet and recited by his companions, and that are required to be recited in Arabic in the Islamic canonical prayers; the same words that have been uttered by successive generations of Muslims in their different lands and throughout the Islamic era. In fact, it is its connection with the Qur'an that has kept the

Arabic language alive and given it an unrivalled position at the centre of the Islamic world, the Arab Middle Eastern and North African countries. The literary language, common to all Arabs, is used for writing, education and formal speech.[1]

Qur'anic Arabic as the Language of Divine Speech

Read! In the name of your Lord who created.

Q. 96:1

This command, sent down to Muhammad in 610 CE, was the first verse of the Qur'an to be revealed. The word *iqra'* ('*Read!*' or '*Recite!*') is an order addressed to Muhammad, linguistically making the source of the speech outside him. God is seen here to speak Himself directly to the Prophet.[2] Later on, other commands, including *qul* ('*Say!*'), which occurs in the Qur'an over 300 times, are addressed to the Prophet. Likewise, he is told to '*convey (balligh) what is sent down (unzila) to you*' (Q. 5:67). Other derivations of the verb forms *nazzala* and *anzala* ('to send down') occur over 300 times in the body of the Qur'an, again stressing the fact that it has been sent down from God. In addition to addressing the Prophet, God also speaks directly to varieties of other people in the Qur'an: the believers who have accepted Islam and those people who have not, whether disbelievers (*al-kāfirūn*), the recipients of earlier revelations (*yā ahla'l-kitāb*, see for example Q. 3:65), the Children of Israel (*yā Banī Isrā'īl*, see for example Q. 2:47) or to mankind in general (*yā ayyuhā'l-nās*, see for example Q. 34:3).

In a further expression of this directness, the Qur'anic discourse often takes the form of God speaking in the first person, as in Q. 2:152, '*Remember Me; I will remember you. Be thankful to Me and never ungrateful.*' More often, God speaks in the first person plural of majesty, as in '*We have sent down the Qur'an Ourself, and We Ourself will guard it*' (Q. 15:9). When God speaks of Himself in the third person, it is normally for the purpose of comparing Him with the presumed gods, 'partners' as seen by the polytheists, to stress that it is Allah, not others who create:

It is God who created you and provided for you, who will cause you to die and then give you life again. Which of your 'partners' can do any one of these things? Glory be to God and exalted be He above the partners they attribute to Him.

Q. 30:40

Thus, the first characteristic of the language of the Qur'an is that it is viewed by Muslims as sacred language. The divine mode of speech gives the Qur'an unique power and gripping effect. As the word of God, the Qur'an has unparalleled status in Arabic and Islam in general and has been crucial in the building of beliefs, laws, morals and nearly all aspects of Islamic culture. When Muslims hear it, they bear in mind the divine instruction: '*Pay attention and listen quietly when the Qur'an is recited, so that you may be given mercy*' (Q. 7:204). In accordance with its pre-eminent status as divine revelation, the Qur'an must be accurately recited according to the particular rules of *tajwīd* (proper recitation); even the recitation of classical Arabic poetry, considered an art form in itself, comes nowhere near the exacting requirements of reciting the Qur'an. Similarly, the act of writing the Qur'an is treated in a very special way. Indeed, the art of Arabic calligraphy was developed especially for writing down the Qur'an and has continued to be used for this purpose over the centuries.[3] Moreover, a copy of the Arabic Qur'an or any part of it is to be handled in a unique way: '*Only the purified can touch it: it is sent down from the Lord of all worlds*' (Q. 56:79). The collected written text of the Qur'an was the first book in the Arabic language. As stated earlier,[4] it was also the starting point around which, and for the service of which, the various branches of Arabic language studies were initiated and developed.

Branches of Islamic knowledge such as *tafsīr* (exegesis of the Qur'an), theology, Islamic law, Sufism, ethics and morals are likewise based on Qur'anic Arabic language, which permeates them. Arab critics drew heavily on the text of the Qur'an, even in their study of principles of literary criticism.

Characteristics of the Language of the Qur'an

As seen above, the foremost characteristic of the language of the Qur'an is that it is seen as sacred language. There are, however, several other concepts fundamental to the Qur'anic message that can be seen in its characteristic use of language and mode of expression.

Guidance

The overriding objective of this divine speech is guidance (*hudā*), a word that occurs over 300 times in the Qur'an. Thus, in the first sura, the *Fātiḥa*, the believers recite, '*Guide us to the straight path*' (Q. 1:6), and immediately at the beginning of the second sura, it is announced that the Qur'an is guidance, '*This is the Scripture in which there is no doubt, containing guidance for those who are mindful of God*' (Q. 2:2).

Clarification

To achieve this guidance, the Qur'an uses clarification (*bayān*), a word that occurs 266 times in the text. The Qur'an describes itself on numerous occasions as making things clear (*mubīn*): '*A light has now come to you from God, and a scripture making things clear, with which God guides to the ways of peace those who follow what pleases Him, bringing them out from darkness into light*' (Q. 5:15–16). To this end, the Qur'an addresses the Prophet: '*We have sent down the scripture to you [Prophet], to clarify everything*' (Q. 16:89). 'Everything', that is, everything pertaining to religion:[5] beliefs, rituals, laws, ethics and all the teachings of Islam. The Prophet is told that the Qur'an was revealed to him to explain to people what had been sent down to them (Q. 16:44) and is instructed: '*Say, "Now the truth has come to you from your Lord: let those who wish to believe in it do so, and let those who wish to reject it do so*"' (Q. 18:29). Thus, the *bayān* of the distinction between truth and error is the Qur'an's primary objective, and on this basis it declares: '*There is no compulsion in religion; truth has become distinct from error*' (Q. 2:256).

Signs and proofs

In making this clarification, the Qur'an makes everything that it says intellectually clear, providing arguments even for the existence of God Himself and His oneness,[6] the prophethood of Muhammad,[7] the Resurrection[8] and Judgement,[9] as well as for its legal and moral teachings. As part of this process, it provides *āyāt*, a word which occurs 382 times, meaning 'signs' or 'proofs':

> *Another of His signs is that He created spouses from among yourselves for you to live with in tranquility: He ordained love and kindness between you. There truly are signs in this for those who reflect. Another of His signs is that He created the heavens and earth, the diversity of your languages and colours. There truly are signs in this for those who know.*
>
> Q. 30:21–2

One of the remarkable characteristics of the language of the Qur'an is that the arguments and signs it uses satisfy the enquiries of those philosophers and intellectuals open to the truth of revelation, and at the same time is found equally to be impressive by ordinary men or women in the street. After all, religion is meant for everybody and such is the 'magical' quality of the language of the Qur'an and the way it is received by Muslims all over the world.

Rational arguments

As al-Rāzī explains, at the time of the revelation, in addition to those who believed in the message, the Prophet Muhammad had to deal with all kinds of people: those who did not believe in an omnipotent God who had power and free will, those who believed in more than one god, those who disbelieved in prophethood and those who did not want to accept the *sharī'a,* in addition to Christians and Jews who had their own beliefs, but did not accept the prophethood of Muhammad.[10] In addressing all of these, the Qur'an produces logical arguments, accentuating the intellectual evidence that runs throughout the Qur'anic discourse. These arguments are often marked by various linguistic devices in the form of formulae such as '*if you are in doubt about ..., then ...*' (*in kuntum fī rayb ... fa-inna ...,* e.g. see Q. 2:23); '*do they say ... ? But the fact is that ...*' (*am yaqulūna ... bal ...,* e.g. see Q. 10:36); '*bring your witnesses then*' (*halumma shuhadā'akum,* e.g. see Q. 6:150); '*bring your evidence*' (*hātū burhānakum,* e.g. see Q. 2111); '*could they not see?*' (*a-fa-lam/a-fa-lā/a-wa-lam yaraw,* e.g. see Q. 20:89); '*did they not see?*' (*a-wa-lam yanẓurū,* e.g. see Q. 7:185); and '*let man reflect*' (*fal-yanẓur al-insān,* see for example Q. 86:5).

Instruction and persuasion

Since the Qur'anic message came to change people's beliefs, it was not sufficient just to argue rationally with them. It requests the Prophet to '*instruct them and speak to them about themselves using penetrating words* (*qawlan balīghan*)' (Q. 4:63). The Qur'an seeks to persuade people to follow its teachings, especially when it is likely that they may think the instructions are hard to follow. An obvious example of this tendency to persuasion can be seen in the passage in Q. 2:183–7, which addresses the obligation to fast in Ramadan, demolishing, one by one, every possible obstacle that might arise in people's minds concerning this matter. Likewise, even as it introduces a legal penalty, a subject that in legal texts is usually presented in sharp, detached language, the Qur'an couches it in persuasive language that elicits compassion. Thus, after prescribing the penalties for murder ('*You who believe, retaliation is prescribed for you* ...' (Q. 2:178)), it continues in the same verse:

but if the culprit is pardoned by his aggrieved brother this shall be adhered to fairly and the culprit shall pay what is due in a good way. This is an alleviation from your Lord and an act of mercy. If anyone then exceeds these limits grievous suffering awaits him.

Q. 2:178

Exhortation and remembrance or reminding (dhikr)

One final device of significance the Qur'an uses to achieve its objective of guidance is that of reminding (*tadhkīr*) its audience. God declares in the Qur'an: '*We have made it easy to learn lessons from the Qur'an: will anyone take heed (muddakir)?*' (Q. 54:17, see also Q. 44:58). The Qur'an describes itself as *dhikr* (remembrance or reminding) and this concept of *dhikr* in its various derivations occurs 255 times in the Qur'an. People are reminded of God Himself (Q. 7:205 and Q. 8:2), of God's favour (Q. 2:231 and Q. 8:26), His power (Q. 19:67), His punishment of earlier nations (Q. 14:5 and Q. 54:17) and of the Hereafter, which occurs regularly throughout the Qur'an.

One feature of *dhikr* in the Qur'an is the multiple use of related material, particularly stories of earlier prophets. At a first glance, this may be seen as mere repetition, but different sections of these stories usually form integral parts of the arguments along with other material in their respective suras, as explained in Chapter 6. The story is repeated, but in each case the material selected is suitable for its context in the sura and the historical context of its revelation. This device ensures that when people hear or read any particular sura in their daily lives, they will usually find in it the employment of sacred history, along with material about God, His power and grace, the Hereafter and so on, so they attain a full picture of the faith which therefore has a most powerful effect.

The Qur'an, as seen above, carries the message of Islam, which is not just a spiritual faith, but a religion that guides and governs all aspects of the Muslim's life. As such, it necessarily includes teachings relating to knowledge of reality (*'ilm*), belief (*'aqīda*), law (*sharī'a*) and ethics and morals (*akhlāq*). Having said this, the basis upon which everything is built is belief, the *'aqīda*, and it is for this reason that this aspect of the revelation occupies the greater part of the Qur'an. As al-Rāzī points out:

Sharī'a provisions in the Qur'an occupy less than 600 verses [out of 6,236]. The rest of the Qur'an is taken up by explaining the oneness of God (*tawḥīd*), the prophethood [of Muhammad] and refuting the claims of pagans and polytheists. As regards the verses that deal with stories, they are intended to show God's wisdom and power.[11]

The Effects of Qur'anic Arabic on Other Muslim Languages and Literatures

It was the Qur'an that took Arabic outside the Arabian Peninsula, making it an international language that displaced local languages in what are now the Arab countries and for several centuries in Muslim Spain. In Persia, Arabic became dominant as the written language for two or three centuries until Persian was reintroduced as the official language under the Samānids.[12]

In fact what is called the Persian language today was born from the introduction of Qur'anic Arabic terms into Middle Persian (prevalent during the Sassanid period up to the seventh century CE). During the Islamic period after the conquest of Persia by the Arab armies, Persians played a major role in the exposition of Arabic grammar; they also wrote numerous works in nearly every field in Arabic and continued to do so even after Persian became the literary, and even scholarly, language of the eastern regions of the Islamic world. It was mostly these scholars, who were masters of Qur'anic Arabic, who introduced so many words and expressions from the Qur'an into Persian. The formal structure of the Qur'an even influenced Persian prosody. It was mostly through Persian that Arabic words penetrated into Turkish languages of the Indian subcontinent such as Sindhi, Punjabi, Gujrati, Bengali and Urdu, not to mention Iranian languages such as Kurdish and Pashtu.

However, even when Arabic ceased to be the primary language of certain parts of the Muslim world, it remained a major source of vocabulary for many other languages, such as Berber, Swahili, Hausa, Malay and Indonesian: 'In all Islamic countries the influence of Arabic is pervasive, because of the highly language-specific nature of Islam, since the revealed book was inimitable, it could not be translated'.[13] In Africa, 'the expansion of Islam brought many of the cultures in the northern half of the continent under the Islamic sphere of influence, which resulted in hundreds of loan-words in the domain of religion, culture and science'.[14] In Hausa, the Qur'anic and other Islamic element show far-reaching effect, and songs of preaching (*wa'azī* – Arabic *wa'ẓ*) constitute what is probably the biggest category in Hausa poetry.[15]

Likewise, the influence of the Qur'an on Swahili literature in East Africa has been profound. The Qur'an in its text 'with its suras, formulas etc., and the influence of Islam as a religion with its values, ethics, stories, and most effectively, poetry, are the areas that bear the most influence'.[16] The three genres of Swahili literature, the novel (*riwaya*), drama (*tamthilia*) and poetry (*shairi*) are all Arabic names. Approximately 50 per cent of the vocabulary of Swahili derives etymologically from Arabic.[17]

In the Ottoman Empire, Turkish became the official language of the state, but at the same time Persian and Arabic were maintained as the languages of culture. 'Between the 15th and 17th centuries, the lexical material of Turkish was almost completely taken from Arabic and Persian.'[18] Even after Ataturk's attempt to purify the Turkish language of Arabic and Persian terms, a large number of loan words from these languages (or from Arabic through Persian) are still present.[19]

It can be said with certainty that, 'of all the languages with which Arabic came into contact, Persian is the one that was most influenced in this process'.[20] As for the Indian subcontinent, 'The impact of Arabic on Persian and other modern Indian languages strongly correlates with the degree of Islamisation which their speakers underwent.'[21] In Bangladesh, 'there is a strong tendency to replace older Sanskrit words with Arabic/Persian loans, especially in the domain of religion'.[22] In Indonesia, where the vast majority are Muslims, Arabic is regarded as the sacred language of their religion, as it is elsewhere in the Islamic world, and its position as a religious language is unshaken. Most Indonesians and also Malaysians have a rudimentary knowledge of Arabic because of their Qur'anic training.[23] In Malay literature, stories such as *Hikayat Iskandar Dzulkarnain* (based on Q. 18:83–98) as well as works of moral guidance and advice show the influence of the Qur'an and its language. One very obvious example of the influence of religious Arabic is the celebrated poem by al-Būṣīrī (d. 696/1295) in praise of the Prophet, known as *The Burda*. This has been adopted as part of the literature of all Muslim peoples of Asia and Africa, has been repeatedly performed and has gained much acclaim. Moreover, Qur'anic vocabulary is an important part of this celebrated poem.[24]

The Qur'an in Daily Life and in Islamic Studies

The Qur'an was, from the beginning, committed to memory by the first Muslims. Throughout Islamic history, many Muslims, both Arabic-speaking and non-Arabic-speaking, men, women and children, have memorised and continued to memorise the whole Qur'an or large parts of it. Nowadays there are international Qur'anic recitation competitions held in Malaysia, Indonesia and Iran, to name but a few countries, sometimes state-funded. The first sura of the Qur'an, *al-Fātiḥa*,[25] which is an essential part of the ritual canonical prayers, is learnt and read in Arabic by Muslims in all parts of the world.[26] This particular sura is recited in Arabic by practising Muslims at least 17 times a day, but other verses and phrases in Arabic are also incorporated into the lives of non-Arabic-speaking Muslims.

In addition to reciting the *Fātiḥa* in Arabic, Muslims all over the world perform all their daily ritual prayers in Arabic, not just the essential Qur'anic text of *Sūrat al-Fātiḥa*, in imitation of the Prophet's example, and in keeping with unbroken tradition. In recent times, Muslims have settled in every continent, including Europe and America. Arabic schools are set up for their children, also mosque schools, where the Qur'an is taught in its original Arabic. It is remarkable that many Muslims from non-Arab countries such as South Asia, Turkey and Africa insist on having a Friday sermon during the congregational prayers in Arabic from the pulpits of mosques in Europe and America, even if they have additional sermons in the local languages. Despite the growing body of Muslim writing on Islam in European languages, Arabic, the language of the Qur'an, still occupies a privileged position that cannot be replaced by any other language.

If we assume that a group of ten Muslims come together from differing linguistic backgrounds, with no common language, they can all pray together, as it is the same Arabic prayer that they all perform. Any of the men among them is, moreover, eligible to lead the prayer. They will also find that they share in common a large amount of Qur'anic vocabulary in Arabic. As the Qur'an and Hadith are in Arabic and are the fundamental sources of Islamic Law and teachings, the main classical works of the different schools of law, which are followed to this day, were all written in Arabic. This means that advanced Qur'anic and Islamic studies in non-Arab Muslim countries are based on Arabic texts written by the followers of all the various schools, that is, Shāfi'ī in South East Asia, for instance, Ḥanafī in South Asia and Turkey, Ja'afarī in Iran and Iraq, Ḥanbalī in

Saudi Arabia and Mālikī in West Africa. Thus the Qur'an has kept Arabic alive in the religious scholarship of non-Arab Muslims.

A great service to the Arabic language and the study of the Qur'an and the Islamic sciences in general was actually rendered by non-Arab Muslims. The most striking example here is Sībawayh (Sībūyah in Persian), who was a Persian and his magnum opus, *al-Kitāb*,[27] has been the first reference point for Arab grammarians throughout the ages. Muslims in the lands of Persia and beyond have contributed great benefits to Arabic grammar, phonology, *tafsīr* (Qur'anic exegesis) and *balāgha* (rhetoric), and have composed works that stand among the best writings in Arabic and Islam. One need only mention names such as al-Zamakhsharī, al-Jurjānī, al-Rāzī and Ibn Jinnī; for Hadith literature there are al-Bukhārī, al-Tirmidhī and al-Nasā'ī; and Abū Ḥanīfa as well as al-Jaṣṣāṣ for *fiqh* (jurisprudence); and, in other sciences, the likes of Ibn Sīnā, al-Fārābī, al-Bīrūnī and many more. All these works were written to serve the Qur'an and Islam.

Even when the people of Persia returned to writing in Persian,[28] the influence of the language of the Qur'an remained a very prominent feature of their language. It is estimated that even now between 50 and 60 per cent of the Persian vocabulary is still derived from Arabic. Not only the vocabulary but also the grammar of Persian, which is an Indo-European language, was affected by Arabic – a phenomenon that is almost an exception to the effects of contacts between languages.[29] The Persian science of *balāgha* was, from the beginning, modelled completely upon the Arabic *balāgha*,[30] which, as seen above, was developed for the study of the language of the Qur'an. The greatest Persian Sufi poet, Jalāl al-Dīn al-Rūmī (d. 672/1273), studied Arabic and religious sciences before turning to Sufism, and even wrote a number of poems in Arabic.[31] The great Persian poet Ḥāfiẓ of Shīrāz (d. 792/1389), as his name indicates, learned the Arabic Qur'an by heart and taught exegesis.[32] Persian Sufi poets often employed Qur'anic themes in their writing. A striking example is 'Abd al-Raḥmān al-Jāmī's (d. 898/1492) treatment of the theme of Yūsuf and Zulaykhā.[33] Even as late as the seventeenth century we find such an important author as Mullā Ṣadrā (d. 1050/1640) writing his greatest works on philosophy and Qur'anic commentary in Arabic. As already mentioned, to a great extent it was thanks to Persian that Arabic words, mostly of Qur'anic origin, which found their way to other languages such as Urdu, Ottoman Turkish and even Malay.

The Persians and the Turks, among others, continue to make a great contribution to Arabic calligraphy. Verses from the Qur'an form the main theme of calligraphy used to adorn mosques and other religious buildings, as well as being used on decorative items to hang in homes and offices. They bring the Qur'anic statements to the attention of Muslims in many situations. For example, on entering a court of justice, they may read in Arabic calligraphy, '*When you judge between people, judge with justice*' (Q. 4:58); in the parliament they will see, '*Their affairs are conducted among them by consultation*' (Q. 42:38); in a military academy they will see, '*Prepare for them whatever force you can muster*' (Q. 8:60); on a marriage certificate they will read, '*Among His signs is that He created spouses from among yourselves so that you may find comfort in them and He ordained love and mercy between you*' (Q. 30:21); on drinking cups, they will read, '*Their Lord has given them a pure drink*' (Q. 76:21); on a lorry in Cairo you may read the prayer said by Noah when his people embarked on the Ark, '*In the name of God may it go and in His name may it arrive*' (Q. 11:41); passengers arriving at the airport in Cairo read Joseph's statement to his parents, '*Enter Egypt safely, God willing*' (Q. 12:99); in many mosques, they read, '*Turn your face to the Sacred Mosque*' (Q. 2:144); and in schools you have, '*Lord, increase my knowledge*' (Q. 20:114). Such calligraphic works, written in Arabic and drawn from the Qur'an, are found in all parts of the Muslim world, which keeps Arabic visible, beautiful and related to the divine text of the Qur'an. It is the Qur'an that gives the Arabic language this unique position and makes Muslims return to it again and again.

The recent Islamic resurgence has also had an effect on the teaching of Arabic in a number of Muslim countries. In Pakistan, in 1977 under President Zia-ul-Haq, the study of Arabic was made compulsory in schools, and although this has not been strictly maintained by later governments, Islamic studies (*Islāmiyyāt*) are still compulsory up to the level of bachelor's degree in all Pakistani educational institutions, and this naturally involves knowledge of Qur'anic Arabic. The already compulsory study of Arabic in Iranian schools was given more emphasis following the Islamic Revolution of 1979 in Iran, and Arabic is also part of the curriculum of madrasas throughout the Islamic word, both in the Middle East and beyond. Beyond this domain, reformers and preachers in the Arab and Muslim world now derive inspiration from the command in the very first revelation, '*Read!*' or '*Recite!*', in their campaigns for a new educational revival among Muslims. This first instruction, '*Read* [or *recite*]*! In the name of your Lord*', lives on in the consciousness of Muslims and continues to influence their languages and literature.[34] The impact of the Qur'an on Arabic and other Islamic languages is an enduring reality that continues to influence the life of Muslims on all levels.

Having covered the Qur'an's impact within the Muslim world, we now move to cover its impact outside the Muslim world in Chapters 12 and 13.

12

English Translations of the Qur'an: The Making of an Image[1]

In this chapter the changing image of the Qur'an in various English translations by native speakers is traced, from Alexander Ross's 1649 *The Alcoran of Mahomet* to Arthur J. Arberry's 1955 *The Koran Interpreted.* These had been preceded by two notable translations of the Qur'an into Latin: the first being *Lex Mahumet pseudoprophete que arabice Alchoran* ... by another earlier Englishman, Robert of Ketton, in 1143,[2] commissioned by the Abbot of Cluny, Peter the Venerable, which influenced the image of the Qur'an in Europe for centuries. The second was *Alcorani textus universus* ... by Ludovico Marracci, published in Padua, 1698,[3] which also had a strong influence on subsequent translations into English, from George Sale's *The Koran: Commonly Called the Alcoran of Mohammed* ...[4] onwards.

The Qur'an in Europe

The first revelation of the Qur'an came in early 610 CE. After this date the revelation arrived gradually until it was completed in 632, shortly before the death of the Prophet Muhammad. Europe had to wait for 511 years before the first Latin translation, the *Lex Mahumet pseudoprophete* by Robert of Ketton, was made in 1143,[5] and even this remained relatively unknown for the next 400 years, until it was printed in Basle in 1543,[6] more than 900 years after that first revelation. Part of the explanation for this is that the Arabs were uninterested in making their Holy Book available to European unbelievers through the medium of translation; to them the Qur'an definitely meant the Arabic and this mindset remained until the second half of the twentieth century. For the Europeans there was another explanation: the power of the Church. As we shall see from the resistance to the translation and publication of the Qur'an, for a long time Islam was considered in Europe to be a Christian heresy. The Qur'an denies the divinity and crucifixion of Christ, even though it attributes to him a very special status as a prophet. It has taken Europe a long time to come round to changing this hostile attitude; indeed, we shall see that it has persisted in one way or another until the present century.

The Europeans were undoubtedly interested in Arabic writings, but this interest was directed towards the natural sciences, rather than religious literature. It was Peter the Venerable, the Abbot of Cluny, who first realised the importance of learning more about Islam. He was dissatisfied with the direction taken by the Crusade movement in his time, in particular the military option advocated by Bernhard of Clairvaux (*c.*1090–1153). While visiting the Cluniac abbey in Toledo, Peter came across two young Europeans, Robert of Ketton and Hermann of Corinth, who were studying the Arabic sciences, and commissioned them to translate a number of texts on Islam. The Qur'an went to Robert. Hermann translated some other works, mainly critical of Islam. Peter's aim in this was to initiate an 'intellectual crusade' using the 'weapons of reason'[7] and a conversion of Muslims to Christianity through preaching. This intention to provide Christians with knowledge of the Qur'an in order to convert Muslims remains a constant through many later translations; the other original aim, which also continued for some centuries was to protect the Christians – and the Church – from the 'Saracen heresy' by refuting it.[8]

Robert of Ketton, the student of Arabic sciences, received support[9] from the Church.[10] He gained the glory of going down in history as the first translator of the Qur'an into Latin. His translation was described as a 'paraphrase', and Norman Daniel wrote:

> Robert was always liable to heighten or exaggerate a harmless text to give it a nasty or licentious sting, or to prefer an improbable but unpleasant interpretation of the meaning to a likely but normal and decent one.[11]

But whatever its defects, it was to prove very influential. Indeed, Ketton's translation of the Qur'an was one of the most important cross-cultural events of the Middle Ages. During the centuries after it appeared, the Latin translation was consulted by clerical scholars, particularly those of the Dominican Order, of which St Thomas Aquinas was an influential member.[12] The special task of this Order became to refute the 'heresy' of Islam,[13] and later, after the unsuccessful attempt by St Francis of Assisi in 1219 to convert the Ayyubid Sultan al-Mālik al-Kāmil at the siege of Damietta, also to attempt to convert the 'Saracens' to Christianity.[14]

Much of the argumentation they used was to claim that the Qur'an was incompatible with the Bible, with philosophy and natural reason. Instead of looking at the Qur'an in itself, they started with the premise that it should be like the Bible and philosophy in content and form and when they did not see this, they vilified it. Take, for example, the arguments of Riccoldo.[15] He found that the Qur'an had chapters named after things like ants (Q. 27, *Sūrat al-Naml*), the spider (Q. 29, *Sūrat al-'Ankabūt*) and smoke (Q. 44, *Sūrat al-Dukhān*), and asserted that these were unsuitable subjects for divine revelation. He considered this as a sign of the Qur'an's irrationality. Furthermore, he claimed, it was full of things that were not worth saying: it repeats things like, 'There is no god but God and believe in the Apostle.'[16] He also regarded it as obscene in that it spoke of 'coitus', and viewed its actual form as unsuitable as scripture:

> The arrangement of the Qur'an is disorderly. There is no order of time by periods and kings as there is in the Old Testament, no narrative order: beginning properly with the praise of God, it slips abruptly into the middle of things, no order of subject-matter and no logical order.[17]

He counted the notion that the Old Testament prophets were Muslims as inherently self-contradictory and the Qur'an's assertion that God did not create the world in play as an absurd point to make (not realising this was in response to the disbelievers of Mecca to refute them), for who would be fool enough to suppose that He had? Another proof of Islamic unreason was that the Qur'an claimed that God prays for Muhammad[18] (resulting from an incorrect translation for 'bless' the Prophet).[19]

In 1542, Johannes Oporinus (1507–68), the great printer, undertook the printing of the *Corpus Toletanum*, edited by Theodor Bibliander, in Basle, and Ketton's translation of the Qur'an was part of this. When the Council of Basle discovered that the Qur'an was being printed, their reaction was divided, so they named expert witnesses to judge on its permissibility. Meanwhile, printing was stopped, the proofs were confiscated and Oporinus was jailed. The expert witnesses were also divided:

> All agreed that the Koran was a heretical book but the three opponents also thought it dangerous if read by dogmatically untrained people, [...] [and that it] ought not to appear in a Christian city.[20]

It was a joint letter from Martin Bucer and Martin Luther that finally broke this deadlock. Martin Luther, who was very interested in 'Turkish writings', had obtained a copy of the *Toletanum Corpus* from the University of Wittenberg, and argued the case for the publication of the Qur'an translation it contained. In pleading for publication, Luther 'stressed the importance to Christianity of a sound knowledge of Islam – not in order to convert Muslim believers, but, on the contrary, to protect certain groups inside the Church from apostasy'.[21]

The Basle Council agreed to this first printed edition of the Qur'an in Europe on condition that neither the name of the City of Basle, nor that of the printer was mentioned in the text; someone from outside Basle had to act as editor and sale of the book was forbidden within city walls.[22] (A similar reaction met the first English translation a century later.) Nevertheless the publication became very successful[23] and the printing and circulation of this Latin translation spurred some on to translate the Qur'an into various European languages. Surprisingly, though, in spite of the fact that it was written by an Englishman, Ketton's Latin translation was not used as a basis for translation into English. The first English translation by Alexander Ross in 1649 was based on the French rendition by Le Sieur du Ryer in 1647.[24] But the image of the Qur'an created by the Latin translation would persist; indeed, the reaction to publishing it would be mirrored in the attempts to prevent the printing of the first English translation by Ross.

Alexander Ross: The Alcoran of Mahomet

The first translator of the Qur'an into English, Alexander Ross, was born in Aberdeen and wrote his translation when he was 'preacher at St Mary's near Southampton, and one of His Majesty's Chaplains (HM Charles I)'. It is said of him that 'He was wont to pit himself against greater writers, [...] and he often indulged in scurrility in his arguments.'[25] Ross did not know any Arabic and based his translation on a French translation from the Arabic published in 1647, we are told, by the Sieur Du Ryer, Lord of

Malezair, and Resident for the King of France in Alexandria, who also visited Istanbul.

The pressure from the authorities, seen earlier in Basle, to suppress the 'danger' of the Qur'an had remained so strong that in 1649 Ross felt it necessary to write a long justification to reassure people that 'Alcoran does not constitute any danger for those who are sound in their faith'.[26] He gave his translation the quaint title, *The Alcoran of Mahomet ... newly Englished, for the satisfaction of all that desire to look into the Turkish vanities,* and incorporated a section on the life of Muhammad and a letter from 'the translator to the Christian reader' justifying his translation of the 'heresy' of 'Mahomet': 'that so viewing thine enemies in their full body, thou mayst the better prepare to encounter and I hope overcome them.'

In this letter, and in the 'Life of Mahomet' and the '*Caveat*' which are appended to the work, Ross heaps abuse on the Qur'an and Muhammad, including all sorts of confused and highly misleading tales and legends all intended to create a repellent image of the Qur'an and Islam. This was intended to ward off those who 'were unwilling this should see the presse'. For Ross these were the newly installed Cromwellian authorities. Like the Basle Council, the English Council of State, spurred on by one Colonel Anthony Weldon, had forbidden the publication of his translation, imprisoned the publisher and seized the copies that had been printed. Nevertheless, after due proceedings instituted by the Council of State, the *Alcoran* finally came out in print on 7 May 1649.

Even in the translation of *Sūrat al-Fātiḥa* (*The Opening,* Q. 1), a short passage, there are a number of errors: in verse 1, he removes the important description of God as *rabb al-'ālamīn* (*Lord of all worlds*); in verse 7 he gives, 'against whom thou hast not been displeased', attributing the displeasure to God when it is not so in Arabic; instead of 'not [the path of] those who have gone astray' he simply says 'We shall not be misled'.

In his translation and in many subsequent translations, the powerful rhythm of the original is lacking and the image of God, so beautiful in Arabic, does not shine through in the English. Nevertheless, we have to give Ross the credit for his pioneering spirit and for starting the tradition of making the Qur'an available in English.

For 83 years, until Sale's translation was published in 1734, Ross's translation was the only version of the Qur'an available in English. The first edition was reprinted twice, and 'there is ample evidence to show that writers and thinkers from all sectors in English society' read it.[27] It was frequently used in seventeenth-century anti-Islamic polemic.

In 1688 another edition was printed, and in 1698, Ross was quoted by the New England preacher Cottom Mather: 'The Qur'an in English had crossed the Atlantic'.[28] It continued to be republished even after Sale's translation appeared, and in 1806 was re-published as 'the First American Edition'.

It is perhaps surprising, in the light of Ross being the only translator of the Qur'an in that period, that Arabists of the time did not undertake any translation of the Qur'an. The first half of the seventeenth century was particularly favourable to the interest in Arabic studies in England. This could be seen in the letter from the Vice Chancellor and Heads of Colleges in Cambridge to Sir Thomas Adams, the founder of the first Chair of Arabic in Cambridge in 1636:

> The work itself wee conceive to tend not only to the advancement of good Literature by bringing to light much knowledge which as yet is lockt upp in that learned tongue; but also to the good service of the King and State in our commerce with those Easterne nations, and in Gods good time to the enlarging of the borders of the Church, and propagation of Christian religion to them who now sitt in darkeness.[29]

In 1630 Archbishop Laud, then Bishop of London, made the first steps to founding the Laudian Chair of Arabic at Oxford. He 'bestowed some 600 Oriental manuscripts on the Bodleian Library in the 1630s, thus establishing Oxford as a major European centre for the study of Oriental languages'.[30] The study of Arabic improved knowledge of the Qur'an and Islam; however, until 1880 when Palmer produced his translation,[31] British academics did not seem to be interested in writing translations of the Qur'an; however, in 1698, a very important scholarly publication appeared in Padua: the Arabic Qur'an with Latin translation and learned commentary by Father Ludovico Marracci, Confessor to Pope Innocent XI, entitled *Alcorani textus universus*.[32] This translation, which took Marracci 40 years to complete, proved to be very influential when it first appeared.[33] Marracci arranged his text as follows:

1. short sections of Qur'anic text;
2. the literal Latin translation;
3. notes containing Muslim interpretations (*tafsīr*);
4. refutation of Islamic doctrines.

Much of the large volume is taken up by material other than the translation of the Qur'an. The refutations often went to great lengths; those relating to the first sura – only five lines in Arabic – take up six and a half pages. Nonetheless, Marracci's work remained a remarkable piece of scholarship and proved to be an invaluable source of Arabic text and commentary for those who had no access to, or insufficient familiarity with, the Arabic language. Marracci's work would have an influential effect on Sale's translation, which is undoubtedly one of the most important in the English language and, as will be seen in the discussion below, also had an influence on Rodwell and Palmer. It marked a great advance on the first Latin translation as Marracci undoubtedly had far greater knowledge of Arabic writings on the Qur'an than Robert of Ketton.

George Sale: *The Koran: Commonly Called the Alcoran of Mohammed*

George Sale (*c.*1697–1734), a solicitor by profession who never left his native country, was the first layman to translate the Qur'an into English. An Arabic translation of the New Testament was commissioned in 1720 by the Society for the Promotion of Christian Knowledge for the use of Syrian Christians at the request of Solomon Negri of Damascus, sent by the Patriarch of Antioch. Negri may have instructed Sale in Arabic, together with a learned Greek named Dadichi from Aleppo.[34] His 1734 translation 'was carried on at leisure times only, amongst the necessary avocations of a troublesome profession'.[35] Judging by his lack of formal education in Arabic, and the fact that there was very little Arabic in his library, especially on the Qur'an, it is difficult, according to Denison Ross, who introduced the 1909 edition of Sale's translation, to assume that Sale's mastery of the Arabic language would have enabled him to translate directly. Denison Ross assumes that such Qur'anic commentaries as al-Zamakhsharī, al-Suyūṭī and al-Bayḍāwī must have been quoted by Sale second hand from Marracci, which included the Arabic material and the Latin translation.[36] Still, Sale produced a fine translation that remained, well into the twentieth century, one of the most enduring in the English language.

As to why Sale, a lawyer, should translate the Qur'an, there seem to be two possible motives: first, his involvement with translating the Bible into Arabic may have increased his interest in Arabic and possibly spurred him on to translate the Qur'an into English, especially considering the sharp criticisms he makes of Ross's translation. Second, as a lawyer, he takes the Qur'an as 'The Mohammedan Law'.[37] In his dedication of the work to Lord Carteret, a royal Privy Councillor, he says that in spite of 'all the detestation with which the name of Mohammed is loaded, [...] I confess I cannot see why he deserves not equal respect [with other conquerors], though not with Moses or Jesus Christ, whose laws came really from heaven'.[38]

Sale condemns the 'writers of the Romish communion' who 'are so far from having done any service in their refutations of Mohammedism, that by endeavouring to defend their idolatry and other superstitions they have rather contributed to the increase of that aversion which the Mohammedans in general have to the Christian Religion, and given them great advantages in the dispute.' He also considered that 'the Protestants alone are able to attack the Koran with success; and for them, I trust, Providence has reserved the glory of its overthrow'.[39]

In spite of this, neither the text of the translation, nor the footnotes betray deliberate intent to denigrate either the Prophet of Islam or the Qur'an. His tone is quite calm and scholarly. Gibbon is reported to have called him 'our honest and learned translator, Sale [...] half a Mussulman'.[40]

In his introduction, Sale justifies the need for a new translation in his comments on his predecessors. Ross, he says, 'being utterly unacquainted with the Arabic, and no great master of the French, has added a number of fresh mistakes of his own to those of Du Ryer; not to mention the meanness of his language, which would make a better book ridiculous'.[41] Of Marracci's translation, he wrote that it:

> adheres to the Arabic idiom too literally to be easily understood, unless I am much deceived, by those who are not versed in the Mohammedan learning. The notes he has added are indeed of great use; but his refutations, which swell the work to a large volume, are of little or none at all.[42]

Then, in his 'Letter to the Reader', he sets out his own approach clearly:

> I have endeavoured to do the Original impartial justice; [...] I have thought myself obliged, indeed, in a piece which pretends to be the Word of God, to keep somewhat scrupulously close to the text; by which means the language may, in some places, seem to express the Arabic a little too literally to be elegant English.[43]

In Sale's translation we witness a remarkable improvement on previous European translations on two fronts: it was by far freer from bias against Islam and the Qur'an that marked the work of his predecessors and many of his successors, whether academics or clerics. Subsequent missionaries felt they had to revise, or even replace, his 'Preliminary Discourse' to compensate, as in the 1877 Boston edition[44] and the 1909 Cairo Arabic Edition of Sale's *Introduction to Islam* by the Nile Mission Press.[45] The second front was Sale's knowledge of Arabic (which Ross totally lacked) and the amount of Islamic material made available to him through translations by European Arabists and Latin translations of Marracci's influential work. His description of the religion of Islam and the life of the Prophet Muhammad, in his 'Preliminary Discourse' to the translation was the first in English to be based on the Arabic sources, particularly the then newly published translation of Abū al-Fidā', printed in Oxford in 1723[46] with a Latin translation.

Another great improvement on previous translations was the way that Sale clarified the sense of various aspects of his text by adding elaboration on the highly concise Arabic of the Qur'an in italics, such as required complements of verbs in English, not essential in Arabic. This definitely made the text easier to understand, even if it rendered the translation prosaic and lacking in English rhythm. In this respect, Sale's translation is clearer and easier to follow than others among the seven translations under discussion here. What is remarkable is that, apart from the archaic pronouns and verb endings, his style still reads today as straightforward and less convoluted and rigid than that of many of the succeeding translators, who obviously thought their translation should sound grander.

There is, however, one tiresome feature that makes it very difficult to locate individual verses in his translation and that is his segmentation of material. His translation of Sura 2, for instance, is written, as are all the other suras, in one single paragraph that runs for 42 pages, without verse numbers. In this, he follows Ross whose Sura 2 takes up 27 pages, all in one paragraph, without breaks or verse numbers, but not Marracci who does break up the text and number the verses.

For 127 years, no other English translation appeared to rival Sale's. He had the field to himself. No other translation has been printed by so many publishers in the United Kingdom and the United States. It is significant that Sale improved the image of the Qur'an on two fronts: he showed less hostility to Islam as a religion and made the text of his Qur'an translation clearer with his explanations.

John Medows Rodwell: *The Koran: Translated from the Arabic*

The next translation to appear was that published by J. M. Rodwell (1808–1900) in 1861.[47] Rodwell graduated from Cambridge with a bachelor's degree in 1830, was ordained deacon at Norwich in 1831 and remained in the clergy from 1850–1900 as Rector of St Ethelburga's in Bishopsgate, London. His uncle, his father-in-law and his son were all clerics. He learned Hebrew from his uncle and acquired elements of Arabic assisted by Catafago.[48] His chief literary works were translations of the Books of Job and Isaiah from the Hebrew and of liturgies from Ethiopic manuscripts and from Coptic. His most important work was the translation of the Qur'an in 1861 under the title, *The Koran: Translated from the Arabic, the suras arranged in chronological order, with notes and index.* His tone and approach can be perceived clearly from his introduction, translation and notes. He rearranged the Qur'anic chapters not in the Islamic canonical order, but according to his idea of their chronological order, based mainly on Nöldeke's dating,[49] but making some of his own choices on thematic order. In his opinion, the Muslim arrangement had been made:

> often with entire disregard to continuity of subject and uniformity of style. The text, therefore, as hitherto arranged, necessarily assumes the form of a most unreadable and incongruous patchwork [...] and conveys no idea whatever of the development and growth of any plan in the mind of the founder of Islam, or of the circumstances by which he was surrounded and influenced.[50]

In this, Ross was echoing the views of medieval clerics. This approach is significant in that it demonstrates clearly how Rodwell and those who followed him were not interested in the Qur'an itself primarily, but in the development of Muhammad's ideas and his sources, particularly when it comes to the relationship of these to the Jewish and Christian scriptures.

The second most obvious feature can be seen in the way his notes relate the Qur'an to the Bible, either to show that Qur'anic material is taken from the Bible, conflicts with the Bible or is inferior in its teaching to the Bible. So the Qur'an is not treated as a text in itself, but as a text for criticism or refutation linked inextricably with the life of the Prophet, as the Gospel is with the life of Jesus. The gospels are biographies of Jesus, and Rodwell, as with other translators, seems to think the Qur'an should likewise follow a linear, chronological pattern, complaining that 'anything approaching to a chronological arrangement was lost sight of'.[51] While repeating many of the calumnies on the character of the Prophet found in earlier writing, Rodwell nevertheless concedes that Muhammad was actuated by a sincere desire to deliver his countrymen from the grossness of its debasing idolatries, but that he 'worked himself up into a belief that he had received a divine call – and that he was carried on by the force of circumstances, and by gradually increasing successes, to believe himself the accredited messenger of Heaven'.[52] He also concedes, like earlier Protestants, that:

> there must be elements both of truth and goodness in the system of which he was the main author, to account for the world-wide phenomenon, that whatever may be the intellectual inferiority (if such is, indeed, the fact) of the Muslim races, the influence of his teaching, aided, it is true, by the vast impulse given to it by the victorious arms of his followers, has now lasted for nearly thirteen centuries, and embraces more than one hundred millions of our race – more than one-tenth part of the inhabitants of the globe.[53]

However, he continues to believe that the Prophet used any means to achieve his aims, 'not even excluding deceit and falsehood, tyranny and unscrupulous violence'.[54] Such views on the Qur'an, the moral character of the Prophet of Islam and the 'intellectual inferiority' of the Muslim races are not supported in Rodwell's work by any evidence of his having read the Arabic text of the Qur'an for itself or Arabic sources in general. We must remember that he lived in the nineteenth century and was busy working as a member of the clergy for 40 years. Nonetheless, he finds it 'hard to justify the strong, vituperative language poured out upon Muhammad's head by Marracci, Prideaux and others'.[55]

Rodwell's description of the style of the Qur'an in his introduction, and in those substituted in the later reprints of 1909 and even 1994, put the reader off the Qur'an. In his notes to the translation, occasionally, while trying to suggest that the Qur'an is inferior to the Bible, he reveals that he has seriously misunderstood crucial Arabic words and expressions. Commenting on '*We do not make distinction between any of His Messengers*' (Q. 2:285), he says this is contradicted by Q. 2:254 as well as several other verses. Q. 2:254 states that God has endowed some prophets more highly than others. The fact is that Q. 2:285 refers to the believers obeying God and not making any distinction between prophets by believing in some and not others (see also Q. 4:150–2). In another example, the believers are described in Q. 23:3 as '*those who turn away from idle talk (laghw)*'; Rodwell translates this as 'who keep aloof from vain words' and says in the footnotes, 'in prayer, Ecclesiastes 5:1, Matthew 4:7 but it may be understood of idle talk generally'. So he relates the Qur'an to the Bible in his reading of it, trying to show biblical sources for Qur'anic words where none exist; for example, *laghw* occurs in the Qur'an ten times, but Rodwell has selected only one particular instance on which to base his argument, while ignoring others which fail to bear it out. In another example, commenting on Q. 18:25, which Rodwell translates as, 'And they tarried in their cave 300 years and nine years over', he states that this figure could not be reconciled with 'the tradition'. He seems to think that this assertion that the sleepers tarried 300 years in their cave is made by the Prophet or the Qur'an when in fact it is part of the various guesses at the extent of their sojourn made by different people at the beginning of Q. 18:22. Verse 25 continues this list after comment to guide the Prophet. This feature of interruption for comments is a recognised general feature.[56] Rodwell should have placed the statement between quotes, as he did with the other guesses the Qur'an presents, but he did not. It should be remembered that the entry on him in the *Dictionary of National Biography* states, 'he acquired elements of Arabic assisted by Catafago'.[57]

Like Ketton, Rodwell sometimes selects such unlikely interpretations of Arabic words to support his views. In his introduction and footnotes Rodwell proves to have taken a retrograde step in his approach to the Qur'an and the image of it he creates compared with Sale's work; however, when we come to his translation, it has made a valuable contribution. Rather than presenting an entire sura, which can run into 40 pages as one single paragraph with no verse numbers, for the first time in English, the material is presented in separate verses with some numbering (every ten verses), which makes it less off-putting and easier to cite. Rodwell's translation, moreover, has rhythm and is more compact than Sales's. He also realised that translation did not mean following exactly the sentence-structure of the source-language, and his translation rearranges certain parts of sentences to show in English where the focus lies in Arabic. In his footnotes we frequently see more literal renditions of specific phrases prefaced by 'lit.', reflecting the fact that in the text itself he adapted the material to suit the English mode of expression and avoid the literalism that has been one of the weakest points in many translations. Although, like Sale, Rodwell adds words in italics to clarify the meaning, these are fewer than Sale's, and he specifically criticises Sale for 'introducing his paraphrastic comments into the body of the text as well as his constant use of Latinised instead of Saxon words'.[58]

Rodwell's translation has had a long life and its effects continue to be felt today. As Carl Ernst has noted:

> This rather theologically biased translation received a boost when it was reprinted in Everyman's Library in 1909 and it is still in print now in canonical order

[of chapters, from 1994 with an introduction by Alan Jones] and very popular with evangelical Christians.[59]

Edward Henry Palmer: *The Qur'ān*

Palmer's translation of the Qur'an was published in 1860, only 20 years after Rodwell's translation appeared, but the difference between the two men and their translations was huge. E. H. Palmer (1840–82) was a Cambridge orphan who, after reaching the sixth form, went to London to work in a city house and picked up French, Italian and other languages. He then returned to Cambridge and, through his acquaintance with a Hindustani lecturer, Sayed Abdullah, acquired Hindu, Persian and Arabic. He read for the Classical Tripos and advanced his knowledge of Arabic through association with Rizq Allāh Ḥassan of Aleppo,[60] following which he catalogued the Persian, Arabic and Turkish manuscripts of Kings and Trinity Colleges and the University Library. On the strength of his publications, he was elected to a fellowship at St John's College Cambridge, which gave him the leisure to travel in the East. This he did under the auspices of the Palestine Exploration Fund and, with some colleagues, made a survey of Sinai. From this he gained excellent contacts with the Bedouin Arabs in the area, to whom he was known as Abdallah Effendi.

Here we have not only the first academic translator of the Qur'an (some 248 years after the establishment of Arabic chairs in British universities), but the first Arabist English translator who had lived among the Arabs and was fully immersed in the spoken language. On his return he resumed his residence at Cambridge, where he lectured in Arabic, Persian and Hindustani concurrently. Palmer was a very fluent writer in Arabic, Persian and Urdu and could compose quite respectable verses in all three.[61] Among his works is the edited and metrical translation into English of the poetical works of Baha-ed-Din Zoheir of Egypt. His translation of the Koran appeared in 1880. Shortly afterwards, in 1882, when Britain invaded Egypt, he was sent on a secret mission to win over the Arabs and stop them attacking the Suez Canal, but was attacked and killed along with his colleagues. The memorial to Palmer is set up in St Paul's Cathedral; he was the only translator of the Qur'an to gain such a distinction.

In Palmer's introduction to his translation of the Qur'an we see a completely different attitude to Islam and the Islamic scripture to that found in previous translations. His 44-page history of the life of the Prophet contains hardly anything Muslims could object to. He was not a cleric; he lived with the Arabs and knew them. He argues forcefully against some of the theses of the earlier authors who 'sought to refute the Qur'an or to repeat the theories [about the Prophet] of imposture and enthusiasm,' saying that 'Even the theory of his being a great political reformer does not contain the whole truth.'[62] Palmer refutes Christian claims that 'the greater part of his revelations were due to the suggestions of a Christian monk,'[63] saying there is no evidence for this. As to the claim that neither the doctrines nor the rites of Islam are original, Palmer answers that:

> No religion, no sacred books of a religion, ever possessed entire originality. [...] The New Testament, it is well known, contains much that is not original. Many of the parables &c., as a late eminent Orientalist once pointed out, are to be found in the Talmud. [...] We know that St. Paul drew upon classic Greek sources for many of his most striking utterances [...] Even the most divine sentiment in the Lord's prayer, "Forgive us our trespasses as we forgive those who trespass against us," is expressed almost in so many words in the advice given by Nestor to the angered Achilles in the first book of Homer's Iliad. Judged then by the standard which we apply to other creeds, Mohammed's religion stands forth as something strikingly new and original.[64]

Unlike Rodwell, who rearranged the suras, Palmer keeps the traditional arrangement which, for him, retains what he calls the 'miscellaneous character of the book, and [...] the one used by the Muslims from the time of Muhammad's successors'.[65] His accompanying notes are minimal, as he gives 'only such as are absolutely necessary for understanding the text'.[66] For more extensive commentaries he refers the reader to Sale's work, which indicates that he felt that more clarification was needed than he himself. A novel feature is the precis he gives of each sura, which is a good and useful aid to understanding the text, although no distinction is made in these precis between central themes and supporting material.

Palmer was perhaps the first to grasp a very important quality of the Arabic Qur'an, that is, its style and rhetorical quality:

> There was nothing antiquated in the style or words, no tricks of speech, pretty conceits or mere poetical embellishment. The metaphor spoke with rude, fierce eloquence in ordinary language. The only rhetorical ornaments [...] are the rhythmical periods and rhymed clauses. [...] To translate this worthily is a most difficult task. Rhyme and rhythm would give the English an artificial ring

from which the Arabic is quite free. The same objection lies against using the phraseology of the Authorised Version of the Bible. [...] to render it by fine or stilted language would be equally foreign to the spirit of the original, while to make it too rude or familiar would be to err equally on the other side. I have therefore endeavoured to take a middle course. I have translated each sentence as literally as the difference in sentence structure between the two languages would allow, and, when possible, I have rendered it word for word.[67]

He objected to the large amount of exegetical material, and very different style of language used in Sale's translation which he felt did not reflect the 'rugged simplicity'[68] of the original. Likewise, he criticised the style of Rodwell's Qur'an translation as being too literary. There is certainly a ring of simplicity about Palmer's translation. The sense is definitely clearer, but the translation does lack the passion and rhythm so essential for the effect of the Qur'an.

From the first edition in 1880, Palmer's translation was always published by the Clarendon Press in Oxford, but in 1928, R. A. Nicholson wrote a new introduction that returns at times to the more combative style of earlier introductions.[69] Through its association with the Clarendon Press, Palmer's translation acquired a wide circulation, with many reprints up to 1965, since when it was replaced by Arberry's 1955 translation. With Palmer's translation the image of the Qur'an witnessed a huge transformation. Fifty years later came another translation, which would again bring about a large shift in the perception of Islam's holy scripture, that of Muhammad Pickthall.

Muhammad Marmaduke Pickthall: *The Meaning of the Glorious Koran*

In 1930, there appeared a new translation which is unique in a sense amongst our group, *The Meaning of the Glorious Koran* by Muhammad Marmaduke Pickthall. Born in London in 1875, the son of a Church of England clergyman, Pickthall was prevented from finishing his education by his poor health. Nevertheless, he learned French, Italian, German and Spanish, and travelled to Syria where he learned Arabic and mixed with Arab society. In 1904, Lord Cromer called him to Egypt and while there he published two books, *Sons of the Nile* and *Veiled Women*, and articles defending Islam and showing its connection with Christianity. He travelled to Turkey and on his return, he declared his conversion to Islam. In 1920 he went to India and participated in the publication of the *Islamic Culture* magazine. Later he became the Imam in London and spent three years on his Qur'an translation, following which he went to Cairo to have it revised by some *'ulamā'* (scholars) there, where he was assisted by Professor M. A. Al-Ghamrāwī, Professor of Medicine under the auspices of the Rector of al-Azhar, M. M. Al-Marāghī.[70] Al-Marāghī and al-Azhar ruled at the time that the words of the Qur'an could not be translated, only their meanings, hence Pickthall's translation was published in 1930 under the title *The Meaning of the Glorious Koran: an Explanatory Translation.* Pickthall was the first to introduce this tradition, which is followed by many Muslim translators in English translations of the Qur'an. Pickthall died in 1936.

Pickthall was a native speaker of English, a novelist and a Muslim. From such a person, one could expect a translation showing due respect to the text of a scripture. This respect for the text was fulfilled, but the style of his translation was not on the same level as previous renditions of the text. This is partly because his primary aim, as explained in his foreword, was 'To present to English readers what Muslims the world over hold to be the meaning of the words of the Koran, and the nature of that Book, in not unworthy language and concisely, with a view to the requirements of English Muslims.[71] He goes on to observe:

> Some of the earlier translations include commentation offensive to Muslims, and almost all employ a style of language which Muslims at once recognise as unworthy. The Koran cannot be translated [...] The book is here rendered almost literally and every effort has been made to choose befitting language. But the result is not the Glorious Koran, that inimitable symphony the very sounds of which move men to tears and ecstasy. It is only an attempt to present the meaning of the Koran – and peradventure something of the charm – in English. It can never take the place of the Koran in Arabic, nor is it meant to do so.[72]

The language he uses is not that of Pickthall the novelist, but rather that of Pickthall the clergyman's son, nurtured on the English style of the Authorised Version of the Bible, and was seen by some English readers to 'parody almost' that style so that 'for many non-Muslim readers [it] is more likely to discourage than attract interest in the Qur'an.'[73] This effect of 'parody' is due largely to the artificial nature of some of the archaisms he uses. This 'befitting language' and his taste which considers that of other translations as unworthy put him in opposition to Palmer's more scholarly view that the Qur'an was written in simple, straightforward Arabic.

Just as his use of biblical archaisms was inappropriate, so too were the many literal renderings he chose, considering the wide divergence in grammar and idioms between English and Arabic, and the Arabic of the Qur'anic style in particular. He must have felt that any linguistic adjustment would be tantamount to tampering with the message, and the fact that he had his translation revised by *'ulamā'* was bound to make it even more literal. Because of this, Arabic grammatical structures and idioms are still much evident in the English he uses. This is somewhat disappointing in view of the fact that he expressly did not call his rendition a translation of the Qur'an, but was the first to use the title *The Meaning of the Glorious Qur'an, an Explanatory Translation.*

Pickthall was also the first to follow the Arabic Qur'an in numbering each verse individually and separately, which makes it the easiest translation so far to cite, but his text is odd at times in that the verse boundaries are different from those of the English sentences. This atomistic approach does not help the reader see thematic units, but rather isolated verses. He provides an introduction to each sura, explaining some of the circumstances of its revelation and its contents, but he uses very few footnotes, solving the problem of pronominal references by inserting the addressee into the text in brackets. All this was very useful and elucidated the meanings.

Pickthall's translation is very popular amongst Muslims who have been driven away from others by the obvious hostility shown by some other translators, or by a perception that, as non-Muslims following a long, hostile tradition towards Islam and the Qur'an, Western translators could not be trusted. Pickthall's translation thus has been continuously in print in both the United Kingdom, and in Arab and Muslim countries, and is distributed free in mosques and recorded on audio cassettes along with the Arabic recitations in many different forms.

Richard Bell: *The Qur'an Translated, with a Critical Rearrangement of the Suras*

Richard Bell (1876–1952) was born in Dumfries and graduated from Edinburgh University in Semitic studies. He was licensed as a Minister of the Church of Scotland and then ordained to a Scottish parish. After serving for 14 years, he was appointed Lecturer in Arabic at Edinburgh University and became Reader in Arabic in 1938 until his retirement in 1947. During his years at Edinburgh University, he was preoccupied with showing how Christianity influenced Islam and with the structure and composition of the Qur'an (among his works is a collection of lectures entitled *The Origin of Islam in its Christian Environment*).[74] *The Qur'an Translated, with a Critical Rearrangement of the Suras* was published in two volumes between 1937 and 1939, followed by his *Introduction to the Qur'an* in 1953. The critical rearrangement of the Qur'anic material he implemented in his translation singles him out among all academics of Qur'anic studies in English and affects the reception, popularity and demand for his translation. This rearrangement was based on 'the hypothesis that the present form of the Qur'an', with its 'dreary welter [...] so often deplored by Western writers', 'rests upon a careful reproduction of a confusion of written documents', rather than upon 'textual defects, or [...] confusion in Muhammad's own thought'.[75] His aim was to reduce what he sees as this confusion of material, taking into account possible 'corrections, interlinear additions, additions on the margin, deletions and substitution, pieces cut off from a passage and wrongly placed, passages written on the back of others and then read continuously, front and back following each other'.[76]

To Muslims this is pure fantasy, since the Qur'an was memorised as a complete corpus right from the time of its origin and recited by a great many Muslims during the life of the Prophet in the traditional order. When it was collated, memorisation was the main criteria for the accuracy of the written text and its arrangement. Moreover, it is clear that, like most translators, Bell, as discussed above, relied mainly on al-Bayḍāwī's (d. 791/1388) *tafsīr*, which was atomistic in character. Had Bell and others used or referred to the work of al-Rāzī (d. 606/1209) and others, they would have seen how the material of the Qur'an fits together, but al-Rāzī was in eight volumes of 700 pages at least, unindexed and rather inaccessible to Bell, certainly not mentioned by him. Be that as it may, Bell himself concedes, as does the editor of his commentary,[77] and Arberry (see below), that his method of reconstruction of the passages on the printed page, 'presented', as Bell says, 'without the arguments which support them',[78] might seem arbitrary, and the author would be the first to admit uncertainty; in fact, the pages of his book are studded with the words 'perhaps', 'probably', 'possibly' and 'maybe'.

Although he rearranged the material within suras, unlike Rodwell before him, Bell kept the suras themselves in their traditional order. He introduces each one with a statement dealing mainly with dating and arrangements, which shows that this was his main preoccupation. He uses an elaborate system of dotted lines, boxes and numbering.[79] This unfortunately made the text confusing and very hard to follow.

The translation itself is straightforward and easy to follow compared with the others so far discussed, and he attempts to maintain some aspect of rhyme, but he relegated translation to a secondary concern in favour of all this rearrangement. He admits, however, that his approach has not worked, and that 'the thorough arrangement of the Qur'an in chronological order remains a complicated problem which must be left to others to solve'.[80] As Arberry said, '[Bell's translation] is virtually unreadable. Certainly one needs to have some detailed knowledge of the text in order to benefit by the arduous exercise of studying his hard laboured pages.'[81]

Perhaps because of this radical approach to the arrangement of the material, and the confusing nature of the text, Bell's translation did not gain popularity and was printed only twice, in 1937 and 1960. In 1991, his commentary on the Qur'an appeared in two volumes,[82] but scholars found it disappointing, failing to add much to his work on the translation, and in fact it was remaindered by the publishers not long after publication. It is perhaps unfair to compare his translation with the others discussed here since it is more a work of deconstruction or 'unravelling', as he puts it, rather than translation, in spite of the title. Bell's preoccupation with the origins of the Qur'an in Christianity and with his fantastic theory about what Muslims did to the text of the Qur'an meant that in the process of his translation the Qur'an itself was neglected.

Arthur J. Arberry: *The Koran Interpreted*

Now we come to the last of our chosen English translators of the Qur'an, Arthur J. Arberry (1905–69), the most notable scholar among the translators discussed in this chapter. He first studied Classics and then Arabic and Persian at Cambridge. In 1932 he was appointed for two years as head of the Department of Classics at the University of Cairo, and this was where he developed his love for the sound of the Qur'an recited in Arabic while listening to an 'old, white-bearded Sheykh who chanted the Koran for the pious delectation of my neighbour'.[83] Back in England he was appointed to the Chair of Persian at London University in 1944, and in 1946 became Professor of Arabic at School of Oriental and African Studies (SOAS). In 1947 he left for Cambridge as Thomas Adams Professor of Arabic, where he stayed until his death in 1969.

Arberry was a very prolific scholar in both Arabic and Persian, contributing to the cataloguing of oriental manuscripts in the India

Office, SOAS and Chester Beatty libraries, translating poetry and prose, and writing about mysticism and mystic poets. He felt that it must be in Britain's interests to strengthen its links with the Islamic world, and was responsible for the introduction of Turkish and Modern Arabic studies and the Middle East Centre in Cambridge. He supervised a great number of Muslim students who remained very loyal to him. Arberry's translation is clearly a labour of love, which, he states, was undertaken:

> at a time of great personal distress, through which it comforted and sustained the writer in a manner for which he will always be grateful. He therefore acknowledges his gratitude to whatever power or Power inspired the man and the Prophet who first recited these scriptures. I pray that this interpretation, poor echo though it is of the glorious original, may instruct, please, and in some degree inspire those who read it.[84]

Arberry called his translation *The Koran Interpreted*, conceding, as he said, 'that the Koran was untranslatable'. He was at pains to study 'the intricate and varied rhythms, which [...] constitute the Koran's undeniable claim to rank amongst the greatest literary masterpieces of mankind'.[85] His motivation for providing a new English translation of his own was that he had noticed 'uniformity and dull monotony' characterising all translations from the seventeenth to the twentieth century, commenting that 'in no previous rendering has a serious attempt been made to imitate those rhetorical and rhythmical patterns which are the glory and the sublimity of the Koran. I am breaking new ground here.'[86]

Arberry keeps to the traditional order of the text, disregarding the view of its composite, fragmentary character, 'wishing to show each Sura as an artistic whole, its often incongruous parts constituting a rich and admirable pattern'.[87] The contrast with Bell here, especially, is striking. While others had previously seen the non-linear, non-narrative nature of the Qur'an as problematic and somehow flawed, Arberry finds its 'incongruity' admirable. In his preface, he explains some of the literary qualities of the Qur'an as he sees them and how he has attempted to render them into English. He hopes, by doing this to show 'that those notorious incongruities and irrelevancies, even those "wearisome repetitions", which have proved such stumbling-blocks in the way of our Western appreciation will vanish in the light of a clearer understanding of the nature of the Muslim scriptures'.[88]

The features he tries to replicate include the rhyming of each verse or 'rhetorical unit'. He explains:

I have called attention to such changes of mood and tempo by making corresponding variations in my own rhythmical patterns. In this fashion I have also striven to isolate and to integrate the diverse sections of which each Sura is composed.[89]

Thus Arberry, conscious of the literary merit of the Arabic, has tried to reproduce some of its rhetorical features. In addition to the features he mentions above, his translation is conveyed in an appealing literary style. Of the seven translators under discussion here, no one comes close to Arberry in terms of his knowledge of Arabic language and literature or Islamic culture. No one has proved able to translate Arabic texts into English as did Arberry, nor were any of them able to produce such an elegant, rhythmic and effective translation as he did. However, there are shortcomings resulting not from lack of ability or skill, but from the approach Arberry took to translation.

Foremost among the problems with this translation is that Arberry chose to present his text without any explanatory notes, because 'notes in plenty are to be found in other versions, and the radiant beauty of the original is not clouded by such vexing interpolations'.[90] However, this causes difficulties because there are numerous pronominal references and historical allusions mentioned very briefly in the Qur'an, known only to those who know the historical background well. He did not give any of this information, either in the introduction to the book or the suras, through either interpolation or footnotes. Montgomery Watt later felt strongly enough about the problems of this lack of contextualisation to publish a *Companion to the Qur'an*[91] based on the Arberry translation in 1967, containing explanatory notes, presented on a sura by sura basis. Another feature that diminishes the effect of his translation was his, at times, excessively close rendering of the Arabic grammatical structures and idioms. As Kenneth Cragg, himself a translator of selected parts of the Qur'an, has rightly pointed out: 'He left his English full of Arabisms, sometimes to the point of oddity and unintelligibility.'[92] For example, he renders Q. 7:71 as 'What, do you dispute with Me regarding names you have named, you and your fathers, touching which God hath sent down never authority?' instead of 'for which God has not revealed any authority', and Q. 20:113 as 'We have turned about in it something of warning' instead of 'We have displayed [in the Qur'an] warning.' However, having said that, Arberry's translation has been praised by Arab scholars, for example, A. L. Tibawi, normally very critical of orientalist scholarship, considers Arberry's translation superior to its predecessors, and says: 'Professor Arberry has to a remarkable degree achieved all he set out to achieve in artistry and interpretation, no less than in technical exactitude.'[93] It is a mark of the esteem in which Arberry's translation is held that it has been widely published, in Britain, America, Pakistan and Iran.

The Making of an Image

The early Christian image of Islam, the Prophet and the Qur'an, as described by Norman Daniel, for example, in his *Islam and the West: The Making of an Image*,[94] was not based on any sound knowledge and contained fantastic ideas about Islam and its Prophet. As Watt has stated: 'Perhaps no man in history has been subjected to more abuse than Muhammad by the Europeans.'[95] The Qur'an itself was portrayed as a 'dangerous book', a barbarous pastiche of the Bible, justifying the excesses of Muhammad, to be read only by the scholars whose job it was to refute it. However, the publication of the Qur'an itself, in translation, from the seventeenth century onwards, and a few of the Arabic sources, has gradually eroded this tissue of fantasy but, with the honourable exceptions of Sale, Palmer, Pickthall and Arberry, the old image persisted for a long time in translations, mainly by means of introductions and footnotes, but also by misinterpretations of the text. Within the translation itself, the effectiveness or otherwise of style and presentation perpetuates the image of the Qur'an as something alien, unclear and disorderly. Relating it to the Bible in content and style has historically affected its image in the West and was a serious distraction from reading and understanding the Qur'an on its own terms, hampering appreciation of its linguistic features and style, which were to a large extent neglected. Misinterpretation and mistranslation, furthermore, affected the understanding of even basic Islamic concepts and terms.

Criteria for Translations

It may be useful at this point to base the following discussion of the merits and demerits of the various translations of the Qur'an addressed in this chapter on various specific criteria. Perhaps many would agree that naturalness in the target language, clarity, accuracy, emotional impact and the objectivity of the translator should be key in any translation of the Qur'an. In what follows, space will only allow for discussion of a limited number of examples.

Naturalness in the target language

In Q. 14:4, God speaks in the plural of majesty: '*We have never sent a messenger who did not use his own people's language to make things clear to them.*' '*His own people's language*' does not here mean only the alphabet or words of the language, but all the linguistic and cultural norms of the target language. Only through following these can things be made clear to people. The English has to be English, not Arabic English, as is obvious from many examples in the existing translations.

An important cause of a translation sounding unnatural is literalism, one of the most common faults, where the translator forces on the English language the norms of the Arabic to one degree or another. Here are some examples:

1. Q. 20:74, is rendered by Pickthall as 'Whoso cometh guilty to his Lord verily for him is Hell', but a more natural English rendition of this verse in my translation is, 'Hell will be the reward of those who return to their Lord as evildoers.'
2. Q. 40:9, is rendered by Pickthall as 'and ward off from them ill deeds; and he from whom thou wardest off ill deeds that day, him verily hast Thou taken into mercy'. More simply, it can be rendered: 'Protect them from all evil deeds: those You protect on that Day from [the punishment for] evil deeds will receive Your mercy'.
3. Q. 74:45, is rendered by Arberry as 'and we plunged along with the plungers', but is (in my translation) rendered as 'we indulged with others [in mocking the believers]', as the figure of speech used in the Qur'an is common and well understood in Arabic, but not in the English.
4. Q. 12:88, rendered as 'fill up to us the measure' by Arberry, is more easily read as 'give us full measure' (my own translation).
5. Q. 17:85, is variously rendered as 'but of knowledge only a little to you is given' (Rodwell) or 'but ye have not knowledge bestowed upon you except a little' (Bell) as well as 'and of knowledge ye have been

vouchsafed but a little' (Pickthall), but can be translated more simply as 'You have only been given a little knowledge'.

6. Q. 2:276, rendered by Rodwell as 'God will bring usury to naught but will increase alms with usury',[96] I have rendered in my translation as 'God blights usury but will bless charitable deeds with multiple increase'.
7. Q. 29:68, rendered by Bell as 'In what is vain then will they believe and for the goodness of Allah be ungrateful!', can be rendered as 'How can they believe in what is false and deny God's blessing?'.

Clarity

Lack of clarity is a common complaint made about English translations of the Qur'an. Clarity is essential because the Qur'an is meant to be a book of guidance; as scripture, it addresses everyone, not just highly intellectual or erudite scholars. If it loses clarity in translation, it is losing something fundamental to its message. Without clarity the message cannot be conveyed. Literalism, archaism and atomism all contribute to lack of clarity. Sometimes more explanation is needed to make the sentences normal in English and show the meaning of very highly concise statements in the Arabic Qur'an, as well as to show the logical connections that may be clear in Arabic according to the rules of conjunction and disjunction (*faṣl wa-waṣl*) in *balāgha* (rhetoric), but that are not clear in English. Another important factor that affects clarity is the rendering of pronouns in Arabic, whether personal, demonstrative or relative, into English. Arabic and English are different in this regard. Sometimes it is essential for a pronoun in Arabic to be replaced by the noun it stands for to make the text clearer for the reader. Pickthall does this, for example in Q. 9:3, 'give tidings (O Muhammad) of a painful doom' and Q. 9:4 'excepting those of the idolaters with whom ye (Muslims) have a treaty'.

Accuracy

The translators addressed in this chapter had varying degrees of knowledge of the Qur'an in Arabic, but the *balāgha* of the Qur'an has not received its due level of attention.[97] Scholars of the Qur'an in English have done a vast amount of work on the chronology of the Qur'an, its sources, foreign vocabulary and teachings, but there are essential elements of the language and style of the Qur'an that have not been sufficiently studied, although these are crucial for an accurate understanding of the text and are part of the criteria for judging the accuracy and effect of the translation.

Wujūh al-Qur'ān

Nor has the vocabulary of the Qur'an received sufficient attention, especially what is known in Arabic Qur'anic Studies as *wujūh al-Qur'ān*, according to which certain words have different meanings depending on the contexts in which they are used. The importance of this feature is that it covers the majority of the basic concepts of the Qur'an, such as *kufr, islām, ẓulm* and *fisq*, and it has long been recognised and addressed extensively in writings within Arabic scholarship on the Qur'an.[98] Even in texts read and quoted by Western scholars, such as *al-burhān fī-ʿulūm al-qur'ān* by Badr al-Dīn al-Zarkashī[99] and *al-itqān fī-ʿulūm al-qur'ān* by Jalāl al-Dīn al-Ṣuyūṭī,[100] there are discussions of *wujūh*; however, English-language scholars and translators do not seem to have given this the necessary attention and consideration. Richard Bell's *Introduction to the Qur'an*, which dedicates a chapter to the language of the Qur'an,[101] does not mention the word *wujūh*. The first non-Muslim scholar who seems to give attention to this feature was the Japanese Toshihiko Izutsu in his 1959 book *The Structure of the Ethical Terms in the Qur'an*, Chapters 9 and 10 on 'Kufr' and 'Words related semantically with Kufr'.[102] Even after this, Alford T. Welch in the second edition of the *Encylopaedia of Islam* (1960–2007),[103] in his long chapter on 'al-Ḳur'ān' does not mention it. In contrast, modern Qur'anic studies in Arabic do give *wujūh* its correct emphasis. For example, Tamman Hassan has identified ten different meanings of the word *kitāb* in the Qur'an.[104] In common with other Western authors, the translators we have covered in this study do not seem to have paid regard to *wujūh*, perhaps in their endeavour to be consistent when consistency is, in fact, the wrong approach, and leads to misunderstanding of the text. The following are a few examples:

1. *Al-Ḥakīm*

   This word occurs in the Qur'an just under 100 times referring mainly to God and sometimes to the Qur'an. The translators habitually give 'Wise' or 'All-Wise', taking it to refer to *ḥikma* ('wisdom') when in fact in many cases it relates more to *ḥukm* ('judgement' or 'decision' by God). In Q. 6:18, among other examples, the context quite clearly shows that *al-ḥakīm* implies decisiveness, not wisdom, contrary to what most translators have chosen (all seven translators discussed here have opted for 'wise'): '*He is the Supreme Master over all His creatures: He is the One who Decides (al-ḥakīm), the All-Aware.*' See also the following examples:

On the Day when He says 'Be!' it will be: His word is the Truth. All control on the Day the Trumpet is blown belongs to Him. He knows the seen and the unseen. He is the One who Decides (al-ḥakīm), the All Aware.

Q. 6:73

If you slide back after clear evidence has come to you, know that God is mighty, and decisive in judgement (ḥakīm).

Q. 2:209

The building they have founded will always be a source of doubt within their hearts until their hearts are cut to pieces. God is all knowing and decisive in judgement (ḥakīm).

Q. 9:110

2. The definite article '*al-*' ('the')
Another important example of *wujūh* is the meaning of the definite article '*al-*', where it can be generic, referring to everything in that class, or it can refer to something just mentioned or understood from the context. In discussing the definite article, Arabic grammar texts refer to the generic '*al-*' (*al al-jinsiyya*), on the one hand, and the *al al-'ahdiyya*, on the other hand, which refers to something already known, understood or spoken about. There are numerous examples of this *al al-'ahdiyya* in the Qur'an and translators mistake it for the generic '*al-*', for example: '*There is no blame on you if you make a hint of intending marriage to these women (khiṭbati'l-nisā')*' (Q. 2:235). The phrase *khiṭbati'l-nisā'* refers to the intention to marry widows before their waiting period is completed, not to all women in general, as interpreted by Bell, Pickthall and Arberry. Rodwell correctly gives 'such' women in his translation. I find it puzzling that few translators were aware of the *al al-'ahdiyya*. Again, in Q. 17:94, on being told by the disbelievers that they would not believe in the Prophet unless he performed many miracles, including making the sky fall down on them in pieces or bringing God and the angels to meet them face to face, the Prophet is instructed to say: '*Praise be to God! Am I anything but a mortal, a messenger?*' Then follows the statement (as rendered by Pickthall): 'And nought prevented mankind from believing when the guidance came unto them, save that they said, "Hath Allah sent a mortal as a messenger?"' According to this, the claim is that the only thing that prevented humankind from believing was that they said,

'How could God have sent a human being as a messenger?' The misinterpretation here is reading the words *nās* as 'mankind' (which it can mean in other contexts) when in fact here it means 'people'. Bell has 'the people', which is better but not accurate enough. The article, '*al-*', refers to the persons just mentioned, so my own translation gives: '*The only thing that has kept these people [of Mecca] from believing, when guidance came to them, was that they said, "How could God have sent a human being as a messenger?"*' This verse, then, refers to an objection often raised by the pagans of Mecca against the prophethood of Muhammad.

3. When in Q. 2:116 the Qur'an describes God as having no child ('*They have asserted, "God has a child (walad)." May He be exalted! No!*'), *walad* is often translated as 'son', which restricts it to the Christian concept, when in fact it also refers to the polytheists' ascription of 'daughters' to God. The interpretation is affected by the modern colloquial usage in Arabic. This is a rich source of misunderstanding of many words.

Things Translators Should Avoid

Naturally translators may fall, whether intentionally or unintentionally, to a greater or lesser extent under the influence of earlier translators, but this can have the adverse effect of perpetuating wrong or inadequate translations. We have already seen that translators continue to translate God's attribute *al-ḥakīm* as 'the Wise', when in many cases the meaning is more to do with His decision and judgement rather than wisdom.

Another pitfall has to do with inappropriate segmentation and punctuation of sentences. One characteristic of Qur'anic Arabic is that it does not contain punctuation marks in the way modern English does. The segmentation of material many translators give does not pay regard to the sense, but rather to the traditional formal layout of the Arabic verses, which can lead to misunderstanding and mistranslation. I will give three examples here:

1. In Q. 6:37, the Qur'an refers to the opponents of the Prophet as being obdurate in their rejection and demands, saying that he should have received a miraculous sign from his Lord. The Prophet is instructed do say, '*God is able to send down a miracle.*' The text continues, with an example of a miracle: '*No kind of beast is there on earth or fowls that flies with its wings, but is a folk like you: nothing have we passed over in the Book: then unto their Lord shall they be gathered*' (Rodwell's translation of Q. 6:38).

The punctuation demanded by the above context is to put a full stop after *'like you'*. Then a new statement by God, '*We have left out nothing in the record of deeds: in the end they will be gathered to their Lord.*' The disbelievers are being warned that all they say is being recorded and they will be held accountable. Without this punctuation it would seem that it is the birds who will be recorded in the book and gathered to their Lord, while the disbelievers are left to say what they like.

2. Q. 5:97, states, according to Arberry's translation:

   God has appointed the Ka'ba the Holy House as an establishment for men, and the Holy month, the offering, and the necklaces – that you may know (li-ta'lamū) that God knows all that is in the heavens and the earth and that God has knowledge of everything.

   Arberry's rendition of *li-ta'lamū* as 'that you may know' is inaccurate. Actually, this is not the '*li-*' of purpose, but an imperative '*li-*'. *Dhālika* in Arabic, before '*li-*', refers to all that has been listed and should have a full stop after it. Then comes the order that they should know that God knows everything. He is watching whether they are obeying or not, and that He has power over everything so that He can punish the disobedient. The following verse (Q. 5:98) states: '*God is terrible in retribution but also all forgiving and merciful.*' It is strange to say that God has ordained all these things listed so that we may know that He knows what is in the heavens and earth; this does not make sense. *Dhālika* in the sense used here is repeated in other places in the Qur'an, for instance, Q. 22:30 and Q. 47:9 and many others. The warning that God knows everything also appears, for example, in Q. 65:13.

3. Q. 18:25, is rendered in Arberry's (and others) translation as: '*And they tarried in their cave three hundred years and to that they added nine years more.*' The first part of the verse should have been put into quotes to show that it is the assumption of people rather than a statement by God: '*[Some say], "The sleepers stayed in their cave for three hundred years," and some added nine more.*'

Antiquated Style

English translators of the Qur'an have historically worked within a cultural atmosphere in which the *Authorized Version of the Bible* with its high level of English was seen to be the model for the language of scripture, in addition to which translators of the Qur'an were writing for people of their own level of literary appreciation. During the nineteenth century, starting from Rodwell, the style of writing any literary text was meant to be of that level. But in 1946, immediately after the war, the Scottish Church led a campaign to modernise the language of the Bible and write a *New English Bible.* Pickthall in particular, who was nurtured on the language of the *Authorized Version,* and being a Muslim who valued the Qur'an highly as the word of God, tried hard to emulate this style. Arabists like Bell and Arberry were actually writing for colleagues, teachers and students of Arabic and Islamic studies, resulting in a translation written in language that was not understood by the majority. The one exception is Palmer who realised that most of the vocabulary of the Qur'an is not obscure or archaic. The fact is that when the Qur'an was first recited to the Prophet's audience, it was understood and appreciated by one and all; not only by Abū Bakr, 'Umar and others of the Arab tribes, but also by Bilāl the Abyssinian, Ṣuhayb the 'Roman' and Salmān the Persian. After all, the intention of the Qur'an was to be understood and to give guidance (*hudā*).

Emotional Impact

Scriptures are meant to change people's minds and lives and for this they need moving language. The Qur'an is the supreme example of moving language in Arabic. This was conceded even by its opponents at the time of the revelation, so much that they said it was 'magic' or poetry.[105]

The Qur'an is a passionate text that does not just give teachings, but strives to deliver its message effectively through various means, including logical arguments that are sometimes extended beyond the boundary of the sentence to run through a number of verses. However, most of the translators discussed here have followed an atomistic approach in their translations, working at the level of the individual verse and starting each new verse as a new paragraph. This weakens the passion that runs through the text.

There is one area of Arabic studies dealing with the rhetoric of the Qur'an, called '*ilm al-ma'ānī.* This is crucial for appreciating the effect of the language of the Qur'an. It is severely lacking in the syllabus of Arabic in British universities. The limited time available is taken up with learning the vocabulary, grammar, history and so on. Moreover, studies on the Qur'an do not seem to be interested in how effective it is in the Arabic, and from earlier centuries many were dismissive of its language and effect. Now and again, one comes across statements, even in the writings of eminent scholars, that show how neglected the Qur'anic *balāgha* is in

Western writing. Some may think that the Qur'an is effective in Arabic mainly because of its rhymes. In fact, this is only one detail.

The passion of the Qur'an is shown in its stylistic features of *balāgha* and is intensified in Arabic through the choice of words, sentence structure, rhythm and sound. Much of this sound effect is lost in translation. The Qur'an is an especially effective text in its own language, as Q. 39:23 itself emphasises:

Allāhu nazzala aḥsana'l-ḥadīthi kitāban mutashābihan mathānīya taqsha'iru minhu julūdu'lladhīna yakhshawna rabbahum. Thumma talīnu julūduhum wa-qulūbuhum ilā dhikri'llāh…

God has sent down the most beautiful teachings: a Scripture that is consistent and draws comparisons; that causes the skins of those in awe of their Lord to quiver. Then their skins and their hearts soften at the mention of God…

Arberry was aware of the aural effect of the Qur'an and made great efforts to convey some of it with his rhythm, alliteration, assonance and general sensitivity to the sound. Take, for example, his rendering of Q. 79:1–5:

By those that pluck out vehemently
and those that draw out violently
by those that swim serenely
and those that outstrip suddenly
By those that direct an affair.

This is a gallant effort to capture some of the effect of the original Arabic but alas, at the expense of the original sense of the words in Arabic, which have cultural connotations, not seen in the English version. In sense, it simply reads '*By the forceful chargers, roving widely, sweeping ahead at full stretch to sort a matter out*'.

Literalism and the atomistic approach with lack of regard for the context, all contributed to making translations of the Qur'an difficult to follow. A few years ago, I ran an experiment by asking my students at the University of London, BA, MA and PhD students, who were native speakers of English, what they thought of existing translations of the Qur'an. They generally said they did not appreciate them because they were unclear and written in language they did not read at school or at university. What was required was clear language, generally understood and intended for a general readership rather than an elite.

Objectivity

Objectivity is essential in studying and translating the Qur'an. An essential part of objectivity is to be equipped with the required level of knowledge of the Arabic language and of the language of the Qur'an with its norms and habits, including *balāgha* (rhetoric) and especially *'ilm al-ma'ānī.* It is only fair, if you wish to make judgement on the Qur'an or translate it that they should be equipped with sufficient knowledge of these basic characteristics of its language and style.

The Qur'an demands adherence to truth, the whole truth, and justice, particularly on the part of people who teach scripture and study it (Q. 3:79) and those who have been entrusted with the Book of God and are witnesses to it (Q. 5:44). Ethical considerations of academic scholarship on any subject demand objectivity.

Conclusion

In this chapter, we have been on a journey, lasting 305 years (1649–1955), to visit seven English translators. These seven had very different backgrounds and agendas: Ross, Rodwell and Bell were Christian clerics, and Bell was also an academic, as were Palmer and Arberry. Sale was a solicitor and Pickthall was an English Muslim novelist. Ross undertook his translation for the satisfaction of those who desired to look into the Turkish vanities and tried to reassure his readers that there was no danger in this. He clearly did not have the qualifications, or the required objectivity for the task, but he should be celebrated for his privileged position of being the first to introduce the Qur'an in English. Sale, on the other hand, intended to produce a better-explained English translation. He could not really have had the required knowledge of Arabic, but relied on Marracci's translation, which helped him a great deal. Sale showed remarkable objectivity for the time and his work was more accurate and clearer but lacking in literary effect. His translation improved the image of Islam, the Prophet and the Qur'an and it enjoyed a long life.

Rodwell's translation, in contrast, was in some respects a retrograde step. He tried to show the historical origins and shortcomings of the Qur'an, thus his objectivity was questionable, but he produced a version written in a better style of English than that of Sale. He was the first to introduce a rearrangement of the Qur'anic material and his quest to show defects showed his own faulty understanding of the Arabic Qur'an. His insufficient knowledge of Arabic and lack of awareness of the very special style of the Qur'an work to the detriment of his translation. Palmer, whose translation came closely after Rodwell's, was, however, the first Arabist among the English translators to show a better understanding of the style of the Qur'an. He was one of the most objective of the translators, improving the image of Islam and the Qur'an further, and his authorial aim was to use direct, balanced language and to refute the claim of lack of originality in the Qur'an. But, in his haste and enthusiasm to prove his opinion about the straightforwardness of the language of the Qur'an, he overlooked its powerful literary effect in Arabic and did not seem to aim for this in English.

Pickthall was the first Muslim to translate the Qur'an into English and his respect for the text shines through. He tried to render it in fitting language, which has been seen by some to be influenced by the *Authorized Version of the Bible.* He added useful clarifications to his translation, but, like all the other translators in our group, fell victim to a degree of literalism that marred the overall effect of his work. He clearly knew good Arabic and received further help in editing from scholars in Egypt. His translation is still widely used by Muslims. In almost direct contrast, Bell's aim above all was to conduct a deconstruction of the text of the Qur'an. In this he showed a lack of objectivity and outlined bizarre views that did not command respect or acceptance from scholars of the Qur'an. Although he had the qualifications and ability to produce good translation, clearer than those of his predecessors, his translation was stunted by his zeal to pursue his strange theories. This is undoubtedly why Bell's has been the only translation since Sale's in 1735 that did not earn acceptability, judging by the small number of reprints.

Last but not least, Arberry was probably the best qualified translator of the whole group, both in terms of his knowledge of Arabic and his proven ability to translate Arabic literature. His appreciation of the effect of the language of the Qur'an was keen and his objectivity was unquestionable. He used a pleasing poetic style, but in his respect for the original, he sometimes followed it too literally for English norms and this contributed to a lack of clarity. The criticism levelled at his translation here is certainly not based on any lack of ability, but is a result of the approach he chose; his desire to stay close in form to the original and to strip the translation of any explanation or footnotes. Those most able to appreciate Arberry are those who already know the Arabic Qur'an and its context well.

In conclusion, it can be said that two things are needed to improve translations and the image of the Qur'an. First, a study of the language and style of the Qur'an that takes into account, and benefits from, knowledge of *balāgha,* the Islamic science developed to identify elements of the matchlessness of the style of the Qur'an and what al-Rāzī has termed *'ādāt al-kitāb al-'azīz* (the [linguistic and stylistic] habits of the noble book); and second, a proper approach to translation itself as detailed above.

Having dealt with the image of the Qur'an in English translations we move now to talk about the effect of English translations on interfaith relations, the subject of Chapter 13.

13

Translations of the Qur'an and Interfaith Relations

Readers of many existing English translations of the Qur'an, who come across such statements as '*O believers, take not Jews and Christians as friends*' (Q. 5:51) and '*Whoso desires another religion than Islam – it will not be accepted of him and in the next world he will be among the losers*' (Q. 3:85),[1] are likely to get the impression that Islam is a rejectionist religion, hostile to other faiths, especially Christianity and Judaism. In this chapter we will consider the effect of English translations of a number of Qur'anic verses that touch on interfaith relations, concentrating in particular on the relations between Muslims, on the one hand, and Jews and Christians, on the other. Before this we will give a general picture of the Qur'anic view of other religions.

The Qur'anic View of Other Religions

The Qur'an affirms to Muhammad the following: '*If your Lord had pleased, He could have made all people into a single community, but they continue to have their differences [...] for He created them to be this way*' (Q. 11:118–19). To those with whom Islam has no common religious ground, Muhammad is asked to declare, '*You have your religion and I have mine*' (Q. 108:3). This is a starting point for the Prophet of Islam to recognise God's plan for the existence of different religions and to know where he and Islam stand in relation to them; however, two particular religious communities have a very special position in the Qur'an: Jews and Christians.

Jews are referred to in the Qur'an as *Banī Isrā'īl* ('Children of Israel') or *Yahūd/ alladhīna hādū*, while Christians are called *al-Naṣārā* (Nazarenes), and they are all collectively referred to as *Ahl al-Kitāb* ('People of the Book'). Calling Jews and Christians by this last name gives them a particular distinction as privileged in having received a divine revelation, whereas the Arabs before the Qur'an had no religious scripture of their own. Their distinction is emphasised in the Qur'an:

Children of Israel, remember how I blessed you and favoured you over other people.

Q. 2:47 and 122

Moses said to his people, 'My people remember God's blessing on you: how He raised prophets among you and appointed kings for you and gave you what He had not given to any other people.'

Q. 5:20

To Moses God spoke directly

Q. 4:164

The Qur'an (Q. 6:83–90) mentions 17 prophets descended from Abraham. God had inspired Abraham to believe in Him alone and '*raised him in rank*' and then granted him children, Isaac and Jacob, each of whom He guided. This is followed by a list of 14 other biblical prophets:

and also some of their forefathers, their offspring and their brothers: We chose them and guided them on a straight path. Such is God's guidance [...] those are the ones to whom We gave the scripture, wisdom and prophethood [...] those were the people God guided. [Prophet] follow the guidance they received.

This guidance was always to believe in the One God. In Q. 10:94 the Prophet is directed: '*If you are in doubt about what We have revealed to you, ask those who have been reading the scripture before you. The Truth has come to you from your Lord.*' Accordingly, the Qur'an addresses Muhammad, saying: '*He has sent the Scripture down to you [Muhammad] with the Truth, confirming what came before it: He sent down the Torah and the Gospel earlier as a guide for people*' (Q. 3:3–4). The Qur'an clearly sets great store on the idea of its confirming (*muṣaddiq*) what came before it, mentioning this term no less than 14 times,[2] two of these showing Jesus confirming the Torah. Thus, there is one consistent message confirmed by all the prophets. In Sura 5 of the Qur'an, one of the last suras to be revealed, God says:

We revealed the Torah with guidance and light, and the prophets, who had submitted to God, judged according to it for the Jews. So did the rabbis and the scholars in accordance with that part of God's Scripture which they were entrusted to preserve and to which they were witnesses. [...] We sent Jesus, son of Mary, in their footsteps, to confirm the Torah that had been sent before him: We gave him the Gospel with guidance, light and confirmation of the Torah. [...] We sent you [Muhammad] the Scripture with the Truth, confirming the Scripture that came before it and protecting it: so judge between them according to what God has sent down.[3]

Q. 5:44, 46 and 48

Far from ignoring or rejecting earlier scriptures, the Qur'an confirms and protects them. The Qur'an never disparages or belittles the earlier scriptures or prophets. At times it criticises the behaviour of some of their followers for not following or upholding them or obeying their messengers. In the Qur'an, God does not say to the Children of Israel, 'Believe in Islam' or 'Believe in the religion of Muhammad,' but '*Believe in the message I have sent down confirming what you already possess. Do not be the first to reject it*' (Q. 2:41).

The Qur'an does of course call on Jews and Christians to accept its teachings, but the Jews and Christians also called on Muslims to become Jews and Christians to find guidance (Q. 2:135–6). Any call to Islam made by the Prophet Muhammad and his followers is governed by the instruction: '*Call people to the way of your Lord with wisdom and good teaching, debate with them in the most courteous way*' (Q. 16:125). At the same time, the Qur'an states: '*Yet most people will not believe, however eagerly you may want them to*' (Q. 12:103).

These verses show that the Qur'an is not a rejectionist text; it acknowledges the religion of the People of the Book and indeed calls on them to judge according to their scriptures, saying:

Those who do not judge according to what God has sent down are rejecting God's teaching.

Q. 5:44

Let the followers of the Gospel judge according to what God has sent down in it. Those who do not judge according to what God has revealed are lawbreakers.

Q. 5:47

Why do they come to you [Muhammad] for judgement when they have the Torah with God's judgement, and even then still turn away? These are not believers.

Q. 5:43

The Qur'an orders Muhammad: '*Say, "People of the Book, you have no true basis [for your religion] unless you uphold the Torah, the Gospel, and that which has been sent down to you from your Lord*"' (Q. 5:68). The Qur'an reports that the Jews and Christians claimed to the Muslims, '*We are the children of God and His beloved ones*' (Q. 5:18); and the Jews claimed that out of all peoples they alone were the friends of God (Q. 62:6). The Qur'an reminds the Muslims that God has not reserved His rewards for one group alone:

It will not be according to your hopes or those of the People of the Book: anyone who does wrong will be requited for it and will find no one to protect or help him against God; anyone, male or female, who does good deeds and is a believer will enter Paradise and will not be wronged by as much as the dip in a date stone.

Q. 4:123–4

Such people specifically claimed that no one would enter Paradise unless they were Jews or Christians (Q. 2:111). The Qur'an does not claim that only the Muslims will enter Paradise. It says:

We have assigned a law and a path to each of you. If God had so willed, He would have made you one community, but He wanted to test you through that which He has given you, so race to do good: you will all return to God and He will make clear to you the matters you differed about.

Q. 5:48

When the Prophet came to Medina, Jews were already living there and he recognised this, seeing them as part of the whole community in Medina within a constitution that gave equal rights and obligations to everyone for the protection of the town.[4] However, with the consolidation of Muslims in Medina and the increase of their power generally, some Jews in Medina resented the newcomers and soon showed hostility towards the Muslims and the Prophet in a number of ways. The Qur'an reports how they tried to turn people away from following Islam, always wishing that they could mislead Muslims (Q. 4:44) and trying to '*turn the believers away from God's path and [...] make it crooked*' (Q. 3:99); mocking Islam, the Islamic call to prayer and the prayer itself (Q. 5:57–8); trying to confuse Muslims and claim to them that certain statements were part of the Qur'an when they were not (Q. 2:79), scheming together to make them turn back:

Some of the People of the Book say [to each other], 'At the beginning of the day, believe in what has been revealed to these believers [the Muslims], then at the end of the day reject it, so that they too may turn back, but do not sincerely believe in anyone unless he follows your own religion'.

Q. 3:72–3

[Prophet] do you not see those people who were given a share of the Scripture before you, how they purchase misguidance and want you [believers], too, to lose the right path?

Q. 4:44

They even mocked God Himself, calling him '*tight-fisted*' (Q. 5:64) and poor when they were rich (Q. 3:181).[5]

The People of the Book demand that you [Prophet] make a book physically come down to them from heaven, but they demanded even more than that of Moses when they said, 'Show us God face to face,' and were struck by the thunderbolt for their presumption.

Q. 4:153

[Prophet], have you considered those [Jews] who claim purity for themselves? No! God purifies whoever He will: no one will be wronged by as much as the husk of a date stone.

Q. 4:49

Worst of all was that some Jews in Medina, when asked by the idolaters of Mecca to pronounce who was better guided, the Muslim believers or themselves, told them they (i.e. the idolaters) were more rightly guided than the believers (Q. 4:51).[6]

As a result of such attitudes, some of the Jewish tribes allied themselves with the Muslims' worst enemies (*al-aḥzāb*) and joined forces to invade Medina and finish off the entire Muslim community, as is recorded in Q. 33:9–26. Most of the criticism of Jews in the Qur'an, apart from the historical references to the Jews at the times of Moses and Jesus, is directed towards these Jews in Medina, not because they were Jews, but for allying themselves with the enemies of the Muslim community.

The collusion against the Muslims between the idolaters and a group of the People of the Book, Jews, was clearly continuous. The Muslims are told:

You are sure to be tested through your possessions and persons; you are sure to hear much that is hurtful from those who were given the Scripture before you and those who associate others with God. If you are steadfast and mindful of God, that is the best course.

Q. 3:186

Qur'anic Criticism of Jews

The Qur'an does not criticise Judaism, but only some Jews, and this is particularly true of Sura 2 and the following four suras. In Q. 2:51–74, the Qur'an speaks of the hard time they gave Moses, but it also criticises all other people who gave their prophets hard times, starting with those to whom Noah, Abraham, Lot, Hūd and Sāliḥ were sent,[7] and ending with the people of Mecca and Medina. The Qur'an uses such material to teach the believers a lesson and, at the same time, encourage them in their times of difficulty by showing that prophets and believers in earlier religions also suffered, but finally triumphed.

The Qur'an criticises a long list of examples of bad behaviour by the Jews (Q. 4:155–61), acts which are forbidden in Judaism and Christianity, too. What the Qur'an blames these Jews for, it also blames the Muslims for, saying, for example, that God will wage war against them if they do not stop taking *ribā* (usury) (Q. 2:275–9). It castigates some Jews for consuming other people's wealth wrongly (Q. 4:162) and also those Muslims who do the same (Q. 4:29–30).

The Qur'an is very careful not to tar everyone with the same brush. It isolates those who do wrong actions, using words like *minhum* ('some of them') and *inna minhum la-farīqan* ('there is a group of them'), *wadda kathirun minhum* ('many of them wish'), *illā qalīlan minhum* ('except for a few of them'), *mina'lladhīna hādū* ('some of the Jews'), *minhum ummatun* ('a group of them'), *min qawmi Mūsā ummatun* ('a group of the people of Moses'). Accordingly the Qur'an emphasises that:

> *they are not all alike. There are some among the People of the Book who are upright, who recite God's revelation during the night, who bow down in worship, who believe in God and the Last Day, who order what is right and forbid what is wrong, who are quick to do good deeds. These people are among the righteous and they will not be denied [the reward] of whatever good deeds they do: God knows exactly who is conscious of Him.*
>
> Q. 3:113–5

The Qur'an mentions praise of the followers of Moses:

> *There is a group among the people of Moses who guide with truth and act justly according to it.*
>
> Q. 7:159

> *We dispersed them over the earth in separate communities – some are righteous and some are less so.*
>
> Q. 7:168

Referring to the Jews in Medina at the time of Muhammad, the Qur'an says:

> *There are People of the Book who, if you [Prophet] entrust them with a heap of gold, will return it to you intact, but there are others of them who, if you entrust them with a single*

dinar, will not return it to you unless you keep standing over them, because they say, 'We are under no obligation towards the gentiles' – they tell a lie against God and they know it. No indeed! God loves those who keep their pledges and are mindful of Him.

Q. 3:75–6

In Q. 62:5, it does not say, 'The Jews are like asses', only those who do not act according to the great privilege of the Torah that they have been given, but carry this precious load and do not benefit from it. In the same way the Qur'an talks about the Arabs who turn away from listening to the Qur'an as being '*like frightened asses fleeing from a lion*' (Q. 74:49–51). So Jews are not criticised for being Jews, and they are not all blamed, only those who misbehaved. In the Qur'an this kind of misbehaviour, whether by Jews, Arabs or anyone else is criticised.

Christians in the Qur'an

The Qur'an talks more about Jews and Moses than about Christians and Jesus. Moses is mentioned 136 times, while Jesus is mentioned by name only 25 times and referred to as Christ (*al-masīḥ*) 11 times. Mary is mentioned 34 times.[8] Part of the explanation for the space it allocates to Moses and the Jews is the role of Pharaoh and his oppression of the Jews, cited as an example of how oppressors meet their end, to warn the oppressors of Mecca and comfort the oppressed Muslims. Another reason is that Judaism, unlike Christianity, has laws which the Qur'an refers to.[9] Furthermore, Jewish clans lived in Medina and had relations with the Muslims during the last ten years of the revelation of the Qur'an, whereas there were not many Christians resident there.

Mary is always honoured in the Qur'an, which emphasises her purity (Q. 3:42–3), innocence and concern when the angel tells her she is to have a child (Q. 3:45 and 47); and her isolation in childbirth and having to face her people and their suspicions afterwards, when she brings the child home (Q. 19:16–29). Jesus himself is well spoken about, even before his birth, as '*highly honoured in this world and the next and one of those brought near [to God]*' (Q. 3:45).

From the beginning, while still an infant, Jesus is described as saying:

'I am a servant of God. He has granted me the Scripture; made me a prophet; made me blessed wherever I may be – He commanded me to pray, to give alms as long as I live, to cherish my mother – He did not make me domineering or graceless. Peace was on me the day I was born, and will be on me the day I die and the day I am raised to life again.'

Q. 19:30–3

From the treatment of the subject it is clear that the Qur'an appeared at a time and place when some Arab Christians at least believed in a doctrine of three gods and that Jesus was literally the son of God.[10] Similarly, when arguing with polytheist Arabs who claimed that God had offspring, the Qur'an asks, '*The Creator of the heavens and earth! How could He have children when He has no spouse?*' (Q. 6:101). When the angel came to Mary to announce the coming of her child, she said to him, '*How can I have a child when no man has touched me? I have not been unchaste.*' (Q. 19:20), so it is clear that everybody understood that a physical relationship was essential to produce offspring. Such a physical relationship between God and a human being was naturally contrary to the Islamic central belief in the One God (in this respect it was not different from the Jewish belief). Jesus himself is represented in the Qur'an as declaring to his people: '*God is my Lord and your Lord, so serve Him: that is a straight path*' (Q. 19:36–7). Similarly, on the Day of Judgement,

> *When God says, 'Jesus, son of Mary, did you say to people, "Take me and my mother as two gods alongside God"?' he will say, 'May You be exalted! I would never say what I had no right to say – if I had said such a thing You would have known it: You know all that is within me, though I do not know what is within You, You alone have full knowledge of things unseen – I told them only what You commanded me to: "Worship God, my Lord and your Lord." I was a witness over them during my time among them. Ever since You took my soul, You alone have been the watcher over them: You are witness to all things and if You punish them, they are Your servants; if You forgive them, You have the power to decide.'*
>
> Q. 5:116–18

The Qur'an is consistent in stressing the belief in one God: '*Say, "He is God the One, God the eternal. He fathered no one nor was He fathered. No one is comparable to Him"*' (Q. 112). Likewise, the Qur'an rejects the belief of some Arabs that the angels were daughters of God and indeed rejects any *shirk* or partnership in divinity with God (so, for example, in Q. 16:57, Q. 18:4–5 and Q. 25:2).[11]

The Qur'an criticises Christians who 'exaggerate in their religion' in raising Jesus above his status as messenger of God, God's word and a spirit from Him:

> *People of the Book, do not go to excess in your religion and do not say anything about God except the truth: the Messiah, Jesus son of Mary was nothing more than a messenger of God, His word directed to Mary, and a spirit from Him.*
>
> Q. 4:171–3

Nonetheless, the Qur'an still considers even these Christians as being People of the Book and gives them, together with the Jews, a special status as believers in God, and Muslims share with them the basic beliefs of religion. They are not called *mushrikūn* like the Arab polytheists. For example, whereas the Qur'an in Q. 2:221 tells Arab Muslim men, '*Do not marry mushrikāt [polytheist women who associate others with God] until they believe*', it says to them in Q. 5:5, '*Chaste women of the People of the Book are lawful to you [in marriage]*'. Such women, who marry Muslim men, are allowed to keep and practice their religion.[12]

Having given this picture of the People of the Book in the Qur'an we now move to see how flawed interpretation and the resulting translation can change the picture and affect interfaith relationships.

Examples of Misleading Interpretations and Translations

I shall select five examples of misinterpretation and explain what gives rise to them:

1. *'Friends'* (awliyā')?

O true believers, take not the Jews or Christians for your friends.

Q. 5:51 (Sale 1734)

'Friends' here stands for *awliyā'* in Arabic. Translators, Muslims and non-Muslims alike, have copied this translation from one generation to the next. *Awliyā'* occurs in the Qur'an 42 times,[13] so it is a major term. *Awliyā'* is the plural of *walī*, which is one of those terms that occur in a variety of meanings, an example of the feature of *wujūh al-qur'ān* as mentioned in Chapter 12. One early Arabic dictionary of *wujūh*[14] gives various meanings for *awliyā'*, including 'friends', but also 'allies', 'supporters' and so on. As in the case of all words associated with *wujūh*, it is the context that determines which of the various meanings should be adopted. This feature appears not to be regarded or appreciated by many translators of the Qur'an.

There are two errors in such translations of Q. 5:51 as the above one: first, a misunderstanding of the meaning of the definite article '*al-*' ('the') in 'the Jews and the Christians'; and second, cutting a short statement off from the entire context before and after.

As for the first point, the definite article '*al-*' is another example of *wujūh*, as mentioned in previous chapters, because it not only has a generic meaning (*jinsiyya*), denoting '*all* Jews and Christians', but can also refer back to specific people already mentioned, as it is the case in Q. 5.49–50, rendering it '*these* Jews and Christians'. This type of '*al-*' is recognised in Arabic grammar and called *'ahdiyya* in contrast to *jinsiyya.* The wider previous context of this passage refers to certain individuals of the People of the Book who came to the Prophet asking him to give judgement.[15] In Q. 5:49–50, he is told to:

judge between them according to what God has sent down. Do not follow their whims and take good care that they do not tempt you away from any of what God has sent down to you. If they turn away, remember that God intends to punish them for some of the sins they have committed: many of them are lawbreakers. Do they want judgement according to the time of pagan ignorance?

These are the specific individuals to whom the reference in the subsequent verse (Q. 5:51) is made.

Reading through the wider passage (Q. 5:49–58) shows that what is involved would not be friendship on the part of Muslims, but desertion from the side of the Muslims and alliance with their enemies, going back on their faith:

Yet you [Prophet] will see the perverse at heart rushing in to them [the aforementioned People of the Book] for protection saying, 'We are afraid fortune may turn against us', but God may well bring about a triumph [...] Then they will rue the secrets they harboured in their hearts and the believers will say, 'Are these the men who swore by God, using their strongest oaths that they were with you?' All they did was in vain. They have lost everything. You who believe, if any of you go back on your faith, God will soon replace you with people He loves and who love Him, people who are humble towards the believers, hard on the disbelievers and who strive in God's way without fearing anyone's reproach. Such is God's favour. [...] Your true allies are God, His Messenger and the believers. [...] Those who turn for protection to God's Messenger and the believers are God's party: God's party is sure to triumph. You who believe, do not take as allies those who ridicule your religion and make fun of it. [...] When you make the call to prayer, they ridicule it and make fun of it.

Q. 5:52–8

'Rushing in', mentioned at the beginning, recalls Q. 5:41:

[Prophet] do not be grieved by those who rush into disbelief – those who say with their mouths, 'We believe,' but have no faith in their hearts, and those Jews who listen eagerly to lies.

Here we have the same groups of people, those apparent Muslims who have sickness in their hearts (the hypocrites) and those Jews who ridiculed the Muslims and gave judgement in favour of the pagans (see 4:47–51). The fact that the Prophet is told not to be grieved by them suggests that collusion between these two groups was ongoing and grieved him. In Q. 5:57, the believers are warned not to be allies to those who mock their religion and their call to prayer, again referring to a group of Jews and disbelievers. In Q. 5:62–3, the same group of Jews is mentioned, who colluded with the disbelievers:

You [Prophet] see many of them rushing into sin and hostility and consuming what is unlawful. How evil their practices are! Why do their rabbis and scholars not forbid them to speak sinfully and consume what is unlawful?

In verse 64 it continues:

The Jews have said, 'God is tight-fisted,' [...] Whenever they kindle the fire of war, God will put it out. They try to spread corruption in the land.

The criticism of this particular group of Jews resumes in verses 81–2:

You [Prophet] see many of them allying themselves with the disbelievers. How terrible is what their souls have stored up for them! [...] If they had believed in God, in the Prophet, and in what was sent down to him, they would never have allied themselves with the disbelievers [...] You [Prophet] are sure to find that the most hostile to believers are the Jews and those who associate other deities with God.

Verse 82 is crucial in our discussion. It can be clearly misunderstood by Muslims and non-Muslims: it declares in an emphatic manner, '*you [Prophet] are sure to find that the most hostile to the believers are the Jews (al-yahūd) and those who associate other deities with God*'. Again, the definite article in *al-yahūd* here is certainly '*ahdiyya* (specific), referring to the same group of people being described at least from verse 41 onwards. It means 'this aforementioned group of Jews who collude with the disbelievers'. The definite article cannot be generic, referring to all Jews since the verse is addressed to Muhammad ('*You are sure to find ...*') in the circumstances described.

Two groups, then, colluded in sharp hostility towards the Muslim believers: one of Jews and one of pagan Arabs. In contrast to these two, vv. 82–3 continue:

you are sure to find that the closest in affection to the believers are those who say, 'We are Christians,' for among them are men devoted to learning and ascetics. These people are not given to arrogance and when they listen to what has been sent down to the Messenger, you will see their eyes overflowing with tears because they recognise the truth in it. They say, 'Our Lord, we believe, so count us among the witnesses.'

Although Christians who held beliefs the Qur'an considers polytheistic are criticised in other parts of Sura 5, vv. 82–3 clearly refer to other Christians who heard the Qur'an and were deeply moved by what they recognised as the truth.

In short, two serious flaws can arise in translations of the verses discussed above: first, misunderstanding of the specific meaning of the definite article '*al-*'; and second, lifting and isolating a word or statement from the context which runs through several verses. These two flaws affect most of the translations of the Qur'an in English.

2. *Apes, Pigs and Donkeys*

Another mistake is the result of the failure to distinguish between figurative and literal expressions,[16] as in Q. 7:163–6 referring to a group of Jews in a village by the sea who broke the Sabbath by fishing.

When they ignored [the warning] they were given, We saved those who forbade evil, and punished the wrongdoers severely because of their disobedience. When, in their arrogance, they persisted in doing what they had been forbidden to do, We said to them, 'Be apes! Be outcasts!'

These people are also mentioned in Q. 2:65 and presumably, although not by name, in Q. 5:60. 'Be apes' is a figure of speech for 'be like apes', a metaphor in place of a simile. Exactly the same formula is used referring to the Arabs in Mecca who denied the Resurrection (Q. 17:50–1): '*Say, "Be stone or iron or something you think is harder"*'. Clearly, this is not literal. Moreover, turning people into apes or any other animal is not known in the Qur'an to be part of the punishment God inflicts on anyone. In Q. 29:40, after mentioning a number of prophets and the punishments brought on their opponents, God says: '*We punished each one of them for their sins. Some We struck with a violent storm; some were overcome by a sudden blast; some We made the earth swallow; and some We drowned.*' These are the types of punishment the Qur'an lists and it is therefore inconceivable that God would turn a group of people into apes because they deployed their fishing nets on Friday to be collected on Sunday after the Sabbath, so that they were not seen to break the Sabbath. Such a crafty strategy could not bring about so incredible a punishment. Yet, people, including many Muslim exegetes in the past, saw this as an actual transformation.[17] What it really means is, 'Carry on behaving like apes [and pigs] if you want to'. It applies only to the group of people referred to.

Another example to be mentioned here is: '*The likeness of those who have been loaded with the Torah, then they have not carried it, is as the likeness of an ass carrying books*' (Arberry's translation of Q. 62:5). It should be noted that the verse does not say, 'the Jews are like asses', but refers to a group of Jews in Medina at the time of the Prophet who behaved in a way contrary to the teachings of the Torah (Q. 5:44). The Qur'an here maintains the divine status of the Torah, making its ruling the ruling of God and condemns only those who do not live by it. Likewise, Arabs who turn away from the Qur'an are likened to asses running away from a lion (Q. 74:49–51).[18]

Errors of interpretation here arise from *ta'mīm al-khāṣṣ*, generalising what applies only to a specific individual or group.

3. Jizya

As explained in Chapter 3, the much-misinterpreted[19] *jizya* (Q. 9:29) was actually a tax collected from non-Muslim members of the Muslim state in correlation with the *zakāh* collected from Muslims. Only when non-Muslims refused to pay were the Muslims given permission to enforce payment by fighting, just as the Caliph Abū Bakr later enforced payment of *zakāh* on Muslim defaulters (see Chapter 3).

4. *Islam*

True religion with God is Islam.

Q. 3:19 (Arberry)

Whoso desires another religion than Islam, it will not be accepted of him. In the next world he shall be among the losers.

Q. 3:85 (Arberry)

Most Muslims and non-Muslims take this to refer to Islam, the religion preached by the Prophet Muhammad. It is of course understandable for a Muslim to believe that Islam is the true religion of God and that if they were to seek any other religion it would not be accepted from them. But it is clear from the context that these two statements refer in fact to *islām* in the older generic sense of total devotion to the One God and not joining anyone or anything with Him. In this sense, all the prophets before and including Muhammad, speak of themselves and are referred to in the Qur'an as Muslims. The root verb *aslama* means to make one's religion free (*salīm*) from any trace of polytheism. The great medieval commentator al-Rāzī cites Ibn al-Anbārī as saying, '"Muslim" means someone who makes his worship totally to God.'[20] In Q. 2:131 Abraham's Lord says to him, '*aslim*' ('*Devote yourself!*') and Abraham says, '*aslamtu li'l-rabbi'l-'ālamīn*' ('*I devote myself to the Lord of all the worlds*'). Al-Aṣamm explains that *aslim* means 'Make your worship pure, free from any trace of polytheism'.[21] This is confirmed in a number of verses in the Qur'an itself:

Abraham entrusted his sons, and so did Jacob, saying, 'My sons, God has chosen your religion for you, so make sure you devote yourselves to Him (muslimūn) to your dying moment.'

Q. 2:132

They say [to Muhammad and his followers], 'Become Jews or Christians and you will be rightly guided.' Say [Muhammad], 'No. Ours is the religion of Abraham, the upright, who did not worship any god beside God. We believe in God and in what was sent down to us and what was sent down to Abraham, Ishmael, Isaac, Jacob and the tribes and what was given to Moses, Jesus and all the prophets by their Lord. We make no distinction between any of them and we are devoted to Him (muslimūn).'

Q. 2:135–6

Say [Muhammad], 'My Lord has guided me to a straight path, an upright religion, the faith of Abraham, a man of pure faith. He was not an idolater.' Say, 'My prayers and devotions, my living and my dying, are all for God, Lord of the Worlds; He has no partner. This is what I was commanded and I am the first[22] *to devote myself to Him (awwal al-muslimīn).'*

Q. 6:161–3

Abraham prayed to God, while building the first house of worship to the One God with his son Ishmael: '*Lord, make us both devoted to You (muslimayni laka). Make our descendants into a community devoted to You (muslimatan laka)*' (Q. 2:128). It is clear from the contexts of the verses cited above that the senses of *aslama* and *muslimūn*, as of *islām*, relate to unadulterated devotion to the One God. However, like many other terms in the Qur'an, *aslama* has different *wujūh*, one of which is also 'to submit'. This is clear in Sura 49, verse 14: '*The desert Arabs say, "We have faith." [Prophet] say to them, "You do not have faith. What you should say instead is 'We have submitted (aslamnā),' for faith has not yet entered your hearts."*'

So the two categorical statements in Q. 3:19 ('*True religion with God is Islam*') and Q. 3:85 ('*Whoso desires another religion than Islam, it will not be accepted of him*'), which are normally understood as restricting true religion to the followers of Muhammad, while any others will not be accepted, do not really lead to the conclusion they are assumed to lead to. A flawed reading of them also entails a flawed interfaith understanding. On the contrary, they show the unity of all prophets in following *islām* in the generic sense. One way of making this clear could be to spell this word with a lower case 'i' as *islām*.

5. Kufr

Kufr, a noun derived from the verb *kafara*, 'to cover, hide', is another major term in the Qur'an that has *wujūh*. In one sense it means 'to be ungrateful'.[23] Other meanings include 'to disbelieve', 'to deny God's existence', 'to deny God', 'to blaspheme' as well as 'to be an infidel'.[24] Accordingly, care should be taken by translators to select the appropriate meaning. When the Qur'an says that Christians or Jews *kafarū*, it can mean they 'denied' the message of Muhammad, as in Q. 98:1. But it is unlikely to think that the Qur'an would say that the Jews or Christians *kafarū* in the sense of denying God or disbelieving in Him as atheists and pagans do. When the Qur'an states, '*Those who say God is the Messiah, son of Mary kafarū*' (Q. 5:72) or '*Those who say God is one of three kafarū*' (Q. 5:73), *kafarū* means 'defy the truth about God', that is, His absolute unity as held by Islam and Judaism, rather than meaning 'deny God'. The Qur'an always considers Christians as People of the Book in spite of these doctrines and gives them a special status as has been pointed out earlier, so the word *kafarū* cannot mean 'disbelieve in God'. Yet, some translators use misleading phrases like 'have disbelieved' (Sahih International)[25] or 'are unbelievers' (Arberry and Fakhry[26]). Asad[27] uses 'deny the truth'.

Conclusion

The fact is that in the last suras to be revealed, in spite of all the tensions between the Muslims in Medina and the Jewish and Christian communities, and in spite of all the criticisms levelled at some Jews and Christians, the Qur'an still affirms, when addressing the Children of Israel, '*God has favoured you above others*' (Q. 2:122) and '*We have sent down the Torah with light and guidance*' (Q. 5:44), and to both the Jews and Christians, '*People of the Book, you have no true basis [for your religion] unless you uphold the Torah, the Gospel, and what has been revealed to you from your Lord*' (Q. 5:68).

We have seen how translators can misinterpret and therefore mistranslate crucial terms that lead to misunderstandings between Muslims and believers in other faiths, but we should reiterate that the Qur'an honours Moses and the Torah as well as Jesus and the Gospel, and calls on Jews and Christians to judge according to their own scriptures. From Sura 2 onwards it lists the great favours shown to the Children of Israel by God. The Qur'an is very careful in making its statements about Jews and Christians, not tarring them all with the same brush, but identifying those who showed hostility to Islam and its Prophet, clearly for political reasons, some of whom allied themselves with the polytheists and hypocrites, the two main opponent groups of Islam and the Prophet. The Qur'an respects those whom God has favoured with a share of the Scripture, that is, the People of the Book. Translations should reflect this.

In this chapter we have dealt with misunderstandings of the Qur'anic attitude towards other religions that arise out of misinterpreting and mistranslating the Qur'an into English. In the previous chapters of this book it has been seen that misinterpreting and mistranslating the Qur'an give inaccurate pictures of the Qur'an and Islam, which also adversely affect the relationship between Islam and other faiths. This is the challenge facing those equipped with understanding of the language and style of the Qur'an and with the necessary objectivity of true scholarship.

God took a pledge from those who were given the scripture, 'Make it known to people; do not conceal it'

Q. 3:187

Conclusion

The general theme of this book is 'Exploring the Qur'an: Images and Reality'. Its chapters explore only a few examples of the ways the Qur'an is misread, but the subject is really much wider than this. If one surveys the books and articles in English on the Qur'an, even over the last ten years for instance, it becomes clear that, apart from a few honourable exceptions, the majority do not actually explore the real text of the Arabic Qur'an. Instead they concentrate on what some exegetes, past and present, or others have said on one issue or another or talk about subjects such as the sources of the Qur'an, faults in the Qur'an and so on. As long as this practice continues, the Qur'an itself will be neglected in such works and the traditional distorted images of it will continue.

A movement away from this towards the Qur'an itself is needed. In addition to this, a proper treatment of the text would require abandoning literalism, atomism and disregard for the context and of what the Qur'an says to explain itself. The whole text in its entirety should be taken as a guide. Study of the *balāgha* (rhetoric) and especially *'ilm al-ma'ānī* (study of meanings), as well as what al-Rāzī termed *'ādāt al-kitāb al-'azīz* (the linguistic and stylistic habits of the noble Qur'an) have all been sorely neglected, even by some eminent scholars. Indeed, we need to add to and expand these sciences in the light of advanced knowledge of modern linguistics.

In the area of translation, regard needs to be paid to the Qur'anic criteria of prophets being sent to teach in the languages of their own people to make things clear to them, so the translations should also be in the language of the target cultures, with all their norms and cultural associations. Literalism, in its various forms, has been shown, in Chapters 12 and 13, to be the main source of inadequacy in English translations, with a negative effect on all the criteria of naturalness, accuracy, clarity and effect.

Objectivity is essential in studying and translating the Qur'an. The Qur'an demands adherence to truth, the whole truth and justice, particularly on the part of people who teach scripture and study it (Q. 3:79) and those who have been entrusted with the Book of God and are witnesses to it (Q. 5:44).

Translators and scholars should guard against automatically following 'what our forefathers did' but should deal closely with the Arabic text of the Qur'an: '*Will they not ponder on the Qur'an?*' (Q. 47:24).

Notes

Chapter 1 The 'Sword Verse' Myth

1 Michael Cook, *The Koran: A Very Short Introduction* (Oxford; New York, 2000), p. 34. It will be clear from the discussion in this chapter that he is relying on *tafsīr* rather than the text. See also Chapter 3 where Ella Landau-Tasseron is identified as doing the same thing.
2 Ibid., p. 33.
3 Pope Benedict's lecture at Regensburg on 12 September 2006 entitled *Faith, Reason and the University: Memories and Reflections*, p. 2. Available at http://w2.vatican.va/content/benedict-xvi/en/speeches/2006/september/documents/hf_ben-xvi_spe_20060912_university-regensburg.html (accessed 5 April 2016).
4 Muhammad Ibn Isḥāq, *The Life of Muhammad*, trans. A. Guillaume (Oxford, 1955), p. 504.
5 Ibid., p. 310. The Prophet is reported to have said: 'If the Quraysh were to offer me any plan that preserved family ties, I would readily concede it to them.'
6 Ibn Isḥāq, *The Life of Muhammad.* p. 494; Ibn Hishām, *Sīra Nabawiyya*, p. 543. In addition to the original treaty, further treaties were made (no dates given), including, in particular, that no one should be barred from getting to the Ka'ba and that no one should be terrorised during the Sacred Months.
7 Ibid., p. 548.
8 Fakhruddin Al-Rāzī, *al-Tafsīr al-kabīr* (Beirut, n.d.), Vol. 15, pp. 217–18; Abū Ḥayyān, Gharnati, *al-Baḥr al-muḥīṭ* (Beirut, 1983), Vol. 5, pp. 7–8. There was a precedent for this, three years earlier, before Hudaybiyya (6 AH). Thus, in Q. 48:12, we find, 'You thought that the Messenger and the believers would never return to their families and this thought warmed your hearts. Your thoughts are evil for you are corrupt people.'

9 According to the Qur'an, the Ka'ba was built by Abraham and Ishmael to be the centre of *tawḥīd*, worship of the One God. Abraham was instructed by God, '*Do not assign partners to Me. Purify My house for those who circle around it, those who stand to pray and those who bow and prostrate themselves*' (Q. 22:26). Q. 9:28 states: '*Believers, those who ascribe partners to God are truly unclean: do not let them come near the Sacred Mosque after this year.*'

10 The Hadith is from al-Bukhārī, *Ṣaḥiḥ*, Ḥajj, 67.

11 This teaching appears throughout the Qur'an.

12 Q. 9:4 and 11.

13 Al-Rāzī, *al-Tafsīr al-kabīr*, Vol. 2, p. 218; Abū Ḥayyān, *al-Baḥr al-muḥīṭ*, Vol. 5, p. 9.

14 Ibid., Vol. 15, p. 225.

15 Muhammad A. Ṣāliḥ, *Tafsīr al-nuṣūṣ fī'l-fiqh al-islāmī*, Al-Maktab al-Islamī (Beirut, 1993), p. 239; Tammām Hassān, *al-Bayān fī rawā'i' al-qur'ān* (*'Ālam al-kutub*, Cairo, 1993), Vol. 1, p. 181.

16 Al-Rāzī, *al-Tafsīr al-kabīr*, Vol. 5, pp. 107–8. See also the commentary of Aḥmad ibn 'Abdullāh ibn Ḥumayd on *Sharḥ al-Maḥallī 'alā'l-waraqāt*, section on *amr*. Available at: www.dr-mahmoud.com. Others have argued that permissibility should be deduced from the context.

17 This is agreed by all jurists. See Muhammad Adib Ṣāliḥ, *Tafsīr al-nuṣūṣ fī'l-fiqh al-islāmī*, Vol. 2, p. 237.

18 Al-Rāzī's work: *al-Tafsīr al-kabīr*. Part 15, p. 225.

19 Sayyid Quṭb, *Fī ẓilāl al-qur'ān Dar al-shuyukh* (Cairo, 1985), Vol. 3, p. 1601.

20 See Muhammad A. S. Abdel Haleem, *The Quran: A New Translation* (Oxford, 2010), footnote to Q. 2:191.

21 Al-Rāzī (*al-Tafsīr al-kabīr*, Vol. 15, p. 225) reports that Farrā' interprets this to mean, 'they should be prevented from reaching the Sacred House.' Al-Qurṭubī (*Jāmi' li-aḥkām al-Qur'ān* (Beirut, 2000), Vol. 8, p. 47) takes it to mean, 'stop them entering your land and coming to you unless you permit them to do so and they come with the safety-permit you grant them.'

22 See Elsaid Badawi and Muhammad Haleem, *An Arabic–English Dictionary of Qur'anic Usage* (Leiden, 2007), p. 100, meaning VII, as in Q. 4:136.

23 *Illā* is used in this context five times in the Qur'an: Q. 3:98, Q. 4:146, Q. 5:34, Q. 24:5 and Q. 25:70. Q. 5:34, for instance, stipulates the penalty for highway robbery, then says, '*unless they repent before you overpower them*'.

24 Al-Rāzī, *al-Tafsīr al-kabīr*, Vol. 11, pp. 3–5.

25 This clearly refers to a later treaty than the one at Hudaybiyya.

26 See Abdel Haleem, *The Quran*, Introduction, p. xxiii. This is one of very few areas where the Qur'an goes into specific details and exceptions. Others areas include rights, such as those of inheritance, and prohibitions, such

as the details of who one cannot marry, and in whose company a woman does not have to cover herself completely.

27 This is similar to Q. 8:61–2 where Muslims were instructed to accept an offer of peace, even if the disbelievers happened to renege later.

28 After sexual intercourse or menstruation.

29 Because 'tourism' and trade around the mosque might cease.

30 That is, inside or outside the Sanctuary. See Muhammad A. S. Abdel Haleem, *The Quran*, p. 21.

31 Abraham was instructed by God to purify the House (Q. 22:26).

32 Quoted by al-Rāzī, *al-Tafsīr al-kabīr*, Vol. 7 (Beirut, n.d.), pp. 14–15. Any edition contains this information in the discussion of Q. 2:256.

33 Ibid., p. 14.

34 Ismail Ibn Kathīr, *Tafsīr al-qur'ān al-'aẓīm* (Beirut, 1992), Vol. 1, p. 333.

35 Here the author seriously distorts the intent of the verse. 'Them' in 'fight them' actually refers to those who fight Muslims (Q. 2:190). 'The religion is God's' means that people are free to worship God without being persecuted for it.

36 Pope Benedict at the University of Regensburg on 12 September 2006. Available at http://w2.vatican.va/content/benedict-xvi/en/speeches/2006/september/documents/hf_ben-xvi_spe_20060912_university-regensburg.html (accessed 5 April 2016).

37 Mūsā Shāhīn Lāshīn, *Al-la'ālī' al-ḥisān fī 'ulūm al-qur'ān* (Cairo, 1982), pp. 196–8.

38 David S. Powers, 'The Exegetical Genre: *nāsikh al-Qur'ān wa-mansūkhuhu*', in A. Rippin (ed.), *Approaches to the History of Interpretation of the Quran* (Oxford, 1988), p. 122.

39 Lāshīn, *Al-la'ālī' al-ḥisān*, pp. 210–13.

40 Powers, 'The Exegetical Genre', p. 123.

41 See Hibat Allāh Ibn Salāma, *Al-nāsikh wa'l-mansūkh* (Beirut, 1986), p. 9.

42 Ibid., p. 98.

43 Ibid., pp. 94–5.

44 Ibid., p. 99.

45 This verse is part of a long section in Sura 2 addressed to the Children of Israel, including nearly 80 verses, starting with verse 40.

46 Ibn Salāma, *Al-nāsikh*, pp. 32–3.

47 Ibid., p. 152.

48 Ibid., p. 191.

49 Ibid., p. 111.

50 Other verses he sees as 'abrogated' by the 'Sword Verse' include: '*Let not what they say sadden you, [Prophet] We know what they conceal and what they reveal*' (Q. 36:76); '*God will gather us together, and to Him we shall all return*'

(Q. 42:15; ibid., p. 155); and '*Be steadfast, like those messengers of firm resolve*' (Q. 46:35; ibid., p. 164).

51 Ibid., p. 209.

52 Tape 1: Rules of Jihad, Transcript p. 445, 21:32 by the prosecution in the case against Sheikh Faisal; Tape 6: The Declaration of War, Transcript p. 1909 [not found online April 2016].

53 Interestingly, Jesus, in Matthew 10:34, does use it: 'Do not suppose that I have come to bring peace to the earth, but a sword.'

Chapter 2 Qur'anic *Jizya*: Tax Defaulters

1 Caliph Abū Bakr, on his decision to fight Arab Muslim tribes who refused to pay *zakāh* after the death of the Prophet (Ṣāliḥ bin 'Abd al-'Azīz Āl al-Shaykh (ed.), *al-Kutub al-sitta* (Riyadh, 1999), p. 606).

2 Arthur J. Arberry, *The Koran Interpreted* (Oxford, 1964), p. 183. I must point out that Arberry's is one of the best translations of the Qur'an into the English language.

3 Their criticism relies, as we shall see, upon the meaning as understood in some classical sources and as sometimes applied in history.

4 Michael Cook, *The Koran: A Very Short Introduction* (Oxford; New York, 2000), p. 33.

5 Ibid.

6 Michael Cook found it opaque (ibid., p. 34).

7 See Abū Abdullah al-Qurṭubī, *al-Jāmi' li-aḥkām al-Qur'ān* (Beirut, 2000), Vol. 4, p. 70; Sayyid Quṭb, *Fī ẓilāl al-Qur'ān* (Cairo, 1985), p. 1,632.

8 Al-Rāzī, *al-Tafsīr al-kabīr* (Beirut, n.d.), part 16, p. 29.

9 Abū Ḥayyān records the view from al-Kirmānī that the People of the Book describe God in a way that does not befit Him, and another view from al-Zajjāj that they assign a child to Him, that they have changed their scriptures, have made unlawful what God made lawful and made lawful what He made unlawful. A third view, from Ibn 'Aṭiyya, was that they had abandoned the Islamic *sharī'a*, which they should have accepted (Abū Ḥayyān, *al-Baḥr al-muḥīṭ* (Beirut, 1993), Vol. 5, p. 30).

10 Ezzedine Ibrahim and Denys Johnson-Davies (trans.), *Al-Nawawī's Forty Hadith* (Damascus, 1977), p. 61.

11 Some say this refers to the Prophet Muhammad, others say it refers to God's messenger whom they claim to follow, meaning that they disagree in belief and practice with their own religion (Nāṣir al-Dīn al-Bayḍāwī, *Tafsīr* (Beirut, 1988), Vol. 1, p. 401; see also al-Rāzī, *al-Tafsīr al-kabīr*, part 16, p. 29).

12 Abū Ḥayyān, *al-Baḥr al-muḥīṭ*, Vol. 5, p. 30.

13 Al-Qurṭubī, *al-Jāmiʿ li-aḥkām al-Qur'ān* (Beirut, 1999), Vol. 4, p. 72.
14 Abū Ḥayyān, *al-Baḥr al-muḥīṭ*, Vol. 5, p. 30.
15 Al-Bayḍāwī, *Tafsīr*, Vol. 1, p. 401.
16 For example, King Solomon wrote, 'It is better that you should not vow than that you should vow and not pay' (Ecclesiastes 5:5).
17 Nessim J. Dawood, *The Koran, Translated with Notes* (London, 1990), p. 136.
18 Alan Jones, *The Qur'ān Translated into English* (Exeter, 2007).
19 Majduddīn Al-Fayrūzabādī, *al-Qamūs al-muḥīṭ*, reprint (Beirut, 1952), Vol. 4, p. 227.
20 *Al-Muʿjam al-wasīṭ* (Cairo, 1972); al-Rāzī, *al-Tafsīr al-kabīr*, Vol. 8, p. 29.
21 Indeed, in support of this, Muḥammad ibn al-Ṭayyib al-Bāqillānī (d. 403/1013) in his *Tamhīd* (Beirut, 1987) has a section on the *iʿjāz al-Qur'ān*, and in it he introduces a hypothetical question which an opponent might ask concerning whether one can be certain if the Prophet challenged the Arabs to produce a work like the Qur'an. His response to this question is this: '*yuʿlam dhālika iḍtirāran min dīnihi wa-qawlihi*', namely 'it is known necessarily by virtue of his conduct and statements'. So a translation which states 'they do not conduct themselves appropriately' fits the context linguistically and relatively.
22 See Paul L. Heck, 'Poll tax', in J. D. McAuliffe (ed.), *Encyclopaedia of the Qur'ān* (Leiden, 2004).
23 Muḥammad ʿImāra, *al-Islām wa'l-ʿaqalliyyāt* (Cairo, 2003), p. 15.
24 Ibid.
25 Ibid.
26 ʿAbd al-Karīm Zaydān, *Aḥkām al-dhimmiyyīn wa'l-musta'manīn fī dār al-Islām* (Beirut, 1976), p. 155, quoting *al-Kharāj* by Abū Yūsuf and *Tārīkh al-Balādhurī*, pp. 283–4.
27 Abū Ḥayyān, *al-Baḥr al-muḥīṭ*, Vol. 5, p. 31; al-Bayḍāwī (*Tafsīr*, Vol. 1, pp. 401–2) gives a list of six.
28 Abu al-Qasim al-Zamakhsharī, *Tafsīr al-kashshāf* (Beirut, n.d.), Vol. 2, p. 185.
29 Abū Ḥayyān, *al-Baḥr al-muḥīṭ*.
30 Al-Ṭabarī, *Tafsīr al-Ṭabarī* (Beirut, 1999), Vol. 6, p. 349.
31 Abū Ḥayyān, *al-Baḥr al-muḥīṭ*, Vol. 5, p. 31.
32 Al-Bayḍāwī, *Tafsīr*, Vol. 1, p. 402. Attribution to Ibn ʿAbbās is regarded as unreliable and should be subjected to close scrutiny. The very same statement is attributed in Abū Ḥayyān to al-Kalbī. On two other occasions in the Qur'an, where *ṣāghirūn* is used, it occurs first in a context of Iblīs who was too arrogant to bow down to Adam: '*I am better than him. You created me from fire and him from clay.' God said, 'Get down from here. This is no place for your arrogance (tatakabbara fīhā). Get out. You are one of the ṣāghirīn*'

(Q. 7:12–13). In the second instance (Q. 27:31), Solomon gives his emissary a message to the Queen of Sheba: '*Do not put yourselves above me, and come to me (a-lā ta'lū 'alayya wa-a'tūnī)*'. In Q. 27:37, when she did not respond as requested, he says, '*We shall certainly come upon them with irresistible forces and drive them from their land ṣāghirīn*'. In both cases *ṣāghirīn* comes in response to someone putting themselves above obeying an order.

33 Tirmidhi, *Sunan*, Buyū', 74.

34 See Yūsuf al-Qaraḍāwī, *Ghayr al-muslimīn fī mujtama' al-islāmī* (Cairo, 1977), pp. 45–52, quoting reliable authorities such as al-Farrāj, Abū Yūsuf and al-Bukhārī.

35 E. W. Lane, *An Arabic–English Lexicon,* 8 vols (Libraire du Liban, Beirut 1968); Hans Wehr, *Arabic–English Dictionary of Modern Written Arabic,* ed. J. M. Cowan (Otto Harrasowitz, Wiesbaden German 1979).

36 Heck, 'Poll tax.', in Jane Dammen McAuliffe (ed.), *Encyclopaedia of the Qur'ān* (Georgetown University, Washington DC, Brill Online, 2016). Available at http://referenceworks.brillonline.com/entries/encyclopaedia-of-the-quran/poll-tax-EQSIM_00333 (accessed 8 April 2016).

37 Al-Rāzī, *al-Tafsīr al-kabīr,* part 16, p. 30.

38 Al-Ṭabarī, *Tafsīr,* Vol. 6, p. 349.

39 Al-Rāzī, *al-Tafsīr al-kabīr,* part 16, p. 30.

40 Al-Wāḥidī, *Asbāb al-nuzūl* (Cairo, 1315/1897).

41 Al-Suyūṭī, *Tafsīr al-Jalālayn* (Baghdad, n.d.), pp. 251–2.

42 Abū Ḥayyān, *al-Baḥr al-muḥīṭ,* Vol. 5, p. 30.

43 Ibid.

44 Abū Dawūd, *al-Kutub al-sitta, Bāb jihād* 82, p. 1,416.

45 Abū Yūsuf, *Kitāb al-kharaj* (Beirut, n.d.), p. 126; Abū Yūsuf Ya'qūb, *Kitab-ul-kharaj = Islamic Revenue Code,* trans. Abid Ahmad Ali and Abdul Hameed Siddiqui (Lahore, 1979), p. 254.

46 Al-Qurṭubī (*al-Jāmi',* Vol. 4, p. 73) states, 'whoever disputes violently in paying over his *jizya* should be disciplined and the *jizya* taken from him *ṣāghiran.*' Further on, he states, 'If the imam makes an agreement with the people of a town or a fortress, and then they break the agreement and refuse to pay the *jizya* they should pay and do not submit to the rule of Islam, without them being oppressed and without the imam doing them wrong or tyrannising them, they should be fought for the *jizya.*'

47 Ibid., Vol. 4, pp. 7–8.

48 Ibn 'Abbās is reported to have named four rabbis who had said that Ezra was the son of God, commenting that 'no Jews now make such a claim'. Abū Hayyān (*al-Baḥr al-muḥīṭ,* Vol. 5, p. 31) takes the fact that some Jews made such a claim as being confirmed in that this verse was read to the

Jews in Medina and they did not reject it or say it was not true, eager though they were normally to reject things said in the Qur'an.

49 Al-Rāzī, *al-Tafsīr al-kabīr*, part 16, pp. 33 ff.

50 Sayyid Quṭb, *Fī ẓilāl al-Qur'ān*, Vol. 3, pp. 1,632 ff.

51 Ibn Mājah, *Sunan Ibn Mājah* (in ālih bin 'Abd al-'Azīz (ed.), *al-Kutub al-sitta*), *Fitan* 3, p. 2,712.

52 See Chapter 3, Qur'anic Jihad.

53 See Aḥmad al-Hāshimī, *Jawāhir al-balāgha* (Beirut, 1986), pp. 131–2.

54 If it is argued that the *jizya* was still discriminatory and made the payers into second class citizens, the alternative of forcing Jews and Christians to engage in Islamic *jihād* and to pay *zakāt*, which is a pillar of Islam, would have been against their basic right to practise their own religions.

55 The fact that Muslim jurists and exegetes later on misinterpreted and misapplied the Qur'anic teachings does not negate the Qur'anic stand.

56 'Imāra, *al-Islām*, p. 15.

57 Abū Dawūd, quoted in al-Qurṭubī, *al-Jāmi'*, Vol. 4, p. 74.

58 Indeed, there is even a Prophetic tradition cited by Ibn Mājah in which it is stated that Muslims are in the '*dhimma* of God'; the tradition states that 'whoever prays the morning prayer is in God's (*dhimma*) protection' (*Sunan Ibn Mājah, Bāb al-Muslimūn fī dhimmat Allāh, ḥadīth* no. 3,947, p. 2,713). So in some ways it has sacred connotations.

59 I reiterate that my discussion here is based only on the Qur'an and not how some Muslim societies have behaved in the past or now according to their circumstances.

Chapter 3 Qur'anic *Jihād*

1 Muḥammad Fu'ād 'Abd al-Bāqī, *al-Mu'jam al-mufaḥras li-alfāẓ al-Qur'ān al-karīm*, many editions. Ella Landau-Tasseron, in the chapter on 'Jihād' in the *Encyclopaedia of the Qur'ān*, simply quotes the figure as 35, but this includes repetitions within the same verse of the verb and its adverb (e.g. see Q. 25:52: *wa-jāhidhum bihi jihādan kabīran* ('*strive hard against them with the Qur'an*'). See also Q. 22:78 and Q. 29:6) and is based on mechanical calculation, which gives an exaggerated impression of its frequency of occurrence.

2 For a Prophetic Hadith on this, see *Ṣaḥīḥ Muslim, Īmān*, p. 80.

3 Nessim J. Dawood (*The Koran* (London, 1990)), in contrast, translates the usage in this verse as 'fight them [...] most strenuously'. This not only isolates the verse from its textual context, with its adjacent verses, which has nothing to do with violence, but also contradicts the historical context of this Meccan sura, which has nothing to do with military *jihād*. In similar vein, Reuven Firestone describes this usage of *jihād* as given as

'an aggressive context, in combination with the imperative' (see Reuven Firestone, 'Jihād' in Andrew Rippin (ed.), *The Blackwell Companion to the Qur'ān* (Oxford, 2006), pp. 308–20, at p. 311).

4 Dawood, *The Koran.* This ignores the historical and textual context of this verse and flies in the face of the well-recognised feature of *wujūh al-Qur'ān* (the multiplicity of meaning of certain Qur'anic terms).

5 e.g. Q. 8:72, Q. 9:211 and Q. 61:11; however, context is the ultimate decider of meaning.

6 See Q. 16:41 and 110, Q. 29:56 and Q. 4:97–100. A boycott was also imposed on the Prophet and his clan. With mounting pressure and having lost his main supporters, his wife, Khadīja, and uncle, Abū Ṭālib, he began to look beyond Mecca for people to accept his message, and in two years some pilgrims from Yathrib (later Medina) accepted the new religion.

7 Pope Benedict XVI in his Regensburg Speech, 2006. Available at http://www.vatican.va/holy_father/benedict_xvi/speeches/2006/september/documents/hf_ben-xvi_spe_20060912_university-regensburg_en.html (accessed 8 April 2016).

8 For more on this aspect of Qur'anic rhetoric, see Muhammad A. S. Abdel Haleem, 'How to Read the Qur'an: *Sūrat al-Ḥadīd* (Q. 57)', *Journal of Qur'anic Studies* 10 (2008), pp. 124–31.

9 See James J. Busuttil, '"Slay them wherever you find them": Humanitarian law in Islam', *Revue de droit pénal militaire et de droit de la guerre* 30 (1991), pp. 113–40.

10 See Ella Landau-Tasseron, 'Jihād', *Encyclopaedia of the Qur'an* (Leiden, 2006), Vol. 3, p. 35. Reuven Firestone has used the same mechanism with 'them', cutting it off from what it refers to in Q. 8:56 (see Firestone, 'Jihād' op. cit. p. 312).

11 Fakhr al-Dīn al-Rāzī, *al-Tafsīr al-kabīr* (Beirut, n.d.), Vol. 5, p. 125; al-Bayḍāwī, *al-Tafsīr* (Beirut, 1998), Vol. 1, p. 108.

12 The concept that fighting should be in the way of God, rather than in the way of *ṭāghūt* ('idolatry', 'tyranny') as the disbelievers do, is also stated clearly in the Qur'an: '*the believers fight for God's cause, while those who reject faith fight for an unjust cause. Fight the allies of Satan: Satan's strategies are truly weak*' (Q. 4:76).

13 Landau-Tasseron, 'Jihād', op. cit. p. 40.

14 For more on this issue, see Chapter 1 on the 'Sword Verse' myth and Chapter 2 on *jizya*.

15 Al-Rāzī, *al-Tafsīr al-kabīr*, Vol. 5, p. 132. He also cites a report by Ibn 'Abbās stating that '*fitna* means *kufr*: disbelief in God. *Kufr* is called *fitna* because it is corruption on earth that leads to injustice and commotion' (ibid., p. 130). However, much of what is attributed to Ibn 'Abbās is open to doubt and the context does not support this interpretation.

16 Arthur J. Arberry, *The Koran Interpreted* (Oxford, 1964), p. 25.
17 Al-Rāzī, *al-Tafsīr al-kabīr*, Vol. 6, p. 35.
18 Al-Rāzī, *al-Tafsīr al-kabīr*, Vol. 5, p. 130.
19 Confirmed in al-Zamakhsharī, *al-Kashshāf* (Beirut, n.d.), Vol. 1, p. 342.
20 Al-Fayrūzabādī, *al-Qamūs al-muḥīṭ* (Cairo, 1952), Vol. 4, p. 227.
21 See Landau-Tasseron, 'Jihād', p. 41.
22 See Chapters 1 and 2 in this book.
23 This is the normal practice of the Qur'an: when it refers to stories of earlier prophets, for example, it does not give personal names to anyone except prophets and angels. See Muhammad A. S. Abdel Haleem, *Understanding the Qur'an: Themes and Style* (London, 2001), p. 152.
24 See also Q. 33:15–21 and Q. 47:20–1.
25 See also Q. 8:9.
26 This verse has been used, isolated from its context and from its reference to the people who kept breaking their treaties, to connect Islam to terrorism; the verb used, *turhibūna,* relates to *irhāb* in modern Arabic, which is used to translate the Western-coined term of 'terrorism'.
27 In recent years, modern Islamic militant movements have considered that Muslim states had abandoned their religious duty and allowed the Muslim lands to be occupied by non-Muslims, without any resistance, so *jihād* has become *al-farīḍa al-ghā'iba* ('the absent religious obligation'). This is the view of such groups as al-Jamā'a al-Islāmiyya in Egypt and al-Qa'ida. They have set up their own *amīrs* (commanders) and followers are expected to obey and carry on *jihād.* There are scholars who take the view that if the Muslim state abandons its obligations, individuals are entitled to take them on. The late Muḥammad al-Ghazālī was asked, in court, in connection with the assassination of a journalist, Faraj Foda, on 8 June 1992 by members of the Jamā'a Islāmiyya, whether individual Muslims may take over the duty of the state when it has failed to restrain an individual from attacking Muslims and Islam. Al-Ghazālī replied that the killing of Farag Foda was in fact the implementation of the punishment against an apostate that the imam has failed to implement.
28 i.e. inside or outside the Sanctuary in Mecca.
29 See Ella Landau-Tasseron, 'Jihād', In *Encyclopaedia of the Qur'an* (Leiden, 2006), Vol. 3, pp. 35–43.
30 This is clear from our discussion of Q. 2:193 which says the same thing.
31 See Chapter 1.
32 See Muḥammad 'Imāra, *al-Gharb wa'l-Islām: ayn al-khatta' wa-ayn al-ṣawāb?* (Cairo, 2004), p. 115, quoting Ibn 'Abd al-Barr, *al-Durrar fī Ikhtiṣār al-maghāzī wa'l-siyar* (Cairo, 1966).

33 ʻImāra goes on, in making his point, to give tables of the victims of Old Testament wars, as 1,635,650 non-Jews and 352,827 Jews, the total being 1,988,477 (he takes this from Muḥammad Jalā' Idrīs, *Falsafat al-ḥarb fī'l-fikr al-dīnī al-Isra'īlī* (Cairo, 2001), pp. 189–91). He then goes on to talk about the religious wars in Western Christian history and gives the number of deaths, as a result of the religious wars waged by Christian churches against other Christians alone, quoting Voltaire, as ten million (from Idrīs, *Falsafat*, p. 126). He continues until the end of the World War II.

34 ʻAbbās Maḥmūd al-ʻAqqād, *Ḥaqā'iq al-Islām wa-abāṭīl ḥusūmihi* (Cairo, 1957), p. 184.

Chapter 4 Qur'anic Paradise

1 The pronouns used to introduce these statements are *man* and *alladhīna*, both of which are particles of generalisation and inclusiveness (*taʻmīm*).

2 There are about 60 citations in the Qur'an of ʻ*āmanū wa-ʻamilū ṣāliḥāt*'. See ʻAbd al-Bāqī, *al-Muʻjam al-mufahras* (Cairo, 1945; reprint Beirut, n.d.), pp. 411–12.

3 Leah Kinberg, 'Paradise', in J. D. McAuliffe (ed.), *Encyclopaedia of the Qur'ān* (Leiden, 2004), Vol. 4, p. 12.

4 Ibid., pp. 13–15.

5 Elsaid M. Badawi and Muhammad A. S. Abdel Haleem, *Arabic–English Dictionary of Qur'anic Usage* (Leiden, 2007), p. 700.

6 Annemarie Schimmel, 'The celestial garden', in E. B. Macdougal and R. Ettinghausen (eds), *The Islamic Garden* (1976), p. 17.

7 John Wansbrough, *Qur'anic Studies* (Oxford, 1979), pp. 25–9.

8 See Muhammad A. S. Abdel Haleem, *Understanding the Qur'an: Themes and Styles* (London, 1999, 2001), pp. 167–81.

9 The Qur'an's explanation makes more sense than all the speculation given by al-Qurṭubī and quoted in Kinberg, 'Paradise', p. 15.

10 Schimmel, 'The celestial garden', pp. 17–18.

11 Ibid., p. 14.

12 Astronomers are always searching for signs of water on planets as the essential basis of all life.

13 These and other special characteristics are shown in all the language used by the Qur'an to describe Paradise. See Abdel Haleem, *Understanding the Qur'an*, pp. 103–5.

14 Nadīm Marʻashlī, *al-Ṣiḥāḥ fī'l-lugha wa'l-ʻulūm* (Beirut, 1974), Vol. 2, p. 615.

15 Academy of the Arabic Language, *Muʻjam al-wasīṭ* (Cairo, 1985), Vol. 2, p. 957.

16 There were no major rivers in Arabia.

17 Schimmel, 'The celestial garden', p. 15.

18 Richard Bell, *The Qur'an Translated with a Critical Rearrangement of the Surahs* (Edinburgh, 1937; reprinted 1960), Vol. 2, p. 515, fn. 1.

19 *Anhār min mā'; wa-anhār min laban; wa-anhār min khamr; wa-anhār min 'asal.*

20 Genesis 2:10. The four rivers here are geographical.

21 Amongst all the luscious gardens and plentiful streams, lofty buildings are provided for believers (Q. 25:75, Q. 29:58 and Q. 39:20).

22 *Taki'a jalasa mutamakkinan* means 'he sat well established in his position'. *Al-muttaka'* is what you sit on, an upholstered chair with a back and two arms. *Al-muttaki'* is he who sits upright on something under him, in an established position (*man istawā qā'idan 'alā wiṭā' mutamakkinan*), Academy of the Arabic Language, *Mu'jam al-wasīṭ*, Vol. 2, p. 1,052.

23 Kinberg, 'Paradise', p. 18.

24 Nadīm Mar'ashlī, *al-Ṣiḥāḥ fi'l-lughah wa'l-'ulūm* (Beirut, 1975), Vol. 2, p. 397.

25 e.g. Schimmel, 'The celestial garden', p. 15.

26 Edward W. Lane, *Arabic–English Lexicon* (Beirut, 1968), Vol. 7, p. 2,616.

27 The guilty person, in contrast, will suffer on his own (Q. 44:44 and 53).

28 On a recent visit to Morocco, the issue of the image of the Islamic Paradise in the West was raised at a meeting with a group of Muslim scholars. The quick reaction was, as I recall: 'We do not take our criteria of what is good Paradise or inferior Paradise from such people. Europeans and Americans consume more food and drink than whole continents in the rest of the world, and they cannot sell anything without having scantily-clad young women advertising it. It must be because they are obsessed with food and women that they pick on this in the Qur'anic Paradise, change the true description and blow it out of all proportion, and do not see the real extent of the spiritual joy and bliss which far outweigh any physical description.' I do not share this view and I hesitated much before putting it in as I certainly do not intend to offend any Western academics who have written on this subject, but finally I thought such academics should be told what a group of *'ulamā'* said about them.

29 Ibn Rushd, *Manāhij al-adilla fī 'aqa'id al-milla*, ed. M. Qasim (Cairo, 1964, 1969), p. 245.

30 Al-'Āmirī, *Kitāb al-I'lām bi-manāqib al-islām*, ed. A. Ghurab (Cairo, 1967), p. 138.

31 Muhammad Abdallah Draz, *Le morale du Coran* (Cairo, 1949), translated from French as *The Moral World of the Qur'an* (London, 2009), pp. 158–65.

32 Arabs described beautiful women as being as precious as ostrich eggs, protected from the dust with feathers.

33 Ibn 'Abbās, as reported in al-Ṭabarī, *Jāmi' al-bayān fī tafsīr al-Qur'ān* (Beirut, 1999), Vol. 1, p. 174.

34 Academy of the Arabic Language, *Al-Mu'jam al-wasīṭ*, p. 915.
35 Leah Kinberg, 'Paradise', see note 4 above.

Chapter 5 Legal Style: Qur'anic *Sharī'a* – Avoiding the Application of the Ultimate Penalties

1 Mahmūd Shaltūt, Introduction. In *Al-Islām: 'aqīda wa-sharī'a* (Cairo, 1990) (see bibliography).
2 Abdelwahhab Khallāf, *'Ilm 'usūl al-fiqh* (Beirut, 1977), p. 33.
3 Q. 4:92.
4 Al-Wāḥidī, *Asbāb al-nuzūl* (Cairo, 1315 AH), p. 33.
5 Ahmad al-Hāshimī, *Jawāhir al-balāgha* (Beirut, 1986), pp. 130–2.
6 Ibn Rushd, *Bidāyat al-mujtahid wa-nihāyat al-muqtaṣid* (Beirut, 1992), pp. 588–9.
7 Fakhr al-Dīn al-Rāzī, *al-Tafsīr al-kabīr* (Beirut, n.d.), part 11, p. 230; al-Bayḍāwī, *Tafsīr* (Beirut, 1988), Vol. 1, p. 266; Ibn Ḥazm was of the opinion that the penalty does not apply if the thief repents (see A. M. al-Aqqad, *Falsafat al-qur'ān* (Cairo, n.d.), pp. 100–1.
8 Ibn Rushd, *Bidāyat*, Vol. 2, p. 586.
9 *Yu'adhdhibu* ('he punishes') is used in the Qur'an for punishment in this world, as is clear in the case of the adultery in Q. 24:2: '*Let their punishment ('adhāb) be witnessed by a group of believers.*'
10 Such jurists apparently rely on the surface meaning of the verse and on Hadith.
11 Muḥammad Salīm El-'Awā, *Fī uṣūl al-niẓām al-jinā'ī al-islāmī* (Cairo, 2006), p. 255.
12 Al-Rāzī, *al-Tafsīr al-kabīr*, Vol. 9, p. 231.
13 Al-Bayḍāwī, *Tafsīr*, Vol. 1, p. 205.
14 Ibid.
15 Al-Rāzī, *al-Tafsīr al-kabīr*, Vol. 9, pp. 235–6.
16 Q. 5:41–4.
17 Al-Rāzī, *al-Tafsīr al-kabīr*, Vol. 11, p. 233; al- Bayḍāwī, *Tafsīr*, Vol. 1, p. 267.
18 Mālik, *al-Muwaṭṭa'*, Book 5, Hadith no. 3,044, p. 1203 (see Arent J. Wensinck, *Concordances et indices de la Tradition Musulmane* (Leiden, 1992), Books III–IV, p. 237.
19 *Ṣaḥīḥ al-Bukhārī*, Aḥkām 39, Ṣulḥ 5, Ḥudūd 3. Also in *Ṣaḥīḥ Muslim*, Ḥudūd 35. See Arent J. Wensinck, *Concordances* ..., Books. I–II, p. 229.
20 El-Awa, *Fī uṣūl al-niẓām*, pp. 301–2.
21 El-Awa, *Fi uṣūl al-niẓām al-jinā'ī al-islāmī* (Cairo, 2006), pp. 301–6.
22 *Ṣaḥīḥ al-Bukhārī*, Book 17, Hadith 4, 205.
23 Kuwait Ministry of Awqaf, *al-Mawsū'a al-fiqhiyya* (Encyclopedia of Islamic Law) (Kuwait, 1993), quoting *Ṣaḥīḥ Muslim*, Vol. 22, p. 126.

24 *Ṣaḥīḥ al-Bukhārī*, Vol. 8, Book 82, no. 812. English translation by Muhsin Khan. Available at http://www.islamtomorrow.com/everything/sahihal-bukhari.pdf (accessed 10 April 2016).
25 *Sunan Abī Dāwūd* Hadith 4377.
26 Mālik, *al-Muwaṭṭa'*, Wensinck, *Concordances*, Vols 5–6, p. 330.
27 Al-Rāzī, *Tafsīr*, Part 23, p. 147.
28 Al-Rāzī, *Tafsīr*, Part 23, pp. 145–7.
29 Ibn Rushd, *Bidāyat*, pp. 563–6.
30 Al-Bayḍāwī, *Tafsīr*, Vol. 1, p. 205.
31 Al-Rāzī, *Tafsīr*, Part 9, p. 232. If we accept the Hadith, however, it clearly seems to be coming as a clarification of Q. 4:15 (keeping them at home). It must therefore have occurred before the revelation of the second verse of *Sūrat al-Nūr*, as was stated by al-Rāzī. This therefore gives us the events as: first, stay at home; second, stoning; and third, abrogation of stoning by *Sūrat al-Nūr* and its replacement with 100 lashes, – rather than the other way around (100 lashes being abrogated by stoning). One can also understand the *sabab al-nuzūl* of Q. 5:41 in this context. Had the punishment in Islam been stoning, the Jews would not have sought the Prophet's judgement. They did so under the belief that he may offer a more lenient ruling. If the ruling in Islam was 100 lashes, this makes sense. If we accept this reasoning, 100 lashes was still the punishment late on, as *Sūrat al-Mā'ida* was one of the last to be revealed. On this occasion, however, the Prophet judged according to the Torah and ordered stoning, as they were Jews merely seeking a way out; the ruling of 100 lashes for Muslims would still stand. It is possible to argue that this change in the ruling through the three stages mentioned above, followed by the stoning of the Jews alluded to in *Sūrat al-Mā'ida* is what has led to the confusion about the order of abrogation and what the final ruling on the subject is.
32 If they are fit for marriage to anyone, they are obviously still alive and not stoned to death.
33 Al-Rāzī, *Tafsīr*, Part 23, p. 134.
34 El-Awa, *Fī uṣūl al-niẓām*, pp. 298–309.
35 Ibn Rushd, *Bidāyat*, Vol. 2, pp. 568–9.
36 *Sunan Tirmidhī*, Ḥudūd, 2. Hadith 1424.
37 Maḥmūd Shaltūt, *al-Islām: 'aqīda wa-sharī'a* (Cairo, 1990), pp. 291–2.
38 Al-Bukhārī, *Kitāb al-I'tiṣām* (many editions).
39 *Nawawī's Forty Hadith*, trans. Ezzedine Ibrahim and Denys Johnson-Davies (Damascus, 1977), Hadith no. 14, p. 59.
40 All the reports on *sabab al-nuzūl* state that these people were Muslims who reverted back to their polytheistic beliefs (al-Rāzī, *Tafsīr*, Vol. 10, pp. 218–19).

41 El-Awa, *Fī uṣūl al-niẓām*, pp.185–7.

42 Ministry of Awqaf and Islamic Affairs, Kuwait, *al-Mawsū'a al-fiqhiyya* (Kuwait, 1992), Vol. 24, p. 34.

43 This is given in Arabic in a nominal sentence: *al-rijālu qawwāmūna 'alā'l-nisā'*. The nominal sentence structure suggests this is the expected situation: husbands support wives.

44 Alfred Guillaume, *The Life of Muhammad: A Translation of Ibn Ishaq's Sirat Rasul Allah* (Oxford, 1955; 4th impression, 1974), p. 651.

45 Another instance of an imperative denoting a permission, not a command is Q. 62:10 giving the believers permission to '*disperse in the land*' after prayer, but expressed in the form of an Arabic imperative (*fa'ntashirū*) (see Chapter 8 section '*Sūrat al-Jumu'a* (Q. 62)').

46 *Ṣaḥīḥ al-Bukhārī*, English translation by Muhsin Khan op. cit., Vol. 8, Book 73, Hadith 68.

47 Muḥammad Nāṣir al-Dīn al-Albānī, in his *Adān al-zifāf fī'l-sunna al-muṭahhara* (4th edition. Al-Maktab al-Islāmī, Beirut, n.d., p. 105), gives al-Sindī's view that *nushūz* on the part of the wife includes '[her] harming the husband and his family by word or by the hand (*īdhā al-zawj wa-ahlihi bi'l-lisān wa'l-yad*)'.

Chapter 6 Euphemistic Style: Sexual Etiquette

1 Pickthall's translation of Q. 2:222.

2 Norman Daniel, *Islam and the West: The Making of an Image* (Oxford, 1993), p. 78.

3 Similarly, in Q. 8:1, they are asking not just about war-gains, but about the distribution of them.

4 Even if it was men who, according to the tradition, asked the Prophet this question, and even if the answer is directed at men, one could argue that the answer given by the Qur'an is also a possible reply to women who desire intercourse with their husbands during their menses.

5 See Yusuf Ali, *The Holy Qur'an: Text, Translation and Commentary* (Lahore, 1969): 'a hurt and a pollution'.

6 See *Qariba al-rajulu zawjatahu jāma'ahā'* in Ibrahim Muṣṭafa et al. (eds), *al-Mu'jam al-wasīṭ*, Academy of the Arabic Language (Beirut, n.d.), p. 723.

7 Compare the Bible, Leviticus 15:19–30, where a menstruating woman is considered 'unclean' and cannot be touched, and certainly cannot engage in intercourse.

8 The question was asked by men and the answer is directed at them.

9 Ministry of Awqaf and Islamic Affairs, *al-Mawsū'a al-fiqhiyya* (Kuwait, 1992), Vol. 35, p. 340.

10 *Sunan al-Dārimī*, *Nikaḥ*, Hadith 45 (many editions).

11 Fakhr al-Dīn al-Rāzī, *al-Tafsīr al-kabīr* (Beirut, n.d.), Part 6, pp. 71–2.

12 Ibid.
13 Ministry of Awqaf, *al-Mawsū'a*, p. 15.
14 See al-Daylami, Abu Abdullah, *Musnad al-Firdaws* 2/55. On returning with Muslim men from a long journey, reaching the outskirts of Medina at nightfall, the Prophet decided to camp outside the city for the night, sending messengers to announce that they were all back, expressly intending that men should not surprise their wives, who might not be prepared for them or might be in a state in which they would not wish to be seen. Al-Bukhārī, *Nikāḥ* 121, in Al al-Sheikh, Salih bin 'Abdel Aziz, *al-kutub al-sitta* (Riyadh, Dar al-Salam, 1999). See also A. M. Al-'Aqqad, *'Abqariyyat Muhammad* (Beirut, Al-Maktabat al-'Asriyya, 2008) p. 94.
15 Ministry of Awqaf, *al-Mawsū'a*, pp. 16–17.
16 Daniel, *Islam and the West*, p. 78.
17 Tammam Hassan, *al-Bayān fī rawā'i' al-qur'ān* (Cairo, 1993).
18 See al-Rāzī, *al-Tafsīr al-kabīr*, Vol. 6, pp. 68–74.
19 Q. 23:5, Q. 24:30–1, Q. 33:35 and Q. 70:29.
20 In our days it is indeed wise to protect these parts from sexually transmitted diseases including HIV and AIDS as well as from the psychological, emotional and social problems caused by illicit contact.
21 Q. 7:16; 24:31, 58.
22 This is *interpreted* in one Hadith to show that covering the face and hands is not necessary.
23 It could also mean jewellery or finery, especially in view of the instruction that women 'should not stamp their feet so as to draw attention to any hidden charms'.
24 Ibrāhīm Muṣṭafa et al., *al-Mu'jam al-wasīṭ* (Cairo, 1960; reprinted Istanbul, 1998), Vol. 1 under *dāna*, p. 299.
25 Pickthall: 'draw their cloaks close around them'; Arberry: 'draw their veils close to them'; Alan Jones: 'draw their robes close to them'.
26 Shaikh Muhammad ibn 'Abdullah al-Subayyal (d. 2012), *Fatāwā wa-rasā'il mukhtāra* (Saudi Arabia, n.d.), pp. 562–3; Shaikh Yusuf al-Qaradawi, *The Lawful and Prohibited in Islam* (USA, 1999): Chapter 3, 'How a Muslim woman should conduct herself'.
27 e.g. 'And let them not stamp their feet so as to reveal what they hide of their adornment' (Pickthall).
28 e.g. *al-Lisan al-Arab* (Cairo, n.d.).
29 As a way of avoiding *fawāḥish* the Prophet advised the men in his community, 'If any one of you sees a woman and is attracted to her, he should go to his wife.' *Saḥīḥ Muslim*, kitāb al-nikāḥ, Hadith 3242. Available at http://www.searchtruth.com/book_display.php?book=008&translator=2&start=0&number=3240 (accessed 10 April 2016).
30 i.e. recognised as a religious woman and not available.

Chapter 7 Narrative Style: Repeating Stories – Noah

1 Abū Isḥāq al-Shāṭibī, *al-Muwafaqāt fī uṣūl al-aḥkām* (Cairo, 1342 AH), Vol. 3, p. 353.

2 Bernhard Heller, 'Nūḥ', in M. Th. Houtsma et al. (eds), *The Encyclopaedia of Islam*, 1st edition (Leiden, 1913–1936), Vol. 6, p. 948 and in P. Bearman et al. (eds), *The Encyclopaedia of Islam*, 2nd edition (Leiden, 1986), Vol. 8, p. 109. Available at http://referenceworks.brillonline.com/entries/encyclopaedia-of-islam-2/nuh-SIM_5966?s.num=0&s.au=%22Heller%2C+B.%22 (accessed 12 December 2015).

3 Richard Bell, *Introduction to the Qur'an* (Edinburgh, 1997), p. 127 and p. 129.

4 David Marshall, 'Punishment stories', in J. D. McAuliffe (ed.), *The Encyclopaedia of the Qur'ān* (Leiden, 2000), Vol. 4, pp. 318–22, p. 318 and p. 320 respectively.

5 Marshall, 'Punishment stories', p. 320.

6 e.g. Q. 42:13, '*In matters of faith, He has laid down for you the same commandments that He gave Noah [...] and which We enjoined on Abraham and Moses and Jesus*', and Q. 4:163, '*We have sent revelation to you [Prophet] as we sent to Noah and the prophets after him, to Abraham, Ishmael*'. There is one exception, in Q. 3:33, when Adam is placed at the head of the list.

7 Theodor Nöldeke, *Tārīkh al-qur'ān*, trans. into Arabic by G. Tāmir (Hildesheim, Zürich, New York, 2004), p. xxxvi. I have adopted Nöldeke's chronological arrangement for the ten Noah accounts as it is generally acknowledged as a sound authority and is widely known and accepted. For the various opinions held by Muslim scholars on the chronology of the Qur'an, see the list in Muhammad Izzat Darwaza, *Sīrat al-rasūl: ṣūra muqtabasa min al-qur'ān al-karīm*, 3rd edition (Qatar, 1979), p. 145. Bell also has a different chronology, for which see Bell, *Introduction to the Qur'an*, pp. 114–20.

8 This partitive '*min*', which indicates that only segments of the stories are revealed and used for specific purposes, appears several times in connection with the stories of earlier prophets (Q. 6:34, Q. 11:120, Q. 19:99 and Q. 28:3).

9 Noah's prophetic mission is said to have lasted for 950 years. For the reiteration of Noah's call to faith, see Q. 7:59, Q. 11:26 and Q. 23:23.

10 Wansbrough, for example, offers as 'a typical instance' the story of Shu'ayb, about which he states that 'the scriptural account exists in three complete versions [...] and in abridged form' in one version, from which he then constructs a nine-element version of the 'complete' story and sets out to count, in a mechanical way, which of these elements are

missing in the accounts and which is least coherent. He concedes that his proposed scheme does not coincide with verse juncture and sequence, but really 'corresponds to a scheme widely attested in the literature of prophetic expression' (John Wansbrough, *Qur'anic Studies: Sources and Methods of Scriptural Interpretation*, London Oriental Series, 31 (Oxford, 1977), p. 21). However, this scheme does not correspond to the text of the Qur'an, nor to the purpose of any of the accounts given.

11 Q. 71:77–81 contains the only description of the nature of this reward in the entire Qur'an.

12 On p. 133 of his *Introduction to the Qur'an*, Bell also asserts that the 'punishment stories' are almost exclusively of temporal and not eschatological punishment, and goes on to say that in Q. 11 there are, exceptionally, references to the Day of Resurrection in the stories of 'Ād, Pharaoh and Abraham.

13 Two examples, both from Noah accounts, are Q. 7:59 and Q. 11:26.

14 In verse 6, the Meccans reject their prophet's message as lies (*fa-qad kadhdhabū*), a refrain which is echoed throughout the sura, in which, with the exception of the first two accounts, all of these stories begin with the phrase '*kadhdhaba … al-mursalīna*' (meaning, 'the people of X rejected the messengers as liars').

15 In the same sura, Muhammad is advised, '*Lower your wing tenderly over the believers who follow you*' (Q. 26:215). Clearly, similar objections had been raised at that time by Meccans, so the context here is objection to, and denial of, the type of followers attracted by Muhammad (see for instance Q. 6:52–4 and Q. 6:68–70).

16 Compare Q. 36:41–2, '*We carried their seed in the laden Ark and made similar things for them to ride upon.*'

17 Compare Q. 6:51–4, Q. 7:188 and Q. 17:90–6.

18 In his chapter in the *Encylopaedia of Islam*, Heller makes the startling assertion that it is Noah, rather than God, who orders the waters to subside: 'When Nūḥ bids the waters be still, the ark lands on Mount Jūdī.' This both misinterprets the word *ablaḥa* as 'be still' rather than 'swallow' and is grammatically unsound. The grammatical phrasing of this passage *wa-qīla yā-arḍu'blaḥī mā'aki* ('*Then it was said, "Earth, swallow up your water"*') has unequivocally been understood by classical commentators and readers of the Qur'an as being God's command, and is an example of the well-known stylistic device used in the Qur'an of presenting God's speech in the passive form. To give just one example, that occurs in the very same passage of this sura, in verse 48, the passive verb *qīla* is again used in this way: *qīla yā-Nūḥu'hbiṭ bi'l-salāmin* ('*And it was said, "Noah, descend in peace from Us"*').

19 Q. 7:59 has *laqad arsalnā Nūḥan ilā qawmihi fa-qāla yāqawmī'budū'llāha mā lakum min ilāhin ghayruhu innī akhāfu 'alaykum 'adhāba yawmin 'aẓīm*; Q. 11:25–6 has *wa-laqad arsalnā Nūḥan ilā qawmihi innī lakum nadhīrun mubīn an lā ta'budū illā'llāha innī akhāfu 'alaykum 'adhāba yawmin alīm*; and Q. 23:23, *wa-laqad arsalnā Nūḥan ilā qawmihi fa-qāla yā-qawmī'budū'llāha mā lakum min ilāhin ghayruhu a-fa-lā tattaqūna.*

20 Al-Bukhārī, *Saḥīḥ* (many editions), *Kitāb al-'ilm*, Book 3, Hadith 1,378.

21 Bernhard Heller, 'Nūḥ', in P. Bearman et al. (eds), *The Encyclopaedia of Islam*, 2nd edition (Leiden, 1986). Available at http://referenceworks.brillonline.com/entries/encyclopaedia-of-islam-2/nuh-SIM_5966?s.num=0&s.au=%22Heller%2C+B.%22 (accessed 12 December 2015).

22 Bell, *Introduction to the Qur'an*, p. 129; Marshall, 'Punishment stories', p. 318.

23 See also Q. 29:15.

24 Al-Shāṭibī, *al-Muwafaqāt*, Vol. 3, pp. 353–8.

25 Muhammad Fu'ad 'Abd al-Bāqī, *al-Mu'jam al-mufahras li-alfāẓ al-qur'ān al-karīm* (Cairo, 1945; reprinted Beirut, n.d.), p. 599.

26 'Abd al-Qāhir al-Jurjānī, *Dalā'il al-i'jāz* (Damascus, 1987), pp. 91–2.

27 Robin C. Ostle (ed.), *Studies in Modern Arabic Literature* (London, 1975), pp. 76–7.

28 Bernhard Heller, 'Nūḥ', in M. Th. Houtsma et al. (eds), *The Encyclopaedia of Islam*, 1st edn (Leiden, 1913–1936). Consulted online on 24 November 2016. http://dx.doi.org/10.1163/2214-871X_ei1_SIM_3519.

29 This is a general statement, which indicates that God will save the believer at any time and gives solace and reassurance to all believers in difficulty.

Chapter 8 Coherent Style: How to Read the Sura

1 Richard Bell, *The Qur'an Translated with a Critical Rearrangement of the Surahs* (Edinburgh, 1937, reprinted 1960).

2 Including Angelika Neuwirth, Neal Robinson, Alan Jones and Muhammad Abdel Haleem.

3 Bell, *The Qur'an*, pp. 579 ff.

4 *Ḥakīm* is normally translated as 'Wise' but, in the context of the preceding attributes, 'the Judicious Decider' is more fitting.

5 Bell, *The Qur'an*, p. 579.

6 It is reported that when the Prophet appeared, the Jews of Medina wrote to the Jews of Khaybar, 'If you follow him we will obey you; if you don't we will do the same.' Those of Khaybar replied, 'We are the sons of the Friend of God. 'Uzay, son of God is from us Jews, and the prophets too.

When was there any prophet among the Arabs? We are more worthy of prophethood than Muhammad, and there is no way we could follow him' (see Abū Ḥayyān, *Tafsīr al-baḥr al-muḥīṭ* (Beirut, 1993), Vol. 8, p. 264).

7 For example, giving prophethood (ibid., p. 263).

8 Abū Ḥayyān is of the view that these are the Jews who were contemporary with the Prophet. They were charged to carry out the Torah's orders and prohibitions and did not (ibid., p. 263).

9 Al-Rāzī, *al-Tafsīr al-kabīr* (Beirut, n.d.), Part 30, p. 5.

10 The use of *al-ummiyyīn* indicates that the verse is specifically directed at the Jews. In other situations, when it is directed at the Muslims, the Qur'an uses the expression *fī-kum/fī-him* or *al-mu'minīn* (Q. 2:129, 151 and Q. 3:164).

11 Bell, *The Qur'an*, p. 579.

12 Alan Jones, *The Qur'ān Translated into English* (Exeter, 2007), p. 518.

13 Jones, Ibid.

14 Al-Bayḍāwī (*Tafsīr* (Beirut, 1988), Vol. 2, p. 493) explains that this is based on the assertion, '*We are the sons of God and His beloved*' (Q. 5:18). Al-Rāzī explains that, according to Ibn 'Abbās, the Prophet invited a group of Jews to Islam and warned them about God's punishment, to which they replied, 'How can you warn us about God's punishment when we are His sons and beloved?' Al-Rāzī continues, 'This relates only to this particular group of Jews' (al-Rāzī, *al-Tafsīr al-kabīr* (Beirut, n.d.), part 11, p. 192).

15 When the Qur'an speaks to the Muslims directly or about the same favour given to them, it does not call them *al-ummiyyīn* (Q. 2:129, 151 and Q. 3:164).

16 Bell asserts, without evidence, that verse 3 was inserted at some later time. Ibid.

17 Bell, ibid.

18 Bell, ibid.

19 Patrick D. Gaffney, 'Friday prayer', in J. D. McAuliffe (ed.), *Encyclopaedia of the Qur'ān* (Leiden, 2005), Vol. 2, pp. 271–2.

20 Bell, ibid. p. 271.

21 Ṣāliḥ b. 'Abd al-'Azīz Āl-Shaykh, *Mawsū'at al-ḥadīth al-sharīf al-kutub al-sitta* (Riyadh, 1999), p. 161.

22 See also Q. 2:267–9 which suggests that what God has is better than any fleeting gain or fear of poverty inspired by Satan.

23 The rhyme scheme, with verses ending in *-īm, -īn* and *-ūn* in Arabic, is a further unifying element.

24 Richard Bell, *The Qur'an*, p. 558.

25 Alan Jones, *The Qur'an: Translated into English*, p. 501.

26 It is true that Nöldeke, too dates verses in his *Geschichte des Qorans* (Göttingen, 1860), but he was writing a history of the Qur'an rather than a translation.
27 Richard Bell, *The Qur'an Translated*, Vol. 2, p. 558.
28 Alan Jones, ibid.
29 The 'dead land' image is frequently used in the Qur'an for the Resurrection, for instance in Q. 22:5 and Q. 41:39.
30 James Robson (trans.), *Mishkat al-masabih* (Lahore, reprint 2006). Available at http://www.dar-us-salam.com/inside/R25-Mishkat.pdf (accessed 24 November 2016).
31 Like those who disbelieve and try to persuade others to disbelieve.
32 See Q. 9:41 and Q. 61:11; compare also Q. 3:186. In Q. 2:195, after the discussion of fighting '*those who attack you*' (verse 191), it says '*give in God's cause and do not contribute to your destruction with your own hands.*' On another occasion the Qur'an castigates the laggards who blamed their friends who died in battle: '*Even if you had resolved to stay at home [and not go out to battle] those of you who were destined to be killed would still have gone out to meet their deaths*' (Q. 3:54).
33 Al-Bukhārī, *al-Ṣaḥīḥ* (many editions) *Kitāb al-jihād*, Hadith 28.
34 This is a common strategy in the Qur'an. It declares, for instance, that '*if God did not repel some people by means of others, many monasteries, churches, synagogues and mosques, where God's name is much invoked, would have been destroyed*' (Q. 22:40). In Q. 2:251, after David kills Goliath the Qur'an says, '*if God did not drive some back by means of others the earth would be completely corrupt.*'
35 The importance of 'iron' here is highlighted by the fact it is the title of the whole sura. Note also how the word 'secretly' in this verse recalls the emphasis on God's infinite knowledge which is repeatedly highlighted at the beginning of the sura.
36 Thus, for example, the obligation to fast in Ramaḍān was introduced in the Qur'an with '*you who believe, fasting is prescribed for you, as it was prescribed for those before you*' (Q. 2:183).
37 In another of the *musabbiḥāt* suras, Q. 62:6, some of the People of the Book claim that they '*out of all people [...] are the friends of God*'.
38 Fakhruddin al-Rāzī, al-*Tafsīr al-kabīr*, for example, Part 7, p. 2; Part 21, p. 10.
39 Aḥmad Ibn Ḥanbal, *Musnad*, Vol. 5, Hadith 26, in A. J. Wensink, *Concordance et Indices de la Tradition Musulmane* (Leiden, 1992), Books V–VI, p. 454. People normally translate the word *qalb* as 'heart', but this is only the first meaning that appears in the dictionary; another meaning is 'core'. The Prophet said, 'Everything has a *qalb*', and this strongly suggests that the meaning is not 'heart', but 'core'.
40 We deal with the views of Richard Bell and Alan Jones below.

41 This is decisive in proving the prophethood of Muhammad; e.g. compare Q. 29:47–51, Q. 26:197 and Q. 11:13. See also al-Rāzī, *al-Tafsīr al-kabīr* (Beirut, n.d.), Vol. 13, part 26, p. 41.

42 Q. 10:31–4, Q. 29:61–3 and Q. 39:3 and 38.

43 The answer to these questions is: '*We know very well what the earth takes away from them: We keep a comprehensive record*' (Q. 50:4).

44 Richard Bell, *The Qur'an*, p. 434.

45 Ibid., Vol. 2, p. 131.

46 Alan Jones, *The Qur'an Translated into English*, p. 402.

47 Jones' (ibid.) assessment that this is simply 'a warning passage' does not give the real focus and intention of this passage.

48 See also the following sura: Q. 37:35–7 has, '*Whenever it was said to them, "There is no deity but God," they became arrogant, and said, "Are we to forsake our gods for a mad poet?" No: he brought the truth and confirmed the earlier messengers.*'

49 Aḥmad Hāshimī, *Jawāhir al-balāgha* (Beirut, 1986), p. 59.

50 Jones, *The Qur'an Translated*, p. 402.

51 Thus he should not be saddened, as stated in verse 76.

52 Jones, following a tradition long held in Western scholarship, reduces the whole story to being a 'punishment story', but what the messengers and the man from the town say actually confirms Muhammad's message and situation. In all 'punishment stories', saving the messengers and the believers are seen by Muslims as being more important (see Q. 10:102–3 and Q. 40:51). Thus, saving Moses and his followers, the resulting revelation of the Torah and the subsequent history of the Jewish nation are seen by Muslims to be more important than drowning Pharaoh at sea.

53 See also Q. 22:5.

54 Similar replies to the question, 'When will the Resurrection be?', are seen elsewhere in the Qur'an. See, for example, Q. 21:38–41, Q. 25:21–30, Q. 36:48–64, Q. 51:12 ff, Q. 67:25–7 and Q. 75:6–15.

55 The interrupting material is not alien, since the whole thrust of the sura is about the Resurrection and Judgement. Interruption of the flow of the discussion at the point of questioning the Day of Resurrection is found in many other places in the Qur'an, such as Q. 51:12–23, Q. 52:9–28 and Q. 69:18–37. The description of the Day is very important to the subject. Since it is only God who knows when the Day will be, it leaves that aside and presents a picture of the event with threats and promises to show them what awaits them.

56 Jones (*The Qur'an Translated*, p. 402) considers verse 69 and the rest of the sura to be a 'peroration', whereas 69–70 are in fact central to the argument from the beginning of the sura.

57 On this, see Q. 21:5, Q. 37:36, Q. 52:30 and Q. 69:41 (‘*It is not the speech of a poet, little do you believe*’).
58 The second half of this verse can also be translated as *‘and they will stand against them as an army’*, compare Q. 28:62–3.
59 See Abdel Haleem Mahmood, *The Creed of Islam* (London, 1976), pp. 71–2, referring to al-Kindī's philosophical *tafsīr* of these verses.
60 Ibid., p. 71–2. See also Q. 40:57 and Q. 50:48.
61 Ibid., p. 71–2.
62 Jones, *The Qur'an Translated*, p. 402.
63 Bell, Ibid.
64 Tammām Ḥassān (*al-Bayān fī mawā'i' al-qur'ān* (Cairo, 2000), Part 2, pp. 395–9) argues, on the basis of comparing different suras in the Qur'an, that the city was Manaf, which is now between Cairo and Saqqara; the two messengers were Moses and Aaron and the third person was an Egyptian who believed alongside Moses.
65 See Chapter 11, ‘The story of Joseph in the Qur'an and the Bible’ in Muhammad A. S. Abdel Haleem, *Understanding the Qur'an: Themes and Style* (London, 2010), pp. 156–7. In the Joseph story, not even the name of his full brother is mentioned in the Qur'an, let alone those of his half-brothers.
66 See Q. 10:22 ff, Q. 31:31–2, Q. 42:32–3, Q. 54:13–14 and Q. 55:24–5.
67 Ibn Ḥanbal, *Musnad* (see note 1).
68 It is commonly believed that when the Prophet had to leave his house by night to flee to Medina, while his opponents were waiting to kill him, he recited these verses and his opponents did not see him leave.
69 Aḥmad Amīn, *Qāmūs al-'ādāt wa'l-taqālīd wa'l-ta'ābīr al-miṣriyya* (Cairo, 1953), p. 284.
70 Al-Rāzī, *al-Tafsīr al-kabīr* (Beirut, n.d.), Vol. 13, Part 26, p. 113.
71 Ibid., Vol. 13, Part 26, p. 113.
72 Al-Bayḍāwī, *Tafsīr* (Beirut, 1988), Vol. 2, p. 288.
73 Ibid., Vol. 2, p. 288.

Chapter 9 Evidential Style: Divine Oaths in the Qur'an

1 This chapter will deal only with studies that have appeared in recent years in English.
2 Ibn al-Qayyim al-Jawziyya, *al-Tibyān fī aqsām al-qur'ān* (Cairo, n.d.), pp.126–32.
3 Ibid., pp. 186–268.
4 Al-Zarkashī, *al-Burhān fī 'ulūm al-qur'ān*, ed. M. A. Ibrahim (Cairo, 1988), pp. 40–6.
5 Al-Suyūṭī, *al-Itqān* (Beirut, 1987), Vol. 2, pp. 370–5.

6 G. R. Smith, 'Oaths in the Qur'an', *Semitics* I (1970), pp. 126–56.
7 Ibid., p. 127.
8 Mustansir Mir, 'The Qur'an oaths: Farahi's interpretation', *Islamic Studies*, Spring Issue, pp. 1–17. Available at http://www.islamic-awareness.org/Quran/Q_Studies/Miroaths.html (accessed 12 April 2016).
9 A. Neuwirth and G. Hawting make no mention of this article in their writings on oaths.
10 Angelika Neuwirth, 'Images and metaphors in the introductory sections of the Meccan suras', in G. R. Hawting and A. A. Shareef (eds), *Approaches to the Qur'an* (New York, 1993), pp. 1–36. A shorter version of this is given in J. D. McAuliffe (ed.), *Encyclopaedia of the Qur'ān* (Leiden, 2004), Vol. 3, pp. 464–8.
11 See discussion below.
12 Neuwirth, 'Images and metaphors', p. 11.
13 Ibid., p. 4.
14 G. R. Hawting, 'Oaths', in J. D. McAuliffe (ed.), *Encyclopaedia of the Qur'ān* (Leiden, 2004), Vol. 3, pp. 561–6.
15 'Compressed grammar' is a valid description but there is nothing unusual at all about the vocabulary.
16 Muhammad A. S. Abdel Haleem, 'Context and internal relationships: Keys to Qur'anic exegesis', in G. R. Hawting and A. A. Shareef (eds), *Approaches to the Qur'an* (New York, 1993), pp. 71–98.
17 Mir ('The Qur'an oaths', p. 4) cites here examples from al-Bayḍāwī, Ibn Kathīr, al-Nisābūrī and Ibn al-Qayyim al-Jawziyya.
18 Al-Rāzī, *al-Tafsīr al-kabīr* (Beirut, n.d.), Part 28, p. 194.
19 Mir, 'The Qur'an oaths', op. cit.
20 Aḥmad al-Hāshimī, *Jawāhir al-balāgha fī'l-ma'ānī wa'l-bayān wa'l-badī'* (Beirut, 1986), pp. 58–9. This gives a handy summary of what all books say about *'ilm al-ma'ānī*, the first of the three branches of *'ilm al-balāgha.*
21 Tammām Ḥassān, *al-Lugha al-'arabiyya: ma'nāhā wa-mabnāhā* (Cairo, 1973), p. 337 and p. 372.
22 Tenets of faith continued to be referred to in the Medinan Qur'an to remind the believers and urge them to action, for example, '*if you truly believe in God and the Last Day*' (Q. 2:232 and Q. 65:2).
23 Mir, 'The Qur'an oaths', pp. 7–9.
24 Neuwirth, 'Images and metaphors'.
25 In the present context see Q. 21:19–26, Q. 34:40–1, Q. 36:149–60 and Q. 78:37–8.
26 Q. 16:57–60, Q. 37:151–7 and Q. 43:15–21.
27 Muhammad A. S. Abdel Haleem, *Understanding the Qur'an: Themes and Style* (London, 2001), Chapter 12.

28 Al-Rāzī, *al-Tafsīr al-kabīr*, Part 26, pp. 116–17.
29 Neuwirth, op. cit.
30 Al-Suyūṭī, *Tafsīr al-Jalālayn* (Baghdad, n.d.), under verse 3 of *Sūrat al-Ḍuḥā*; al-Bayḍawī, *al-Tafsīr* (Beirut, 1998), Vol. 2, pp. 603–4.
31 Al-Rāzī, *al-Tafsīr al-kabīr*, Part 28, p. 279.
32 Abdullah Ibn 'Abbas' suggestion, followed by M. Asad in his translation, that *najm* refers to the gradual unfolding of the Qur'an could be seen to have validity with regard to the statement in verse 3, '*he does not speak from his own desire*' (i.e. the revelation descends on him), but is less relevant to verse 2, '*he has not strayed nor is he deluded*'. This is more the result of being guided when aided by the star. Several Qur'anic references show that such guidance comes from the sun, the moon and the stars.
33 J. Wellhausen and K. Wagtendonk cited by Neuwirth, 'Images and metaphors', p. 35.
34 Whoever does a good deed will have ten times the reward for it (Q. 6:160) and the Meccans are challenged to bring ten suras like the Qur'an (Q. 11:13), which is the maximum number of suras they were ever challenged to bring. The remedy for a certain flaw in the performance of the Hajj is that the person should fast for three days during the Hajj and seven days later at home (*tilka 'ashratun kāmilatun*, 'that is ten complete [days altogether]'; see also Q. 5:89, Q. 7:142 and Q. 28:27).
35 It was also suggested this could mean God, the One and his creatures, which are multiple, or all things which are either *shaf'* or *watr*. In any case, the dichotomy suggests that the situation will change and the hardship will be followed by ease.
36 Using *ḥijr* for 'mind' here suggests it should stop a *taḥjūr* person from impatience or doubt.
37 The Meccan disbelievers challenged the Prophet to make the sky fall down on them in fragments (Q. 17:92).
38 According to this logic, the pronoun in *raj'ihi* in verse 8 should refer to the fluid, but then it would mean 'God is able to put it back in the loin'!
39 This argument is used in other places in the Qur'an: He who created it the first time can do it again (Q. 17:51). In fact, the second creation is easier than the first (Q. 30:27).
40 Academy of the Arabic Language, *Mu'jam alfāẓ al-qur'ān al-karīm* (Cairo, 1988), Vol. 1, p. 477.
41 Neuwirth ('Images and metaphors', p. 25), following Bell's translation, did not find a proper meaning of *raj'* or *ṣad'* and commented 'suggesting a vain security and will lead to a phase of trial'.
42 Al-Suyūṭī, *Tafsīr al-Jalālayn*.
43 Al-Bayḍāwi, *al-Tafsīr*.

44 Neuwirth, op. cit., pp. 9–10.
45 Mir, op. cit. under 'Phenomenal oaths'.
46 Jalāl al-Dīn al-Suyūṭī, Tafsīr, Surat al-Mursalat (77), p. 777.
47 Bayḍāwi, Tafsīr, Sura 77, Vol. 2, p. 556.
48 See *naza'a, nashaṭa, sabaḥa, sabaqa* and *dabbara* in Academy of the Arabic Language, *Mu'jam alfāẓ al-qur'ān al-karīm* (Cairo, 1988) and E. Badawi and M. Abdel Haleem, *Arabic–English Dictionary of Qur'anic Usage* (Leiden, 2007).
49 Even in Arberry, whose translation in general is better than all that preceded it.
50 A. J. Arberry, *The Koran Interpreted* (Oxford, 1964), p. 628.
51 Significantly, *al-'ādiyāt* is placed between *al-zalzala* (Q. 99) and *al-qāri'a* (Q. 101).
52 Al-Rāzī, *al-Tafsīr al-kabīr*, Vol. 15, Part 30, p. 217.
53 A. Neuwirth, G. Hawting, R. Bell and A. Jones.
54 Smith, 'Oaths in the Qur'an', p. 156.
55 See also Sidney Griffith, 'Christian Lore and Arabic Qur'ān: The "Companions of the Cave" in *Sūrat al-Kahf* and in Syriac Christian Tradition', in G.S. Reynolds (ed.), *The Qur'an in its Historical Context*, Routledge Studies in the Qur'an (London, 2008), pp. 109–35, at p. 116.
56 See al-Bayḍawī's (*al-Tafsīr*, p. 427) comments on Q. 51:1–6.
57 Mir, 'The Qur'an oaths', p. 8.
58 Ibid., p. 3.
59 Q. 18:47, Q. 52:10 and Q. 78:20.
60 This oath begins with '*lā*' like all oaths using the verb *uqsimu*, of which there are eight in the Qur'an: Q. 56, Q. 69, Q. 70, Q. 75 (twice), Q. 81, Q. 84, and Q. 90.
61 Al-Rāzī, Tafsīr *Surat Al-Hāqqa*, Part 30, p. 116.
62 See verse 26.
63 Oaths taken in English culture normally have the function of lending support to a claim that is made. 'I swear by my life that what I am telling you is true' or 'I swear by my honour…' say: if I am not telling you the truth, then my life shall be taken away from me – or then I shall lose my honour. So, the function of the oath is, as it is in the Quran, to lend support to a claim, but the thing sworn by ('my life', 'my child's life', 'my honour') is not something that is taken as an image analogous to the image of the claim, as seems to be the case in the Quran. When the Quran says 'By the morning brightness and by the night when it grows still, your Lord has not forsaken you…', it establishes an analogous case between (a) the alternation of night and day and (b) the alteration of the Prophet's situation. So the oath here says 'As much as it is the case that night follows day and they change, it is the case that your situation will change in the same way'.

64 Smith, 'Oaths in the Qur'an', p. 142. Footnotes giving the various meanings suggested by the *mufassirīn* for the *fā'ilāt* adjectives have been omitted.
65 Mir, 'The Qur'an oaths', p. 7.
66 Neuwirth, 'Images and metaphors', pp. 9–10.

Chapter 10 Rhetorical Style: Arabic of the Qur'an

1 John Burton, 'Linguistic errors in the Qur'an', *Journal of Semitic Studies* xxxiii/2 (Autumn 1988), pp. 181–96. See also Muhammad A. S. Abdel Haleem, 'Grammatical shifts for rhetorical purposes: *Iltifāt* and related features in the Qur'an', *Bulletin of the School of Oriental and African Studies* Vol. LV, Part 3 (1992), pp. 423–31.
2 John Wansbrough, *Qur'anic Studies: Sources and Methods of Scriptural Interpretation*, London Oriental Series, 31 (Oxford, 1977), p. 220.
3 Abū 'Ubayda, *Majāz al-qur'ān* (Cairo, 1954), Vol. 1, p. 8. See also Sībawayhī, *al-Kitāb* (Cairo, 1988), Vol. 1, pp. 331–2.
4 Ḍiyā al-Dīn Ibn al-Athīr, *al-Mathal as-sā'ir fī 'adab al-kātib wa'l-shā'ir* (Cairo, 1939).
5 Jalāl al-Dīn al-Suyūṭī, *Itqan fi 'ulūm al-qur'ān* (Cairo, 1987), Vol. 2 p. 348.
6 Muḥammad 'Ubāda, *'Usūr al-ihtijāj fī'l-nahw al-'arabī* (Cairo, 1980), Vol. 1, pp. 68–108.
7 Tammām Ḥassān, *al-Bayān fī rawā'i' al-qur'ān* (Cairo, 1993), p. 283.
8 Ibid., pp. 7–8.
9 Abdel Haleem, 'Grammatical shift', p. 426.
10 Burton, 'Linguistic errors', p. 177.
11 Abū 'Ubayda, *Majāz al-qur'ān*, Vol. 1, p. 165 and p. 173.
12 Badruddin Al-Zarkashī, *al-Burhān fī 'ulūm al-qur'ān* (Cairo, 1957), Vol. 3, p. 325.
13 Abū 'Ubayda, *Majāz al-qur'ān*, Vol. 2, pp. 21–2.
14 Abdel Haleem, 'Grammatical shift', pp. 428–9.
15 Theodor Nöldeke, *Neue Beiträge zur semitischen Sprachwissenschaft* (Strassburg, 1910), p. 13.
16 Ḍiya al-Din Ibn al-'Athīr, *al-Mathal as-sā'ir fī 'adab al-kātib wa'l-shā'ir* (Cairo, 1971), Vol. 2, pp. 43–5.
17 Muhammad A. S. Abdel Haleem, 'Context and internal relationships: Keys to Qur'anic exegesis', in A. A. Shareef and G. R. Hawting (eds), *Approaches to the Qur'an* (London, 1993), p. 431.
18 Tammām Ḥassān, *al-Lugha al-'arabiyya: ma'nāhā wa-mabnāhā* (Cairo, 1973), pp. 243–6; Tammām Ḥassān, *al-Bayān*, pp. 56–7.
19 Ibn Hishām, *Mughnī al-labīb*, ed. 'Amāyra and al-Sayyid (Cairo, 1988).
20 Ḥassān, *al-Bayān*, p. 95.

21 ʻIzzedīn Ibn ʻAbd as-Salām, *Majāz al-qur'ān* (London, 1999). See also Abū ʻUbayda, *Majāz al-qur'ān*, Vol. 1, pp. 26–46 and pp. 261–471.
22 Abu Isḥāq Al-Shāṭibī, *al-Muwāfaqāt fī ʻuṣul al-sharīʻa* (Beirut, 1975), Vol. 3, pp. 353–4.
23 Abdel Haleem, ʻContext', pp. 71–98.
24 ʻAbd al-Razzāq Nawfal, *al-Iʻjāz al-ʻadadī fī'l-qur'ān al-karīm* (Cairo, 1976).
25 See also Ḥassān, *al-Bayān*, Part 2, chapter on *al-ḥiwār*, pp. 275–89.
26 ʻPlace your hand wherever you wish on the text of the Quran and count the number of words in the statements you see. Then compare this to what you consider most eloquent outside the Quran and then compare the amount of meaning in the two texts. Consider further how many words you can drop or replace from the Quran without disturbing the meaning and purpose of the statement' (M. A. Draz, *al-Nabā' al-aẓīm* (Kuwait, 1984), p. 112).
27 See below under the treatment of Arabic calligraphy outside Arabia.
28 Sayyid Quṭb, *al-Taṣwīr al-fannī fī'l-qur'ān* (Cairo, 1966).
29 Ahmad Mukhtar Omar, ʻThe *fāṣila* in the Qur'an: Word, context and meaning', *Journal of Qur'anic Studies* 1 (1999), pp. 220–38.
30 Ḥassān, *al-Bayān*, p. 187.
31 Aḥmad al-Hāshimī, *Jawāhir al-balāgha fī'l-maʻānī wa'l-bayān wa'l-badīʻ* (Beirut, 1986), p. 239.
32 Muḥammad Ḥassan ʻAbd Allāh, *al-Islamiyya wa al-rūḥaniyya fī* ʻadab *Najīb Maḥfūẓ* (Cairo, 2001); Rajā 'al-Naqqāsh, *Najīb Maḥfūẓ: safahat min mudhakkiratihi wa adawa'ja* Muḥammad Ḥassan ʻAbd Allāh, *ala adabihi wa hayatihi* (Cairo, 1998); Abdel Haleem, ʻGrammatical shift', p. 432; Muhammad A. S. Abdel Haleem, *Understanding the Qur'an: Themes and Style* (London, 2001), p. 207, f. 52.

Chapter 11 The Arabic Qur'an in the Muslim World

1 Around the beginning of the twentieth century in Egypt, for instance, there were calls for the adoption of English or of the Roman script for writing, or even the local Arabic dialect of Egypt. These were fiercely rejected because it would have meant severing the connection with the language of the Qur'an and the rich history of Arab-Islamic culture.
2 The angel Gabriel merely transmitted the Qur'an to Muhammad: ʻ*This Qur'an has been sent down to you by the Lord of the Worlds: the Trustworthy Spirit brought it down to your heart, Prophet*' (Q. 28:192–4).
3 See Yasin Hamid Safadi, *Islamic Calligraphy* (London, 1987), 144 pp.; Martin Lings, *Splendours of Qur'anic Calligraphy and Illumination* (Vaduz, Liechtenstein, 2004).

4 See Chapter 9 of this book.
5 Thus the Qur'an is not a book of history, science or literature as such.
6 On His existence, see for example Q. 30:19–27 and Q. 27:60–4. On His oneness, see Q. 17:42–4, Q. 21:21–4 and Q. 27:60–4.
7 See, e.g. Q. 10:16, Q. 21:3–9, Q. 29:48 and Q. 52:30–4.
8 See, e.g. Q. 36:77–82 and Q. 56:57–73.
9 See, e.g. Q. 23:115–16, Q. 38:27–8, Q. 45:21–2 and Q. 95:7–8.
10 Al-Rāzī, *al-Tafsīr al-kabīr* (Beirut, n.d.), Vol. 1, Part 2, p. 90.
11 Ibid., Vol. 1, Part 2, pp. 88–9.
12 i.e. 951–1174 CE.
13 See Kees Versteegh, *The Arabic Language* (Edinburgh, 1997), Chapter on 'Arabic as a world language', pp. 226–40.
14 Ibid., p. 229.
15 Mervyn Hiskett, *A History of Hausa Islamic Verse* (London, 1975), p. 27.
16 Farouk Topan, 'Swahili as a religious language', *Journal of Religion in Africa* xxii/4 (1992), pp. 331–49; Farouk Topan, 'Projecting Islam: Narrative in Swahili poetry', *Journal of African Cultural Studies* xiv/1 (2001), pp. 107–19; Farouk Topan, 'Muslim literature in sub-Saharan Africa', in A. Nanji (ed.), *The Muslim Almanac* (New York, 1996), pp. 365–9.
17 Kees Versteegh, *The Arabic Language*, p. 231.
18 Ibid., p. 231.
19 Ibid., p. 234.
20 Ibid., p. 232.
21 Ibid., p. 237.
22 Ibid.
23 Ibid., p. 238.
24 Christopher Shackle and Stefan Sperl (eds), *Qasida Poetry in Islamic Asia and Africa* (Leiden, 1996), p. 16.
25 See the chapter on *al-Fātiḥah* in Muhammad A. S. Abdel Haleem, *Understanding the Qur'an: Themes and Style* (London, 2001), pp. 15–28.
26 Even though, according to one religious interpretation, it is permissible for those who cannot read Arabic to read the prayers in a foreign tongue, but this rare view is opposed by the vast majority of Muslim experts on Islamic law and is not practised anywhere in the Islamic world.
27 https://archive.org/stream/kitabsibawayh/KitabSibawaih_0#page/no/mode/2up (accessed 24 November 2016).
28 Starting with the Ṭāhirid dynasty (821–73 CE) and continuing under the later dynasties, Saffarid, Samānids and Ghaznāwids. See Muhammad Ghunaimi Hilal, *Mukhtarāt min al-shi'r al-fārisī* (Cairo, 1965), p. 7.

29 Ibid., p. 5.
30 Ibid., p. 9.
31 Ibid., p. 195.
32 Ibid., p. 225.
33 Muhammad Ghunaimi Hilal, *al-Adab al-muqāran* (Cairo, 1977), p. 302.
34 There are now many schools, publishing houses, educational institutions, media outlets and publications called *Iqra'*. For example, a series of publications in Cairo is called *Iqra'*; there is an educational institution in Arabia with branches in other countries including Britain and America called *Iqra'*; and an Arab television channel also bears the same name.

Chapter 12 English Translations of the Qur'an: The Making of an Image

1 This chapter is based on a lecture delivered at SOAS, University of London in 1997.
2 Robert of Ketton, *Lex Mahumet pseudoprophete que arabice Alchoran, id est collectio praeceptorum vocatur,* Paris BnF, MS Arsenal 1162, fols 26–140 and many other manuscripts.
3 Ludovico Marracci, *Alcorani Textus Universus* (Padua, 1698).
4 George Sale, *The Koran: Commonly Called the Alcoran of Mohammed, translated into English immediately from the original Arabic, with explanatory notes, taken from the most approved commentators, to which is prefixed a preliminary discourse* (London, 1734).
5 Ketton, *Lex Mahumet* (op. cit.).
6 Robert of Ketton, *Lex Mahumet...*, edited by Theodor Bibliander in *Muchametis saracenorum principis eiusque successorum vitae, ac doctrina ipseque Alcoran [...].* (Basel, 1550 CE).
7 Giles Constable (ed.), *Letters of Peter the Venerable: Champion of Cluny* (Cambridge, MA; Oxford, UK, 1967), Vol. 1, Ep. 111, p. 298.
8 Peter the Venerable (d. 1159), *Liber contra sectam sive heresim Saracenorum* (*A Book against the Sect or Heresy of the Saracens*).
9 'Although he received support from the Church – he became Archdeacon of Pamplona in 1143 – Robert's preference was for translating scientific rather than theological works. He is known to have studied Euclid and to have translated the work of Al Battani and Avicenna, and it seems that he would not have made the translation for which he is famous, that of the Qur'an, without the encouragement of the French Abbot Peter the Venerable, who wished to have access to Islamic texts.' Available at https://en.wikipedia.org/wiki/Robert_of_Ketton (accessed 24 November 2016).

10 Perhaps he would have done better with the Abbasid caliph al-Ma'mūn in ninth-century Baghdad, who used to give the prominent translators into Arabic the weight of their manuscript in gold.
11 Norman Daniel, *Islam and the West: The Making of an Image* (Edinburgh, 1960), quoted in Oliver Leaman (ed.), *The Qur'an: an Encyclopaedia* (London and New York, 2006), p. 667.
12 Hartmut Bobzin, *Der Koran im Zeitalter der Reformation: Studien zur Frühgeshcichte der Arabistik und Islamkunde in Europa* (Beirut, 1995), p. 61.
13 See, e.g. Riccoldo da Monte Croce, Dominican Monk 1242–1320, *Libellus contra legem saracenorum.* First published in Seville, 1500, under the title *Confutatio Alcorani* (*Confutation of the Koran*). This work was translated into German (*Verlegung des Alcoran*) by Martin Luther in 1542.
14 They later became the chief agents of the Inquisition.
15 Riccoldo da Monte Croce, *Libellius contra legem sarracenorum,* first published in Seville, op. cit. Available at https://en.wikipedia.org/wiki/Riccoldo_da_Monte_di_Croce#Apologetic_writings_against_Islam_and_Judaism (accessed December 2015). See Daniel, *Islam and the West,* p. 78.
16 Daniel, *Islam and the West,* p. 78.
17 Ibid., p. 81.
18 Ibid., p. 85.
19 Ketton literally translated Q. 33:56 (in Latin) as 'God and His angels bless the Prophet'.
20 Hartmut Bobzin, 'Latin translations of the Koran: A short overview', *Der Islam* 70 (1993), p. 196.
21 Ibid., p. 196.
22 Ibid.
23 Ibid.
24 Alexander Ross and André Du Ryer, *The Alcoran of Mahomet, translated out of the Arabick into French/by the Sieur du Ryer, ... and newly Englished, for the satisfaction of all that desire to look into the Turkish vanities* (London, 1688).
25 Sidney Lee (ed.), *Dictionary of National Biography* (London, 1897), p. 252.
26 *Caveat* in Nabil Matar, *Islam in Britain: 1558–1685* (Cambridge, New York, 1998), p. 85.
27 Ibid., pp. 86–7.
28 Ibid., p. 88.
29 Arthur J. Arberry, *Inaugural Lecture at the Cambridge School of Arabic* (n.p., 1948), p. 8.
30 Mordechai Feingold, 'Patrons and professors: The origins and motives of endowments of university chairs – especially the Laudian professorship of Arabic' in G. A. Russell (ed.), *The 'Arabick' Interest of the Natural Philosophers in Seventeenth-Century England* (Leiden, 1994), pp. 109–27.

31 Edward Henry Palmer, *The Qur'an* (Oxford, 1880).
32 Luigi [Ludovico] Marracci, *Alcorani textus universus* (Padua, 1698).
33 E. Denison Ross, 'Ludovico Marracci', *Bulletin of the School of Oriental and African Studies* ii/1 (February 1921), p. 117.
34 Sir Leslie Stephen and Sir Sidney Lee (eds), *Dictionary of National Biography* (Oxford, 1921–22), p. 179.
35 Sale, 'The life of George Sale', in *The Koran: Commonly Called the Alcoran of Mohammed*, p. xii.
36 Sir Edward Denison Ross, 'Introduction', to *The Koran: Translated into English from the original Arabic* by George Sale (London, n.d.), p. ix. 'Marracci not only reproduced the whole of the Arabic text of the Qur'an, fully vocalized, but also displays very extensive reading, and, what is very important and unusual, reproduces the original text, in addition to the Latin rendering, of all the quotations he makes from Arabic authors.'
37 Compare Peter the Venerable's title for the Qur'an in the Toledan Corpus: *Lex Saracenorum* (*The Law of the Saracens*).
38 George Sale, 'Dedication to Lord Carteret', in *The Koran: Commonly Called the Alcoran of Mohammed*, no page number.
39 George Sale, 'To the reader', in *The Koran: Commonly Called The Alcoran of Mohammed*, p. iv. Sale proceeds to outline a strategy for converting the Muslims based on that which the 'worthy bishop Kidder [...] prescribed for the conversion of the Jews, which, *mutatis mutandis*, may be applied to the former [the Muslims] notwithstanding the despicable opinion that the writer, for want of being better acquainted with them, entertained of those people, judging them scarce fit to be argued with.' This amounts to a swingeing critique of the methods attempted so far and which must be avoided: using compulsion, teaching doctrines against common sense, using weak arguments and ill words, quitting articles of the Christian faith in order to gain the Mohammedans (although the Church of Rome 'ought to part with many practices and some doctrines').
40 Stephen and Lee, *Dictionary*, p. 179.
41 G. Sale, 'Letter to the reader', in *The Koran: Commonly Called the Alcoran of Mohammed*, p. vi.
42 Ibid., p. vii.
43 Ibid.
44 George Sale, *The Koran: Commonly Called the Alcoran of Mohammed.* Burnham, 'The Life of Muhammad or the History of that Discourse ... which has subjugated nearly as large a portion of the globe as the religion of Jesus has set at liberty'.
45 The Nile Mission Arabic translation of Sale's *Introduction to Islam* (trans. Hashim al-Arabi (Cairo, 1909), pp. 305–400) added refutations to the notes

and three more chapters, 'including what escaped the knowledge of Sale or it was not his task to do since he only presented the information', that is, 'to show the faults in what Muslim historians and commentators on the Qur'an have said'. It says that Sale was 'so removed from bias that some of his Christian countrymen accused him of having slipped out of Christianity'.

46 Bernard Lewis and Peter Malcolm Holt (eds), *Historical Writing on the Peoples of Asia* (n.p., 1962), p. 299.

47 Rodwell was a contemporary and friend of Charles Darwin.

48 Stephen and Lee, *Dictionary*, p. 304.

49 Theodor Nöldeke, *Geschichte des Qorâns* (Beirut, 2004) in Arabic.

50 John Medows Rodwell, *The Koran translated from the Arabic* (New York and London, 1968), Preface, p. 2. He neglected any study of the language and style of the Qur'an and became busy with his other tasks.

51 Ibid., p. 2.

52 Ibid., pp. 13–14.

53 Ibid., p. 15.

54 Ibid.

55 Ibid.

56 See, for instance, Abū Isḥāq alShāṭibī, *al-Muwāfaqāt fī uṣūl al-sharī'a* (Beirut, 1975), Vol. 3, pp. 353–4.

57 Stephen and Lee, *Dictionary*, p. 304.

58 Rodwell, *The Koran*, Preface, p. 17.

59 Carl Ernst, quoted at Adabiyat@lists.uchicago.edu [email list] (accessed 3 July 2012).

60 Arthur J. Arberry, *The Cambridge School of Arabic: An Inaugural Lecture Delivered on 30 October 1947* (Cambridge, 1948), p. 27.

61 Ibid., p. 28.

62 Palmer, *The Qur'an*, Part I, Chapters I to XVI, Introduction, p. xlvi.

63 Ibid., p. xlviii.

64 Ibid., p. liv.

65 Ibid., p. lxxx.

66 Ibid., p. lxxviii.

67 Ibid.

68 Ibid., p. lxxix.

69 For instance, he says, 'Anyone can see how little its claim to confirm and perfect the teaching of the former prophets is worth' (Palmer, *The Koran*, Introduction, p. vi). This statement shows that Nicholson did not properly understand the Qur'an's assertion that it confirms earlier scriptures. Similarly, Alan Jones, in his introduction to the 1994 edition of Rodwell's translation says, 'It is difficult to reconcile the very specific references to, for example, Muhammad's family (cf. for example 33:28–33) with the belief

that each prophet has received the same message' (p. xxv). The fact is that, in the Arabic Qur'an, confirmation of earlier scriptures does not mean what Nicholson and Jones seem to understand by it, but is confined to the basic beliefs in One God and the concepts of justice and the Last Judgement. See, for instance, 'We never sent any messenger before you [Muhammad] without revealing to him, "There is no God but Me, so serve Me"' (Q. 21:25). Also: 'In matters of faith, He laid down to you the same commandment that He gave Noah, which We have revealed to you [Muhammad] and which We enjoined on Abraham, Moses and Jesus: "Uphold the faith and do not divide into factions in it – what you [Prophet] call upon the idolaters to do is hard for them"' (Q. 42:13). Likewise: 'We sent down to you [Muhammad] the scripture with the truth, confirming the scripture that came before it and as a guardian over them [...] We have assigned a law and a path to each of you' (Q. 5:48). Furthermore: 'The Sabbath was made obligatory only for those who differed about it' (Q. 16:124 and Q. 6:146).

70 'Abd Allāh 'Abbās al-Nadawī, *Tarjamāt ma'ānī al-qur'ān al-karīm* (Jeddah, 1972), pp. 72–3.

71 Muhammad Marmaduke Pickthall, *The Meaning of the Holy Qur'an* (London, 193), Foreword, first page.

72 Ibid., first page.

73 Anthony H. Johns, 'Ellipsis in the Qur'an: A response to Saleh Salim Ali', *Hamdard Islamicus* xviii/2 (1995), pp. 15–23.

74 Richard Bell, The Gunning lectures, Edinburgh University, 1925. Available at http://muhammadanism.com/bell/origin/poooi.htm (accessed 13 April 2016).

75 Richard Bell, *The Qur'an Translated with a Critical Rearrangement of the Surahs* (Edinburgh, 1937), Vol. 1, Preface, p. vi.

76 Ibid., p. vi.

77 Ibid., p. viii.

78 Ibid.

79 Bell's assertions that certain parts of the Suras had hardly anything to do with each other are at complete variance with what can be deduced from the Arabic material. See, for instance, *Sūrat al-*'Alaq (Q. 95), where Bell ignores the verbal and semantic connections between the two parts he distinguishes.

80 Richard Bell, *The Qur'an Translated* (Edinburgh, 1937), C. Edmund Bosworth and M. E. J. Richardson (eds), Vol. 1, Preface, p. vi.

81 Arthur J. Arberry, *The Koran Interpreted: A Translation* (New York, 1996), Preface, p. 23.

82 Richard Bell, op. cit.

83 Arberry, *The Koran Interpreted*, p. 28.

84 Arthur J. Arberry, *The Koran Interpreted* (Oxford, 1964), Introduction, p. xiii.

85 Ibid., p. x.
86 Arberry, Preface to *The Koran Interpreted* (New York, 1996), op. cit. p. 25.
87 Ibid., p. 25.
88 Ibid., p. 28.
89 Ibid., p. 26.
90 Ibid., p. 28.
91 Watt, *Companion to the Qur'an* (Oxford, 1994), 2nd edition.
92 See 'The Qur'an into English: A translator's apology' in Kenneth Cragg, *Readings in the Qur'an* (Brighton, 1999), p. 49.
93 Abdul Latif Tibawi, 'Second critique of English-speaking orientalists and their approach to Islam and the Arabs', *The Islamic Quarterly* xxiii/1 (1979), pp. 3–54.
94 Daniel, *Islam and the West.*
95 William Montgomery Watt, *Muhammad: Prophet and Statesman* (London, 1961), p. 231. See also Thomas Carlyle, *On Heroes, Hero Worship and the Heroic in History: Six Lectures, Reported, With Emendations and Additions* (New York, 1866), p. 39: 'The lies (Western slander) which well-meaning zeal has heaped round this man (Muhammad) are disgraceful to ourselves only.'
96 Rodwell uses less literalism than others, but there are still some examples.
97 Muhammad A. S. Abdel Haleem, 'Grammatical shifts for rhetorical purposes: *Iltifāt* and related features in the Qur'an', *Bulletin of the School of Oriental and African Studies* Vol. LV, Part 3 (1992), pp. 423–31.
98 Two of the earliest studies dedicated to this feature were *al-Wujūh wa-al-naẓā'ir fi al-qur'ān al-karīm* by Ḥatim Ṣāliḥ and *al-wujūh wa'l-naẓā'ir li-alfāẓ kitāb Allāh al-*'azīz by Abū 'Abd Allāh al-Ḥusayn b. Muḥammad al-Damaghānī (d. 478/1085).
99 Al-Zarkashī, *al-Burhān*, Vol. 1, pp. 111–54.
100 Al-Suyūṭī, *al-Itqān*, Vol. 2, pp. 381–92.
101 Richard Bell and William Montgomery Watt, *Introduction to the Qur'an* (Edinburgh, 1970), pp. 82–5.
102 Toshihiko Izutsu, *The Structure of the Ethical Terms in the Qur'an* (Tokyo, 1959), pp. 113–67.
103 A. T. Welch, R. Paret, and J. D. Pearson, 'al-Ḳur'ān', in P. Bearman et al., *Encyclopaedia of Islam*, 2nd edition. http://dx.doi.org/10.1163/1573-3912_islam_COM_0543 (accessed 24 November 2016).
104 Tammām Ḥassān, *al-Bayān fī rawā'i' al-qur'ān* (Cairo, 1993), pp. 429–30.
105 Q. 52:30, Q. 36:69 and passim.

Chapter 13 Translations of the Qur'an and Interfaith Relations

1 Both quotations are from Arthur J. Arberry, *The Koran Interpreted* (London, 1955).

2 Muhammad Fu'ād'Abd al-Bāqī, *al-Mu'jam al-mufahras li-alfāẓ al-qur'ān* (Cairo, 1945), p. 406.

3 This refers to a case where some Jews came to the Prophet to judge between them, hoping he would give them a judgement more lenient than the one in the Torah. See al-Bayḍāwī, *al-Tafsīr* (Beirut, 1988), Vol. 1, p. 267.

4 Alfred Guillaume, *The Life of Muhammad: A Translation of Ibn Ishaq's Sirat Rasul Allah* (Oxford, 1955; 4th impression, 1974), p. 231.

5 This was a retort to Q. 2:245, a verse often used by the Prophet when asking for financial contributions to the cause.

6 This is taken to refer to an actual event in which a group of disbelieving Meccans went to two eminent Jewish figures in Medina for counsel on the truth of Muhammad's teachings and were told that the idolaters were more rightly guided than the Muslims. See al-Bayḍāwī, *al-Tafsīr*, Vol. 1, p. 219.

7 See, for instance, Q. 7:59–170, Q. 11:25–108 and Q. 11:120.

8 'Abd al-Bāqī, *al-Mu'jam*, under 'Maryam'.

9 e.g. dietary laws as in Q. 5:146.

10 See C. Jonn Block, *The Qur'an in Christian-Muslim Dialogue: Historical and Modern Interpretations* (Abingdon, New York, 2014), p. 24.

11 Similarly, the Qur'an does not mention the belief that Jesus died on the cross to take away the original sin and absolve his followers, for two reasons. First, the concept of original sin is alien to the Qur'an. It recounts that Adam erred and God inspired him with the prayer of repentance and accepted his repentance. Second, on the Day of Judgement, '*every soul is held in pledge for its own deeds*' (Q. 74:38), '*and no soul will be able to do anything for another. On that Day, command will belong to God*' (Q. 82:19). Muhammad is instructed to say, 'I have no control over benefit or harm, [even] to myself, except as God may please' (Q. 7:188).

12 Muslims take the view that when Muslim husbands believe in the prophethood of Moses and Jesus, they allow their Christian or Jewish wife to keep her faith and practices, whereas Jewish and Christian husbands, who do not believe in Muhammad and his message with its beliefs and practices, which a Muslim woman should adhere to.

13 Said Badawi and Muhammad A. S. Abdel Haleem, *An Arabic–English Dictionary of Qur'anic Usage* (Leiden, 2007).

14 Hārūn ibn Mūsā (d. *c.*170 AH/786 CE), *al-Wujūh wa-l-naẓā'ir fi-l-qur'ān al-karīm* (Baghdad, 1989).

15 This case involved adultery, hoping the Prophet would give a lighter penalty of lashing instead of stoning. See al-Bayḍāwī, *al-Tafsīr*, Vol. 1, pp. 266–7.

16 See the discussion in Michael Cook, *The Koran: A Very Short Introduction*, op.cit. pp. 98–100.
17 See, for instance, al-Bayḍāwī, *al-Tafsīr*, Vol. 1, p. 67, but he also quotes Mujāhid as disagreeing with his opinion and saying that they were just likened to apes and pigs just as they were likened to the donkey.
18 See Chapter 8, section '*Sūrat al-Jumu'a* (Q. 62)' on the unity of suras.
19 See, for example, Michael Cook, *The Koran: A Very Short Introduction* (Oxford, New York, 2000), pp. 33–4.
20 Al-Rāzī, *al-Tafsīr al-kabīr* (Beirut, n.d.), Part 7, p. 208.
21 Ibid., Part 4, p. 72.
22 'First' here and in other similar contexts in the Qur'an does not mean literally 'first' (compare Q. 7:143, Q. 26:51 and Q. 39:12). Perhaps 'foremost' might be closer to the meaning.
23 Q. 14:7.
24 Badawi and Haleem, *Dictionary*, p. 809.
25 Saheeh International, *The Qur'an: Arabic Text with Corresponding English Meanings* (Jeddah, 2004).
26 Majīd Fakhry, *An Interpretation of the Qur'an: English Translation of the Meanings: A Bilingual Edition* (New York, 2004).
27 Muhammad Asad, *The Message of the Qur'an* (Gibraltar, London, 1980).

Bibliography

'Abd al-Barr, Ibn, *al-Durrar fī Ikhtiṣār al-maghāzī wa'l-siyar* (Cairo, 1966).

'Abd Allāh, Muḥammad Ḥassan, *'Alā adabihi wa ḥayātihi* (Cairo, 1998).

———. *Al-Islāmiyya wa'l-riyāya fī 'adab Najīb Maḥfūẓ* (Cairo, 2001).

Abdel Haleem, M. A. S., 'Grammatical shift for rhetorical purposes: *Iltifāt* and related features in the Qur'an', *Bulletin of the School of Oriental and African Studies* Vol. LV, Part 3 (1992), pp. 423–31.

———. 'Context and internal relationships: Keys to Qur'anic exegesis', in G. R. Hawting and A. A. Shareef (eds), *Approaches to the Qur'an* (New York, 1993), pp. 71–98.

———. *Understanding the Qur'an: Themes and Styles* (London, 1999, 2001).

———. 'How to read the Qur'an: *Sūrat al-Ḥadīd* (Q. 57)', *Journal of Qur'anic Studies* 10 (2008) (see Chapter 8, section 'Sūrat al-Hadīd (Q. 57)' below).

———. *The Quran: A New Translation* (Oxford, 2010).

———. 'Qur'anic *"jihad"*: A linguistic and contextual analysis', *Journal of Qur'anic Studies* 12 (2010), pp. 147–66.

'Ali, Yusuf, *The Holy Qur'an: Text, Translation and Commentary* (Lahore, 1969), p. 10, *Sunan al-Dārimī, Nikaḥ*, Hadith 45 (many editions).

Āl Shaikh, Salih bin 'Abdel Aziz, *al-kutub al-sitta* (Riyadh, Dar al-Salam, 1999).

———. *Mawsū'at al-ḥadīth al-sharīf al-kutub al-sitta* (Riyadh, 1999).

Amīn, Aḥmad, *Qāmūs al-'ādāt wa'l-taqālīd wa'l-ta'ābīr al-miṣriyya* (Cairo, 1953).

'Āmirī, Abu al-Hassan Muhammad ibn Yusuf al-, *Kitāb al-I'lām bi-manāqib al-islām*, ed. A. Ghurab (Cairo, 1967).

'Aqqad, 'Abbās Maḥmūd, *Falsafat al-qur'ān* (Cairo, n.d.).

———. *Ḥaqā'iq al-Islām wa-abāṭīl ḥusūmihi* (Cairo, 1957).

———. *'Abqariyyat Muhammad* (Beirut, Al-Maktabat al-'Asriyya, 2008).

Arabi, The Nile Mission Arabic translation of Sale's *Introduction to Islam*, trans. Hashim al-Arabi (Cairo, 1909).

Arberry, Arthur J., *The Koran Interpreted* (Oxford, 1964).

———. Inaugural Lecture at the Cambridge School of Arabic (Cambridge, 1948).

Asad, Muhammad, *The Message of the Qur'an* (Gibraltar, London, 1980).

Athīr, Ḍiyā al-Dīn Ibn, *al-Mathal as-sā'ir fī 'adab al-kātib wa'l-shā'ir* (Cairo, 1939).

'Awā, Muḥammad Salīm El-, *Fī uṣūl al-niẓām al-jinā'ī al-islāmī* (Cairo, 2006).

Awqaf, Kuwait Ministry of Awqaf, *al-Mawsū'a al-fiqhiyya* (Encyclopedia of Islamic Law) (Kuwait, 1993).

Badawi, Elsaid M. and Abdel Haleem, Muhammad A. S., *Arabic–English Dictionary of Qur'anic Usage* (Leiden, 2007).

Balādhūrī, Aḥmad Ibn Yaḥyā al-, [*Tārīkh*] *Kitāb Futūh al-Buldān* (Book of the Conquests of the Lands). Translation by P. K. Ḥitti (volume I: 1916) and F. C. Murgotten (volume II: 1924) Brill, Leiden.

Bāqī, Muhammad Fu'ad 'Abd al-, *al-Mu'jam al-mufahras li-alfāẓ al-qur'ān al-karīm* (Cairo, 1945; reprinted Beirut, n.d.).

Bāqillānī, Muḥammad ibn al-ayyib al- (d. 403/1013), *Kitāb tamhīd al-awā'il wa-talkhīṣ al-dalā'il* (Beirut, 1987).

Bayḍāwī, Nāṣir al-Dīn Abū al-Khayr 'Abdullāh ibn 'Umar al-, *Tafsīr* (Beirut, 1988).

Bearman, P., et al. (eds), *The Encyclopaedia of Islam*, 2nd edition (Leiden, 1986). Available at http://referenceworks.brillonline.com/entries/encyclopaedia-of-islam-2/nuh-SIM_5966?s.num=0&s.au=%22Heller%2C+B.%22 (accessed 12 December 2015).

Bell, Richard, *The Qur'an Translated with a Critical Rearrangement of the Surahs* (Edinburgh, 1937; reprinted 1960).

———. *Introduction to the Qur'an* (Edinburgh, 1997).

———. 'The origin of Islam in its Christian environment', in *The Gunning Lectures* (Edinburgh University, 1925). Available at http://muhammadanism.com/bell/origin/poooi.htm (accessed 13 April 2016).

Benedict, Pope Benedict's Lecture at Regensburg on 12 September 2006, *Faith, Reason and the University: Memories and Reflections*. Available at http://w2.vatican.va/content/benedict-xvi/en/speeches/2006/september/documents/hf_ben-xvi_spe_20060912_university-regensburg.html (accessed 5 April 2016).

Block, C. Jonn, *The Qur'an in Christian-Muslim Dialogue: Historical and Modern Interpretations* (Abingdon, New York, 2014).

Bobzin, Hartmut, 'Latin Translations of the Koran: A Short Overview', *Der Islam* 70 (1993).

———. *Der Koran im Zeitalter der Reformation: Studien zur Frühgeshcichte der Arabistik und Islamkunde in Europa* (Beirut, 1995), p. 61.

Bukhārī, *Ṣaḥīḥ al-Bukhārī*, English translation by Muhsin Khan. Available at http://www.islamtomorrow.com/everything/sahihalbukhari.pdf (accessed 10 April 2016).

Burton, John, 'Linguistic errors in the Qur'an', *Journal of Semitic Studies*, xxxiii/2 (Autumn 1988), pp. 181–96.

Busuttil, James J., '"Slay them wherever you find them": Humanitarian law in Islam', *Revue de droit pénal militaire et de droit de la guerre*, 30 (Brussels, 1991).

Carlyle, Thomas, *On Heroes, Hero Worship and the Heroic in History: Six Lectures, Reported, With Emendations and Additions* (New York, 1866).

Constable, Giles (ed.), *Letters of Peter the Venerable: Champion of Cluny* (Cambridge MA, Oxford, 1967).

Cook, Michael, *The Koran: A Very Short Introduction* (Oxford, New York, 2000).

Cragg, Kenneth, 'The Qur'an into English: A translator's apology', in Kenneth Cragg, *Readings in the Qur'an* (Brighton, 1999).

Damaghānī, Abū 'Abd Allāh al-Ḥusayn b. Muḥammad al- (d. 478/1085), *Iṣlāḥ al-wujūh wa'l-naẓā'ir fī'l-Qur'ān al-Karīm* (1970).

Daniel, Norman, *Islam and the West: The Making of an Image* (Oxford, 1993).

Darwaza, Muhammad Izzat, *Sīrat al-rasūl: ṣūra muqtabasa min al-qur'ān al-karīm*, 3rd edition (Qatar, 1979).

Dawood, Nessim J., *The Koran, Translated with Notes* (London, 1990).

Daylami, Abu Abdullah, *Musnad al-Firdaws.*

Denison Ross, Edward, 'Ludovico Marracci', *Bulletin of the School of Oriental and African Studies* ii/1 (February 1921).

———. Introduction to *The Koran: Translated into English from the original Arabic* by George Sale (London, n.d.).

Draz, Muhammad Abdallah, *al-Nabā' al-aẓīm* (Kuwait, 1984).

———. *Le morale du Coran* (Cairo, 1949), translated from French as *The Moral World of the Qur'an* (London, 2009).

Fakhry, Majīd, *An Interpretation of the Qur'an: English Translation of the Meanings: A Bilingual Edition* (New York, 2004).

Fayrūzabādī, Majd al-Dīn Muḥammad ibn Isḥāq al- (d. 1414), *al-Qamūs al-muḥīṭ*, reprint (Beirut, 1952).

Feingold, Mordechai, 'Patrons and professors: The origins and motives of endowments of university chairs – especially the Laudian Professorship of Arabic' in G. A. Russell (ed.), *The 'Arabick' Interest of the Natural Philosophers in Seventeenth-Century England* (Leiden, 1994).

Firestone, Reuven, 'Jihād' in Andrew Rippin (ed.), *The Blackwell Companion to the Qur'ān* (Oxford, 2006), pp. 308–20, at p. 311.

Gaffney, Patrick D., 'Friday Prayer', in J. D. McAuliffe (ed.), *Encyclopaedia of the Qur'ān* (Leiden, 2005), Vol. 2, pp. 271–2.
Griffith, Sidney, 'Christian lore and Arabic Qur'ān: The "Companions of the Cave" in *Sūrat al-Kahf* and in Syriac Christian tradition', in G. S. Reynolds (ed.), *The Qur'an in its Historical Context*, Routledge Studies in the Qur'an (London, 2008), pp. 109–35.
Guillaume, Alfred (trans.), *The Life of Muhammad: A Translation of Ibn Ishaq's Sirat Rasul Allah* (Oxford, 1955; 4th impression, 1974).
Ḥanbal, Ibn, *Musnad* (1993) (numerous editions).
Hāshimī, Aḥmad al-, *Jawāhir al-balāgha* (Beirut, 1986).
———. *al-Bayān fī rawā'i' al-qur'ān* (Cairo, 1993).
Ḥassān, Tammām, *al-Lugha al-'arabiyya: ma'nāhā wa-mabnāhā* (Cairo, 1973).
Hawting, G. R., 'Oaths', in J. D. McAuliffe (ed.), *Encyclopaedia of the Qur'ān* (Leiden, 2004), Vol. 3, pp. 561–6.
Hawting, Gerald R. and Shareef, A. A. (eds), *Approaches to the Qur'an* (New York, 1993).
Ḥayyān, Gharnati, *al-Baḥr al-muḥīṭ* (Beirut, 1983).
Heck, Paul L., 'Poll tax', in J. D. McAuliffe (ed.), *Encyclopaedia of the Qur'ān* (Leiden, 2004).
Heller, Bernhard, 'Nūḥ', in M. Th. Houtsma et al. (eds), *The Encyclopaedia of Islam*, 1st edition (Leiden, 1913–1936).
Hilal, Muhammad Ghunaimi, *Mukhtarāt min al-shi'r al-fārisī* (Cairo, 1965).
———. *al-Adab al-muqāran* (Cairo, 1977).
Hishām, Abdullah ibn Yūsuf ibn, *Mughnī al-labīb*, Māzin Mubārak, Muḥammad 'Alī Ḥamd Allāh, Volume 1 (1969).
Hishām, Abu Muhammad 'Abdu'l-Malik Ibn (d. 833 CE), *Sīra Nabawiyya*. Available at https://archive.org/details/SeerahIbnHisham (accessed April 2016).
Hiskett, Mervyn, *A History of Hausa Islamic Verse* (London, 1975).
Houtsma, Martijn Theodoor et al. (eds), *The Encyclopaedia of Islam*, 1st edition (Leiden, 1913–36).
Ḥumayd, Aḥmad ibn 'Abdullāh ibn, On *Sharḥ al-Maḥallī 'alā'l-waraqāt*. Available at www.dr-mahmoud.com (in Arabic) (accessed 24 November 2016).
Ibrahim, Ezzedine and Denys Johnson-Davies (trans.) *Al-Nawawī's Forty Hadith* (Damascus, 1977).
'Imāra, Muḥammad, *al-Islām wa'l-'aqalliyyāt* (Cairo, 2003).
———. *al-Gharb wa'l-Islām: ayn al-khatta' wa-ayn al-ṣawāb?* (Cairo, 2004).
Izutsu, Toshihiko, *The Structure of the Ethical Terms in the Qur'an* (Tokyo, 1959).
Jawziyya, Muhammad ibn Abu Bakr, also known as Ibn al-Qayyim al-Jawziyya, *al-Tibyān fī aqsām al-qur'ān* (Cairo, n.d.).

Johns, Anthony H., 'Ellipsis in the Qur'an: A response to Saleh Salim Ali', *Hamdard Islamicus* xviii/2 (1995), pp. 15–23.

Jones, Alan, *The Qur'ān Translated into English* (Exeter, 2007).

Jurjānī, 'Abd al-Qāhir al-, *Dalā'il al-i'jāz* (Damascus, 1987).

Kathīr, Ismā'īl Ibn, *Tafsīr al-qur'ān al-'aẓīm* (Beirut, 1992).

Ketton, Robert of, *Lex Mahumet pseudoprophete que arabice Alchoran, id est collectio praeceptorum vocatur,* Paris BnF, MS Arsenal 1162, fols 26–140 and many other manuscripts.

———. *Lex Mahumet* ..., ed. Theodor Bibliander, in *Muchametis saracenorum principis eiusque successorum vitae, ac doctrina ipseque Alcoran* [...] (Basel, 1550 CE).

Khallāf, Abdelwahhab, *'Ilm 'usūl al-fiqh* (Beirut, 1977).

Khiyār, Muḥammad ibn Isḥāq ibn Yasār ibn, *The Life of Muhammad* translated by A. Guillaume (Oxford, 1955).

Kinberg, Leah, 'Paradise', in J. D. McAuliffe (ed.), *Encyclopaedia of the Qur'ān* (Leiden, 2004), Vol. 4, pp. 12–20.

Landau-Tasseron, Ella, 'Jihād' in *The Encyclopaedia of the Qur'ān* (Leiden, 2004) Vol. 3, pp. 35–43.

Lane, Edward W., *Arabic–English Lexicon* (London, 1863).

Lāshīn, Mūsā Shāhīn, *Al-la'āli' al-ḥisān fī 'ulūm al-qur'ān* (Cairo, 1982).

Lee, Sidney (ed.), *Dictionary of National Biography* (London, 1897).

Lewis, Bernard and Holt, Peter Malcolm (eds), *Historical Writing on the Peoples of Asia* (n.p., 1962).

Lings, Martin, *Splendours of Qur'anic Calligraphy and Illumination* (Vaduz, Liechtenstein, 2004).

Lisān al-'Arab (Cairo, n.d.).

Mahmoud, Abdel Haleem, *The Creed of Islam* (London, 1976).

Mājah, Ibn Mājah, *Sunan Ibn Mājah.*

Mālik, *al-Muwaṭṭa'* (many editions).

Mar'ashlī, Nadīm, *al-Ṣiḥāḥ fī'l-lugha wa'l-'ulūm* (Beirut, 1974).

Marracci, Luigi [Ludovico], *Alcorani textus universus* (Padua, 1698).

Marshall, David, 'Punishment stories', in J. D. McAuliffe (ed.), *The Encyclopaedia of the Qur'ān* (Leiden, 2000), Vol. 4, pp. 318–22.

Matar, Nabil, *Islam in Britain: 1558–1685* (Cambridge, New York, 1998).

McAuliffe, Jane Dammen (ed.), *Encyclopaedia of the Qur'ān* (Leiden, 2004).

Mir, Mustansir, 'The Qur'an oaths: Farāhī's interpretation', *Islamic Studies* (Spring Issue, 1990), pp. 1–17. Available at http://www.islamic-awareness.org/Quran/Q_Studies/Miroaths.html (accessed 12 April 2016).

Monte Croce, Riccoldo da, Dominican monk 1242–1320, *Libellus contra legem saracenorum.* First published in Seville, 1500, under the title *Confutatio Alcorani* (*Confutation of the Koran*). This work was translated into German (*Verlegung des Alcoran*) by Martin Luther in 1542. See also https://en.

wikipedia.org/wiki/Riccoldo_da_Monte_di_Croce#Apologetic_writings_against_Islam_and_Judaism (accessed 24 November 2016).

Mūsā, Hārūn ibn (d. c.AH 170/786 CE), *al-Wujūh wa'l-naẓā'ir fī'l-Qur'ān al-karīm* (Baghdad, 1989).

Muslim, *Ṣaḥīḥ Muslim*, trans. Abd-al-Hamid Siddiqui. Available at http://www.islamtomorrow.com/everything/sahihmuslim.pdf (accessed April 2016).

Muṣṭafa Ibrāhīm Muṣṭafa et al., *al-Mu'jam al-wasīṭ* (Cairo, 1960; reprinted Istanbul, 1998).

Nadawī, 'Abd Allāh 'Abbās al-, *Tarjamāt ma'ānī al-qur'ān al-karīm* (Jeddah, 1972).

Naqqāsh, Rajā' al- and Maḥfūẓ, Najīb, *Safahat min mudhakkiratihi wa adawa'ja* (Cairo, 1998).

Nawfal, 'Abd al-Razzāq, *al-I'jāz al-'adadī fī'l-qur'ān al-karīm* (Cairo, 1976).

Nawawī, al-, *Matn al-arba'īn,* trans. E. Ibrahim and D. Johnson-Davies (Damascus, 1977).

Neuwirth, Angelika, 'Images and metaphors in the introductory sections of the Meccan suras', in G. R. Hawting and A. A. Shareef (eds), *Approaches to the Qur'an* (New York, 1993), pp. 1–36. A shorter version of this is given in J. D. McAuliffe (ed.), *Encyclopaedia of the Qur'ān* (Leiden, 2004), Vol. 3, pp. 464–8.

Nöldeke, Theodor, *Neue Beiträge zur semitischen Sprachwissenschaft* (Strassburg, 1910).

———. *Tārīkh al-qur'ān,* trans. into Arabic by G. Tāmir (Hildesheim, Zürich, New York, 2004).

———. *Geschichte des Qorâns* (Beirut, 2004) (in German).

Omar, Ahmad Mukhtar, 'The *fāṣila* in the Qur'an: Word, context and meaning', *Journal of Qur'anic Studies* 1:1 (1999), pp. 220–38.

Ostle, Robin C. (ed.), *Studies in Modern Arabic Literature* (London, 1975).

Palmer, Edward Henry, *The Qur'an* (Oxford, 1880).

Pickthall, Muhammad Marmaduke, *The Meaning of the Holy Qur'an* (London, 1930).

Powers, David S., 'The exegetical genre: *nāsikh al-Qur'ān wa-mansūkhuhu*', in A. Rippin (ed.), *Approaches to the History of Interpretation of the Quran* (Oxford, 1988), pp. 341–59.

Qaraḍāwī, Yūsuf al-, *Ghayr al-muslimīn fī-mujtama' al-islāmī* (Cairo, 1977).

Qurṭubī, Abū 'Abdullāh al-, *Jāmi' li-aḥkām al-Qur'ān* (Beirut, 2000).

Quṭb, Sayyid, *al-Taṣwīr al-fannī fī'l-qur'ān* (Cairo, 1966).

———. *Fī ẓilāl al-qur'ān* Dar al-shuyukh (Cairo, 1985).

Rāzī, Fakhr al-Dīn al-, *al-Tafsīr al-kabīr,* also known as *Mafātīḥ al-Ghayb* (Beirut, n.d.).

Reynolds, Gabriel Said (ed.), *The Qur'an in its Historical Context,* Routledge Studies in the Qur'an (London, 2008).

Robson, James (trans.), *Mishkat al-masabih* (Lahore, reprint 2006). Available at http://www.dar-us-salam.com/inside/R25-Mishkat.pdf (accessed 24 November 2016).

Rodwell John Medows Rodwell, *The Koran translated from the Arabic* (New York and London, 1968.

Rushd, 'Abū l-Walīd Muḥammad Ibn 'Aḥmad Ibn, *Manāhij al-adilla fī 'aqa'id al-milla*, ed. M. Qāsim (Cairo, 1964, 1969).

———. *Bidāyat al-mujtahid wa-nihāyat al-muqtaṣid* (Beirut, 1992).

Ṣafadi, Yasīn Hamid, *Islamic Calligraphy* (London, 1987), 144 pp.

Saheeh International, *The Qur'an: Arabic Text with Corresponding English Meanings* (Jeddah, 2004).

Salām, 'Izzedīn Ibn 'Abd al-, *Majāz al-qur'ān* (London, 1999). See also Abū 'Ubayda, *Majāz al-qur'ān.*

Salāma, Hibat Allāh Ibn, *Al-nāsikh wa'l-mansūkh* (Beirut, 1986).

Sale, George, *The Koran: Commonly Called the Alcoran of Mohammed, translated into English immediately from the original Arabic, with explanatory notes, taken from the most approved commentators, to which is prefixed a preliminary discourse* (London, 1734).

Ṣāliḥ, Muhammad Adib, *Tafsīr al-nuṣūṣ fī'l-fiqh al-islāmī: dirāsa muqarana li-manāhij al-'ulama' fī istinbāt al-aḥkām min nuṣūs al-Kitāb* (Beirut, 1993).

Schimmel, Annemarie, 'The celestial garden', in E. B. Macdougal and R. Ettinghausen (eds), *The Islamic Garden* (1976, out of print).

Shackle, Christopher and Sperl, Stefan (eds), *Qasida Poetry in Islamic Asia and Africa* (Leiden, 1996).

Shaltūt, Maḥmūd, *al-Islām: 'aqīda wa-sharī'a* (Cairo, 1990).

Shāṭibī, Abū Isḥāq al-, *al-Muwafaqāt fī uṣūl al-aḥkām* (Cairo, 1342 AH).

Shaykh, Ṣālih bin 'Abd al-'Azīz Āl al- (ed.), *al-Kutub al-sitta* (Riyadh, 1999).

Sībawayhī, Abū Bishr 'Amr ibn 'Uthmān ibn Qanbar Al-Baṣrī (c. 760–796 CE) (commonly known as Sībawayhī), *al-Kitāb al-Nahw* (Cairo, 1988).

Smith, G. Rex, 'Oaths in the Qur'an', *Semitics* I (1970), pp. 126–56.

Stephen, Sir Leslie and Lee, Sir Sidney (eds), *Dictionary of National Biography* (Oxford, 1921–22).

Subayyal, Shaikh Muhammad ibn 'Abdullah al- (d. 2012), *Fatāwā wa-rasā'il mukhtāra* (Saudi Arabia, n.d.), pp. 562–3.

Suyūṭī, Jalāl al-Dīn al-, *Tafsīr al-Jalālayn* (Baghdad, n.d.).

———. *al-Itqān fi 'ulūm al-qur'ān* (Beirut, 1987). English translation by Hamid Lagar, Michael Schub and Ayman Abdel Haleem, *The Perfect Guide to the Sciences of the Qur'ān*, Vol. 1 (Reading, 2011).

Ṭabarī, al-, *Tafsīr al-Ṭabarī* (Beirut, 1999).

———. *Jāmi' al-bayān fī tafsīr al-Qur'ān.* http://rissc.jo/tafsir/Al_Jalalain_Eng.pdf (accessed 24 November 2016).

Tibāwī, 'Abdul Laṭīf, 'Second critique of English-speaking orientalists and their approach to Islam and the Arabs', *The Islamic Quarterly* xxiii/1 (1979), pp. 3–54.

Tirmidhī, Abu 'Isa Muhammad ibn 'Īsa al-, *Jāmi' at-Tirmidhī* known as *Sunan* (many editions).

Topan, Farouk, 'Swahili as a religious language', *Journal of Religion in Africa* xxii/4 (1992), pp. 331–49.

———. 'Muslim literature in sub-Saharan Africa', in A. Nanji (ed.), *The Muslim Almanac* (New York, 1996), pp. 365–9.

———. 'Projecting Islam: Narrative in Swahili poetry', *Journal of African Cultural Studies,* xiv/1 (2001), pp. 107–19.

'Ubāda, Muḥammad, *'Usūr al-ihtijāj fī'l-nahw al-'arabī* (Cairo, 1980).

'Ubayda, Abū (d. AH 210/825 CE), *Majāz al-qur'ān* (Cairo, 1954), Vol. 1, p. 8.

Venerable, Peter the (d. 1159), *Liber contra sectam sive heresim Saracenorum* (A Book against the Sect or Heresy of the Saracens).

Versteegh, Kees, 'Arabic as a world language', in *The Arabic Language* (Columbia University Press, 2001).

Wāḥidī, 'Alī ibn Aḥmad al-, *Asbāb al-nuzūl* (Cairo, AH 1315/1898 CE). English translation PDF available at http://www.altafsir.com/Books/Asbab%20 Al-Nuzul%20by%20Al-Wahidi.pdf (accessed 24 November 2016).

Wansbrough, John, *Qur'anic Studies: Sources and Methods of Scriptural Interpretation* (Oxford, 1979).

Watt, William Montgomery, *Muhammad: Prophet and Statesman* (London, 1961).

Wensinck, Arent J., *Concordances et indices de la Tradition Musulmane* (Leiden, 1992).

Yūsuf, Abū, *Kitāb al-kharaj* (Beirut, n.d.), p. 126.

Yūsuf, Ya'qūb Abū, *Kitab-ul-kharaj = Islamic Revenue Code,* trans. Abid Ahmad Ali and Abdul Hameed Siddiqui (Lahore, 1979), p. 254.

Zamakhsharī, Abū al-Qāsim Maḥmūd b. 'Umar al-, *Tafsīr al-kashshāf* (Beirut, n.d.).

Zarkashī, Badr al-Dīn al-, *al-Burhān fī 'ulūm al-qur'ān,* ed. M. A. Ibrahim (Cairo, 1988).

Zaydān, 'Abd al-Karīm, *Aḥkām al-dhimmiyyīn wa'l-musta'manīn fī dār al-Islām* (Beirut, 1976).

Index

Arabic names beginning with 'al-' or 'Ibn' are indexed under the second element.
n = endnote. *t* = table/diagram.

Ibn 'Abbās, Abdullah 35, 85, 99, 305*n32*, 306–7*n48*, 308*n15*, 319*n14*, 324*n32*
Abdullah, Sayed 261
abrogation 18–25, 26–7, 55; Islamic commentaries 22–5, 101; non-Islamic commentaries 18–22, 20–2; and stoning penalty 97, 101; see also *naskh*
Abū Bakr, Caliph 9, 29, 42, 47, 57–8, 277, 295
Abū Hanifa 93, 94
Abū Ḥayyān al-Gharnāṭī 31, 34–5, 36, 37, 45, 304*n9*, 305*n32*, 306–7*n48*, 319*n8*
Abū Hurayra 99
Abū Mansūr al-'Āmirī, 82
Abū Muslim 19, 95
Abū 'Ubayda 34, 45, 213–14
Abū Zahra, Muhammad 102
Adams, Sir Thomas 254
adultery see *zinā*
Africa, influence of Arabic in 243–4
agreements, keeping/breaking of 32, 38, 41, 46
'Ā'isha (wife of Muhammad) 97
alcohol, consumption of 31; punishment for excess 107; Qur'anic disapproval 106–7
'Alī ibn Abi Talib, Caliph 9, 308*n6*
amputation of body parts, as legal punishment 92, 93–4; juristic debates 94
Ibn al-Anbārī 295
angels; oaths (debatably) sworn by 182–3, 196; oaths sworn to existence of 206; presence in Paradise 82
animals, idolaters compared to 166–7; *see also* 'asses'; horses
apostasy 104–6; as no ground for fighting 105–6; penalties for 105; Qur'anic references 104
al-'Aqqād, 'Abbās Maḥmūd 66–7
Arabic (language) 213–34; calligraphy 239, 246–7; centrality of Qur'an to study of 214–15, 233–4, 237–8; grammar 215–19, 224–5; impact on other Muslim languages/literature 243–4; as language of divine speech 237–9; linguistics 214–15; literary criticism 214; literature 233–4; study in British universities 254, 277–8; teaching of 214–15, 245–6, 247–8
Al-Araby, Abdullah 20–1
Arberry, Arthur J. 10, 29, 30, 43, 56, 197, 249, 263, 266, 267–70, 280, 295, 297; academic career 267–8, 279; features of translation 268–9, 278; problems of translation 269–70, 271, 274, 276, 277; use of rhyme 269
Asbaq (Christian slave) 20
'asses', non-observers likened to 142–4, 289, 295
Ibn al-'Atāqī 23
Ibn al-Athīr 214, 220–1
atomism 36, 178, 183, 193–4, 266; objections to 184, 194, 196, 199
awliyā' ('friends'), interpretation of 291–4
Al-Azhar University, Cairo 89, 214–15, 264

Badr, battle of (623 CE/2 AH) 17
Bangladesh 244
al-Bāqillānī, Muḥammad ibn al-Ṭayyib 305*n21*
Basle, Council of 251–2

al-Bayḍāwī 31, 37, 55, 95, 173, 183–4, 194, 195, 197, 255, 266, 319*n14*
beating, as punishment; for adultery/fornication 98, 100–1, 102; for intoxication 107; within marriage *see* domestic violence; restrictions on severity 100; for slander 103
belief; as condition for entry to Paradise 71–3; 'in God and the Last Day', rhetorical use of 30–1, 43
Bell, Richard 79; biography 265–6, 279; errors/misunderstandings 141–2, 144, 148, 149, 156, 158, 271–2, 274, 333*n79*; preconceptions 141, 149, 160; on 'punishment' theme in Noah story 119, 120, 132, 317*n12*; Qur'an translation/structural commentary 141–2, 144, 145, 148–9, 160, 265–7, 273; reliance on conjecture 141, 148, 160, 266
Benedict XVI, Pope 8, 21
Bible, Qur'an compared with Deuteronomy 66–7; Genesis (Noah) 132–5, 140; Leviticus 314*n7*; by medieval scholars 251; by Victorian scholars 258–9, 270
Bibliander, Theodor 251
Bilāl Ibn Rabah (the Abyssinian) 277
Bucer, Martin 252
al-Bukhārī 112
Burton, John 213, 218
al-Būsīrī, *The Burda* 244
Busuttil, James 54

calligraphy 239, 246–7
Carteret, Lord 255
Christians 289–91; nomenclature 284
Clairvaux, Bernard of 250
compulsion (in religion), prohibition on 18–21, 105, 240
Cook, Michael 7–8, 10, 11–14, 18, 25, 30, 43
Cragg, Kenneth 269
Cromer, Lord 263
Crusades 250

Daniel, Norman 250, 270
Darwaza, Muhammad Azza 102
Dawood, Nessim J. 32, 50, 55, 56–7, 307–8*n3*
day, oaths sworn by 200–1
declension *(I'rāb)* 217–19
definite article; as binder 223; range of meanings 274–5, 291–2
al-Dehlawi, Shah Waliullah 23
dhikr (remembrance) 242–3
dhimma (protection), significance of 45–6
Dhū'l-Ḥijja, month of 187–8
dīn, range of meanings 32
divorce 30
domestic violence 107–9; (alleged) permissibility under *sharī'a* 107–8; (limited) Qur'anic sanctioning 108; Prophetic disapproval 109
Draz, Muhammad Abdallah 231, 327*n26*
du Ryer, André, Sieur 252–3, 256

earth, oaths sworn by 191–3
Egypt; legal system 91; popular culture 139; suggested change to Western alphabet 327*n1*
El-'Awā, Muḥammad Salīm 99
Encyclopaedia of Islam 119, 131, 317*n18*
Encyclopaedia of the Qur'ān 86
Ernst, Carl 260–1
'even and the odd,' oath sworn by 187–8
extremism, Qur'anic interpretation based in 1, 12, 18–19, 21, 25, 309*n27*

fadl (divine favour) 142–4, 157
al-Faisal, Sheikh Abdullah 25
Farāhī, Ḥamīd al-Dīn 'Abd al-Ḥamīd 178–9, 180, 195, 202
al-Fārisī 23
al-Fayrūzabādī 32
al-Fidā, Abū 257
fighting; circumstances permitting 51–2, 56–8, 67; distinguished from killing 21; gifts in support of 153–4; proper objects of 58–9; Qur'anic justifications 52–8; strategy/tactics 58–9, 61–3; see also *qitāl*; self-defence
Firestone, Reuven 307–8*n3*
Five Pillars of Islam 51
Foda, Faraj 309*n27*
food and drink, in Paradise 80, 82
fornication see *zinā*
Forrest, Trevor William *see* al-Faisal, Sheikh Abdullah
Francis of Assisi, St 251
fruit, oaths sworn by 201–2

al-Ghāmidiyya (confessed adulteress) 98–9
Al-Ghamrāwī, M. A., Prof. 264
al-Ghazālī, Muḥammad 309*n27*
Gibbon, Edward 256
God, oaths sworn in name of 204–5; *see also* oaths (divine); oneness (of God)
good deeds, as condition for entry to Paradise 71, 73–4; in combination with belief 73; listing of 73–4
grammar/syntax, Qur'anic 215–28, 233–4; abnormal syntax 227; (apparent)

errors 218–19; binding elements 219–24; concordance 224; context 227–8; declension 217–19; definite article, use of 223, 274–5; departures from rules of 218–19, 220–3, 233 (see also *iltifāt*); morphology 216–17; omissions 217, 223, 226; parenthesis, use of 227; particles 224; pronouns, use of 220–3; repetition, use of 219–20; syntactic relations 216; syntagmatic requirement 225–7; word order 224–5; *see also* rhetorical features
Grimme, Hubert 79

hadd see *ḥudūd*
Ḥadith 30, 35–6, 38, 131; on adultery/fornication 100–1, 313*n31*; on apostasy 105
Hāfiẓ of Shīrāz 246
hands, amputation of *see* amputation
Hassan, Rizq Allāh 261
Ḥassan, Tammām 232–3, 273, 322*n64*
Ḥausa (African language), influence of Arabic/Qur'an 243–4
Hawting, G. R. 179
Ibn Ḥazm 94
head of state, responsibilities of 63–4
Heller, Bernard 131, 317*n18*
Hermann of Corinth 250
ḥirāba (highway robbery) 90, 92
homosexuality 95–6
Horovitz, Josef 79
horses, oaths sworn by 196–8
Hudaybiyya, Treaty of (628 CE/6 AH) 8–9, 24, 65–6, 301*n6*
ḥudūd (serious crimes, 'limits set by God') 91–109; deterrent intent of penalties 92, 93, 109; inapplicability on non-Muslim States 107; mitigation of penalties 93, 102, 103–4, 107; non-Qur'anic 104–8; offences covered by 90; Qur'anic source for penalties 91–2; repentance for 92, 93–4, 96; *see also* amputation; *ḥirāba; qadhf; sariqa*; stoning; *zinā*

iltifāt (grammatical shift for rhetorical purposes) 218–19, 233; pronomial 220–3; types of 221
imagery, Qur'anic use of 231–2
'Imāra, Muḥammad 33–4, 310*n33*
imperative, range of meanings 11–12
Indian subcontinent, languages of 243, 244
Innocent XI, Pope 254
interfaith relations 4, 46–7, 283–98; misinterpretations/mistranslations 291–8; Qur'anic approach to 283–91
Ibn Isḥāq 26
islām, etymology/significance 295–6
Izutsu, Toshihiko 273
'Izzedīn Ibn 'Abd as-Salām 226

al-Jamā'a al-Islāmiyya 309*n27*
al-Jāmī, 'Abd al-Raḥmān 246
janna/jannāt (garden/Paradise) 75–8; etymology 75–6; *jannatān* (two gardens) 77–8; singular *vs.* plural forms 76–7
Al-Jawziyya, ibn al-Qayyim 178
Jesus, treatment in Qur'an 289–90
Jews; hostility to Islam (in Medina) 286–7, 288–9, 318–19*n6*; moral distinctions among 142–6, 287–9, 292–3, 294–5; nomenclature 284
jihād 2, 47, 49–68; anti-Islamic misconceptions 67–8; battle tactics 61–3; as business of state 63–4; castigation of failure to commit to 60–1; consistency of Qur'anic teachings 64–7; divorce from original meaning 49; and entry into Paradise 74–5; etymology 49; extremist Muslim misconceptions 67–8; literal meaning 49; military, restrictions on recourse to 67–8; military *vs.* non-military 49–50, 67; misinterpretations 53–4, 55–7, 65–6, 67–8; mistranslations 21–2, 50; preparation of forces 62–3; Qur'anic exhortations to 59–61; Qur'anic usages 49–51; range of meanings 49–51
jizya (tribute); breaking of agreement to pay 32, 38, 41; etymology 33; exemptions 33–4, 38–9; in lieu of military service 33–4, 42, 45; mistranslations 33, 295; payment procedure 35–6; Qur'anic significance 45; refunding 34, 45; services/privileges granted in return for 33–4, 45–6; *see also* *jizya* verse
jizya verse (Q 9:29) 2, 27, 29–47, 57–8, 295; on breaking of agreements 32, 38, 41; context 39; crucial terms, meaning/significance 45–7; *dīn*, significance of 32, 43–4; humility/submission, treatment of 35–7, 44–5; Islamic exegeses 30–1, 32–3, 34, 36–7, 41; juristic interpretations 36; linguistic

analysis 43–5; literal interpretations 30–1; *min*, significance of 32–3, 44; mistranslations 32, 33; Occasion of Revelation *(sabab al-nuzūl)* 37–43; 'out of hand', significance of 34–5; range of interpretations 34–7, 43–4; restricted applicability 40–3; translations 29, 42–3
Jones, Alan 32, 144, 148–9, 156, 158, 160, 162, 168, 261, 321*n52*, 332–3*n69*
Judgement, Day of 119, 151–2; divine oaths sworn to 204–7; referencing in Noah story 121, 124; unavoidability 69–70, 174–5
al-Jurjānī, 'Abd al-Qāhir 138, 214

kabad (burden of responsibility) 200
Ibn Kathīr, Ismā'il 20
Ketton, Robert of 249, 250–1, 252, 255, 260, 329*n9*
Khadīja (wife of Muhammad) 308*n6*
al-Khafīf, 'Ali 102
Khawārij (splinter group) 101–2
killing (of non-Muslims); 'fighting' distinguished from 21; restrictions on 13–16, 17–18, 54–5

Landau-Tasseron, Ella 54
Lane, Edward W. 36, 81
lashes *see* beating
Laud, William, Archbishop 254
legs, covering of 116, 117
Luther, Martin 252

Mahfouz, Najib 233–4
Mā'iz (confessed adulterer) 98–9
Malaysia/Malay language 243, 244
Mālik Ibn Anas 93
al-Mālik al-Kāmil, Sultan 251
al-Ma'mūn, Caliph 330*n10*
Mansur, 'Ali, Councillor 102
Manuel II Palaeologus, (Byzantine) Emperor 21–2
marital relations *see* domestic violence; *nushūz*; sexual relations; *zinā*
Marracci, Ludovico 249, 254–5, 256, 257, 279
Al-Marrāghī, M. M., Prof. 264
Marshall, David 119–20, 124, 131, 132
Mather, Cottom 254
Mecca; departure from *see* Medina, relocation to; hostility experienced by first Muslims 51–2, 121, 129, 189, 190, 199–200, 317*n14*; oaths sworn by 199–200
Medina, relocation to 51–2, 59, 129, 286, 308*n6*, 322*n68*; (alleged) increase in militancy following 20–1, 51; formation of Muslim State 63–4; social relations following 113
memorisation, of Qur'anic text 233–4, 245, 266
menstruation 111–12, 115, 116–17, 314*n4*
Messenger (of God), application of 31–2, 43, 304*n11*
Mir, Mustansir 178–9
moon, oaths sworn by 200–1,206–7
morphology 216–17; departures by addition 217; departures by omission 217
Muhammad, the Prophet; (alleged) imposition of stoning penalty 96–7, 98–9; analogies with earlier prophets 122, 125–6, 127, 128–30, 136–8, 139; comments on *Sūrat Yā Sīn* 158, 171–2; divine oaths as to prophethood 184–91; final pilgrimage/death 26, 64, 249; on marital relations 109, 113, 315*n14*; marriages 97, 98, 109; misrepresentations 21; negotiation of Hudaybiyya Treaty 8–9; preference for mitigation of punishments 14, 99–100, 103–4; Qur'anic exhortations to/regarding 147–8, 154–5, 161–3, 166, 199–200, 233, 241–2, 285–6; relocation to Medina 51–2; role as head of state 63–4; on taxation/protection 45–6; unbelievers' denial of/challenges to 158–9, 161–2, 166,174–5, 190; on unnecessary killing 14
Mullā Ṣadrā 246
Muslim world; influence of Qur'an 3–4, 237–48; popular culture 139–40, 172–3, 185

al-Naḥḥās 23
naskh ('abrogation') 22–5, 26–7; exegetical interpretations 22–5; juristic interpretations 22; mistranslations 22; number of verses affected by 22–3
Negri, Solomon 255
Neuwirth, Angelika 179, 182, 195, 202, 210–11
Nicholson, R. A. 263, 332–3*n69*
night, oaths sworn by 184–5, 187–8, 200–1, 206–7
Noah, Qura'nic accounts of 119–40, 164; (apparent) repetitiveness 135–8; brief versions 127, 128–9, 135; contrasted with biblical version 132–5, 140; differences between

135–8; (limited) focus on punishment 119, 122, 124–5, 126, 132–5, 139–40; in modern popular culture 138, 247; number/order 120–1, 120*t*; parallels with Muhammad 122, 125–6, 127, 128–30, 136–8, 137*t*, 139; physical description of Flood 121–2; principal themes 121–31; referenced in Arabic literature 138–9; references to drowning 122–3, 124–5, 126, 131–2, 138, 139–40; selection of evildoers *(al-mala')* 131–2, 139–40; treatment of divine mercy 122–3, 126, 127, 130–1; treatment of unbelievers' responses 123–6, 127–8, 129–30, 131, 136
Nöldeke, Theodor 120, 121, 130, 179, 213, 220, 258, 316*n7*, 320*n26*
nushūz (marital impropriety) 107–9, 314*n47*

oaths, form/function in Arabic culture 177, 181, 208; compared with English 325*n63*; *see also* oaths (divine)
oaths (divine) 161–2, 177–211; differing interpretations 183–4, 187–8, 193–4, 198–9, 203–4; function 181–2, 208–9, 325*n63*; grammar/vocabulary 177, 185, 189–90; internal 204–7; in Muslim popular culture 185; objects sworn by 183–4, 185–9, 191–205, 208–9; proposed reclassification 180; quantity/location 181; serial 193–8; studies in Arabic 178, 193–4; studies in English 178–9, 209–11; subjects: oneness of God 182–4; prophethood of Muhammad 184–91; Resurrection 191–204; target audience 182; translations 197
obscenity, Qur'an accused of 111
oneness (of God); centrality to Islamic belief 181, 289–91; oath sworn to 182–3
Oporinus, Johannes 251–2
oppression, permissibility of armed resistance to 57, 67
Ottoman Empire 244

Pakistan 247
Palmer, E. H. 254, 255, 261–3, 270; academic career 261, 279; non-Qur'an translations 261; qualities of translation 262–3, 277, 280
Paradise 2, 68, 69–86; angelic presence 82; components 78–80; female presence 70, 80–2, 85; figurative language 85–6; food and drink 80, 82; location 75; physical condition of inhabitants 81; physical/spiritual rewards 82–5; qualifications for entry 70–4; reuniting of families 70, 81, 83; role of *jihād* 74–5; terminology 75–8; Western misrepresentations 80–1, 82, 86, 311*n28*; *see also* belief; good deeds; *janna/jannāt*; Judgement; Resurrection
parent and offspring, oath sworn by 199–200
pen, oaths sworn by 185–6, 209
penal code see *sharī'a*
People of the Book 283–91, 297–8; beliefs ascribed to 30–1; conduct required by own beliefs 31–2; defined 29, 46; denial/resentment of Muhammad 142–3, 157, 158–9; distinctions between 39, 40–3, 142–3; distinguished from polytheists 40; entry into Paradise 72–3; exemptions from military service 33–4; nomenclature 284; (prohibition on) humiliation 35–6; rights under Islamic law 46–7; *see also* Christians; Jews
permissibility, distinguished from imperative 11–12
persecution (of Muslims) 188–9
Persian (language); calligraphy 246–7; influence of Arabic/Qur'an 243, 246; literature 246
Peter the Venerable, Abbot 249, 250
Pickthall, Muhammad Marmaduke 263–5, 270, 279; characteristics of translation 264–5, 271–2, 274, 277, 279, 280
polytheists *(mushrik)*; distinguished from People of the Book 40; limited applicability of term 7, 9, 18, 20, 26, 55, 58; mistranslations/misunderstandings 18; Muslim obligations relating to 7–8, 11–18, 24, 26; verses addressed to 79, 126, 181–2
poverty, compassionate treatments of 38–9
private parts, covering of 115–16
pronouns 220–3; demonstrative 223; gender agreement 222–3; grammatical rules 220; omission 223; Qur'anic departures from rules 220–3
protection, Islamic concept of 45–6

qadhf (slander) 90, 102–4; penalties 100, 103
al-Qaffāl 19–20
qiṣāṣ (retribution); compensation as

alternative to 90, 91; offences liable for 90; scale of penalties 91
qitāl (fighting); distinguished from *jihād* 50; Qur'anic teachings on 52, 60, 64, 66
Qur'an; acceptance of other religions 283–7, 297–8; as basis of Arabic scholarship 214–15, 233–4, 237–8; chronology of composition 120; commentaries on specific subjects *see jihād*; oaths (divine); Paradise; Resurrection; *sharī'a*; compared with Old Testament 66–7, 132–5, 140; criticisms by Western scholars/translators 111, 114, 250–1, 253, 270; forms of discourse 239–43; guidance, as central aim 169–70, 213, 239–40, 272; on interfaith relationships 46–7; language *see* Arabic; grammar/syntax; rhetorical features; linguistic analysis 1–2; Meccan *vs.* Medinan Suras 20–1, 49, 60, 79, 104, 105–6, 120, 187; memorisation 233–4, 245, 266; misinterpretations 1, 111; oaths sworn by 161–2, 189–90; on protection 45–6; rational justification of teachings 52–3, 119, 133, 167–8, 170–1, 172, 240–1; reactive nature 38; sections of special significance 158, 172–4; specific sections see *jizya* verse; *Sūrat al-Ḥadīd; Sūrat al-Jumu'a; Sūrat Yā Sīn*; 'Sword Verse'; structure 141–75; study requirements 299–300; *see also* style
al-Qurṭubī, Abū Abdallah 39–40, 302*n21*, 306*n46*
Quṭb, Sayyid 12

Ramadan 187–8, 241, 320*n36*
al-Rāzī, Fakhruddin 12, 37, 54, 93, 95–7, 101, 135, 156, 173, 180, 184, 186, 206, 217, 240, 241, 266, 295, 299, 319*n14*
recitation, of Qur'an 245
repentance; penalty imposed in spite of 93–4, 103; penalty mitigated on grounds of 92, 93, 96, 312*n7*; for sexual misconduct 96; for slander 103; for theft 92, 93–4; for unbelief 13–14
Resurrection; centrality to Islamic belief 69–70, 174, 181–2; divine oaths sworn by 198–9; divine oaths sworn to 191–207; Quran'ic arguments for 159–60, 161, 163–4, 167–8, 171–2, 174–5, 191–3; Quran'ic depictions 161, 165; unbelievers' objections to 159, 174–5
rhetorical features (of Qur'an) 228–33; adjectives, use of 229; affective sentences 228; conciseness 231; contrast 229–30; dialogue/direct speech 230–1; emphasis 229; generalisation 229; imagery 231–2; memorability 233; rhyme 232, 320*n23*; rhythm 232–3; stories/parables 230; verbal sentences 229
rhyme, Qur'anic use of 232, 320*n23*
Riccoldo of Monte Croce 251
Rodwell, J. M. 255, 257–61, 266; biographical background 257–8, 279; flaws in translation 259–60, 263, 271–2, 275, 279–80
Ross, Alexander 249, 252–5, 257, 279; flaws in translation 253, 256
Ross, Edward Denison 255, 331*n36*
al-Rūmī, Jalāl al-Dīn 246
Ibn Rushd 82

Sacred Months 11
Ibn Salāma, Hibat Allāh 8, 23–5
Sale, George 249, 253, 254, 255–7, 260, 263, 270, 279, 331*n39*; criticisms of earlier translators 256; qualities of translation 256–7
Salmān al-Fārisī (the Persian) 277
al-Ṣāmit, 'Ubāda b. 100–1
sariqa (theft) 90, 93–4; application of penalty despite repentance 93–4
al-Sayāb, B. S. 138–9
Schimmel, Annemarie 77–8, 79
self-defence; arguments for 52–3; circumstances permitting 51–2, 53, 56–7, 67; limits on 53; permitted methods 53
sexual relations 111–17; delicacy of approach, recommended 113; euphemistic style of discussion 112, 114–15, 117; extramarital see *zinā*; Meccan *vs.* Medinan approach 113; times to abstain from 111–12, 115, 116–17
al-Shāfi'ī, Abū 'Abdullah 93
Shaltūt, Mahmūd 89
sharī'a 86, 89–109, 241–2; legal/religious meanings 89–90; literal meaning 89; types of penalty 90–1; see also *ḥudūd; qiṣāṣ; ta'zīr*
al-Shāṭibī 119
sky, oaths sworn by 191–3, 203–4
slander see *qadhf*
Smith, G.R. 178, 199, 202, 209–10

stars, oaths sworn by 186–7, 191–2
stoning, as penalty for adultery/fornication 96–102, 313*n31*; absence from Qur'an 98, 102; (alleged) imposition by early leaders 96–7, 98–9; modern support for 99; objections to 101–2
style; coherent 3, 148, 155–8, 169–71 (*see also* Qur'an: structure); euphemistic 3, 112, 114–15, 117 (*see also* sexual relations); evidential 3 (*see also* oaths (divine)); legal 3 (see also *sharī'a*); narrative 3 (*see also* Noah); rhetorical 3 (*see also* grammar/ syntax, Qur'anic)
Suhayb ar-Rūmi ('the Roman') 277
sun, oaths sworn by 184–5, 200–1
Sūrat al-Fātiḥa (Q. 1), memorisation/ recitation 245
Sūrat al-Ḥadīd (Q. 57) 148–58; calls/ arguments for giving to God 150–1, 152–4; glorification of God 149–50; on hypocrites 151–2; structural coherence 155–8; vocabulary 156, 157
Sūrat al-Jumu'a (Q. 62) 141–8; exhortation to Prophet 147–8; structural coherence 147–8; treatment of *faḍl* (favour) 142–4; treatment of religious observance 142–7
Sūrat Yā Sīn (Q. 36) 158–75; as 'Core of the Qur'an' 158, 171–2, 320*n39*; in popular culture 172–3; special importance 158, 172–4; structural unity 168–9; structure 160–9; style 169–71; themes 158–60; Verses 1-12 161–2; Verses 13-32 161, 163; Verses 33-48 161, 163–5; Verses 49-65 161, 165; Verses 66-68 161, 165–6; Verses 69-70 161, 166; Verses 71-76 161, 166–7; Verses 77-83 161, 167–8; vocabulary 159–60, 168–9
al-Suyuṭī, Jalāl al-Dīn 23, 37, 178, 184, 193–4, 195, 203–4, 214, 255, 273
Swahili, influence of Arabic/Qur'an on 244
'Sword Verse' (Q 9:5) 2, 7–27, 64; (alleged) abrogation of other verses 18–25; cited as example of Islamic aggression 11–18, 26; contextualisation 25–6, 55; historical background 8–10; limited applicability 10–12, 25–6, 55, 58; misinterpretations 10–27; misnaming 11–14; mistranslations 11–14; non-innovative nature 17–18; restrictions on killing imperative 13–16; textual analysis 10–17

al-Ṭabarī 35, 37
taxation 29–47; modern Arabic systems 36, 47; obligations of People of the Book 31–2; see also *jizya; jizya* verse; *zakāh*
ta'zīr (deterrent penalties) 90–1, 104
'ten nights', oath sworn by 187–8
theft see *sariqa*
Thomas Aquinas, St 251
Tibawi, A. L. 270
'tilth' (fields), women as 111–14; as expression of respect 113–14
Torah, law of 96–7
torture, undergone by Muslims 188–9
translations(s) 141–75, 249–81; accuracy 272–6; antiquated style 276–7; clarity 272; criteria 270–9; early history 249–52; emotional impact 277–8; errors/misunderstandings 1, 3–4, 7, 11–14, 251, 253, 259–60, 266–7, 291–8, 299–300; influence of Authorized Version 276–7; literalism 271–2, 299–300; naturalness (in target language) 271–2; objectivity 279, 300; pitfalls 275–6; status compared to original 237
trees, as component of Paradise 79–80
Turkish (language) 244; calligraphy 246–7

'Umar, Caliph 20, 38–9, 277; imposition of legal penalties 97, 107

wa, (mis)translation of 13
al-Wāḥidī 37
Wansbrough, John 77, 121, 213, 316–17*n10*
al-Wāqidī 26
water, symbolic significance of 89; as metaphor for divine revelation 131; in Paradise 78–9
Watt, Montgomery 269, 270
Wehr, Hans 36
Welch, Alford T. 273
Weldon, Anthony, Col. 253
whipping *see* beating
winds, oaths sworn by 193–6, 209–11
wine *see* alcohol
women; alleged degradation in Qur'an 111, 114, 117; dress codes 115–16, 117; presence in Paradise 70, 80–2, 85; punishment for adultery/ fornication 95–6; Qur'anic expressions of respect for 113–14, 117; as 'tilth' (fields) 111–14;

see also domestic violence; menstruation; *nushūz; zinā*
wujūh al-Qur'ān (words with different meanings according to context) 273–4, 291–2

zakāh (Muslim tax) 51; distinguished from *jizya* 45, 46; refusal to pay 57–8
al-Zarkashī, Badr al-Dīn 178, 273
al-Zamakhsharī 34, 36, 255
Zia-ul-Haq, President 247
zinā (fornication/adultery) 90, 94–102; age/experience of guilty parties 97–8; evidence/witnesses 100, 102; 'hurt' (physical *vs.* spiritual), as penalty 95–6; introduction of worldly penalties 94–5, 96; nature of, defined 95–6; penalties for 94–5, 97–102; penalties for false accusations of 98, 100; Qur'anic prohibition 94–5; *see also* stoning
zīna (ornaments/physical charms) 115–16
Zoheir, Baha-ed-Din 261
al-Zuhrī 22–3